DŌGEN KIGEN
Mystical Realist

HEE-JIN KIM

DŌGEN KIGEN
Mystical Realist

Foreword by Robert Aitken

The University of Arizona Press • Tucson

Revised Edition 1987
Originally published (1975, 1980)
as Monograph No. XXIX for the
Association for Asian Studies

THE UNIVERSITY OF ARIZONA PRESS
Copyright © 1975, 1987
The Arizona Board of Regents
All Rights Reserved

Designed by Kaelin Chappell
This book was set in 11 on 13 Linotron 202 Bembo.
Manufactured in the U.S.A.

Library of Congress Cataloging-in-Publication Data

Kim, Hee-Jin.
  Dōgen Kigen, mystical realist.

  (Monographs of the Association for Asian Studies;
no. 29)
  Bibliography: p.
  Includes index.
  1. Dōgen, 1200–1253. I. Title. II. Series.
BQ9449.D657K56 1987   294.3'927   87-10928
ISBN 0-8165-1025-3 (alk. paper)

British Library Cataloguing in Publication data are available.

To those friends
who helped me understand Dōgen

CONTENTS

The Way of Dōgen Zenji

HEE-JIN KIM'S *Dōgen Kigen—Mystical Realist* was the first comprehensive study in English of Dōgen Zenji's writings, and for the past twelve years, it has served as the principal English language reference for those Dōgen scholars who work from his thirteenth-century Japanese and for Western Zen students reading translations of his writings. This revised edition appears in a scholarly setting that now includes many new translations and studies of Dōgen, and thus it is most welcome.

Dōgen wrote at the outermost edge of human communication, touching with every sentence such mysteries as self and other, self and non-self, meditation and realization, the temporal and the timeless, forms and the void. He moved freely from the acceptance of a particular mode as complete in itself to an acknowledgment of its complementarity with others, to a presentation of its unity with all things—and back again. He wrote of the attitude necessary for understanding, of the practice required, of the various insights that emerge, and of the many pitfalls. He did not generally write for beginners—most of his points require very careful study, and a few of them elude almost everybody. These challenges are compounded by his creative use of the Japanese language of his time. It has been said that he wrote in "Dōgenese," for he made verbs of nouns, nouns of verbs, created new metaphors, and manipulated old sayings to present his particular understanding.

Thus the writings of Dōgen are an immense challenge to anyone seeking to explicate them in English, but Dr. Kim does a masterful job. In this Foreword, I do not presume to explicate Dr. Kim's words, but offer a personal perspective of Dōgen in the hope that it might serve as access to Dr. Kim's incisive scholarship.

I choose as my theme a key passage in the "Genjō Kōan," the essay which Dōgen placed at the head of his great collection of talks and essays, the *Shōbōgenzō,* using Dr. Kim's translation:

To study the Way is to study the self. To study the self is to forget the self. To forget the self is to be enlightened by all things of the universe. To be enlightened by all things of the universe is to cast off the body and mind of the self as well as those of others. Even the traces of enlightenment are wiped out, and life with traceless enlightenment goes on for ever and ever.

To study the Way is to study the self. Asian languages offer the same options as English for the meaning of the word "study." "A Study of Whitehead" would be the presentation of an understanding of Whitehead. Thus the first sentence of the passage quoted also means, "To understand the Way is to understand the self."

The term "Way" is a translation of *Dō* in Japanese, *Tao* in Chinese. It is the ideograph used to identify the central doctrine of Taoism and its basic text, the *Tao te ching.* Kumarajiva and his colleagues in the early fifth century selected *Tao* as a translation of Dharma, a key Sanskrit Buddhist term meaning "law," or "way of the universe and its phenomena," or simply "phenomena." In Dōgen's view, all phenomena are the Buddha Dharma—the way of the universe as understood through Buddhist practice.

Indeed, for Dōgen, to study and understand the Buddha Way is to practice the Buddha Way, and to practice the Buddha Way is to have the self practice. It is important to understand that practice, like study, is both action and attainment. Modes of practice: zazen (Zen meditation), realization, and the careful works that transcend realization—all these are complete in themselves, and they are also means for further completion. They are aspects of a single act at any particular moment, and they are also stages that appear in the course of time.

As to the self, it has no abiding nature, and "kisses the joy as it flies." It is the Buddha coming forth now as a woman, now as a youth, now as a child, now as an old man, now as an animal, a plant, or a cloud. However, animals and plants and clouds cannot "study" in Dōgen's sense, so in this context, Dōgen intends the human being that can focus the self and make personal the vast and fathomless void, the infinitely varied beings, and their marvelous harmony.

To study the self is to forget the self. Here Dōgen sets forth the nature of practice. My teacher, Yamada Kōun Rōshi, has said, "Zen practice is a matter of forgetting the self in the act of uniting with something." To unite with something is to find it altogether vivid, like the thrush, say, singing in the guava grove. There is just that song, a point of no dimension—of cosmic dimension. The "sole self" is forgotten. This is something like the athlete who is completely involved in catching the ball, freed of self-doubt and thoughts of attainment, at the same time aware of the other players and their positions. Using this same human ability on one's meditation cushions is the great Way of realization. It must be distinguished from thinking *about* something. When you are occupied in thinking, you are shrouded by your thoughts, and the universe is shut out.

There are other analogies for gathering oneself in a single act of religious practice, freeing oneself of doubt and attainment. Simone Weil sets forth the academic analogy:

Contemplating an object fixedly with the mind, asking myself "What is it?" without thinking of any other object relating to it or to anything else, for hours on end.[1]

Dōgen often uses the phrase, "mustering the body and mind" to understand oneself and the world. Using Dr. Kim's translation of a later passage in the "Genjō Kōan":

Mustering our bodies and minds we see things, and mustering our bodies and minds we hear sounds, thereby we understand them intimately. However, it is not like a reflection dwelling in the mirror, nor is it like the moon and the water. As one side is illumined, the other is darkened.

This mustering is zazen—and also the activity of the Zen student who is grounded in zazen. Dr. Kim quotes Dōgen writing elsewhere in the *Shōbōgenzō:*

The Buddhas and Tathāgatas have an ancient way—unequaled and natural— to transmit the wondrous Dharma through personal encounter and to realize supreme enlightenment. As it is imparted impeccably from Buddha to Buddha, its criterion is the samādhi of self-fulfilling activity.

For playing joyfully in such a samādhi, the upright sitting in meditation is the right gate.

With the practice of zazen, mustering body and mind, we understand a thing intimately by seeing or hearing, and the self is forgotten. This kind of understanding is not by simile, it is not a representation, like the moon in the water, but is a brilliant presentation of the thing itself, and a complete personal acceptance. One side is illumined. There is only that thrush. At the same time, the universe is present in the shadow. The other players are still there.

To forget the self is to be enlightened by all things of the universe. The term "enlightened" is *shō,* the same *shō* found in *inka shōmei,* the document given to a senior student by a master confirming him or her as a teacher. The thrush confirms you, enlightens you, but be careful not to give "enlightenment" anything more than provisional status. It is likely to be just a peep into the nature of things. Nonetheless, "One impulse from a vernal wood" or the Morning Star shining over the Bodhi tree is a communication. It works the other way, from the self to the object, but the result is different, as Dōgen makes clear earlier in the "Genjō Kōan":

That the self advances and confirms the myriad things is called delusion; that the myriad things advance and confirm the self is enlightenment.[2]

The way of research and analysis is "called" delusion. Don't condemn it, Dōgen is saying. By advancing and confirming and throwing light upon all things of the universe, you reach intellectual understanding. However, when you forget yourself in mustering body and mind in the act of practice, there is only that particular act, in that particular breath-moment. Then, as Dr. Kim says, the whole universe is created in and through that act. With this you experience the things of the universe. They are your confirmation, your enlightenment.

To be enlightened by all things of the universe is to cast off the body and mind of the self as well as those of others. When you focus body and mind with all your inquiring spirit upon a single matter, the self is forgotten. The myriad things communicate their wisdom with their forms and sounds, and the emptiness, harmony, and uniqueness of the ephemeral self and the world are understood clearly. This is reminiscent of Paul's "putting off the old man"—not merely forgetting but dying to the self.

Casting off body and mind should not be confused with self-denial. Many people suppose that they must get rid of the self. The Buddha too went through a phase of asceticism, avoiding food and sleep in an effort to overcome his desires. Such a path has a dead end, as the Buddha and others have found. We need food and sleep in

order to cast off body and mind. The Way is gnostic rather than
ascetic.

Finally, as Dōgen says, when you cast off body and mind, all other
beings have the same experience. One version of the Buddha's exclamation under the Bodhi tree reads, "I and all beings have at this
moment entered the Way!" This does not mean, "All beings can now
come along." Rather, at the Buddha's experience, all beings simultaneously cast off body and mind.

When Hsüeh-fêng and Yen-t'ou were on pilgrimage together, they became
snowbound in the village of Wushantien. This gave them time for an extended dialogue, during which Hsüeh-fêng recounted his various spiritual
experiences. Yen-t'ou exclaimed, "Haven't you heard the old saying, 'What
enters from the gate [that is, by intellection] cannot be the family treasure?'"
Hsüeh-fêng suddenly had deep realization and exclaimed, "At this moment,
Wushantien has become enlightened!"[3]

With his exclamation, Yen-t'ou cast off body and mind. Simultaneously, Hsüeh-fêng did the same. The whole village was likewise affected, proving Bell's theorum a thousand years and more before Bell.

Even traces of enlightenment are wiped out, and life with traceless en-
lightenment goes on for ever and ever. Wiping away the intimations of
pride that come with a realization experience are the ultimate steps of
Zen practice, steps that never end. They form the Way of the Bodhisattva, polishing the mind of compassion, engaging in the travail of
the world, "entering the marketplace with bliss-bestowing hands."
Over and over in kōan practice, the Zen student works through the
lesson of casting off, casting off.

A monk said to Chao-chou, "I have just entered this monastery. Please
teach me."
  Chao-chou said, "Have you eaten your rice gruel?"
  The monk said, "Yes, I have."
  Chao-chou said, "Wash your bowl."[4]

"Have you eaten your essential food?" "Yes, I have." "If so, wipe
that idea of attainment away!" For our limited purposes this would
be an explication of Chao-chou's meaning. What is left after body
and mind are cast off? Endlessly casting off—ongoing practice. The
"Genjō Kōan" ends with the story:

When the Zen teacher Pao-chê of Ma-ku was fanning himself, a monk asked
him, "The nature of wind is constant, and there is no place it does not reach.
Why then do you fan yourself?"

Pao-chê said, "You only know that the nature of wind is constant. You don't yet know the meaning of its reaching every place."

The monk asked, "What is the meaning of its reaching every place?"

Pao-chê only fanned himself. The monk bowed deeply.

The nature of the wind is Buddha nature, "pervading the whole universe." The monk's question is an old one. If all beings by nature are Buddha, why should one strive for enlightenment? Dōgen himself asked such a question in his youth, and his doubts fueled his search for a true teacher. Pao-chê takes the monk's words: "reaching every place" as a figure of speech for Zen Buddhist practice that brings forth what is already there. As Dōgen says in his comment to this story—the final words of the "Genjō Kōan":

Confirmation of the Buddha Dharma, the correct transmission of the vital Way, is like this. If you say that one should not use a fan because the wind is constant, that there will be a wind even when one does not use a fan, then you fail to understand either constancy or the nature of the wind. It is because the nature of the wind is constant that the wind of the Buddha House brings forth the gold of the earth and ripens the kefir of the long river.

The wind of the Buddha house, the practice of zazen, realization, and going beyond realization, is altogether in accord with the wind of the universe, the Buddha Mind. As Dōgen says elsewhere, "The Dharma wheel turns from the beginning. There is neither surplus nor lack. The whole universe is moistened with nectar, and the truth is ready to harvest."[5] The harvesting of truth, the practice of forgetting the self, the practice of realizing forms and sounds intimately, the practice of polishing our mind of compassion—this is our joyous task.

ROBERT AITKEN
Koko An Zendo, Honolulu

FOR NEARLY six decades since D. T. Suzuki published his first series of *Essays in Zen Buddhism* in 1927, Zen has been taking root
firmly in Western culture and continuing to grow steadily both in its
dissemination and in its depth of understanding. Indeed Suzuki's introduction of Zen to the West was one of the epoch-making events in
Western cultural history, and it became rightfully the beginning of a
great experiment which has been going on ever since, although not
without some whimsical and misguided by-products in the course of
its evolutionary process.

If Zen has a universal element that transcends historical and cultural bounds, it should be nurtured here in the West with its own distinctive marks and imprints. Just as Zen has evolved differently in the
different countries of East Asia and Vietnam, so does it transform
itself into the "Western Zen" (or "American Zen" for that matter)
which is on the verge of emergence today. By the sheer number of
publications in this field, by the mushrooming growth of meditation
centers all over the Western countries, by its impact upon such fields
as art, philosophy, psychology, religion, and folk culture, we can
readily witness the intensity and fervor of this cultural experiment.

Under such circumstances the present study on Dōgen, though it
is none other than a prolegomenon, aims in a modest way to fulfil a
twofold function: to contribute to the evolution of Western Zen as
well as to a better understanding of Zen in general. Quite obviously,
these two goals are mutually related and reinforcing.

Today systematic study of Dōgen in the West is virtually nonexistent, which means that Western knowledge of Zen is painfully fragmentary, not only in quantity, but, more importantly, in quality. In recent years some sporadic attempts have been made to acquaint the West with Dōgen, but these cover only a tiny portion of the entire corpus of his philosophy and religion. It is our hope that the study of Dōgen's Zen will remedy the situation and lead to a more complete understanding of Zen.

On the other hand, I am of the opinion that it is high time for Western students to deal with Zen as a historical religion in its concrete historical, philosophical, moral, and cultural context—not to isolate it from them. After all, Zen is a cultural and historical product. I feel strongly that such an approach to Zen is imperative to the maturity of Western Zen (or any Zen for that matter), and this work endeavors to apply it seriously to the study of Dōgen. It might surprise many readers that such a historical consciousness is quite in accord with Dōgen's belief that fidelity to history is the way to transcend it.

The present work draws heavily upon, and is greatly indebted to, Japanese scholarship in Dōgen studies, which has diversified so much in recent years that materials and findings are indeed bewildering to the beginning student of Dōgen. This book endeavors to add to this scholarship through systematic efforts to elucidate Dōgen's life and thought with an acute awareness of certain issues which are relevant and vital in relation to current thinking in philosophy and religion. In this respect, Dōgen's thought sheds light on some vitally important issues in a surprisingly modern way. Here I am not implying that Dōgen anticipated fully and completely what we now know. Yet, despite his remoteness from us in terms of age and culture, his messages are infinitely richer and more complex than we might at first think.

It has been my persistent conviction that we can avoid making either a strict philosopher or a pious religionist of Dōgen and can understand him totally in a humanistic context. Be that as it may, it is my sincere hope that the present work will stimulate students to delve further into Dōgen.

Throughout this study I used *Dōgen zenji zenshū* (edited by Ōkubo Dōshū) as the basis of my research and translation. In view of the current status of Western acquaintance with Dōgen, I have attempted to render as many literal translations of his writings as possible even at the expense of stylistic quality. Most of these appear here for the first time in English. In an introductory work such as this, translations are of necessity highly selective and fragmentary, and it is well-nigh unavoidable to lay primary, if not sole, emphasis upon *Shōbōgenzō*.

The Japanese reading of Buddhist terms is extremely confusing even among Buddhist scholars. In order to avoid unnecessary chaos, I adopted the customary Sōtō way of reading them rather than the one which is suggested in Ōkubo's aforementioned *Zenshū*. Thus, for example, I used *uji* instead of *yūji*, *datsuraku* instead of *totsuraku*, *konshin* instead of *unjin*, *gato* instead of *wazu*, and so forth. I consulted frequently with *Shōbōgenzō yōgo sakuin* (edited by Katō Shūkō) and *Zengaku jiten* (edited by Jimbo Nyoten and Andō Bun'ei) for the reading of important terms which were used in this work.

My indebtedness and gratitude to many friends for making this study possible are too great to be adequately expressed in words.

I wish to acknowledge, above all, the unfailing assistance and encouragement of Professor John A. Hutchison, given throughout this project; indeed, it might not have been completed without him.

The Blaisdell Institute, Claremont Graduate School and the School of Theology were kind and generous enough to invite me to Claremont to teach and do research on Dōgen in 1970 to 1972. I am deeply grateful to these three institutions for providing necessary funds.

I also extend my special gratitude to Dr. Yamada Reirin, the former abbot of the Los Angeles Zenshūji temple, who initially guided me to Dōgen's *Shōbōgenzō*; to Professors Nakamura Hajime, Masunaga Reihō, and Abe Masao in Japan for their kind assistance through correspondence; to Professors Floyd H. Ross, Herbert W. Schneider, Margaret Dornish, and Katō Kazumitsu for their invaluable comments and suggestions.

For my research I used resources from the Komazawa University Library in Tokyo, the Honnold Library in Claremont, the UCLA Oriental Library, the library of the Los Angeles Zenshūji temple, the Hinomoto Library of Tenrikyō Church in Los Angeles, the library of the Blaisdell Institute, and the Orientalia section of the University of Oregon. I thank each of them for their kindness and cooperation in the use of their collections.

I should not forget to mention the moral support I received from the members of the Department of Religious Studies and the Asian Studies Committee, University of Oregon, when this work was in its final stage of preparation. My gratitude extends to them.

I wish to express my thanks to Dale Pryor of Eugene, Oregon, for her careful and competent work of editing, proofreading, indexing, and making thoughtful suggestions; to Dorothy Banker Turner and Anne Holmes for their assistance in various ways at different stages of this project; and to Mary Armes for typing the final copy for photo reproduction. I also thank the Association for Asian Studies at the University of Arizona and the University of Arizona Press for their cooperation and skill in the publication of this book.

HEE-JIN KIM

DŌGEN KIGEN
Mystical Realist

ONE

Toward a
Total Understanding
of Zen

D URING THE past several decades the significance of Dōgen's thought—not only for the history of Buddhist thought but also for the history of ideas at large—has been increasingly recognized, though belatedly, by a growing number of students both inside and outside of the Sōtō sectarian circle in Japan. Masunaga Reihō, a leading Dōgen scholar in the Sōtō sect, for example, characterizes Dōgen as "the unique religious personality" with "incomparable depth of thought."[1] Among those singing his praises outside the sect is Tanabe Hajime, one of the most prominent Japanese philosophers, who exalts Dōgen almost ecstatically, calling him "a great metaphysical thinker," and appraising his thought in the *Shōbōgenzō* (*Treasury of the True Dharma Eye*), Dōgen's magnum opus, as "the culmination of dialectical thinking" and "the precursor of Japanese philosophy." "Indeed," says Tanabe, "his thought seems to have already had an insight into, and to have made a declaration of, the direction to which the systematic thought of today's philosophy should move."[2] Even a foreign student of Zen Buddhism concurs with these claims in observing that Dōgen "belongs among the great creative figures of humankind."[3] It is not difficult for us to glean such praises and eulogies from various sources—they are perhaps more frequent than criticisms of Dōgen. A sudden rise in Dōgen studies in scholarly circles and an unprecedented enthusiasm among intellectuals for the past several decades seem to indicate that, after the initial shock of the discovery of a virtually unknown thinker, the "popularity" of Dōgen has been steadily growing in the post-war period.

Credit for causing the "initial shock" in Dōgen studies should go to Watsuji Tetsurō, a leading cultural historian, who brought Dōgen to light from his cloistered confinement in the Sōtō sect. In his now famous essay "Shamon Dōgen" ("Dōgen, a Monk") written in 1926, Watsuji declared:

I am not here insisting that my own interpretation is the only one on the truth of Dōgen itself, in the understanding of which I am least confident. I can safely say, however, that a new path of interpretation has been opened up here, to say the least. Henceforth Dōgen is no longer "Dōgen, the founder of the sect," but, our Dōgen. The reason I dare make such an arrogant statement is that I know Dōgen has been killed thus far in the Sōtō sect.[4]

Deceptively meager as it may have been in its size, Watsuji's essay was a bombshell, openly revolting against sectarian injustice to Dōgen and challenging many younger minds to engage in Dōgen studies without being fettered by sectarian concerns. This revolt, in the spirit of making Dōgen "our Dōgen," was cheered and welcomed even by some insiders of the Sōtō sect, although there was also much sectarian resistance and indifference. This was the beginning of Dōgen studies in the genuinely modern sense.

For some seven hundred years prior to 1926 Dōgen studies had been limited to the sectarian scholars, who were not equipped with modern methodologies and philosophical reflections but only with apologetic concerns and confessional hermeneutics. Dōgen was venerated pietistically but never studied critically. For the sake of convenience we can divide the history of Dōgen studies into the following periods: (1) the period of institutional expansion (1253–1660), (2) the period of sectarian studies (1660–1868), (3) the period of continued stagnation (1868–1926), (4) the period of awakening (1926–1945), and (5) the period of steady maturity (1945–the present). Let us briefly examine these stages.[5]

To begin with, the first period, from immediately after Dōgen's death to about 1660, is characterized by the institutional expansion of the Sōtō sect. It had started modestly in the Hokuriku regions and gradually extended throughout the country due to the shrewd accommodation policies of Keizan Jōkin (1268–1325) and his two most able disciples, Gasan Jōseki (1275–1365) and Meihō Sotetsu (1277–1350). These men adopted certain aspects of esoteric Buddhism and folk tradition, such as a syncretistic mountain religion called *shugendō,* endeavoring in this way to come in close contact with the people. These accommodative and popularizing policies were certainly not in accord with Dōgen's style of Zen, which was designed for the training of monastics in a "puristic" and "puritanic" spirit, as we shall see later; on the other hand, Sōtō Zen after the death of Dōgen shunned the aristocratic and bureaucratic Gozan Zen in Kyōto and Kamakura and thrived primarily among farmers, the common people, and powerful clans in the regions and provinces remote from the centers of the Gozan Zen establishment. During this period three different editions of Dōgen's *Shōbōgenzō* appeared: Ejō's seventy-five-chapter edition, Giun's sixty-chapter edition (1329), and Bonsei's eighty-four-chapter edition (1419). Kenzei wrote his famous *Kenzeiki (The Record of Kenzei),* a biography of Dōgen which influenced all other biographies in the subsequent years. *Kikigaki (The Record of Dōgen's Expositions)* by Senne and *Shō (Selected Commentaries; 1303–8)* by Kyōgō, both commentaries on the *Shōbōgenzō,* were of great importance because they were based on these two disciples' direct acquaintance with Dōgen. Generally speaking, however, the sectarian scholars in this period relegated the *Shōbōgenzō* to oblivion in favor of the study of Chinese Zen Buddhism (such as the doctrine of Five Ranks). It was the dark age of sectarian studies.[6]

The second period started sometime in the middle of the seventeenth century when we see the emergence (or resurgence) of the so-called "sectarian studies" (*shūgaku*) and the rise of the "sectarian restoration movement" (*shūtō-fukko-undō*) led by such leaders as Gesshū Sōko (1618–1696), Manzan Dōhaku (1636–1715), Tenkei Denson (1648–1735), and Menzan Zuihō (1683–1769), who attempted to rescue the sect from confusion and corruption and to restore the rigor and purity of Dōgen Zen. Thus, Dōgen's works were printed, the monastic rules of Dōgen and Keizan published, and a fresh enthusiasm for scholarly studies encouraged. It was in this period that the *Shōbōgenzō* was for the first time rigorously studied and by these sectarian scholars, though previously Dōgen's minor works had been primarily studied. Several commentaries on the *Shōbōgenzō* were written: Tenkei's *Benchū (A Commentary with Critical Notes)* in 1730, Menzan's *Monge (Menzan's Lectures)* in the 1760s and *Shōtenroku (A Study on the Sources of Terms, Names and Events in the Shōbōgenzō)* in 1759, Honkō's *Sanchū (A Commentary)* in 1793, Zōkai's *Shiki (Personal Comments)* in circa 1779, and so on. Kōzen edited the ninety-five-chapter edition (Kōzen-bon) of the *Shōbōgenzō* in 1690. However, the sectarian studies in Sōtō Zen, like other sectarian studies of Buddhist sects at that time, were severely limited by the governmental control and supervision of the Tokugawa regime which was interested in nothing but the utilization and exploitation of religion to maintain the status quo of the feudalistic order. No freedom of thought existed; sectarian orthodoxies were articulated, stereotyped, and defended.[7]

The third period was marked by the advent of the Meiji Restoration (1868), at which time Japan broke away from feudalism and apparently became well-nigh intoxicated—at least for a time—by anything Western.[8] Yet as Kagamishima Hiroyuki observes, Sōtō sectarian scholarship at that time was moved by no more than "the inertia of the Tokugawa period."[9] Dōgen (unlike Shinran and Nichiren) was little known to the Japanese at large.[10] The only works of great importance produced during this period were *Keiteki* (*A Guide on the Right Path*), an authoritative commentary on the *Shōbōgenzō* by Nishiari Bokusan (1821–1910),[11] and the *Sōtō kyōkai shushōgi* (*The Principles of Practice and Enlightenment of the Sōtō Order*; 1890), an anthology of selected passages from the *Shōbōgenzō* for the believers of Sōtō Zen.[12]

The fourth period began in the 1920s with Watsuji's aforementioned essay. As we have noted, this essay freed Dōgen from the monopoly of sectarian studies, awakened the sectarian scholars from their dogmatic slumber, and incited enthusiasm and passion for Dōgen as a spiritual mentor of humankind. In 1935, nine years after the publication of Watsuji's essay, Akiyama Hanji published *Dōgen no kenkyū* (*A Study on Dōgen*) in which he systematically addressed himself to Dōgen's thought with a special emphasis on ontology in relation to Western philosophical traditions. (This remains the most comprehensive study of Dōgen's thought.)[13] A few years later, in 1939, Tanabe Hajime, as cited before, wrote a short book entitled *Shōbōgenzō no tetsugaku-shikan* (*The Philosophy of Shōbōgenzō: A Personal View*) in which he professed to have been awakened to the intellectual capacity of the Japanese through Dōgen's philosophical tenacity and exactitude.[14] As is clear from the foregoing observations, Watsuji, Akiyama, and Tanabe were primarily interested in Dōgen as a thinker, and hence in his philosophical contributions. However, Hashida Kunihiko, who was a physiologist at Tokyo University, approached Dōgen as the advocate of religious practice, rather than as a philosopher, in his *Shōbōgenzō shakui* (*A Commentary on Shōbōgenzō*), the first volume of which appeared in 1939.[15] His impact was to free Dōgen further from the sectarian monopoly.

As a result of the nonsectarian awakening, two distinctive camps were formed: that of sectarian studies and that of nonsectarian studies of Dōgen. The impact of the latter upon the former is evident, though there have also been many rebuttals and countercriticisms, and the tension between the two factions has persisted until today. Major controversies can be summarized as follows:[16] (1) Dōgen was seen by the nonsectarian student as an independent thinker in the history of thought, and *Shōbōgenzō* was seen as his spiritual and intellectual testimony, not as sectarian scripture. The sectarian student, on the other hand, vigorously defending a special form of religious tradition nurtured in the sect as an invaluable heritage, saw Dōgen as a religionist, and above all, as the founder of the Sōtō sect (*shūso*), and *Shōbōgenzō* as the scripture of the sect, not as a philosophical treatise. (2) Dōgen was understood by the nonsectarian student primarily from the standpoint of *Shōbōgenzō;* their sectarian friends would not accept this position, feeling that though it is a major work, it is by no means the only work of importance. The nonsectarians tended to emphasize philosophical ideas, whereas the sectarians emphasized religious faith and monastic cult. And finally, (3) nonsectarian students were primarily concerned with the contemporary significance of Dōgen in relation to a changing world situation, though, in fact, they were more often than not reading their own philosophical views into Dōgen, largely as a result of neglecting the historico-social context in which Dōgen's thought evolved. One of the most authoritative answers on the part of the sectarian camp to the nonsectarian interpretation of Dōgen was Etō Sokuō's *Shūso to shiteno Dōgen zenji* (*Dōgen Zenji as the Founder of the Sōtō Sect*; 1944), in which, as its title suggests, Dōgen was interpreted as the founder of the sect whose Zen emphasized enlightenment *and* faith (quite a new emphasis in Zen tradition).[17] It was also during this period that a number of critical editions of Dōgen's various works were produced: among others, Ōkubo Dōshū's *Teihon Dōgen zenji zenshū* (*A Definitive Collection of Dōgen's Complete Works*; 1944) and Etō Sokuō's *Shōbōgenzō* in three volumes (1939–43) are important. The latter, especially, published in a popular edition, appealed to a wide audience. By and large, the creative interaction between the two camps until the end of World War II seems to have been good for Dōgen studies.

The post-war period marks a new maturity in Dōgen studies. The previous distinction between the two camps has persisted but is now less significant, for, in the shared search for understanding, differences have become matters of emphasis rather than of principle. More importantly, however, both sectarian and nonsectarian students of Dōgen have been confronted with an entirely new world situation in which traditional values and methodologies have been radically challenged. Dōgen studies have now reached a new phase in which both parties are compelled to cooperate and transform one another so as to contribute to the common task of engendering better self-understanding in an emerging world community. Thus recent study shows intensified efforts to place Dōgen in the historical, social, and cultural contexts in which his thought was formed rather than to study his thought in the abstract, though philosophical treatment is still being carried out. Ienaga Saburō's "Dōgen no shūkyō no re-kishiteki seikaku" ("A Historical Character of Dōgen's Religion") in his *Chūsei Bukkyō shisōshi kenkyū* (*Studies in the History of Medieval Japanese Buddhist Thought*; 1955), Takeuchi Michio's *Dōgen* (1962), Takahashi Masanobu's *Dōgen no jissentetsugaku kōzō* (*The Structure of Dōgen's Practical Philosophy*; 1967), Etō Sokuō's *Shōbōgenzō josetsu: Bendōwa gikai* (*Prolegomena to the Shōbōgenzō: An Exposition of Bendōwa*; 1959), Ōkubo Dōshū's monumental collection of Dōgen's entire works, *Dōgen zenji zenshū* (*The Complete Works of Dōgen Zenji*; 1969–70), which reflects the findings and results of recent Dōgen studies, and a legion of other important works and articles have been written in this period.[18] In addition to the study of *Shōbōgenzō* which characterized the pre-war period, Dōgen's other writings have been investigated, and probed for linguistic, textual, and literary data.[19] Furthermore, there have appeared several different translations of Dōgen's works in colloquial Japanese that have disseminated Dōgen's thought rapidly among the Japanese populace. In short, Dōgen studies have diversified, broadened, and improved considerably in their scope, precision, and methodology in the post-war period. The quantity and quality of scholarly output in this area are highly promising.

Once we turn our eyes from Japan to the Western scene, we find that virtually nothing has been introduced concerning Dōgen.[20] Masunaga is justified in saying: "Western knowledge of Zen seldom extends to the Sōtō style—the style of the larger Zen sect in Japan."[21] Obviously ignorance of Sōtō Zen is tantamount to ignorance of Dōgen, its founder. The scholarship of Zen Buddhism in the West has chiefly relied upon D. T. Suzuki's brilliant introduction of many invaluable texts and his own interpretation of them, based primarily on Rinzai Zen in which Suzuki was nurtured. Overshadowed by Suzuki's brilliance and reputation, the Sōtō tradition has been treated like a stepchild of Zen in the West. Perhaps this situation has been aggravated by the extreme difficulty of presenting Dōgen's thought in a form intelligible to the Western mind. His language and thought are forbiddingly difficult and subtle, yet irresistibly intriguing, and more often than not, exasperate the students of Dōgen, who tend to alternate between hope and despair. Nevertheless East–West cooperative efforts to translate and disseminate Dōgen's works are continuing.[22]

Having established the historical background of Dōgen studies, though in barest outline, allow me to make my basic assumptions explicit before embarking on this investigation.

First, Zen Buddhism is not a monolithic religion with a mystical slant, as it might appear superficially from the reading of Suzuki's works. Although it has an unmistakable "family resemblance" to other East Asian religions, it also contains elements and traits diverse and rich enough to surprise even those who are initiated into Zen. Furthermore, Zen is still in the making. The belief that Zen embodies a mystical extremism characterized by irrationality, eccentricity, and obscurantism is a flagrant error.[23] Many of these allegedly Zen qualities are exaggerations or misinterpretations, resulting in a distorted image of Zen. Dōgen, as we shall see later, conceived of Zen quite differently—his style of Zen was "rational," "analytic," "exact," though these adjectives should be rightly understood only in a sense different from that of Western philosophical tradition. A total understanding of Zen is urgently called for today, and Dōgen studies are an integral part of such a task, which means that Zen must be studied in the total context of Buddhism as well as in the context of the general history of religions.[24]

Second, Dōgen was a religious thinker, not merely or even primarily a philosopher. As we have mentioned previously, nonsectarian students of Dōgen were often mistaken in viewing him as a philosopher who attempted to build a philosophical system. On the contrary, even Dōgen's most philosophic moments were permeated by his practical, religious concern, against the background of which his philosophic activities stand out most clearly in their truest significance. What Dōgen presents to us is not a well-defined, well-knit philosophical system, but rather a loose nexus of exquisite mytho-poeic imaginings and profound philosophic visions, in the flowing style of medieval Japanese, studded sparsely with classical Chinese prose and verse. A rare combination of vision and analysis in Dōgen's thought has dazzled many a student, so much so that many have lost sight of its deeper matrix—his religious, especially cultic, concern, that is, a passionate search for liberation through concrete activities and expressions. Thus philosophy for Dōgen was an integral part of religion and ritual.

Third, religion, examined from the phenomenological standpoint, is our nonrational activity in search of the ultimate meaning of existence. We do not wish to enter an elaborate discussion of recent phenomenological investigations of religious phenomena at this point, but merely to draw on the general agreement with which historians of religions, social scientists, and religious thinkers concur regarding the nature and function of religion.[25] Religion, then, is not something reducible to purely intellectual world-views, utilitarian functions, and the like, nor is it something explainable in terms of the needs of immediate existence and survival, but, at its most serious and creative level, it is our attempt to free ourselves for a symbolic reality, through mythopoeic visions and cultic activities. Human nature is most fruitfully understood in terms of *animal symbolicum* and *homo ludens*.[26] Religion is intimately related to myth-making and playful activities—thus, nonintellectual, nonutilitarian, and nonethical—at its core. The modern proclivity to view religion strictly from the scientific, theological, and ethical standpoints misses the deeper psychometaphysical forces operating in religious aspirations. The moral, intellectual, and utilitarian values of religion can only be adequately appreciated in this broader context. We shall keep this fundamental insight in mind throughout our subsequent investigation.

Fourth, religious thought, like any other intellectual endeavor, employs concepts and symbols bequeathed from a particular religious and cultural tradition, which mediate between our inner aspirations and the cultural and socioeconomic conditions of a given age. Religious thought cannot dispense with the interaction of metaphysical visions and historical forces—mutually limiting, conditioning, and transforming. Thus historico-cultural and philosophico-phenomenological conditions cannot be divorced from one another in any adequate intellectual history. In our present study of Dōgen's thought we are not only concerned with the historical forces within which Dōgen's thought evolved but also with the structure of his experience and thought, with its own subtle logic. While thought is not reducible to history, it cannot be isolated from it either—being radically conditioned and hence relative even at its core. For even the phenomenology of emptiness, however ahistorical it may be alleged to be, has, after all, a history. Thus, the history of any religious thought must do full justice to the fact that irreducible character and radical conditionality are paradoxically allied and merged in the structure of the object of investigation. We have to come to terms with such peculiarities of religious thought and history, and accordingly we shall probe into the philosophical and experiential aspects of Dōgen's thought.[27]

Fifth, Dōgen was obviously a child of the age (i.e., medieval Japan) and of the Buddhist tradition, and his intellectual horizon was limited to the catholic Buddhism which he envisioned, as we shall discuss later. Traditionally minded as he may have been, Dōgen has attracted many contemporary philosophers and religious thinkers who regard him as surprisingly "modern," as we have already illustrated in the case of Tanabe Hajime. The philosophically minded students of Dōgen, however, have made a mistake, more often than not, in seeing significance divorced from history, resulting in mere subjectivity rather than in an objective understanding of Dōgen's thought. Thus our assumption in this study is, although it may sound too platitudinous even to mention, that significance and history must be in a creative tension.

Lastly, and related to the preceding assumption, is this: our approach does not attempt to be exhaustive but to present a perspective through which the character of Dōgen's thought can be illuminated systematically. We are not looking for a system in Dōgen; there is none. In this respect our study is highly selective and subjective, but it is at the same time supported by textual and historical evidence. We shall attempt to expound the two fundamental structural elements of Dōgen's thought, namely, meditation and wisdom, and to see their nature and function in the context of the total. The meanings of these two terms will gradually be made clear in the course of our study. Moreover, these terms are associated in Dōgen's thought with the ideas of activity (*gyōji*) and expression (*dōtoku*) which will prove to be central throughout this work.

With these assumptions in mind we shall undertake the study of

Dōgen as a human being—neither merely the founder of the sect nor merely a philosopher—who struggled to seek a mode of existence and freedom for himself and for others, with his personal yearnings and frustrations, fears and hopes, in the midst of chaotic and tumultuous Kamakura Japan. By so doing we hope to see the Dōgen who, while confined to a particular religious and cultural tradition, nevertheless envisioned values which are germane to the evolution of humanity.

TWO

Dōgen's Life

RELIGION is a symbolic model with symbols, values, beliefs, and practices which enable us, individually and collectively, to attain spiritual liberation and to grasp the meaning of existence. These elements of the symbolic model, in turn, are intricately interwoven with the conditions of our biological and psychological makeup as well as with sociocultural and historical conditions. Thus the net result constitutes a unique texture of the individual's symbolic reality.

Dōgen inherited the symbolic model of Buddhism through his upbringing, studies, and training in Japan and China, and accordingly his thought moved within the framework of this model. Some basic values of Buddhism, especially of Zen, are evident in his life and thought, yet they are modified through his personal influence as well as by the social and cultural conditions of the early Kamakura period of Japan in which he lived. In what follows, I shall attempt to review and understand some significant features of Dōgen's life so as to pave the way to understanding his thought.[1] Dōgen's life may be considered in the following distinctive periods: early childhood (1200–1212); apprenticeship in Buddhism (1212–27), which may be subdivided into the spiritual struggle at Hiei and Kenninji (1212–23) and study in China (1223–27); and the creative period in Japan after his return from China until his death (1227–53), which may be divided into the Yamashiro period and the Echizen period which started in 1243. Before we embark on the account of Dōgen's spiritual pilgrimage, we shall observe briefly the social background of the age in which Dōgen's life and thought occurred.

The Historical and Social Background of the Early Kamakura Period

The first half of the thirteenth century, that is the early Kamakura period, in which Dōgen lived and died, and its immediately preceding phase of the Heian period, had several important features relevant to our investigation of Dōgen's life and thought. They can be explained in terms of nobility-warrior power struggle, the corrupted situation of Buddhism, and traditional folk movements of the masses.

There were two opposing social forces in Japan in those days: the court nobility in Kyōto and the military class in Kamakura. The court aristocracy (the imperial-Fujiwara complex) had been already advancing towards its breakdown by the end of the Heian period. Now far removed from the erstwhile "glory and splendor" (*eiga*) of Fujiwara no Michinaga, they had desperately clung to whatever vestiges were left to them of their declining power, which was to be ended by their demise in the Jōkyū War in 1221. Their life was very similar to that of the Heian aristocracy described in *Genji-monogatari* (*The Tale of Genji*). Their activities centered exclusively around political pursuits, amorous adventures, and poetic and artistic indulgence—contingent on the wealth and leisure derived from enormous holdings of tax-free estates (*shōen*). Perhaps no society in human history emphasized aesthetic refinement and sensibility more than the circle of court nobles of Japan in those days. As Ivan Morris aptly observes, "Upper-class Heian life was punctuated with poetry from beginning to end, and no important event was complete without it."[2] With this aestheticism were associated the two fundamentally related sentiments of the age—the sense of the affective quality of life and the world (*mono no aware*), and the sense of impermanence (*mujō*). Despite its outward pomposity, the aristocratic way of life was permeated by the awareness of beauty shadowed by the sense of the sorrow of existence because of the inherently ephemeral character of beauty. They grasped something religious in the beautiful, and vice versa. Beauty inspired in them a religious feeling, a sense of the ultimate limits of life, of impermanence and death; religion, likewise, appealed to them for aesthetic, rather than ethical, reasons.[3] Their lot in this life was interpreted as resulting from karma or fate (*sukuse* or *suguse*) to which they resigned themselves. They were indifferent to the masses, as if their ethical sensibilities were in inverse proportion to their aesthetic sensibilities.[4] Dōgen's life and thought can be adequately understood only against this decadent, overly refined aristocratic tradition into which he was born.

After a decisive victory over the Tairas at the battle of Dannoura in 1185, the Minamoto family took hegemony over Japan by establishing the feudal government (*bakufu*) in 1192 and set the pattern for the rising samurai class with its gradually emerging way of life known as "the way of warriors" (*bushidō*). (In its earlier stage the way of warriors seems to have been a far cry from the romanticized picture of its later developments in the Tokugawa period—greedy, predatory, ruthlessly calculating, a strict business dealing with little or no sense of absolute loyalty and sacrifice.)[5] The Minamotos moved basically within the old political framework. They enforced powers delegated to them by the imperial house but were the de facto rulers of Japan without attempting to displace the imperial house. In this respect they followed the precedents set by the Fujiwaras. Warriors were culturally "provincial," looked down on by the aristocrats; yet their economic, military, and political powers were steadily growing and becoming consolidated, and they were gradually emerging as a class separate from both the aristocrats and the farmers, merchants, and artisans. The martial arts were their profession, and they were acutely aware of the ultimate meaning of their profession—the destruction of human lives.[6]

The incredible complexity of the political situation in which both aristocratic and military classes were helplessly enmeshed is aptly described by a historian as follows:

One finds in thirteenth century Japan an emperor who was a mere puppet in the hands of a retired emperor and of a great court family, the Fujiwaras, who together controlled a government, completely dominated by the private government of the Shōgun—who in turn was a puppet in the hands of the Hōjō regent. The man behind the throne had become a series of men, each in turn controlled by the man behind himself.[7]

In addition to this chaotic political situation were the infinitely complicated transactions involving tax-free estates—perhaps the most significant economic institution to mold Japanese life from the latter part of the eighth century to the end of the sixteenth century.[8] By the end of the Heian era some eighty percent of the rice land in the country belonged to the manorial system,[9] over which court nobles and samurai warriors fought for control. Also conspicuous in this power struggle were the religious orders. Their entanglement in this grim situation had many sordid psychological and social ramifications.

During the Heian period religious institutions accumulated huge tax-free estates which had to be protected by an oxymoronic Japanese institution, the armed monastics (*sōhei*). Since the middle of the tenth century, major Buddhist monasteries such as the Enryakuji temple on Mt. Hiei, the Onjōji temple in Miidera, the Tōdaiji and the Kōfu-kuji temples in Nara had had standing armies and resorted to military means to solve their conflicts with other religious institutions and with the government. They had destroyed rival monasteries, demonstrated in the streets of the capital, presented their petitions to the imperial court by force (*gōso*), and engaged in many other flagrant militant actions.[10] Although the wealth, prestige, and power of some established monasteries undoubtedly increased, their moral, intellectual, and religious life was dangerously disintegrating. Armed monastics were very active during Dōgen's lifetime.

Another characteristic of Buddhism in this period was its inseparable association with the Heian aristocracy. One of the most conspicuous examples of this was the monopolization of all the important posts in the monastic centers by the members of the imperial house and the Fujiwara family. This resulted in the formation of clerical cliques (*monzeki*) which excluded non-Fujiwara aspirants. Earlier, as a political career in the court had become exceedingly difficult owing to the swelling numbers of the Fujiwara family, some took the profession of monastics with little or no religious motivation as the next surest way to wealth and power. In addition, at many monastic centers the activities revolved around magico-religious rites and prayers (*kaji-kitō*) of esoteric Buddhism for the protection of the nation and the welfare of privileged families of the court aristocracy. The complete secularization (meaning aristocratization) of Buddhism with no distinction between the Buddha-law (*buppō*) and the secular law (*ōbō*) had been firmly established when Dōgen entered Mt. Hiei for study in his youth.[11]

In this period, the Buddhist doctrine of the Three Ages (*shō-zō-matsu no sanjisetsu*) was widely accepted. The Three Ages were the Age of Right Law (*shōbō*) in which the genuinely authentic Dharma (universal truth and righteousness) prevailed, the Age of Imitative Law (*zōbō*) in which mere forms of Dharma dominated, and the Age of Degenerate Law (*mappō*) in which Dharma was entirely decayed. In the first, teaching, practice, and attainment of enlightenment prevailed; in the second, teaching and practice alone; and in the third only teaching. The Age of Degenerate Law, as interpreted by some circles of Buddhism in Japan, was believed to have begun in 1052.[12] This calculation was accepted by both the aristocrats and the general populace; the Buddhist leaders of the time based their diagnosis of the current religious situation upon this doctrine.[13] This belief was reinforced by incessant earthquakes, fires, murders, epidemics, and famines in the late Heian and early Kamakura periods. Thus was produced a historical consciousness based on a sense of "apocalyptic crisis" and a conviction of the utter wretchedness and helplessness of humankind, with the concomitant sense of spiritual exigency that led to faith in the unfailing compassion and grace of Amida Buddha.[14]

Dōgen, while utilizing the scheme of the Three Ages, rejected such romantic pessimism as regards human nature and history, because to him human nature possessed the elements of both greatness and wretchedness, regardless of time and place. Thus he remarked:

The ancient sages were not necessarily of sturdy build, nor were all the forebears richly endowed. It has not been long since the death of Śākyamuni Buddha, and when we consider Buddha's lifetime, not all people were superior: there were both sheep and goats. Among monastics some were unimaginable villains and others were of the lowest character.[15]

Whether human beings are great or wretched is determined not by external conditions but by our manner of dealing with each other.[16] This doctrine was relevant to Dōgen to the extent that it diagnosed the mass spiritual crisis of his time and aided individuals in confronting this crisis. Otherwise, it was nothing but a symptom of human failure to deal with life and the world.[17]

As we turn our attention from the affairs of nobles, warriors, and relgionists to those of the masses, we observe that the farmers, merchants, and artisans at that time were in a downtrodden state, though they had been gaining social and economic powers. The corruption and indifference of the ruling classes, chaotic social and political conditions, and omnipresent sufferings and miseries led these disinherited people towards something radically new that promised to revitalize their spiritual life. Their primitive yearnings had been more often than not associated with various folk-traditional undercurrents that were deeper than Buddhist and Confucian religious ideologies.[18]

In particular, the so-called "holy men" (*hijiri*)—with shamanistic, magico-religious practices and beliefs—were active among the masses from the latter part of the tenth century on, disseminating "the essential importance of individual faith and unworldliness"[19] at odds with insitutional Buddhism. As Hori emphasizes, the *hijiri* movement was essentially folk-traditional, anti-authoritarian, anti-secular, paving the foundation for new Kamakura Buddhism, especially Pure Realm Buddhism. Lay monastics (*shami*) also increased in number and quietly engaged in a spiritual revitalization of the common people.[20] In an important sense these holy men and lay monastics were the precursors of Kamakura Buddhism, which could be regarded as the cultic and intellectual purification and crystallization of the passionate personal faith advocated by them.

Dōgen's Zen Buddhism was no exception in that it was a part of this general process which was already taking place in medieval Japan.[21] In addition, the folk tradition of Japan had many other features which are relevant to our subject matter—especially, the tradition of *dōzoku* (a kind of kinship system) in the social structure of Japan, and the tradition of mountain asceticism and purification which was deeply rooted in the Japanese folk mentality.[22] Perhaps no Kamakura Buddhist would appear more remote from folk tradition than Dōgen—anti-magical, elitist, eremitic—yet, after all, his was a religion of the people which came into being and sustained itself by drawing its creativity and vitality from a source deeper and more indigenous than the enfeebled ideologies and adventures of aristocratic tradition.

Early Childhood: Initiation into Impermanence

Dōgen was born in Kyōto on January 2, 1200, perhaps as an illegitimate son of Koga Michichika and the daughter of Fujiwara Motofusa. He was among eleven sons and three daughters of Michichika. The Koga (or Minamoto) family was descended from Prince Tomohira, son of Emperor Murakami (r. 946–57) and during the lifetime of Michichika, then the Lord Keeper of the Privy Seal, the family was at the height of its power and prosperity and controlled both the dominating power of the Fujiwara family and the pro-shōgun force within the courtly circle in Kyōto. In addition, Michichika stood unparalleled in the literary circle (the Murakami Genji's literary fame was well known) and was unfailingly devoted to the imperial family (the Murakami Genji had the tradition of fighting for the restoration of the imperial rule). His mother was a beautiful, yet ill-fated woman who, according to one account, was married to Kiso Yoshinaka, separated from him, and later remarried to Koga Michichika.[23]

Michichika died suddenly on October 21, 1202, when Dōgen was only two years of age. After the death of his father, Dōgen was raised by his mother and his half-brother, Michitomo, in a culturally over-refined atmosphere, with his brothers and sisters, many of whom had occupied eminent positions in the imperial court and were well versed in poetry and classics. It is not difficult to imagine that Dōgen must have been systematically educated in the Chinese as well as the Japanese classics, and well trained in literary skills and techniques which were the sine qua non of aristocratic life. Dōgen himself recalled later: "In my boyhood I studied history and literature enthusiastically."[24] Also he wrote:

As a result of my predilection for study from childhood, I am prone even now to examine the rhetorical expressions of non-Buddhist classics and to consult the *Wên-hsüan* [an anthology of classical proses and verses]. But I believe that such a thing is irrelevant and should be discarded once and for all.[25]

Dōgen urged his disciples to pay attention not so much to the rhetoric, however prestigious it might be, as to the content of the writing under study. However, Dōgen's sensitivity to language must have been cultivated in a refined literary environment, as evidenced by his poetic excellence, his fondness of the use of a flowing medieval Japanese style rather than a Chinese style, his instruction on "loving speech" (*aigo*), and his deep insight into the nature of language and symbols in human thought. Dōgen eschewed vainglorious aestheticism, but never relinquished poetic sensibility.

At the age of seven, in 1207, Dōgen lost his mother, who at her death left an earnest request for him to seek the truth of Buddhism by becoming a monastic and to strive to relieve the tragic sufferings of humanity.[26] Unlike his father's death which took place when he was only two, his mother's death must have been a serious blow to his fragile and sensitive mind. We are told that in the midst of profound grief Dōgen experienced the impermanence of all things as he watched the ascending incense at his mother's funeral service.[27]

This experience left indelible impressions upon Dōgen's tender mind which no doubt determined the direction he took in his subsequent spiritual journey. Later Dōgen emphasized, time and again, the intimate relation between the desire for enlightenment (*bodaishin*) and the awareness of impermanence (*mujō*) and death.[28] To Dōgen the lucid understanding of life and the thorough penetration into death (*ryōshō-tasshi*), a total understanding of the meaning (*dōri*) of impermanence and death, were the alpha and omega of religion. Dōgen understood the impermanent character of life in religious and metaphysical terms rather than in psychological or aesthetic ones, and he lived out this understanding in monastic life. Dōgen's way of life was not a sentimental flight from, but a compassionate understanding of, the intolerable reality of existence.

Five years after his mother's death, Dōgen was confronted by another crisis. After he was orphaned, Dōgen was adopted by Fujiwara Moroie, his mother's younger brother, who at over forty years of age did not yet have an heir and consequently wanted to train Dōgen for this honor.[29] This meant the promise of a brilliant career for Dōgen in the tradition of the Fujiwara hegemony, even though the Fujiwara hegemony had been declining at the time. In the spring of 1212 Moroie was planning to have a *gempuku* ceremony for Dōgen as a token of initiation into aristocratic manhood. At this juncture Dōgen had to choose either to become a monastic or to follow his uncle's desire. Dōgen's decision was to become a monastic, and he visited Ryōkan,[30] another uncle on his mother's side, in the Onjōji temple at the foot of Mt. Hiei for an intelligent settlement of the matter. Deeply moved by Dōgen's determination and the seriousness of his motivation, Ryōkan recommended him to study at the Senkōbō at Yokawa-Hannyadani on Mt. Hiei, one of the most renowned centers of Buddhist studies at that time. Upon hearing the news of Dōgen's decision to enter into the monastic's life, Moroie was greatly disappointed.

To Dōgen there was no conflict between his decision and his filial piety to Moroie, for, as he saw it, to study Buddhism was to fulfill his duty to Moroie. He wrote that filial piety should not be limited to one's parents alone but extended to all sentient beings, and further said: "To follow the Way obediently in our living from day to day and in our study from moment to moment—that is the truest filial piety."[31] In a more revealing statement which was indicative of his unique style of Zen, Dōgen wrote:

Even the Buddhas and ancestors are not without tender feeling and affection (*on'ai*) but they have thrown them away. The Buddhas and ancestors, too, are not lacking various bonds, yet they have renounced them. Even though you hold them dear, the direct and indirect conditions of self and other are not to be clung to; therefore, if you do not forsake the bonds of affection, they in turn should desert you. If you must care for tender feeling, treat it with compassion; to treat it with compassion means to resolutely relinquish it.[32]

Thus: "The students of Buddhism should not study Dharma for their own profit but only for the sake of Dharma."[33] The Way for the sake of the Way—relentless as it may have sounded—was the core of Dōgen's spiritual search from the very beginning to the very end.

Apprenticeship in Buddhism

In April 1213, Dōgen's ordination ceremony was administered by Kōen, abbot of the Enryakuji temple on Mt. Hiei.[34] Thereafter Dōgen delved deeply into a systematic study of Buddhist sūtras at the Senkōbō. No more favorable educational environment could be found in those days than that at Hiei. Dōgen devoured these studies with his gifted mind. His earnestness in the search for truth at that time and thereafter can be glimpsed in the emphasis he placed on the need to live seriously. Some twenty years later, Dōgen repeatedly wrote in his *Shōbōgenzō zuimonki*: "The arising and decaying of all things occurs swiftly; birth-and-death is gravely important" (*mujō-jinsoku shōji-jidai*). The impermanence of existence did not lead him to fatalism nor to the pessimism which was so pervasive in that age; on the contrary it led him to heightened vitality in the search for the Way. Dōgen admonished: "Having a transient life, you should not engage in anything other than the Way."[35] And further he wrote:

In a Chinese classic it is said: "I shall be content even to die in the evening if only I hear the Way in the morning." Even if you were to die by starvation or by cold, you ought to follow the Way even a day or even an hour. How many times might we be born again and die again in an infinitude of aeons and rebirths? Such a hope is nothing but a blind attachment to the worldly conditions. Die of starvation in following the Way once and for all in this very life, and you shall attain eternal peace and tranquility. . . . If you do not seek enlightenment here and now on the pretext of the Age of Degenerate Law or wretchedness, in what birth are you to attain it?[36]

And: "At each moment do not rely upon tomorrow. Think of this day and this hour only, and of being faithful to the Way while given a life even just for today, for the next moment is uncertain and unknown."[37] Elsewhere Dōgen stated:

The student of Buddhism should think of the inevitability of dying. While the truth is too obvious to be thought in those words, you should not waste your precious time by doing useless things, but instead do worthwhile things. Of many worthwhile things, just one—indeed all else is futile— is vitally important: the way of life of the Buddhas and ancestors (*busso no anri*).[38]

"Today's life does not guarantee tomorrow's. The possibility and danger of dying are always at hand."[39] These statements, though written much later in his life, reflect unmistakably the seriousness of the religious enterprise Dōgen undertook at the Senkōbō after his initiation into Buddhism.

While he was studying the sūtras at the Senkōbō, Dōgen was confronted with an apparently insoluble question which, according to the biographies of Dōgen,[40] was as follows:

As I study both the exoteric and the esoteric schools of Buddhism, they maintain that human beings are endowed with the Dharma-nature by birth. If this is the case, why did the Buddhas of all ages—undoubtedly in possession of enlightenment—find it necessary to seek enlightenment and engage in spiritual practice?

And no one on Mt. Hiei could give a satisfactory answer to this spiritual skepticism. The question itself, however, was of such magnitude in Dōgen's spiritual struggle that he was thereafter restless until he found an answer once and for all in 1225 from Ju-ching at the T'ien-t'ung monastery.

Dōgen's question was concerned with the time-honored Mahāyāna doctrines of original enlightenment (*hongaku*) and acquired enlightenment (*shikaku*). The doctrine of original enlightenment was propounded primarily by Tendai Buddhism, which was responsible for the synthesis of diverse currents of Buddhist thought, such as Tendai, Kegon, Shingon, and Zen. Although the doctrine itself was as old as the early history of Mahāyāna Buddhism,[41] its most radical interpretation was formulated in Japan during the Heian and Kamakura periods, for the most part by Tendai thinkers, who pressed the doctrine to its logical extremity.[42] Several aspects of the doctrine were as follows: Original enlightenment was eternal in that it was not a temporal occurrence that had a beginning and an end in time. The opposites, such as enlightenment and delusion, life and death, being and non-being, one and many, were dialectically negated and in turn affirmed without minimizing their respective absolute status. Related to this was the unity of enlightenment and practice, in which emphasis was placed not upon special forms of religious discipline so much as upon the activities of daily life. The metaphysical status of phenomenon (*ji*) was now construed as primary in contrast to that of principle (*ri*); accordingly, the existential actualities of a given situation acquire supreme importance. Things, events, and values as they exist in actuality were eternalized not as the manifestations of principle but precisely by virtue of the intrinsic status of the phenomena themselves. Doctrinal studies were held in disrepute, and instead, an instantaneous liberation here and now through faith in original enlightenment was assured.[43]

In addition, the doctrine of original enlightenment was accompanied by a cognate doctrine of "this body itself is Buddha" (*sokushin-jōbutsu*), which was likewise radicalized by Japanese Buddhism. This accepted the immediate enlightenment of the psycho-physical existence with all its particularities, which were not a finger pointing to the moon but the moon itself, or to put it differently, not the accommodative manifestations of the Body of Law (*Dharmakāya*; *hosshin*), but the Body of Law itself. This doctrine of esoteric Buddhism, whether the Shingon version or the Tendai, was influential in the current ethos. Thus, mundane existence was sanctified, which was the same result effected by the doctrine of original enlightenment.[44]

The doctrines of original enlightenment and of "this-body-itself-is-Buddha" went hand in hand in reinforcing the efficacy of faith, the absolutization of phenomena, and the instantaneous attainment of liberation. When one denied any metaphysical hiatus between principle and phenomenon, however, even the profoundest Mahāyāna doctrines became dangerously indistinguishable from a crude and irresponsible acceptance of whatever existed in the world, at the sacrifice of spiritual exertions. In fact, a number of dangerous misinterpretations of these doctrines were rampant toward the close of the Heian period, and especially flagrant among worldly minded Buddhist monastics who attempted to rationalize the pursuit of their selfish interests.

Furthermore, an exclusive claim of faith, which required no strenuous religious and moral exertions, was too readily associated with the antinomian cynicism inspired by the Age of Degenerate Law.

It is noteworthy that this moral, intellectual, and religious crisis coincided with the heyday of the doctrines of original enlightenment and "this-body-itself-is-Buddha." The latter unwittingly served as a religious rationalization for the apathetic state of affairs. The significance of Dōgen's original question at Mt. Hiei and his endeavors thereafter can be properly understood only in view of his acute sense of this crisis in the age in which he lived.

If we were primordially enlightened and consequently liberated here and now within this body-mind existence, then why did we have to exert ourselves at all? What was the significance of intellectual, moral, cultic, and religious activities and endeavors? Dōgen did not question the truth of original enlightenment but believed it with his whole heart and mind. But he did question the significance of the activities that constituted human existence. Thus the question amounted to asking, "What is the meaning of existence?"

With the question unsolved, Dōgen finally left Hiei when Kōen resigned as abbot.[45] He brought the question to Kōin (1145–1216) at the Onjōji temple in Miidera in the province of Ōmi. However, he found Kōin unable to answer his question; instead, the latter referred the young man to Eisai (1141–1215) who had returned from China to found Rinzai Zen and who resided at the Kenninji temple in Kyōto.[46] Dōgen later wrote:

As a result of the desire for enlightenment which was first aroused in my mind through the awareness of the impermanence of existence, I travelled extensively to various places and, finally having descended Mt. Hiei to practice the Way, settled at the Kenninji temple. Until then I had met neither a right teacher nor a good friend and consequently had gone astray and had erroneous thoughts.[47]

Dōgen apparently visited Eisai at the Kenninji temple in 1214.[48] Founded by Eisai in 1202, the Kenninji temple was at that time not only the center of Zen but also the center of studies on Tendai, Shingon, and other schools of Buddhism. Indeed, Kenninji was a rival of Hiei. Hence visiting Eisai under such circumstances must have been a bold venture for a young man of only fourteen. At any rate, "Dōgen entered Eisai's school and heard Rinzai Zen Buddhism for the first time."[49] Despite the fact that there was an extremely short length of time between Dōgen's visit in 1214 and Eisai's death in 1215, and that Dōgen probably could not have had frequent and intimate personal contacts with Eisai because the latter busied himself in propagating

Zen between Kyōto and Kamakura, Eisai's lasting influence on Dōgen cannot be denied.[50] In any event, the Kenninji visit was only one
on the agenda of Dōgen's extensive travelling.[51] His willingness to
learn from a variety of sources indicates his moral courage as well as
his intellectual openness, and reveals his "intersectarian" approach to
Buddhism which was to revitalize religion in his time.

After three years' wandering, Dōgen again settled at the Kenninji
temple in 1217 to receive the instructions of Myōzen (1184–1225)
and stayed there until 1223 when he left for China to study. During
this period Dōgen must have studied Rinzai Zen systematically; at the
same time a warm relationship between Myōzen and Dōgen developed as they studied together as teacher and disciple. It may be fair to
say that Dōgen's knowledge about Zen Buddhism was acquired from
Myōzen, who was the highest-ranking disciple of Eisai and his successor. Some ten years later Dōgen wrote about Myōzen with respect
and affection: "Myōzen zenji, the chief disciple of the founder Eisai—
he alone transmitted the supreme Dharma rightly. None of the others
could equal him in this respect."[52] Thus six years' study under Myōzen
in which he was constantly encouraged and assisted by the teacher
must have been as strenuous as the study he had had at Hiei.

Yet Dōgen could not erase a feeling of dissatisfaction. He reminisced later:

Although my teachers were just as distinguished as any other leader in the
scholarship of Buddhism, they taught me to become famous in the nation
and to be honored by the whole world. Thus in my study of Buddhism, I
thought, above all, to become equal to ancient wise ones of this country and
to those who held the title of Great Teacher (*daishi*). As I read afterwards
[Hui-chao's] *Kao-sêng-ch'uan* (*Biographies of Eminent Buddhist Monastics*) and
[Tao-hsüan's] *Hsü-kao-sêng-ch'uan* (*Further Biographies of Eminent Buddhist
Monastics*) and others, and studied eminent Buddhist monastics and scholars
of the great T'ang dynasty, I came to realize that they differed from what my
teachers taught. What is more, I realized that thoughts such as mine, according to their treatises and biographies, were loathed by these people. Having
contemplated the nature of the matter at last, I thought to myself I should
have rather felt humbled by ancient sages and future good men and women
than elated by the praise of despicable contemporaries. As for an aspiration
for greatness, I wished to emulate the greatness of Indian and Chinese monastics and scholars rather than my countryfolk. Also I should have aspired
to be equal to the gods of heavens and invisible worlds, Buddhas and
bodhisattvas. In view of such a realization, the holders of the title of Great

Teacher in this country seemed to me worthless, like earthen tiles, and my whole life was changed completely.[53]

This summarizes Dōgen's more than ten years' spiritual struggle at Hiei and Kenninji. His original question remained unanswered; he could not find a right teacher, and the general circumstances of Japanese Buddhism of the time were unfavorable to him. As to the failure to find a right teacher (*shōshi*), Dōgen wrote:

Right teachers have not appeared in our country since olden times. How can we tell this? Observe their utterances. They are like those who try to fathom the source of a stream by scooping up a handful of water. Although ancient teachers of this country wrote books, taught disciples, and expounded teachings to humans and gods, their speeches were green and their expressions yet immature. They did not attain the summit of an intellectual grasp of doctrines, much less the neighborhood of enlightenment. They merely transmitted words and letters, while their disciples recited names and sounds. Day and night they counted others' riches for nothing. Herein lies my charge against the ancient teachers. Thus some led people to seek enlightenment outside the conditions of mind, while still some others led them to desire rebirth in other lands. Confusions arise from and delusions originate in this. . . . Alas, Buddhism has not yet been disseminated in this tiny remote country, and right teachers have not yet appeared. If you want to study the best of Buddhism, you should consult the scholarship of China far away and reflect thoroughly on the living path that transcends the deluded mind. When you don't meet a right teacher, it is better not to study Buddhism at all.[54]

Uttered by a man of an essentially conservative frame of mind, these words were a startling attack on the immaturity of contemporary Japanese Buddhism.

Perhaps as a result of this disillusionment, the possibility (or more appropriately the necessity) of study in China, which had been originally suggested by Kōin, might have emerged in Dōgen's mind as the next step necessary for the fulfilment of his search for truth. Or as Takeuchi surmises, the Jōkyū (or Shōkyū) War in 1221 with all its miseries and sufferings—especially the banishment of three ex-emperors (all were related to Dōgen's family), countless bloody executions, and the involvement of armed monastics—may have prompted Dōgen to decide to study in China.[55] Dōgen brought the matter to Myōzen, and both seem to have begun preparing to study abroad immediately after the Jōkyū War.[56] Thus, after due formalities, a party of Myōzen,

Dōgen, and others left the Kenninji temple on February 22, 1223, and toward the end of March set sail from Hakata in Chikuzen for China.

The party's voyage on the East China Sea was not always smooth. Particularly for Dōgen—a man of frail physical frame who had probably not had any previous experience on board a ship, the voyage must have been a tough one.[57] Early in April the ship arrived at Ch'ingyüan-fu in Ming-chou (now the province of Chekiang). While Myōzen immediately entered the Ching-tê-ssŭ temple on Mt. T'ient'ung, Dōgen lived on the ship, visited various other temples, and observed the Chinese customs, until early July when he could enroll at the Ching-tê-ssŭ temple.[58]

While Dōgen was living on board, an old Chinese monk, sixty-one years of age, visited the ship in order to get Japanese *shiitake* (a kind of mushroom for soup). He was the chief cook at the monastery on Mt. Ayüwang (Yüwang) which was situated some eighty-five miles from where the ship was anchored. In the course of a lively conversation, Dōgen, paying courtesy to the old man, asked him to stay overnight and talk some more. The old man, however, declined and insisted on returning to the monastery immediately after he bought the *shiitake*. Dōgen apparently could not understand why this man had to return in such a hurry despite the fact that the monastic food, in Dōgen's view, could readily be prepared by other cooks without him. To this puzzlement of Dōgen, the old man said: "The reason for my being the chief cook at such an old age is that I regard this duty as the practice of the Way (*bendō*) for the rest of my life. How can I leave my practice to other persons? Besides I did not obtain permission for staying out." Then Dōgen asked: "Why are you, a person of advanced age, engaged in such a troublesome task as the chief cook rather than in practicing zazen or reading the kōans of old masters? Is there any worthwhile thing in your work?" To this question, the old monk laughed loudly, saying: "You, a good man from a foreign country, perhaps do not understand what the practice of the Way is, nor what words and letters (*monji*) are." Upon hearing this old man's remark, Dōgen was "all of a sudden shocked and ashamed profoundly." Promising Dōgen to discuss the matter some day in the future, the old man disappeared hurriedly into the gathering dusk.[59]

In early July 1223 Dōgen at last left the ship and enrolled at the Ching-tê-ssŭ temple on Mt. T'ien-t'ung where Wu-chi Liao-p'ai

(d. 1224) was abbot. This was the same temple where Eisai had once studied, being one of the "Five Mountains" regarded as the most important centers of Zen Buddhism in China. It was supported by the Chinese royal court and the population of monastics was said to be always no less than one thousand.[60]

It was one day in July soon after Dōgen's enrollment at the Ching-tê-ssŭ temple that the second meeting took place between Dōgen and the old chief cook.[61] The old man was then about to retire from his post at the Ayūwang monastery and leave for his native village. The two picked up their discussion where they had left off previously. Dōgen asked: "What are words and letters?" The answer came: "One, two, three, four, five." "What is the practice of the Way, then?" asked Dōgen. "Nothing is concealed throughout the entire universe" (*henkai-fuzōzō*) was the old man's reply. Their lively discussion continued without their knowing where to end it. Dōgen wrote later:

Just as the words and letters I have seen thus far are one, two, three, four, five, so the words and letters I see now are also six, seven, eight, nine, ten. The monastics of future generations will be able to come to understand a non-discriminative Zen (*ichimizen*) based on words and letters, if they devote efforts to spiritual practice by seeing the universe through words and letters, and words and letters through the universe.[62]

The encounters with the old chief cook on these two occasions were decisive events in Dōgen's subsequent life and thought. It was during these encounters that he had the realization which he had been groping toward regarding the relationship between practice and language, between deeds and words, between activities and expressions, and more specifically, with respect to the place of words and letters (*monji*) in the scheme of things. Unlike other Zen Buddhists of the time, Dōgen recognized not only the limits and dangers of language, but more importantly, the possibility of using it for liberation in spiritual matters by understanding the "reason of words and letters" (*monji no dōri*). To him language and symbols were not to circumscribe but potentially to open up reality; consequently, they were to be reinstated in their legitimate place within the total context of human spiritual endeavors.

At this juncture it is worthwhile to review the place of Buddhism in general and Zen (Ch'an) in particular in the Sung period. When Dōgen visited China, it was nearly a century after the establishment of the Southern Sung (1127–1279) with its capital in Hangchow (Lin-an) which governed central and southern China. (Northern China was controlled by the Chin.) China suffered constant threats of foreign invasion, internal political factionalism, and military weakness while it enjoyed the same unprecedented economic, technological, and cultural leadership as before. Neo-Confuciansim was the predominant ideology of the day and was destined to become the official learning of China. Buddhism had been steadily declining in those days as compared with the golden age of Buddhism in the Sui-T'ang era (581–907), owing to several factors. Ch'en observes the following:[63] (1) the moral degeneration of monastic communities due to the sale of monasterial certificates and of honorary clerical titles by the Chinese government in order to cope with its severe financial difficulties; (2) the rise of Neo-Confucianism to intellectual eminence; (3) the civil service examination system that lured many able men to the study of the Confucian classics for prestige and power; (4) the popularity of the Zen and Pure Realm schools of Buddhism which tended to be anti-textual and anti-scholastic and did not produce great thinkers comparable to those of the T'ang period; (5) the decline of Buddhism in India during the eleventh and twelfth centuries, resulting in the end of cultural exchange between Indian and Chinese Buddhists. Despite all this, the Zen and Pure Realm schools were still active, and particularly Zen enjoyed the highest esteem.[64] Although Neo-Confucianists rejected Zen, their thought contained Buddhist and Zen elements, and the culture of the period owed as much to Zen Buddhism as to Neo-Confucianism.[65] Moreover, Zen communities were expanding physically and their economic activities were ever vigorous. Nevertheless, Zen lacked the rigor, authenticity, and brilliance it had had in the previous period and showed its inner impoverishment and decay.[66] Moreover, Zen teachers began to meddle with politics, and Zen monasteries became centers of social and political life.[67]

Dōgen himself wrote on various occasions concerning this state of affairs of Zen Buddhism which he witnessed during his stay in China. For example:

Those who allegedly study vinaya today in the great country of Sung drink heavily and are intoxicated, in contradiction to the name of śrāvaka—yet they neither are ashamed of, nor have regret for, nor are aware of, the fact that they are transmitting a family heritage entirely foreign to their own tradition.[68]

Although there are in China a great number of those who proclaim themselves to be the descendants of the Buddhas and ancestors, there are few who
study truth and accordingly there are few who teach truth. . . . Thus those
people who have not the slightest idea of what the great Way of the Buddhas
and ancestors is now become the teachers of monastics.[69]

. . . In the country of Sung lately there are those who call themselves Zen
teachers. However, they do not understand the wealth and depth of Dharma
and are inexperienced. Reciting a few words of Lin-chi and Yün-mên, they
take them for the whole truth of Buddhism. If Buddhism had been ex-
hausted by a few words of Lin-chi and Yün-mên, it could not have survived
till today. . . . These people, stupid and foolish, cannot comprehend the
spirit of the sūtras, slander them arbitrarily, and neglect to study them.
Truly they are to be called heretics.[70]

These forthright criticisms were made as a result of Dōgen's keen observations of Zen Buddhism in China. As these quotations amply
show, the religious situation in China was not too far from what Dōgen had observed in his own country.

Another aspect of contemporary Buddhism and Zen which Dōgen
criticized was a theory of "the unity of three religions" (sankyō-itchi)
of Confucianism, Taoism, and Buddhism which was advocated not
only outside but even within the Buddhist circle, probably because
the survival of Buddhism was guaranteed only by its coming to
terms with Confucianism and Taoism under extremely unfavorable
conditions. Dōgen witnessed a number of those who held this popular view:

Lately, a number of the shallow-minded in the country of Sung do not
understand the purport and substance [of the doctrine of "All things themselves are ultimate reality" (shohō-jissō)] and regard the statements of ultimate reality (jissō) as false. Furthermore, they study the doctrines of Lao-tzŭ
and Chuang-tzŭ, maintaining that they are the same as the Way of the Buddhas and ancestors. Also there is a view of the unity of Confucianism, Taoism, and Buddhism. Some say that the three are just like the three legs of a
tripod kettle which cannot stand upright if it lacks even one leg. There is
nothing comparable to the foolishness of such a view.[71]

Apart from the general state of Buddhism and Zen, Dōgen's criticism was directed primarily at the Lin-chi (Rinzai) sect which was
popular at that time. As Dōgen wrote, "In the country of Sung today
the Lin-chi sect alone prevails everywhere."[72] Of the two separate
lines of transmission in the sect, the line of Huang-lung Hui-nan
(1002–1069) and the line of Yang-ch'i Fang-hui (992–1049), the latter

brought forth the highest development in Chinese Zen Buddhism. Although Dōgen was already familiar with the Huang-lung line, transmitted by Eisai, which he had studied at the Kenninji temple, what he encountered in China was the Yang-ch'i tradition, whose best-known representative was Ta-hui Tsung-kao (1089–1163). Dōgen denounced him and his followers relentlessly; he may have been prejudiced sometimes, yet his primary reason seems to have been their involvement with political and other secular interests and concerns, and their transcendentalistic interpretation of Zen which we shall have an occasion to investigate later.[73]

It is easy to understand Dōgen's great disappointment with the general conditions of Buddhism and particularly of Zen in China. Although he stayed at the Ching-tê-ssŭ temple for nearly two years under Wu-chi Liao-p'ai, Dōgen's spiritual needs were not fully satisfied. Thus, while he was at the Ching-tê-ssŭ temple, Dōgen seems to have visited various nearby Zen monasteries.[74] Upon Wu-chi's death toward the end of 1224, Dōgen left Mt. T'ien-t'ung and began travelling extensively, visiting the various temples and monasteries of the "Five Mountains" and studying the characteristics of the "Five Houses" of Chinese Zen Buddhism. As a result of this wandering, Dōgen gained firsthand acquaintance with Chinese Buddhism but still did not find a right teacher.[75]

With a thoroughly discontented heart, Dōgen wanted to return home after realizing the futility of staying in China any longer, and he set out to pay his last visit to Mt. T'ien-t'ung where Myōzen had been ill for some time.[76] On the way to T'ien-t'ung, Dōgen learned of the death of his former teacher, Wu-chi Liao-p'ai, and his heart was greatly saddened. While revisiting the Ching-shan Wan-shou-ssŭ temple, Dōgen met an old monk who informed him that Ju-ching (1163–1228), well-known as a peerless master in Zen Buddhism, had been appointed abbot of the Mt. T'ien-t'ung monastery by the Chinese royal court, and who urged him to see Ju-ching as soon as possible.

It was May 1, 1225, when Dōgen met Ju-ching at long last at Miao-kao-t'ai, the latter's private quarters.[77] "I met Master Ju-ching face to face. This was an encounter between a man and a man," so wrote Dōgen later.[78] Ju-ching's reception was warm as if a loving father welcomed his beloved son, and he told Dōgen to visit him and to ask questions freely at his own private quarters at any time without the slightest ceremony. This availability in a great teacher rekindled in the young inquiring mind a burning desire for truth.[79] How earnestly Dōgen had longed for such a meeting with a right teacher! As we have observed before, Dōgen once went so far as to say: "When you don't meet a right teacher, it is better not to study Buddhism at all."[80] He also wrote: "Without meeting a right teacher, you do not hear the right Dharma."[81] Dōgen was convinced that the actualization or perfection of Dharma largely depended upon the ability and competence of a teacher to shape the disciple as an artisan shapes raw material.[82]

More importantly, however, the personal encounter was absolutely necessary in Dōgen's view, for Dharma did not emerge in a vacuum, but invariably emerged in a concrete social context, in which persons were significantly related to one another.[83] "When a person meets a person, intimate words are heard and deciphered."[84] The season was ripe so that the mystery of Dharma unfolded itself decisively in the meeting between Ju-ching and Dōgen on Mt. T'ien-t'ung.

Ju-ching, a native of Yüeh-chou, left there at the age of nineteen, travelled around all over China, visited Zen temples and monasteries, and studied Buddhism under various teachers. Later he became a disciple of Tsu-an (or Chih-chien) on Mt. Hsüeh-t'ou and attained enlightenment. Then he went on a pilgrimage throughout the country for nearly forty years and presided over various famous monasteries such as Ch'ing-liang in Chien-k'ang, Shui-yen in T'ai-chou, Ching-tz'ŭ in Lin-an, Shui-yen in Ming-chou, Ching-tz'ŭ again, and lastly T'ien-t'ung. Although the T'ien-t'ung monastery was traditionally presided over by abbots of the Lin-chi sect, Ju-ching belonged to the tradition of the Ts'ao-tung (Sōtō) sect, and more specifically, to the Chen-hsieh line of that sect in China.[85]

We are told that during this period Ju-ching never failed, even a single day, to practice zazen, the traditional form of Buddhist meditation which emphasizes an upright lotus posture, steady breathing, and mental freedom from all attachments, desires, concepts, and judgments. Ju-ching devoted so much time to zazen that the flesh of his buttocks broke out in sores time and again; yet at such a time he would practice it more earnestly.[86] Ju-ching's educational method reflected this disciplinary rigorism and monastic asceticism. As Dōgen wrote:

When I stayed once at the T'ien-t'ung monastery, I saw that Ju-ching, accompanied by other elders in the monastics' hall, used to practice zazen until eleven o'clock in the evening and start it towards dawn as early as two-thirty or three; and this he never failed to practice even a single night.[87]

This uncompromising rigor, whether towards himself or towards his disciples, was combined with utter sincerity and personal warmth. Dōgen recounted the following moving episode:

Ju-ching, my former teacher and abbot of the T'ien-t'ung monastery, admonished those who had fallen asleep during zazen practice in the monastics' hall, striking them with his shoe and scolding with harsh words. Nevertheless monks rejoiced in being struck by the teacher and admired him.

Once he spoke to the congregation in the hall: "At such an advanced age I should now retire from the monastic community, seclude myself in a cottage, and care for my remaining days. However, I am in the office of abbot as your leader in order to help each of you break delusions and find the Way. For this reason I sometimes utter scolding words and sometimes strike with a bamboo rod, though it should be done very carefully. On the other hand, it is a method to educate people in the place of Buddha. So brothers, forgive me with compassion." Thereupon all the monks wept.[88]

Thus, Dōgen had an unreservedly high regard for his teacher who advocated "zazen-only" (*shikan-taza*), which later became the heart of Dōgen's religion and philosophy:

True, there are throughout the country of great Sung not merely a hundred or two but thousands of those who allegedly advocate the practice of meditation and thereby profess to be remote descendants of the ancestors. However, I hear of none who exhort zazen-only. Throughout China only Master Ju-ching [is an exception].[89]

The central religious and philosophical idea of Ju-ching's zazen-only was the "body-mind cast off" (*shinjin-datsuraku*)—the phrase repeated by Dōgen tirelessly throughout his works.

Furthermore, Ju-ching was famous for his rare quality of disinterestedness in the worldly fame and gain which had corrupted the Buddhism of the time to the marrow. Dōgen observed:

My former teacher neither approached an emperor nor met one. No intimate acquaintance with ministers and governmental officials was made. Not only did he decline the purple robe and the title of Great Teacher but he also did not wear any colorfully mottled one all his life—instead always a black robe or a simple one-piece gown, whether in the lecture sessions or in the private sessions.[90]

Ju-ching was utterly indifferent to pecuniary gains, and Dōgen professed to witness this quality in his teacher alone, and in none other.[91]

Ju-ching opposed strongly the sectarian spirit within Zen Buddhism. The so-called "Five Houses" of Zen in the Sung period were in the state of a family feud, although the Lin-chi sect predominated all others. Ju-ching, though nurtured in the Ts'ao-tung tradition, detested sectarian biases and divisions and even disliked using the name of Zen as opposed to other Buddhist sects and schools. He aimed at the catholicity of Buddhism at large. We can glimpse Ju-ching's thought from the following descriptions of Dōgen's:

My former teacher, Ju-ching, once gave a sermon to monastics: "In recent times people assert seriously that there are distinct traditions of Yün-mên, Fa-yen, Wei-yang, Lin-chi, and Ts'ao-tung. This is neither Buddhism, nor the teaching of the Buddhas and ancestors."

Such a realization of the Way can be found not even once in a millenium, but Teacher alone does comprehend it. Nor is it heard in the ten quarters of the universe, but Teacher alone does hear it.[92]

And then:

It ought to be clear that nothing could be more seriously mistaken than to call it "a school of Zen." Foolish persons lament as if they failed in Buddhist scholarship on account of not having the designation of school or sect after the fashion of "school of realism," "school of nihilism," etc. Such is not the Way of Buddhism. No one ever called it the school of Zen.

Nevertheless, mediocre persons in recent times are foolish enough not to understand the old tradition and, having no instructions from erstwhile Buddhas, maintain erroneously that there are five distinct traditions in [Zen] Buddhism. This is the degeneration of nature. And no one has yet appeared to save this situation except my teacher, Ju-ching, who was the first one to be greatly concerned with it. Thus humanity has been fortunate; Dharma has deepened.[93]

Ju-ching also opposed the popular view of the unity of three religions. Its syncretistic tendencies must have been quite unpalatable to his purist religious principles.[94]

What emerges out of our examination of Dōgen's *Hōkyōki, Shōbō-genzō,* and other works concerning Ju-ching's character and thought is clear. He was a strong, dynamic, charismatic personality who had an uncompromising passion for the monastic asceticism of zazen-only as the sine qua non of Buddhism. Buddhism should be subservient to nothing of worldly power and glory; rather it should be content with the virtue of poverty and live quietly in deep mountains. Dharma must be sought for the sake of Dharma. He opposed strongly the then prevalent sectarianism in Buddhism in general and Zen in particular. Ju-ching sought a catholic Buddhism free from sectarian divisions. In brief, he was the embodiment of the idealism and purity of Zen monasticism which was the rightly transmitted Buddhadharma (*shōden no buppō*). These tenets (though no doubt selected by Dōgen with his own emphasis) were very likely Ju-ching's, and Dōgen enthusiastically accepted and faithfully transmitted them, transforming them through his own distinctive Japanese ethos.[95]

Dōgen deemed Ju-ching to be the right teacher he had been seeking. According to Dōgen, a right teacher is described as follows:

A right teacher is one who, regardless of old age or prestige, comprehends the right Dharma clearly and receives the certification of a true teacher. He/she gives no precedence to words and letters or to intellectual understanding. With an unusual ability and an extraordinary will power, he/she neither clings to selfishness nor indulges in sentimentality. He/she is the individual in whom living and understanding correspond to each other (*gyōge-sōō*).[96]

Dōgen must have recollected his mentor's character and thought as he wrote these statements some ten years later. True, Ju-ching fitted the foregoing criteria for the right teacher, or perhaps vice versa. More often than not, Dōgen exalted and adored this teacher—with tears of gratitude and joy—so much so that we are given the impression of rhetoric getting the upper hand on factual description.[97] Yet we still cannot but acknowledge the picture of a towering personality who shaped decisively the destiny of Dōgen's subsequent life.

What is most significant, however, is Dōgen's absolute devotion to the person whom he considered to be the right teacher, and consequently the authority and tradition the teacher represented. Such was the case in spite of his equally indomitable defiance of political power and authority, and furthermore in spite of his respect for intellectual independence.[98]

In turn, Ju-ching admired his Japanese disciple and once asked him to become his assistant, saying: "In spite of being a foreigner, you, Dōgen, are a man of superior character." Dōgen, however, "positively declined the offer."[99]

Thus the teacher and the disciple studied and practiced together for two years (1225–1227) in an almost ideal rapport. This, however, should not suggest a complete absence of conflicts between them. Dōgen later acknowledged that conflicts between teacher and disciple were a necessary condition for the right transmission of Dharma. He wrote: "The common endeavor of teacher and disciple in practice and understanding constitute vines of the Buddhas and ancestors (*bus-so no kattō*), that is, the life force of the skin-flesh-bones-marrow of Dharma (*hiniku-kotsuzui no meimyaku*)."[100] "Vines" in the traditional Zen parlance referred to doctrinal sophistries, intellectual entanglements and conflicts. Dōgen saw, contrary to the Zen tradition, the positive values of such conflicts in the personal encounter of teacher and disciple. Both teacher and disciple grow together through such vines.

Under Ju-ching, Dōgen studied and practiced meditation without sparing himself. Dōgen recalled later:

After hearing this truth [the sole importance of zazen] from the instruction of my former teacher of T'ien-t'ung, I practiced zazen day and night. When other monastics gave up zazen temporarily for fear that they might fall ill at the time of extreme heat or cold, I thought to myself then: "I should still devote myself to zazen even to the point of death from the attack of a disease. If I do not practice zazen even without illness, what is the use of taking care of my body? I shall be quite satisfied to die from a disease. What good fortune it is to practice zazen under such a great teacher of the great country of Sung, to end my life, and to be disposed by good monastics . . ." Thinking thus continuously, I resolutely sat in zazen day and night, and no illness came at all.[101]

Dōgen's apprenticeship matured daily in such an uncompromising asceticism.

A decisive moment of enlightenment in Dōgen's life came at long last. It happened during an early morning zazen session on a certain day of *geango* (i.e., the three-month intensive meditational session between April 16 and July 15) in 1225.[102] In the course of meditation, a monk next to Dōgen inadvertently had fallen asleep. Upon noticing the monk, Ju-ching thundered at him: "In zazen it is imperative to cast off the body and mind. How could you indulge in sleeping?" This remark shook Dōgen's whole being to its very foundation, and then an inexpressible, ecstatic joy engulfed the heart of Dōgen. In Ju-ching's private quarters on the same morning Dōgen offered incense and worshipped Buddha. At this unusual action on the part of Dōgen, Ju-ching asked: "What is the incense-burning for?" The disciple exuberantly answered: "My body and mind are cast off!" "The body and mind are cast off" (*shinjin-datsuraku*), joined the teacher, "cast off are the body and mind" (*datsuraku-shinjin*). Thus Ju-ching acknowledged the authenticity of Dōgen's enlightenment.[103]

This event, apparently sudden and revolutionary, was not an isolated one but the necessary fruition of Dōgen's long spiritual struggle. What Dōgen's mind had consciously and unconsciously groped for and reflected upon finally took shape dramatically in these unique circumstances. Furthermore, it was at this moment that the question with which Dōgen had lived since his residence on Mt. Hiei was finally resolved.[104] The significance of the key notion "casting off the body-mind" in the context of Dōgen's life and thought was that zazen-only, as the mythic-cultic archetype, symbolic of the totality of the self and the world, represented that through which Buddha-nature became embodied; to cast off the body-mind did not nullify historical and social existence so much as put it into action so that it could be the self-creative and self-expressive embodiment of Buddha-nature. Being "cast off," however, concrete human existence was fashioned in the mode of absolute freedom—purposeless, goalless, objectless, meaningless. Buddha-nature was not to be enfolded in, but to unfold through, human activities and expressions. The meaning of existence was finally freed and authenticated with its human-all-too-human conditions only if and when it was lived co-eternally with absolute meaninglessness.

What was taking place then in Dōgen's mind was a radical de-mythologizing and, in turn, remythologizing of the whole Buddhist symbol-complex of original enlightenment, the Buddha-nature, emptiness, and other related ideas and practices. The crux of his revolutionary vision lay in a realistic affirmation and transformation of what was relative, finite, and temporal in a nondualistic vision of the self and the world. To understand duality lucidly and penetrate it thoroughly within a nondualistic mode of existence was Dōgen's final solution. His remaining life consisted of his intellectual, moral, and cultic efforts to enact and elucidate this vision in the specific historical and social conditions of his time.

On September 18, 1225, Ju-ching conferred upon Dōgen the official certificate of the ancestral succession to the Chen-hsieh line of the Ts'ao-tung sect. On this day the sect saw the succession of a Japanese monk for the first time in the history of Chinese Buddhism.

One day in 1227 Dōgen expressed to Ju-ching his intention of returning to Japan; the latter gave him the sacerdotal robe transmitted from the time of Fu-yung Tao-chiai (1043–1118), the genealogical document of ancestral succession,[105] his own portrait,[106] and other precious objects. Except for these objects which he received from Ju-ching, Dōgen returned to Japan literally "empty handed" (*kūshu-*

genkyō). Unlike other Buddhists who had previously studied in China, Dōgen brought home with him no sūtras, no images, and no documents. His sole "souvenir" presented to his countrymen was his own body and mind, his total existence, now completely liberated and transformed. He himself was the surest evidence of Dharma. Thus, Dōgen transmitted the Chen-hsieh line of Sōtō Zen to Japan. The date of Dōgen's return to Japan was probably sometime in the fall of 1227. Ju-ching died a year later on July 17, 1228.

Meanwhile, Myōzen, who had been studying at the T'ien-t'ung monastery ever since his arrival in China, died on May 27, 1225, soon after Dōgen met Ju-ching. Dōgen brought Myōzen's remains to Japan with him and very soon thereafter wrote *Sharisōdenki* (*Account of the Death of Myōzen Zenji*).

Dōgen concluded the period of this apprenticeship with the following:

Further, I went to great Sung, visited good teachers throughout the province of Chekiang, and investigated the various traditions of the Five Houses. Finally, I became the disciple of Ju-ching on T'ai-pai fêng [the Ching-tê-ssŭ temple on Mt. T'ien-t'ung], and the great matter of my entire life (*isshō sangaku no daiji*) was thus resolved.[107]

Transmission and Transformation of the Way in Japan

Upon his arrival in Japan Dōgen immediately returned to the Kenninji temple after four years' absence. The chaotic situation he had witnessed before had not changed much. In fact, it was worse than ever in every respect.[108] Dōgen, however, expressed his sense of mission this way: "In the first year of the Shao-ting era [1228–1233] of the Sung dynasty I returned to my native place [Kyōto] and vowed to propagate Dharma and save all beings of the world. I felt then that a heavy load was on my shoulders."[109] In the fall of the same year Dōgen wrote *Fukan-zazengi* (*General Advice on the Principles of Zazen*), which might be regarded as the manifesto of Dōgen's "new" Buddhism in reaction to the established Buddhism of Japan. At the beginning of the book, Dōgen proclaimed:

If the Way works spontaneously everywhere, why do we separate practice and enlightenment? If the supreme teaching is free, why do we waste our time on the means of attaining it? Inasmuch as the whole truth has nothing to do with dust, why do we believe in the means of wiping it away? The Way is not separate from here and now; so what is the use of getting a foothold on practice? However, when there is even the slightest gap between two opposites, they are poles asunder like heaven and earth. When love and hate are differentiated even imperceptively, we are doomed to lose the Buddha-mind. It should be perfectly clear that an infinite recurrence of rebirth is due to our mental discrimination, while illusions and delusions of this world arise from an incessant persistence of selfish deliberation. If you wish to surpass even the pinnacle of spiritual advancement, you should understand clearly the here-and-now as it is (*jikige no jōtō*). Even if you boast of your understanding of Dharma and are richly gifted in enlightenment, even if you attain the Way and illuminate your mind, even if you are about to enter the realm of enlightenment with a soaring spirit, you are still short of the absolute freedom in which enlightenment itself is transcended (*shusshin no ro*). Although Buddha was endowed with great native wisdom, he sat in zazen six years. Bodhidharma bequeathed to us the legacy of the Buddha-mind, yet still sat facing a wall for nine years. Such were the ancient sages. Why cannot we practice like them? Therefore, desist from pursuing words and letters intellectually and reflect upon your self inwardly (*ekō-henshō*). Thus your body and mind shall be cast off naturally and your original nature (*honrai no memmoku*) shall be realized. If you wish to attain it, be diligent in zazen at once.[110]

The above statement indicated the direction and character of Dōgen's thought and activity in the subsequent period of his life. In the simplest and purest form of zazen-only, Dōgen found the essence and prototype of Buddhist *cultus* as well as *mythos*, and the crystallization of practice and enlightenment.

Dōgen stayed at the Kenninji temple for three years. In the meantime, as the peculiarities of his Zen became manifest in his teaching and education of disciples, and his name became more and more famous, enmity from both Hiei and Kenninji seems to have been aggravated. It was perhaps this enmity that led Dōgen eventually to move in 1230 to an abandoned temple called An'yōin in Fukakusa.[111] While in the An'yōin temple, Dōgen wrote *Shōbōgenzō*, "Bendowa," which expounded his basic tenets in the form of eighteen questions and answers. Expanding the basic thought of *Fukan-zazengi*, Dōgen made clear the purpose of his writing this chapter which was also applicable to all his subsequent writings:

In our country principles of the practice of zazen have not yet been transmitted. This is a sad situation for those who try to understand zazen. For this reason I have endeavored to organize what I learned in China, to transcribe some wise teachers' teachings, and thereby to impart them to those who wish to practice and understand zazen.[112]

Thus, with *Fukan-zazengi* and the "Bendōwa" chapter was laid the cornerstone of Dōgen's whole religious and philosophical citadel. Upon this foundation Dōgen's Zen Buddhism, though initially transplanted from China, gradually developed into a distinctively Japanese form which was the product of the symbolic model Dōgen inherited from Buddhist tradition (which will be greatly elaborated later on), his own idiosyncrasies, and the social and historical peculiarities of thirteenth-century Japan. The Way was transmitted and transformed.

As the number of his followers had daily increased, Dōgen moved again in 1233, this time to the Kannon-dōriin temple in Fukakusa which had been built as the Gokurakuji temple and maintained by the Fujiwara family for generations. Dōgen's life at this place for the following ten years (1233–43) was his most creative period, literary and otherwise: he expanded the original Kannon-dōriin into the Kōshō-hōrinji temple, accepted Koun Ejō (1198–1280) as his disciple and the head monk (*shuso*) of the temple,[113] and wrote forty-four chapters of *Shōbōgenzō*, including such crucially important chapters as "Genjō-kōan," "Busshō," and *Eihei shoso gakudō-yōjinshū* and *Tenzo-kyōkun*. These events were not separate but were intimately interconnected with each other.

In the winter of 1234 Ejō became a disciple of Dōgen. From the age of seventeen Ejō had studied such schools of Buddhism as Tendai, Shingon, Kusha (Abhidharmakośa), Jōjitsu (Satyasiddhi), Hossō (Yogācāra), etc., on Mt. Hiei, and later the Pure Realm school from Shōkū (1147–1247),[114] and Zen Buddhism from Kakuan of Tōno-mine. Thus Ejō was already well versed in Buddhism in general. He probably met Dōgen for the first time immediately after the latter returned from China. Although Ejō was two years older than Dōgen, he must have been impressed by Dōgen's fresh interpretation of Buddhism in general and Zen in particular. Two years after this first meeting Ejō became Dōgen's disciple. For nearly twenty years thereafter, until Dōgen's death, teacher and disciple worked together to found Sōtō Zen in Japan. The timing of Ejō's discipleship was crucially important: Dōgen needed an able co-worker for the education of disciples, administration of the temple, and also for the pending project of the founding of the Kōshōji temple.

In December 1235, Dōgen started a fund-raising campaign for the building of a new monastics' hall (*sōdō*), the center of monastic activities. In light of the calamitous circumstances of the time, this drive must have been far from easy; yet the completion of the monastics' hall was accomplished in the fall of the following year. In *Shōbōgenzō zuimonki* Ejō reported the following remarks made by Dōgen:

> It should not be thought, necessarily, to be for the growth of Buddhism that we now campaign for the building fund of the monastics' hall and take pains with that project. At present the number of students is still small, so, instead of doing nothing and wasting time, I want to offer an opportunity for those who have gone astray to get acquainted with Buddhism and, at the same time, to provide a place for monastics' practice of zazen. Also there should be no regret even if the original project is not completed. I will not be distressed even if people in the future, seeing just one pillar I have built, think that despite my intentions I failed to finish it.[115]

On October 15, 1236, the opening ceremony of the monastics' hall was successfully held and the temple was named officially Kōshō-hōrinji temple. As we shall see, this was an epoch-making event in the history of Japanese Zen Buddhism, because it was the realization of Po-chang's envisionment in which the monastics' hall was the center of monastic life. On December 29, Dōgen appointed Ejō to be the head monk whose function was to assist the abbot in all educational as well as religious matters of the monastic community. At the same time Ejō delivered his first sermon in place of Dōgen.[116] About a year later the Dharma hall (*hattō*) was added to the temple through the efforts of Shōgaku zenni. Thus, combined with the Buddha hall (*butsuden*) which had existed from the beginning, Dōgen's dream was realized, for in his view the monastics' hall, the Dharma hall, and the Buddha hall were the three most important buildings of a monastic community.[117] The Kōshō-hōrinji temple was gradually emerging as one of the most powerful centers of Buddhism in Japan.

Dōgen opened his monastic community for everyone, regardless of intelligence, social status, sex, or profession. His religion was through and through the religion of the people, as were other "new" Kamakura Buddhist sects. His logic of universalism was thoroughgoing, if not always consistent. Dōgen wrote: "In their excess of mercy the Buddhas and ancestors have opened the boundless gate of compassion (*kōdai no jimon*) so that all sentient beings may be led into enlightenment. Who in the heavens and on earth cannot enter it?"[118] Also Dōgen proclaimed like Shinran: "There is a very easy way to become a Buddha." [119] From such a standpoint Dōgen wrote further: "Zazen-only is of foremost importance for the growth of a Zen monastic. Through the practice of zazen, irrespective of intelligence, one will mature naturally." [120] He also said:

The true learning of the Way is not dependent on one's native intelligence or acquired learning, nor on cleverness or quickness. This should not be construed as an exhortation to become like the blind, the deaf, or the fool. Truth does not employ erudition and high intelligence, so do not despair of being endowed with slowness and inferior intelligence. For the true learning of the Way should be easy. [121]

Similar statements are replete in Dōgen's works. Despite his aristocratic origin and philosophical erudition nothing was more alien to his thought than social condescension or intellectual arrogance.

Dōgen's religion abolished the separation between monastics and lay persons. "Those who regard mundane life as an obstacle to Dharma know only that there is no Dharma in secular activities; they do not yet know that no secular activities exist in Dharma." [122] Monastics and laity are in essence one and the same. "It [enlightenment] depends," wrote Dōgen, "solely upon whether you have a sincere desire to seek it, not upon whether you live in a monastery or in the secular world." [123]

Nevertheless Dōgen also stated as follows:

Of all the Buddhas in the three periods and in the ten quarters not a single Buddha attained Buddhahood through the secular life. Because of those Buddhas of the past, monasticism and ordination have their merits. Sentient beings' attainment of the Way necessarily depends upon entering into the monastic's life and receiving the precepts. Indeed the monastic's life and the vow to observe the precepts, being the unchanging law of Buddhas, are possessed of boundless merits. Although in the sacred teachings there is the view which advocates the attainment of Buddhahood through the secular life, it is not the rightly transmitted teaching. . . . What the Buddhas and ancestors have rightly transmitted is to become a Buddha through monasticism. [124]

 He went so far as to say that "even if a monastic violates the precepts, he/she is superior to a lay person who does not break his/her precepts." [125] Thus these passages pose one of the thorniest problems in Dōgen studies—his view on monasticism and laity.

However, as we shall see in more detail later, Dōgen held, from the very beginning to the very end, that "homelessness" was the ideal possibility or model of rightly transmitted Buddhism, which transcended both the monastic's life and the householder's life in their ordinary senses; Dōgen's universalism was envisioned in terms of monastic elitism.[126] That is to say, Dōgen held up the monastic life as a challenge to his Buddhist contemporaries as well as to the secularists of the time. The monastic life was not a withdrawal from the world, but a challenge, an invitation, a recommendation to the world. It is in this light that we understand Dōgen's idealization of monasticism and his relentless demand that he and his disciples pursue the Way for the sake of the Way without accommodating worldly interests and concerns. Fundamentally speaking, the ideal of monasticism was the ideal of every human being; to be born was the initiation into the monastic's life. He wrote:

> Therefore, whether we are heavenly beings, humans, rulers, or all the officials, whether we are laypeople, monastics, servants, or brutes, we should uphold Buddhist precepts and rightly transmit the monastics' robes in order to become the children of Buddha. Indeed this is the shortest way to rightly enter the rank of Buddha.[127]

This was quite different from the approaches taken by his contemporaries such as Shinran and Nichiren. While the latter were equally anti-secular and anti-authoritarian, they approached the matter of liberation by adapting the Way to the levels of the common people (*taiki-seppō*) who were living in the Age of Degenerate Law. The easy path (*igyō*), advocated in terms of the recitation of "Namu-Amida-Butsu" (*myōgō*) and "Namu-Myōhō-Rengekyō" (*daimoku*), was "superior" to other methods precisely because it was superlatively adapted to the religious situation of the age. It was the means of these leaders involving themselves with human existence.

On the other hand, accommodating himself to inferior and mediocre minds had little appeal for Dōgen. In this respect Dōgen retained his aristocratic elitism, while at the same time he detested any flattering association with power and authority. It must be remembered that at this time incessant earthquakes, epidemics, fires, famines, social unrest, and so forth, had brought incalculable suffering upon the entire populace. Yet, unlike Shinran and Nichiren, Dōgen seems to have been well-nigh impervious to all this, not because he lacked compassion but because his compassion was modulated in a different key, as it were, though such a view of compassion is no doubt vulnerable to the criticism that it is misplaced and inhuman.

Dōgen repudiated, at least in principle, religious discrimination between the sexes. To the question of whether zazen can be practiced by man and woman in the secular life or should be practiced only by a monk, Dōgen answered: "The understanding of Dharma, as the ancestors taught, does not depend on differences in sex and in rank."[128] His case for the equality of sexes was most eloquently stated in the following:

Some people, foolish in the extreme, also think of woman as nothing but the object of sensual pleasures, and see her this way without ever correcting their view. A Buddhist should not do so. If man detests woman as the sexual object, she must detest him for the same reason. Both man and woman become objects, thus being equally involved in defilement.[129]

Dōgen continues:

What charge is there against woman? What virtue is there in man? There are wicked men in the world; there are virtuous women in the world. The desire to hear Dharma and the search for enlightenment do not necessarily rely on a difference in sex.[130]

Thus, Dōgen ridicules the Buddhist practice of "no admittance to woman" (*nyonin-kinzei*) as "a laughable matter in Japan."[131]

The rapid expansion of Dōgen's Buddhism can be seen in the fact that an annex (*jūundō*) had to be added to the monastics' hall already in 1239. In commemoration of this event, Dōgen wrote twenty-one instructions on life in the annex in his *Kannon-dōri Kōshō-gokokuji jūundōshiki*, which begins with the statement: "Those who have believing minds and give up desire for worldly fame and gain shall enter. Those who lack sincerity shall not join; entering mistakenly, they shall depart after due deliberation." And: "The congregation in the hall should be in harmony with one another just like milk and water, and endeavor to live by the Way." The book ends with this remark: "The foregoing instructions are the body and mind of the Buddhas and ancestors: revere and follow them."[132]

In 1241 such able disciples as Ekan, Gikai (1219–1309), Giin, Gien, Gijun, and others (who had been the disciples of Dainichibō Nōnin) joined Dōgen's community. It is significant to note that Dainichibō Nōnin was the forerunner among Japanese Buddhists to establish a "pure Zen" (*junsui-zen*) in contrast to the traditional "mixed Zen" (*kenju-zen*).

Thus the primitive order of the Sōtō sect in Japan was formed with deep commitment to pure Zen. As we shall see, Dōgen wished to establish Zen Buddhism, unadulterated, full-fledged, and clearly distinguished from all non-Zen schools of Buddhism, as well as from those Zen schools which had been admixed with esoteric Buddhism. Thus viewed, Dōgen, like Dainichibō Nōnin, was passionately puristic in this respect, and indomitably independent of all Buddhist schools.

It also should be noted that Hatano Yoshishige, a well-known member of the supreme court of the shogunate in Rokuhara, became a devout follower of Dōgen and himself entered into monkhood eventually. Hatano played an important role in the further development of Dōgen's religion.

The founding of the Kōshō-hōrinji temple and Ejō's assistance must have given Dōgen a favorable opportunity for the unfoldment of the creative literary activity to which we have referred previously. The core of Dōgen's thought seems to have matured during this period.

As time went on, Dōgen himself must have felt compelled to define his own position more articulately in order to distinguish it from other schools of Buddhism. As we have noted already, he criticized Buddhism, both established and new, unflinchingly. Early in his career he criticized Pure Realm Buddhism unduly:

Do you know the merits attained by the reading of sūtras and the practice of nembutsu? It is most pitiful that some believe in the virtue of just moving the tongue or of raising the voice. Taking them for Dharma, they become more and more remote from it. . . . To try to realize the Way by way of nembutsu—moving the mouth foolishly ten million times—can be compared to the attempt to leave for Yüeh [south] by orienting the thill of your cart towards the north. . . . Lifting the voice incessantly is just like a frog croaking day and night in a rice pad in the springtime. It is after all futile, too.[133]

In the context of his criticism of such schools as Hokke, Kegon, and Shingon, Dōgen wrote: "A Buddhist should neither argue superiority or inferiority of doctrines, nor settle disputes over depth or shallowness of teachings, but only know authenticity or inauthenticity of practice."[134] And Dōgen relentlessly criticized the Buddhists of these schools, calling them "the scholars who count words and letters" (*monji o kazouru gakusha*). Dōgen sharply set himself apart from scholastically oriented Buddhism by characterizing his own religion as being intent upon the authenticity of practice for which he had a burning sense of mission and a stubborn purism.

Coupled with his rising popularity, this stubbornness and sense of mission did not fail to irritate the traditionally minded Buddhists, especially those on Mt. Hiei. Thus Dōgen's position at the Kōshō-hōrinji temple became increasingly threatened by the traditionalists. At the same time, however, Dōgen was offered an attractive invitation by Hōjō Yasutoki to visit Kamakura but flatly refused it, perhaps because his anti-authoritarian spirit was too unconquerable to allow him to accept.[135]

Despite all this, he dedicated *Gokoku shōbōgi* (*Significance of the Right Dharma for the Protection of the Nation*) to the imperial authority. This gesture touched off Hiei's furies against Dōgen. Here he seems to have followed the footsteps of other Japanese Buddhists and/or the loyal family tradition of the Murakami Genji. He too was deeply involved with other reglionists, as well as with nobles and warriors—the well-known tripartite camps of the upper echelon of Kamakura Japan.

A proposal to move the monastic headquarters to the province of Echizen was made by Hatano Yoshishige, who offered his own property in the province for the site of a new monastery. Dōgen's acceptance of this offer seems to have been hastened by several factors: (1) As we have seen, the pressures of established Buddhism led Dōgen to the realization that the original vision of his monastic ideal was insurmountably difficult to carry out in the current surroundings.[136] (2) As Furuta contends, his sense of rivalry with the Rinzai sect, particularly with Enni Ben'en (1202–1280) of the Tōfukuji temple—Dōgen's most powerful contemporary—might have driven him to a more self-conscious effort to establish Sōtō Zen as opposed to Rinzai Zen despite his advocacy of a catholic Buddhism. Significantly enough, his anti-Rinzai remarks became especially frequent around 1243 and thereafter.[137] (3) Dōgen was more and more reminded of Ju-ching's instruction: "Do not stay in the center of cities or towns. Do not be friendly with rulers and state ministers. Dwell in the deep mountains and valleys to realize the true nature of humanity."[138] (4) Dōgen's unquenchable yearnings for nature rather than urban commotion must have grown in this period as we surmise from his exaltation of mountains and waters (*sansui*): "From timeless beginning have mountains been the habitat of great sages. Wise ones and holy persons have all made mountains their secret chambers and their bodies and minds; by them mountains are fulfilled."[139] And finally, (5) all these circumstances and factors reinforced his original belief in ascetic Buddhism (*shukke-Bukkyō*), rather than mundane Buddhism (*zaike-Bukkyō*). Ascetic Buddhism had consistently been the model of Buddhism for Dōgen from the very beginning. Sadly, Dōgen must have realized the impracticability of his ideal of universal monasticism in the mundane world, and perhaps with a tinge of pessimism, must have been attracted increasingly to the community of a select few in order to exemplify his utopian vision.

This shift in emphasis, not in principle, contrasts significantly with his earlier position, namely, the dissemination and popularization of zazen in Japan as widely as possible. Nevertheless, this stress on elitism rather than universalism did not imply in the slightest the disownment of his determination to change the world as much as the self. On this account we must not minimize the social significance of monastic asceticism.

On July 30, 1243, Dōgen arrived in the province of Echizen and immediately entered a small temple called Kippōji, which had long been in a state of desolation. The Kōshōji temple, on the other hand, was left to his disciple Gijun. Dōgen stayed at the Kippōji temple, and occasionally went to Yamashibu to preach. Although the Kippōji period lasted only about a year, Dōgen, secluded from the world by heavy snow, preached and worked as energetically as ever, thus producing twenty-nine chapters of *Shōbōgenzō*. This indicates that Dōgen was still at the height of his literary productivity.

In the meantime, Hatano Yoshishige and other lay disciples had been engaged in the construction of the Daibutsuji temple, to which Dōgen moved on July 18, 1244. The Dharma hall and the monastics' hall were built in rapid succession. In April, 1245, Dōgen announced the observance of the *geango* period for the first time in the history of the new headquarters.

On June 15, 1246, Dōgen changed the name of the Daibutsuji to the Eiheiji temple. "Eihei" meant "eternal peace" and was the name of the era in the Later Han dynasty during which Buddhism was said to have been introduced to China. Thus, Dōgen signalled the introduction to Japan of the eternal peace of Buddhism. He at last realized his long-cherished dream: the establishment of an ideal monastic community, as envisioned by Po-chang Huai-hai (720–814), in the bosom of mountains and waters. Echizen was an ideal place for such a purpose, for it was physically remote from Kyōto and Kamakura, hence free from the established Buddhism, the imperial–Fujiwara power complex, and the warrior class. Thus, the Eiheiji temple became the symbol of the "center of the world" (*axis mundi*) in the religion of Dōgen and his followers.[140]

In the Daibutsuji-Eiheiji period Dōgen wrote only eight chapters of *Shōbōgenzō*. He directed his efforts primarily to the formulation and guidance of moral precepts and disciplinary rules for the monastic community rather than to the exposition of his thought. This period was characterized by his concentration on the ritualization of every aspect of monastic life. He wrote, for example, *Taidaiko-goge-jarihō* (1244), which established the sixty-two rules of behavior for junior members of the monastic community in relation to senior members who had received the training for five years or more; *Nihonkoku Echizen Eiheiji chiji-shingi* (1246), in which the six administrative leaders were instructed with respect to their treatment of inferiors (in contrast to *Taidaiko-goge-jarihō*, this was written for the monastic leaders); *Bendōhō* (circa 1244–46), containing minute instructions concerning early morning zazen, morning zazen, early evening zazen, and evening zazen, all aspects of daily life in the monastics' hall such as washing the face, wearing the robe, the way to sleep; *Eiheiji jikuimmon* (1246), in which Dōgen exalted the spiritual significance of preparing and taking a meal (his instructions were permeated by his notion that eating itself was a spiritual matter); *Fushuku-hampō* (circa 1246–53), which specified, in minute detail, mealtime manners and rules presenting Dōgen's metaphysics of eating, in which food and Dharma were nondually one; *Kichijōzan Eiheiji shuryō-shingi* (1249), in which Dōgen formulated the code of conduct in the monastic library which was regarded by him as the center of intellectual life;[141] and *Eiheiji jūryo seiki* (1249) in which he admonished disciples not to be involved with or cater to political and religious powers. Such formulations of morality and cult were directly derived from his conception of the sanctity of every aspect of life; they were regarded as free expressions of Buddha-nature rather than as rules and codes that bound the lives of ordinary monastics.

Thus the Eiheiji monastery was an exclusive religious and educational community of the very best seekers who had an unflinching determination to grow in the wisdom and compassion of the bodhisattva way and thus become members in the family tradition of the Buddhas and ancestors (*busso no kafū*).[142] This community was also designated as the community of truth (*shinjitsu-sō*), the community of peace and harmony (*wagō-sō*), or the community of purity (*shōjō-sō*).

For about seven months between August 3, 1247, and March 13, 1248, Dōgen preached before Hōjō Tokiyori of the Kamakura government, but declined his offer of property in the Echizen province.[143] In view of his rejection of Yasutoki's invitation, Dōgen's Kamakura visit may be construed as self-contradictory, but he seems to have complied with Hatano Yoshishige's earnest request.[144] There are different speculations concerning what Dōgen recommended to or discussed with Tokiyori during his stay in Kamakura; the question is still open to further investigation.[145]

In 1250 the ex-emperor Gosaga sent an offer to Dōgen to bestow a purple robe upon him. Dōgen declined more than once, but finally accepted on imperial insistence. However, Dōgen never wore the robe till the end of his life.[146] From about 1250 on, he suffered from ill health and his participation in monastic activities was greatly hampered. His condition worsened around the summer of 1252. Yet on January 6, 1253, Dōgen wrote *Shōbōgenzō*, "Hachi-dainingaku," which was his last message given to his disciples in anticipation of his approaching death. According to remarks by Gien and Ejō, inserted at the end of this chapter, Dōgen hoped to compose a total of one hundred chapters for *Shōbōgenzō*, but could not accomplish it. Ejō wrote: "Unfortunately we cannot see a one-hundred chapter version. This is a matter for deep regret."[147]

On July 14, Dōgen appointed Ejō to be his successor as the head of the Eiheiji monastery. Following Hatano Yoshishige's advice, Dōgen finally reluctantly left Echizen for Kyōto, on August 5, accompanied by Ejō and several other disciples, in order to seek medical care. He was treated at the home of his lay disciple Kakunen in Kyōto; however, his illness, perhaps aggravated by the journey, was already too advanced to be cured by any medical treatment.

On August 28, Dōgen bade farewell to his grieving disciples and died in the posture of zazen.

THREE

Activity, Expression, and Understanding

IT IS often said that meditation and wisdom are the foot and eye of Buddhism. Wisdom is never conceived apart from meditation, and vice versa. This inseparability is clearly stated in such statements as: "There is no meditation for one who is without wisdom, no wisdom for one without meditation; one in whom there are meditation and wisdom, one indeed is close to nirvāṇa,"[1] and "When meditation and wisdom are equal, one sees all things."[2] No matter what the precise meanings of the two, and no matter what their relationship is, their mutual inseparability seems to differentiate Buddhism from the general tradition of Western philosophy and religious thought. In fact, we may even say, though at the risk of oversimplification, that the history of Buddhist thought consists of various interpretations of meditation and wisdom and their relationship. Thus the Buddhist symbolic model has meditation and wisdom as its primary structural elements.[3]

Dōgen was no exception to this tradition. Although his thought was enormously complex, subtle, and elusive, meditation and wisdom still remained as the fundamental structural elements of his thought. It is for this reason that the analysis of these two polar concepts in the total context of Dōgen's thought is imperative for its elucidation and understanding. In this chapter, therefore, it will be our purpose to examine this problem.

The Rightly Transmitted Buddha–Dharma

As we have seen before, Dōgen studied Sōtō Zen for two years under Ju-ching who belonged to the Chen-hsieh line of that tradition, and he was proud of his truthful transmission of Ju-ching's teachings to Japan. Despite his frequent attacks on Rinzai Zen, particularly Ta-hui Tsung-kao and his followers, in an unduly harsh, sectarian manner, and moreover, despite his criticisms of other Buddhist sects and schools, we can reasonably maintain that Dōgen's intention was not to establish any particular sect or school of Buddhism or Zen but to disseminate what he called the "rightly transmitted Buddha-dharma" (*shōden no buppō*), which transcended all sectarian divisions and divisiveness. The Buddha-dharma that was rightly transmitted was neither the body of creeds, nor the content of certain experiences, nor any Absolute, nor a return to the letter of Buddha's teachings, or the like; it was the symbolic expression of the spirit of Śākyamuni the Buddha which opened up the mysteries and horizons of Buddha-nature and which was the rationale for sectarian differentiations.

Thus, he rejected the fashionable distinctions between Zen and other Buddhist schools, that is, between the school of the Buddha-mind (*busshin-shū*), and the schools of the Buddha-word (*butsugo-shū*),[4] between Tathāgata Zen (*nyorai-shōjō-zen* or *nyorai-zen*) and Ancestral Zen (*soshi-zen*),[5] between "Kōan-introspection" Zen (*kanna-zen*) and "Silent-illumination" Zen (*mokushō-zen*),[6] and so on.

His views on these matters are amply discussed and expounded in a number of chapters of *Shōbōgenzō* and other writings. First of all, Dōgen severely criticizes designations such as "Zen sect" (*zenshū*), "Zen ancestors" (*zenso*), "Zen students" (*zensu*), "Bodhidharma sect" (*daruma-shū*), and the like. They are said to be the "violations of the Way" and the "enemies of the Buddhas and ancestors."[7] Moreover, Dōgen denounces the so-called "Five Houses" of Chinese Zen Buddhism and warns that Lin-chi's "Three Mysteries and Three Essentials" (*sangen-san'yō*), "Four Arrangements of Subject and Object" (*shiryōken*), "Fourfold Precedence and Subsequence of Light and Activity" (*shishōyū*). Yün-mên's "Three Phrases" (*sanku*), Tung-shan's "Five Ranks" (*goi*), and similar doctrines of various Zen traditions are "mad expressions." He levels his criticism at each of the Five Houses, not excepting his own Sōtō sect.[8] Analogously, he considers the designation of the school of the Buddha-mind, in contrast to the school of the Buddha-word, to be preposterous and false. All these sectarian distinctions are a "grave offence," bringing "impiety" and "disgrace" to the Buddhas and ancestors, and ultimately they can be traced back to a lack of "seeking the Way to its roots" and of the spirit of "longing for antiquity," as well as to the "confused state of the worldly mind."[9]

When Dōgen visited China during the Southern Sung period, it was the heyday of Ancestral Zen and of the method of kōan introspection under the leadership of the followers of Ta-hui Tsung-kao. Dōgen witnessed a number of Zen Buddhists who categorically denounced the scriptural and doctrinal studies. Ancestral Zen seems to have reached its most extreme form at the time of Lin-chi I-hsüan (d. 866), Tê-shan Hsüan-chien (780–865), and Yang-shan Hui-chi (814–890), and its extremity must have still been quite flagrant during Dōgen's stay in China.[10]

Under such circumstances Dōgen endeavored to go beyond any arbitrary distinction between Ancestral Zen and Tathāgata Zen to the spirit of Buddha himself, and advocated the necessity of the study of both traditional scriptures and the records of Zen ancestors. This stand was taken in opposition to the traditional Zen principle, "a special tradition outside the scriptures" (*kyōge-betsuden*), which set apart Ancestral Zen from Tathāgata Zen. At one place Dōgen wrote: "Do not misunderstand Buddhism by believing the erroneous principle 'a special tradition outside the scriptures'."[11] And he wrote:

The view that sūtras are not Dharma neither takes into account the time when the Buddhas and ancestors used the sūtras nor the time when they left them behind as a result of their study. It fails to recognize the degree of intimacy between the Buddhas and ancestors and the sūtras.[12]

You should tell them [those who reject sūtras]: "If sūtras are to be discarded as you advocate, you should abandon the Buddha-mind and the Buddha-body as well; if you are to throw Buddha's body-mind away, you should do so with the offspring of Buddha [all sentient beings], and in turn with the Buddha-way. Repudiating the Buddha-way, can you avoid rejecting the ancestral way?"[13]

A special tradition outside the scriptures, in Dōgen's view, does not exclude that tradition which is expounded in the scriptures. Both scriptural tradition and a special tradition are legitimate parts of his rightly transmitted Buddhism. In a similar fashion he placed strictures on other Zen tenets such as "no dependence upon words and letters" (*furyū-monji*), "direct pointing at the human mind" (*jikishi-ninshin*), "seeing into one's own nature and the attainment of Buddha-hood" (*kenshō-jōbutsu*), etc.[14]

It is necessary for us to distinguish between Kōan-introspection Zen and Silent-illumination Zen. As we are going to see in more detail later, Dōgen's "zazen-only" (*shikan-taza*) is closer to the Silent-illumination Zen of Sōtō Zen than to the Kōan-introspection Zen of Rinzai Zen, and his criticisms of the latter are more frequent and devastating than of the former. However, his reasons for such criticisms are based on his conception of the rightly transmitted Buddha-dharma. This point is demonstrated by his alteration of Hung-chih Chêng-chüeh's *Tso-ch'an-chên (Admonitions of Zazen)*—despite his whole-hearted admiration for this great teacher of Silent-illumination Zen in Sung China.[15] As Etō's comparative analysis shows, Dōgen's position is clearly differentiated from Hung-chih's in that the former emphasizes actional realization in contrast to the latter's intuitionistic illumination.[16] In short, both Kōan-introspection Zen and Silent-illumination Zen are criticized by Dōgen on the basis of his criterion—the rightly transmitted Buddha-dharma, which will be discussed shortly.

In the same vein, Dōgen views both Mahāyāna Buddhism and Theravāda Buddhism from this vantage point, though he is not altogether free of scornful remarks about the latter. However, he is remarkably free of the complacency and wishful thinking which are typical of Mahāyānist thinkers. For example, the Four Fruits (of the Theravāda path, i.e., stream-winner, once-returner, never-returner, and arahat), according to Dōgen, are not stages of spiritual progress, but enlightenment itself.[17] Likewise the Thirty-seven Stages to enlightenment (*saptatriṃśad bodhipākṣikā dharmāḥ*; *sanjūshichihon-bodaibumpō*) are reinterpreted by Dōgen in such a way that they are now the thirty-seven virtues *of* enlightenment—in Dōgen's own words, "the eyeballs, nostrils, skin-flesh-bones-marrow, hands, feet, and faces of the Buddhas and ancestors."[18] The arahat ideal is said to be identical in its soteriological intention with the ideal of Buddhas and bodhisattvas, that is, supreme enlightenment (*anuttara-samyak-saṃbodhi*).[19] All in all, "There is neither Mahāyāna nor Hīnayāna in the activities of a monastic."[20]

In the foregoing observations we have seen Dōgen's endeavor, through his notion of the rightly transmitted Buddha-dharma, to vindicate what he deemed to be the spirit of Śākyamuni Buddha himself, whom Dōgen thought was not only the historical Buddha but the cosmic Buddha, subsuming and transcending all the Buddhas. We shall say more on this matter later. What Dōgen attempted was not a mere return to or recapitulation of Buddha's teachings but a radical reexpression and reenactment of them. Thus his notion of the rightly transmitted Buddha-dharma involved a thorough demythologizing and remythologizing.

Then what is the criterion of the rightly transmitted Buddha-dharma? Dōgen states:

The Buddhas and Tathāgatas have an excellent way—unequalled and natural—to transmit the wondrous Dharma through personal encounter and to realize supreme enlightenment. As it is imparted impeccably from Buddha to Buddha, its criterion is the samādhi of self-fulfilling activity (*jijuyū-zammai*).

For playing joyfully in such a samādhi (*kono zammai ni yuke suruni*), the upright sitting in meditation is the right gate.[21]

The samādhi of self-fulfilling activity is often used in Buddhism in contrast to the samādhi of other-fulfilling activity (*tajuyū-zammai*). The former refers to that samādhi which is concerned with the self-enjoyment of the Body of Law (*Dharmakāya*; *hosshin*) without relating itself to other sentient beings, whereas the latter refers to that samādhi which is concerned with the enjoyment and fulfillment of others through the accommodation of the Body of Law to the needs and states of sentient beings in myriad forms, such as the Body of Enjoyment (*Sambhogakāya*; *hōjin*) and the Body of Transformations (*Nirmāṇakāya*; *ōjin*). (Briefly, the Body of Law refers to the transcendental Buddha, beyond time and space; the Body of Enjoyment, the mythic bodhisattvas; the Body of Transformations, the physical existence lived by the Buddha. This will be further developed later.) In the context of Dōgen's thought, the samādhi of self-fulfilling activity signifies the samādhi which at once negates and subsumes self and other—the Body of Law (or essence) on the one hand, and the Body of Enjoyment and the Body of Transformations (or accommodation) on the other. It refers to an absolute freedom of self-realization absent any dualism of antitheses. The crucially important thing to note, however, is that in Dōgen, opposites or dualities are not obliterated or even blurred; they are not so much transcended as realized. The absolute freedom in question here is that freedom which realizes itself in duality, not apart from it.

The criterion of the samādhi of self-fulfilling activity is not an abstract principle but itself a mode of activity. Thus Dōgen writes as noted previously: "A Buddhist should neither argue superiority or inferiority of doctrines, nor settle disputes over depth or shallowness of teachings, but only know authenticity or inauthenticity of practice."[22] The significance of this statement can be adequately appreciated if seen in the context of the current evolutionary classification of Buddhist teachings (*kyōsō-hanjaku*) or in the prevalent devolutionary view of history, that is, the doctrine of the Age of Degenerate Law (*mappō*). Dōgen rejected both, contending that the former was based on an arbitrary and complacent scheme of developmental stages of doctrines, and the latter on a faulty interpretation of the human nature and historical process. Instead, Dōgen found the criterion of truth and authenticity in a special quality of experience, or more accurately, of activity, which is epitomized in the samādhi of self-fulfilling activity.

This idea of the samādhi of self-fulfilling activity is inseparable from Dōgen's other fundamental thoughts. His conception of the rightly transmitted Buddha-dharma links this with the unity of practice and enlightenment (*shushō-ittō* or *shushō-ichinyo*), the casting-off of body and mind (*shinjin-datsuraku*), non-thinking (*hishiryō*), the total exertion (*gūjin*), abiding in a Dharma-position (*jū-hōi*), and so forth.

From this perspective, Dōgen interprets the entire history of Buddhism:

Śākyamuni Buddha and Mahākāśyapa lived by practice based on enlightenment (*shōjō no shu*): Bodhidharma and Hui-nêng were likewise guided by practice based on enlightenment. There is no exception in the way Dharma has been kept alive.[23]

One might wonder whether Dōgen was historically accurate with respect to the Indian teachers in whose view meditation seems to have been, primarily if not exclusively, a means to the attainment of enlightenment. However, concerning Chinese Buddhism, Dōgen seems to have rightly understood the general tenor of Hui-nêng (638–713), who is often said to have revolutionized Chinese Zen thought. Hui-nêng maintained the unity of meditation (*ting*) and wisdom (*hui*) comparing them to "substance" and "function" or to a "lamp" and "light," respectively.[24] He rejected the contemplative and instrumental view of meditation and the intellectualistic and substantialistic view of wisdom, whereby the unity of meditation and wisdom was understood in terms of activity. Dōgen took very seriously thoughts such as these that were implied by certain elements in Hui-nêng's teachings. On the other hand, Dōgen severely criticized the idea of "seeing into one's own nature" (*kenshō*) and went so far as to regard the *Platform Sūtra* as a spurious work and not the words of the sixth ancestor.[25] We can safely conjecture that Dōgen must have read a presently unknown Sung edition of this work which might have been highly idealistically oriented (as compared with the Tun-huang text which Dōgen did not know) and revolted against such elements which seem to have been associated with the view (of Kōan-introspection Zen of the time) that interpreted "seeing" and "one's own nature," in "seeing into one's own nature," dualistically. From his own standpoint, the activity of seeing was itself one's own nature.[26] Be that as it may, Dōgen, an ardent admirer of Hui-nêng, selected certain elements consistent with his conception of the rightly transmitted Buddha-dharma and was clearly intent on restoring those which according to him constituted the spirit of Hui-nêng and the essence of Buddhism.

Furthermore, Dōgen believed that the rightly transmitted Buddha-dharma was most authentically transmitted by and in Ju-ching's life and thought. That is, Dōgen generalized an interpretation of the history and essence of Buddhism in such a way that the rightly transmitted Buddha-dharma was bequeathed from Śākyamuni Buddha through Bodhidharma, Hui-nêng and his followers, to Ju-ching, and finally to Dōgen himself. This genealogy is traced back even to the primordial time of the Seven Buddhas of the past. To Dōgen the search for reason (*dōri*) consisted, to a considerable extent, in the longing for antiquity (*bōko*). He once said: "To practice and understand the way of ancient Buddhas is to realize it [in ourselves]. They [abide] from generation to generation. Although the 'ancient Buddha' in question is synonymous with 'old' in [the duality of] new and old, it also transcends, yet is faithful to, the ancient and the modern."[27] Fidelity to history was the way to transcend it. Here we see Dōgen's sense of mission in the history of transmission of the Way, and in the traditionalism, purism, and classicism which were dominant elements in his thought.

Dōgen's conception of the rightly transmitted Buddha-dharma has posed many complicated problems for students of the history of Buddhist thought, particularly in the relation of his idea to Japanese Tendai Buddhism of the late Heian and early Kamakura period and Chinese Zen Buddhism of the Sung period. I am inclined to think with Kagamishima Genryū that Dōgen was critical of both the view of Japanese Tendai "fideism," which had the premise of original enlightenment but denied the necessity of practice, and the view of Sung Chinese Zen which accepted practice based on original enlightenment in principle, yet retained (even with Ju-ching, according to Kagamishima) the vestiges of the dualistic view of acquired enlightenment.[28] Thus Dōgen endeavored to overcome the difficulties and inconsistencies of both Japanese and Chinese Buddhist and Zen traditions by advancing the view of practice based on original enlightenment not only in principle but in fact—a radicalization of the nonduality of practice and enlightenment in his own version of mystical realism which shall be elucidated throughout this work.

Zazen-Only: The Prototype of Absolute Meaninglessness

The crucial importance of meditation in Buddhist tradition has been increasingly acknowledged by many Buddhist students in recent times. Some quotations from various sources will demonstrate this point: "Meditational practices constitute the very core of the Buddhist approach to life."[29] "Meditation is the alpha and the omega of Buddhism."[30] "This acceptance of meditation as central to Buddhist practices is a common bond through which it may be possible for Theravāda and Mahāyāna to grow closer together in the future."[31] Although meditation is the common core of Buddhism, there are many different interpretations of it. Thus the history of Buddhism is co-extensive with the history of various conceptions and interpretations of meditation.[32]

Meditation or zazen, as a structural element of Dōgen's symbolic model, has an absolute simplicity in its form, yet is in its content impregnated with psycho-metaphysical and ethico-religious values and meanings—the crystallization of the creative possibilities of absolute emptiness. More importantly for our purpose, however, meditation in Dōgen is the prototype of religious thought and action—prototypical in the sense that it is, in its form and content, the compendium and paradigm of all activities (*gyōji*) and expressions (*dōtoku*) expounded later in this chapter. That is to say, Dōgen's zazen-only (*shikan-taza*) epitomizes the whole body of his religio-philosophical and cultic-moral visions and enactments. In this respect Dōgen's whole works—written or otherwise—are simply footnotes on zazen-only.[33]

When Dōgen returned from China in 1227, he immediately promulgated *Fukan-zazengi* in which he attempted to correct what he felt were errors made by Ch'ang-lu Tsung-che in his *Ch'an-yüan-ch'ing-kuei* (*Zen Monastic Rules*) and thereby to restore the spirit of the monastic ideal envisioned by Po-chang Huai-hai (720–814).[34] The central theme of *Fukan-zazengi* was zazen-only. Physically, this is no more than sitting upright in the cross-legged posture and meditating with a relaxed disposition. Dōgen instructs as follows:

For the practice of zazen a quiet room is recommended, while food and drink must be taken in moderation. Free yourself from all attachments, and bring to rest the ten thousand things. Think of neither good nor evil and judge not right or wrong. Stop the operation of mind, of will, and of consciousness (*shin-i-shiki*); bring to an end all desires, all concepts and judgments. To sit in zazen, put down a thick pillow and on top of this a second one. Thereafter one may choose either a full or half cross-legged position. In the full position (*kekka-fuza*) one places the right foot on the left thigh and the left foot on the right thigh. In the half position (*hanka-fuza*) only the left foot is placed upon the right thigh. Robe and belt should be worn loosely, but in order. Next the right hand rests on the left foot, while the back of the left hand rests in the palm of the right.

The two thumbs are placed in juxtaposition. The body must be maintained upright in zazen, without inclining to the left or to the right, forward or backward. Ears and shoulders, nose and navel must be aligned. The tongue is to be kept against the palate, lips and teeth are firmly closed, while the eyes are to be always open. After the bodily position is in order, also regulate your breathing. If a thought arises, take note of it and then dismiss it. When you forget all attachments steadfastly, you will become zazen itself naturally. This is the art of zazen. Zazen is the Dharma-gate of great repose and joy.[35]

The physical aspects of Dōgen's zazen are almost identical with Tsung-che's.[36] However, in Dōgen's thought, such a physical form is identified with the "whole truth of Buddhism" (*buppō no zendō*) or with the "right gate of Buddhism" (*buppō no shōmon*). Zazen for Dōgen is not one among many spiritual practices but the very best of all practices; accordingly, incense burning, worship, nembutsu, confession, and recitation of the sūtras are unnecessary.[37] Dōgen's exaltation of zazen and its virtues is almost ecstatic, as we see in the following:

[A meditator] passes beyond the entire universe at full speed and is greatly honored in the abode of the Buddhas and ancestors—[this is due to] zazen in the full cross-legged position (*kekka-fuza*). Treading upon the heads of heretics and demons, [one] becomes an initiate (*kochūnin*) in the secret chamber of the Buddhas and ancestors—[because of] zazen in the full position. This one truth alone [enables the individual] to transcend the furthest bounds of the Buddhas and ancestors. This is why they are engrossed in it and nothing else.[38]

Thus, zazen-only is called "the samādhi of samādhis" (*ōzammai*).

Dōgen justifies zazen-only by observing the commonality of this method, by means of which alone all the Buddhas and ancestors have attained enlightenment.[39] He appeals here simply to the undeniable historical fact. To the question of why sitting alone among the "four postures" of standing, walking, sitting, and lying down is especially chosen for spiritual practice, Dōgen argues:

We cannot comprehend fully the way in which all the Buddhas since olden times have practiced and attained enlightenment one after another. Looking for reasons [for adopting the sitting posture of zazen], you should know that it has been universally applied by Buddhists; beyond this, no further [reasons] should be asked. However, the ancestors have spoken highly of zazen as the Dharma-gate of repose and joy. Perhaps sitting is the most restful and balanced of the four postures. Indeed, not only one or two Buddhas but all the Buddhas and ancestors have followed the practice.[40]

Hence, the historical reason that all the Buddhas and ancestors have practiced it plus the psycho-physical reason that it is a form of ascesis best fitted for "repose and joy" (*anraku*) are presented here. Repose and joy, in this connection, are not idle sitting, but heightened awareness and aliveness.[41]

In connection with his justification of zazen, Dōgen contends that it is neither one of the Threefold Way of morality, meditation, and wisdom, nor one of the Six Perfections (*pāramitās*) of bodhisattvahood of almsgiving, morality, patience, vigor, meditation, and wisdom.[42] Zazen in Dōgen's rightly transmitted Buddha-dharma is zazen-only which is the primordial form of Buddhist spiritual life bound to no particular school, yet from which all schools and sects are derived. The corollary of this position is to reject any practice of zazen mixed with other practices or disciplines such as Shingon *mantra* and Tendai *śamatha-vipaśyanā* (*sikan*): "Indeed, unless one concentrates on one thing, one cannot attain the one wisdom [of Buddha],"[43] admonishes Dōgen.

Despite such arguments, this justification is incomplete unless the content of zazen-only is fully expounded. As we have noted earlier, the external form of Dōgen's zazen was not much different from Tsung-che's; their interpretations, however, differed markedly. Dōgen carefully scrutinized those portions of Tsung-che's document which were inconsistent with his view—those magical and instrumental views of zazen, for Tsung-che entertained the idea that zazen was a means to the attainment of magical yogic powers.[44] Furthermore, Dōgen continually refined his principles of zazen over the years so as to make them more internally consistent.[45] Dōgen also benefited from Hung-chih's *Tso-ch'an-chên,* whereby, as we have discussed before, he shifted from the latter's quietistic and contemplative orientation to his own actional and realizational orientation. Dōgen's most mature thought on zazen was presented in the popular edition of *Fukanzazengi,* "Zazengi" and "Zazenshin" of *Shōbōgenzō,* and *Bendōhō.*[46]

Dōgen's conception of zazen-only, then, is a reinterpretation of Chinese Zen of the Sung period (along with other forms of Buddhist meditation which he studied) which roots out "impure" and inconsistent elements and reinforces others germane to his view. The net result was a radically different conception of zazen in its content and significance. In brief, the samādhi of self-fulfilling activity, as the criterion of the rightly transmitted Buddha-dharma, means that the matter of supreme importance in religion is not abstract doctrines and theories so much as lived experience and activity which is crystallized in zazen-only.

The content of zazen-only can be considered from various standpoints. In the first place, zazen-only should be construed neither as obliterating experiences at the conscious level nor as advocating absorption in an undifferentiated realm. Dōgen has said:

Free yourself from all attachments, and bring to rest the ten thousand things. Think of neither good nor evil and judge not right or wrong. Stop the operation of mind, of will, and of consciousness (*shin-i-shiki*); bring to an end all desires, all concepts and judgements.[47]

It is a pity that they [those who tried to formulate the rules and principles of zazen] spent their whole lives visiting and staying in monasteries all over the country, yet failed to work out a single sitting, and that their sitting was altogether alienated from their true selves and their efforts no longer realized their true selves. The reason is not that meditators necessarily feel averse to their body-mind but that these individuals do not truly endeavor in zazen, hence are precipitously intoxicated in the midst of delusion. Their formulations are examples of merely "returning to the origin, back to the source" (*gengen-hempon*) and of attempts at vainly "stopping thoughts in abysmal quietude" (*sokuryo-gyōjaku*).[48]

Needless to say, zazen differs from mere dreams, fantasies, reveries, or compensatory projections, though Dōgen has something to say about these aspects of human experience, too, as we shall see on a later occasion. "Dispersion" at the conscious level and "dark sinking" at the unconscious level must be avoided, since common to both are confusions and chaos. In short, the confusion and chaos of differentiation and undifferentiation are redeemed; thereby we are liberated from the tyranny of the two for a new mode of thinking.

The problem is further expounded in his treatment of "thinking" (*shiryō*), "not-thinking" (*fu-shiryō*), and "non-thinking" (*hi-shiryō*) in connection with the story of Yüeh-shan Wêi-yen (745–828).[49] Dōgen writes:

While thinking in unmoving zazen (*gotsu-gotchi no shiryō*) has been taught by more than one person, Yüeh-shan's way is incomparably superior. It refers to "Think of this not-thinking." Thinking may be the skin-flesh-bones-marrow [of zazen]; likewise at times not-thinking may be the skin-flesh-bones-marrow [of zazen].

The monastic said: "How can I think of not-thinking? Not-thinking, though indeed time-honored, can be restated as "How's Thinking" (*ikan-shiryō*). Cannot there be thinking in the unmoving zazen? When you delve into the unmoving zazen deeply, you cannot but understand it. Unless you are extremely short-sighted, you should be able to scrutinize the unmoving zazen and have some thought on it.

Great Teacher [Yüeh-shan] said: "Non-thinking."

While one uses non-thinking translucently, to think of not-thinking is necessarily realized in and through non-thinking. There is "Who" in non-thinking; the "Who" maintains my self. Even though it is I that sits adamantly in zazen, it is not just thinking but none other than the totality of the unmoving zazen itself. If the unmoving zazen is what it is, how can it think of itself as its object?

Therefore, the unmoving zazen is not measured by Buddhas, by dharmas, by enlightenment, or by any comprehension.[50]

Here, Dōgen speaks of the thought of unmoving sitting in meditation (*gotsugotchi*), through which "thinking of not-thinking" is said to be realized. The function of *non*-thinking is not just to transcend both thinking and not-thinking, but to realize both, in the absolutely simple and singular act of immovable sitting itself. Ultimately, there is nothing but the act of immovable sitting in meditation which itself is the thought of immovable sitting in meditation. In other words, non-thinking is beyond thinking and not-thinking; nonetheless it is the form—a very special form of thinking beyond thinking and not-thinking, that is, thinking of not-thinking. Thus in Dōgen's conception of zazen-only, non-thinking is used not transcendentally so much as realizationally; it is objectless, subjectless, formless, goalless, purposeless. But it is not identical with a vacuum, void of intellectual content. What zazen-only does is not the elimination of intelligence but the realization of it. Furthermore, what intelligence does in zazen-only is to unfold, rather than to circumscribe, the mysteries of existence. Dōgen calls this "How's Thinking."[51]

In this connection the following points must be kept in mind. First, as we have said regarding Dōgen's reservation about Hung-chih, non-thinking should not be identified with mystical contemplation or illumination. For that matter, it is neither a philosophical contemplation (*theoria*) of eidetic forms, nor the experience of mystical union (*unio mystica*), nor a pantheistic apprehension of the self and the world. As Dōgen untiringly emphasizes, the Way is realized in and through the body.[52] Non-thinking has its roots firmly fixed in the most concrete physical matrix. Secondly, non-thinking is the essence of the samādhi of self-fulfilling activity—the bliss of enlightenment which Buddha himself enjoys (*jiju-hōraku*) and which is often referred to as joyous play (*yuke* or *yuge*). It is the activity of *homo ludens* par excellence in absolute inner freedom, being prototypical of the truth that whatever exists itself is its own raison d'être. Thirdly, thinking and not-thinking are said to be realized through emptiness;[53] and non-thinking is said to be right thought (*shōshiyui* or *shōshiryō*).[54] Thus emptiness, non-thinking, and right thought are interchangeably used by Dōgen. However, right thought here is post-logical. When, and only when, non-thinking is realized, is the authenticity of thought established. Finally, a characteristic of Dōgen's thought is that he uses a number of interrogatives in the Sung colloquial language in order to express his profound metaphysical ideas such as *shimo* or *somo* (what, how, which) and other related expressions. "How's Thinking" in the previous quotation is an example. As we shall examine more fully later, these interrogatives, along with the idea of emptiness and non-thinking, are significant in indicating that zazen for Dōgen is ultimately the expression of an eternal quest for the meaning of existence which is, paradoxically enough, meaningless— thus living the meaning of meaninglessness. This is Zen.[55]

In the second place, the content of zazen-only can be considered in terms of the unity of practice and enlightenment (*shushō-ichinyo, shushō-ittō,* or *honshō-myōshu*). This principle is succinctly stated as follows:

The view that practice and enlightenment are not one is heretical. In the Buddha-dharma they are one. Inasmuch as practice is based on enlightenment, the practice of a beginner is entirely that of original enlightenment. Therefore, in giving the instruction for practice, a Zen teacher advises his/ her disciples not to seek enlightenment beyond practice, for practice itself is original enlightenment. Because it is already enlightenment of practice, there is no end to enlightenment; because it is already practice of enlightenment, there is no beginning to practice.[56]

Thus, zazen-only is called "practice based on enlightenment" (*shōjō no shu*) in contrast to "practice prior to enlightenment" (*shōzen no shu*). Or practice is said to be "pure" or "undefiled" (*fuzenna no*), when it is not defiled by the dualism of practice and enlightenment in the means-end relationship. This is equivalent to the casting-off of the body-mind (*shinjin-datsuraku*). The act of sitting in meditation seeks no longer to attain a special state of consciousness, nor to become a Buddha, and consequently is called the "kōan realized in life" (*genjō-kōan* or *kōan-genjō*).[57] The attempt to attain enlightenment through zazen, or through the introspection of kōan, is the "meditation of awaiting enlightenment" (*taigo-zen*) or "acquired meditation" (*shūzen*).

The unity of practice and enlightenment does not wipe out the distinction between the two; the tension between them exists always, yet remains pure. Dōgen quotes often with approval what Nan-yüeh Huai-jang (677–744) answered to Hui-nêng (638–713), "Practice and enlightenment are not obliterated but undefiled."[58] Here we need to exercise utmost care in understanding this statement which epitomizes the crux of Dōgen's way of thinking. In Dōgen's view, the samādhi of self-fulfilling activity in its absolute purity is that very psycho-metaphysical activity, undefiled by and unattached to dualistic categories, events, and things, that our perception and intellect creates, while living with them and using dualities. For the dualistic world remains real, not dissolved. Therefore, the unity in question does not replace distinction but is unobstructed by it; it is post-critical, not pre-critical. Confronted with thought and reality, the mind is ever vigilant, deconceptualizing and deontologizing them as circumstances demand, and thereby attaining the state of absolute freedom and purity.

In the third place, zazen-only cannot be fully understood apart from the consideration of faith—the element fundamentally important in Dōgen's thought. If enlightenment is realized at the moment one sits in meditation, does this, nonetheless, allow some latitude for degrees of intellectual depth and stages of spiritual progress, that is, infinite individual variations and differences? Dōgen's answer is affirmative and provides faith for it. Previously, we have noted Dōgen's view that even the practice of a beginner is entirely made up of original enlightenment because practice is based on enlightenment, and that what matters most in religion is the authenticity of practice. Supporting such a view are statements like the following: "The Way is the Way, all the same, whether at the time of the initial desire for enlightenment or at the time of the final culmination of enlightenment. At the beginning, the middle, and the end of it is equally the Way."[59] "The practice of a beginner is entirely that of original enlightenment."[60] In stating this, Dōgen does not imply that faith precedes enlightenment or is eventually replaced by enlightenment. Throughout the ongoing advance in enlightenment (*bukkōjōji*), faith and enlightenment, or believing and seeing, are twin companions of emptiness and Buddha-nature.

From Dōgen's standpoint the psychological distinction between "once-born" and "twice-born" types of religious experience of William James is less important; instead, he is concerned with the logical structure of the samādhi of self-fulfilling activity, which is the criterion for spiritual authenticity. Thus for Dōgen faith lies in original enlightenment, and enlightenment comes from original faith. He writes:

It is imperative for those who practice the Way to believe in it. Those who have faith in the Way should know for certain that they are unfailingly in the Way from the very beginning—thus free from confusions, delusions, and disarray, as well as from additions, subtractions, and errors. Believing in this manner and penetrating the Way thus, practice it accordingly. Such is fundamental to learning the Way.[61]

The virtue of faith [in the exposition of the "Five Virtues" of faith, vigor, mindfulness, concentration, and wisdom] is engendered neither by the self nor by others. Because it is [generated] neither by forcing oneself nor by one's contrivance, neither by being coerced by others nor by fitting in a self-made norm, faith has been imparted intimately through ancestors in India and China. Faith is so called when the entire body becomes faith itself (*konshin-jishin*). Faith is one with the fruit of enlightenment; the fruit of enlightenment is one with faith. If it is not the fruit of enlightenment, faith is not realized. On account of this, it is said [in the *Mahāprajñāpāramitā-śāstra* by Nāgārjuna] that faith is the entrance to the ocean of Dharma. Indeed where faith is attained, there is the realization of the Buddhas and ancestors.[62]

Faith and enlightenment are often regarded as two antithetical ideas, so much so that Zen Buddhism is mistakenly thought to be exclusively the religion of enlightenment, faith being an inferior or even a foreign element, or at best a preliminary to enlightenment.[63] But in Dōgen's thought, faith and enlightenment interpenetrate each other so that without one the other cannot be fully meaningful. The inferior status of faith is repudiated once and for all; it now becomes the very core of enlightenment.[64]

In the fourth place, and lastly, zazen-only as the samādhi of self-fulfilling activity is intimately related to the principle of "the total exertion of a single thing" (*ippō-gūjin*), expressed in such favorite statements of Dōgen as "as one side is illumined, the other is darkened" (*ippō o shōsuru toki wa ippō wa kurashi*) and "the total experience of a single thing is one with that of all things" (*ippōtsū kore mambōtsū nari*). This principle is also inseparably associated with another cognate principle—"to abide in a Dharma-position" (*jū-hōi*)—which becomes crucially important, especially in connection with Dōgen's view of time. At one place Dōgen succinctly explains "the total experience of a single thing" (*ippōtsū*) as follows:

"The total experience of a single thing" does not deprive a thing of its own unique particularity. It places a thing neither against others nor against none. To place a thing against none is another form of dualistic obstruction. When total experience is realized unobstructedly (*tsū o shite tsū no ge nakara-shimuruni*), the total experience of a single thing is the same as the total experience of all things. A single total experience is a single thing in its totality. The total experience of a single thing is one with that of all things.[65]

An action, an event, a thing, or a being is chosen not dualistically, that is, as an action among actions, an event among events, and so forth, in a causal, hierarchical, evolutionary, or means–end model, but non–dualistically as the absolute action, as the absolute event, abiding in the Dharma-position of the absolute now discrete from before and after—there is nothing but that particular event which consumes the whole universe, and ultimately even this is emptied. Throughout this investigation we shall endeavor to demonstrate how important this idea is in Dōgen's thought. Suffice it to say for now that zazen-only is prototypical of such a *nondualistic choice* for existence at a given moment. Choice and nondualism are not a contradiction in terms. Herein lies the crux of Dōgen's mystical realism which is neither transcendental nor immanental in the conventional fashion but properly to be called realizational. Furthermore, as the model of zazen-only itself indicates, the solution is not merely intellectual but cultic and actional.

The content of zazen-only, as we have observed thus far in its diverse apsects, is what distinguishes Dōgen's meditation from other forms of meditation. Dōgen simplified, purified, enriched, and radicalized the content of zazen—methodologically, metaphysically, religiously—though his view was greatly influenced by Chinese and Japanese Buddhist tradition, especially by Zen and Tendai. Indeed, to Dōgen zazen-only was at once metaphor and reality.

Creative Activities

The prototype of zazen-only has two aspects: activities (*gyōji*) and expressions (*dōtoku*). As will become clearer, both are interchangeably used in Dōgen's thought, although we shall use, purely for convenience's sake, "activities" in connection with cultic and moral activities, and "expressions" in relation to intellectual and philosophic endeavors. But after all, expressions are expressive activities, activities are active expressions. Both are the self-activities and self-expressions (*jidōshu*) of Buddha-nature.

The necessity of activities is shown by Dōgen's analyses and interpretations of some traditional kōan stories. There is a famous story of Nan-yüeh's polishing a tile to make a mirror. The story runs something like this: Ma-tsu Tao-i (709–788) was practicing meditation every day. The teacher Nanyüeh Huai-jang (677–744) happened to see him and questioned him thus: "What is your aim in practicing zazen?" "My aim is to become a Buddha," came the answer. Next the teacher picked up a tile and began to polish it on a stone in front of the hermitage where Ma-tsu had been meditating. Bewildered by this strange act, Ma-tsu asked: "What is Teacher doing?" "I am polishing this tile to make a mirror." "How can you make a mirror by polishing a tile?" The teacher's reply was: "Likewise, how can you become a Buddha by practicing zazen?"[66]

Commenting on this story, Dōgen gives an unconventional interpretation which is characteristic of his treatment of other kōan stories as well. He contends in effect that the story advocated not only the Zen dictum "Do not attempt to become a Buddha" (*fuzu-sabutsu*) but, more importantly, the necessity of zazen undefiled. He writes:

Indeed we do know that when a tile, as it is being polished, becomes a mirror, Ma-tsu becomes a Buddha. When Ma-tsu becomes a Buddha, Ma-tsu becomes Ma-tsu instantly. When Ma-tsu becomes Ma-tsu, zazen becomes zazen immediately. Therefore, the tradition of making a mirror by polishing a tile has been kept alive in the core of ancient Buddhas.[67]

In the activity of zazen undefiled, a tile and a mirror, Ma-tsu and Buddha are one, though not dissolved. The tile is not transformed into the mirror, but the tile *is* the mirror; the act of polishing the tile itself is to unfold the purity of the mirror. Consequently, zazen, likened to the act of polishing the tile in this case, is nothing other than the unfolding enactment of original enlightenment, that is, the mirror. At one level, Dōgen affirms the conventional interpretation of the story, but at another he penetrates the matter far more deeply so that the story is now seen to have an entirely new significance. The real issue is not whether to meditate but how to meditate; the *how* is obviously not a matter of technique so much as a matter of authenticity.

Hence the following becomes meaningful:

Although this Dharma inheres in each of us in abundance, it does not become visible without practice, nor is it realized without enlightenment. If you let it go, it fills your hand; yet it transcends one and many. If you talk about it, it fills your mouth; yet it is infinite in space and time.[68]

Unless we take risks and choose to act, Buddha-nature never becomes visible, audible, tangible. Prior to human (and other sentient and insentient beings') creative activities and expressions, Buddha-nature cannot be said to exist in terms of potentialities, innate ideas, and so forth.[69] This is why Dōgen says: "The logic of Buddha-nature is such that it is provided not before becoming a Buddha, but afterwards. Buddha-nature and becoming a Buddha always occur simultaneously."[70] Only when we create our own identity through our body and mind, only then does Buddha-nature create itself.

Another example will elucidate the matter further:

Ma-ku Pao-ch'e was fanning himself one day when a monastic came and asked: "The nature of the wind is abiding and universally present. Why do you still use your fan?"

The teacher's answer was: "You know only the nature of the wind as abiding; you do not yet know the truth of its being universally present."

The monastic said: "What is the truth of its being universally present?"

The teacher only fanned himself without a word.

And the monastic saluted him.[71]

The monastic's intellectual grasp of the nature of the wind misses its crucially important characteristic, because the nature of the wind is such that it cannot be conceptualized or contemplated but is instead to be actualized; furthermore, it is not potentiality being actualized, but rather actuality creating itself through the act of fanning. Being a Buddha must be tested ever afresh by being an active Buddha (*gyōbu-tsu*). This is precisely what Dōgen meant by saying: "Buddha-nature and becoming a Buddha always occur simultaneously."[72] And also: "If you have attained enlightenment, you should not halt the practice of the Way by thinking of your present state as final. For the Way is infinite. Exert yourself in the Way ever more even after enlightenment."[73]

Inasmuch as the concept of activity in Dōgen's thought is primarily a religious rather than a philosophical one, as regards religious practice and discipline, it is naturally closely related to his treatment of the traditional theories of the Buddha-body (*buddha-kāya: busshin*)—a most representative formulation of which is the so-called "Threefold Body of Buddha"—and to his own conception of the active Buddha.

The Threefold Body of Buddha consists of the Body of Law (*Dhar-makāya; hosshin*), the Body of Enjoyment (*Saṃbhogakāya; hōjin*), and the Body of Transformations (*Nirmāṇakāya; ōjin*). The Body of Law is the transcendental body of Buddha which is utterly beyond time and space, formless, impersonal, immutable, being confined to itself. It is designated by such words as emptiness, thusness, Dharma-nature, and so on, and apprehended by prajñā. The Body of Law is primarily the subject of metaphysical speculation. The Body of Enjoyment refers to the "mythopoeic" body of Buddha which enables mythic figures such as bodhisattvas to enjoy the rewards of their merits and vows to save sentient beings. It is at once transcendental and phenomenal, at once historical and supra-historical, consistent with the Mahāyāna spirit of "neither abiding in nirvāṇa nor abiding in saṃsāra" and with the dual nature of Buddha as both emptiness and compassion. Amida Buddha of Pure Realm Buddhism is a classical example of the Body of Enjoyment. The Body of Transformations is the physical and historical body of Buddha who lived in about the sixth century B.C.E. and preached Dharma to his disciples. In the evolution of various theories of the Buddha-body, the Body of Enjoyment was introduced relatively later in order to reconcile the theory of two Buddha-bodies, that is, the Body of Law and the Body of Transformations.[74] In the structure of Buddhist experience, however, these three bodies represent one living reality of Buddha-dharma.

Be that as it may, it is also undeniable that the traditional doctrine of the Threefold Body of Buddha has a strong tendency to relegate historical and empirical realities to a metaphysically inferior status. Thus the historicity of the Body of Transformations is only superficially historical, because the life of Śākyamuni Buddha, for example, is construed as the "appearance" of the Body of Law, and his conducts on this earth as "make-believe acts" to guide the deluded sentient beings. As Sangharakshita notes, "In the system as a whole, however, Gautama the Buddha occupies a distinctly subordinate, indeed almost insignificant position, and one is often left with the impression that the Mahāyāna could now get on quite well without Him."[75] To be sure, Dharma in Buddhism means always Buddha-dharma, indicating a certain relation to the historical Buddha; yet the latter never means the once-and-for-all event of Person that qualitatively sets itself apart from all other historical events. Śākyamuni Buddha is not solely the historical person who was awakened to Dharma and has been revered as the initiator of turning the wheel of Dharma; he is also one of the innumerable transcendental Buddhas in the three periods of past, present, and future and in all the realms of the universe. By and large, the predominant propensity in Mahāyāna Buddhism has been to deemphasize or even obscure the historicity of Śākyamuni Buddha; its historical mooring, if any, has been tenuous. However, the situation changes significantly in Theravāda Buddhism.

Such a characterization of the doctrine of the Buddha-body may seem unfair to Mahāyāna Buddhism, but such an understanding seems to have been what made Dōgen, at least, unhappy about the traditional conception, when he proposed his own view.

When he speaks of the pantheon of Buddhas, Tathāgatas, and bodhisattvas, Dōgen is not too different from other Buddhists. He en-
joined his disciples to reverently recite the names of the ten Buddhas
every day: Birushana-butsu (Vairocana Buddha) as the Body of Law,
Rushana-butsu as the Body of Enjoyment, Śākyamuni Buddha, Mi-
roku (Maitreya), all the Buddhas in the three periods and the ten
quarters, Monju (Mañjuśrī), Fugen (Samantabhadra), Kanzeon or
Kannon (Avalokiteśvara), all the bodhisattvas and mahasattvas, and
Mahā-prajñā-pāramitā.[76] Thus Dōgen was definitely in line with the
general Buddhist tradition of emphasizing these Buddhas in speaking
of Buddha-dharma.

However, Dōgen's overriding emphasis was on the historical Buddha—Śākyamuni Buddha—in whom all the Buddhas and bodhisattvas are represented as his myriad forms. Śākyamuni Buddha is a historical person—an absolutely unadulterated, concrete human being,
and the same historical person is Buddha-dharma as well. Thus the
historical Buddha becomes the prototype of Buddha-dharma in Dōgen's thought.[77] He is no longer an apparitional or assumed body of
the Body of Law in some interpretations of the doctrine. Dōgen rejects the logic of hierarchical degrees of being, and instead takes the
historicity of Buddha seriously. From this standpoint Dōgen has this
to say:

Truly you should know that although Śākyamuni the person (*ningen no shaka*)
endeavors at this moment to liberate sentient beings [on this earth], Śākyamuni of the Tuṣita Heaven (*jōten no shaka*) is now transforming heavens. The
student of Buddhism should understand that, while Śākyamuni the person
has an infinite variety of expressions, activities, and sermons, they constitute
glowing lights and auspicious signs in the human realm which is just one
corner [of the universe]. Do not be foolish enough to fail to see an infinite
variety of edifying activity on the part of Śākyamuni of the Tuṣita Heaven.[78]

Although the transcendental Buddha is talked about along with the
historical Buddha, they are no longer conceived in the traditional
logic of, say, the Threefold Body of Buddha but in the logic of
Dōgen's mystical realism. In Dōgen's use of "Śākyamuni Buddha"
(Shakamuni-butsu) the historical Buddha and the transcendental Buddha are inseparably intertwined with each other.[79] It is also in this
context that Dōgen declares that the past Buddhas are the disciples of
Śākyamuni Buddha[80] and that all the Buddhas are necessarily Śākyamuni Buddha.[81]

The prototypical character of Sākyamuni Buddha as the historical existence as well as the cosmic existence is further and more clearly developed in Dōgen's view of the active Buddha (*gyōbutsu*), in which activity (*gyō*) and Buddhahood (*butsu*) are nondualistically one and the same. Dōgen maintains:

All the Buddhas necessarily enact majestic activities (*igi*). Such is the active Buddha. The active Buddha is not the Buddha of the Body of Enjoyment (*hōbutsu*), or the Buddha of the Body of Transformations (*kebutsu*), or the Buddha of the Body of Law (*jishōshin-butsu*), or the Buddha of the other-directed Body of Enjoyment (*tashōshin-butsu*). It is neither acquired enlightenment (*shikaku*) nor original enlightenment (*hongaku*); it is neither the apprehension of one's nature nor that of emptiness. [The active Buddha is not static and contemplative as these terms might suggest.] No Buddha—none of these Buddhas—can ever equal the active Buddha. Note that all Buddhas active in the Way do not await enlightenment. The active Buddha alone is thoroughly familiar with the affairs of the realm of ongoing enlightenment. The Buddhas of the Body of Law and the like have never dreamed of such a thing.[82]

One characteristic of the active Buddha is the "actual" Buddha which differs from mere appearance. Dōgen equates the active Buddha with the "true human body" (*shinjitsu-nintai*) and maintains: "The meaning of 'true' [in 'the entire earth is the true human body'] is the actual body. You should know that the entire earth (*jindaichi*) is not our temporary appearance but our genuine human body."[83] Thus the active Buddha is actual in the sense that it is absolutely concrete with no metaphysically inferior status attributed to it. For this reason, the active Buddha guards against "binding one's self without a rope" (*mujō-jibaku*)—the victimization of the self by its own created mental constructs, especially by Buddha and Dharma. So Dōgen admonishes, on the "bonds of Buddha" (*butsu-baku*) and the "bonds of Dharma" (*hō-baku*):

Unless you are the active Buddha, you will never be liberated from the bonds of Buddha and the bonds of Dharma and will be entangled with the demons of Buddha (*butsuma*) and the demons of Dharma (*hōma*).

The "bonds of Buddha" means to understand enlightenment abstractly and hence to be bound by intellectual views and theoretical understanding. . . . This is likened to binding one's self without a rope. The rope, so long without a break, is like the vines that entwine a tree to its death, or like living vainly in the cave of the conceptual Buddha. Humans do not know that the Body of Law is diseased and the Body of Enjoyment is troubled.

Those scholars of doctrines, sūtras, and śāstras, who heard the Way from a distance, even say that an intellectual view of the Dharma-nature arises in the Dharma-nature itself, and that this is due to ignorance. When they speak of an abstract thinking of the Dharma-nature occurring in the Dharma-nature, they do not attribute this to the bonds of the Dharma-nature, but instead, they pile the bonds of ignorance on top of them. They are not aware of the existence of the bonds of the Dharma-nature. Although they are pitiful on this account, they realize the bonds of ignorance piled up, and this realization must work as a seed for the arising of aspiration to enlightenment. The active Buddha has never been bound by such bonds.[84]

While Buddha and Dharma are conventionally thought to be liberating forces unchallenged and unchallengeable, Dōgen recognizes the fact that they may become bonds as dangerous and sinister as the bonds of ignorance. Although Dōgen frequently uses the traditional terms of the Threefold Body doctrine and related ideas in his writings, they are used in the context of his advocacy of the active Buddha, which is actual in an unadulterated historical concreteness, free of any monistic vestiges. When Dōgen refers to the historical Buddha and the eternal Buddha, he means the active Buddha.

The conception of the active Buddha expands to cosmic dimensions. "Buddha's activities take place with the entire earth and with all sentient beings. If they are not with all existences, they are not yet the activities of Buddha."[85] "An infinite number of Buddhas reside in a speck of dust."[86] The active Buddha is the Buddha of the three periods and the ten quarters.[87] In short, Buddhas abound spatially and temporally. Dōgen further writes:

Do not measure or judge the great Way [the active Buddha] in terms of the quantity of Buddhas [the Threefold Body of Buddha]. For the latter is a part of the former; it is like a flower blooming in the spring. Do not grope for or deliberate on the majesty of the active Buddha with the capacity of the mind. The latter is a facet of the former. It is likened to the world: A blade of grass is undoubtedly the mind of the Buddhas and ancestors; it is a piece imprinted by the traces of the active Buddha. Although the capacity of the mind is regarded as embodying an infinite quantity of Buddhas, to appreciate the forms and movements of the active Buddha would be indeed far more than it is capable of. Since the active Buddha cannot be fathomed by amount, it is immeasurable, inexhaustible, and transcends any number.[88]

The "majestic activities" (*igi*) of the active Buddha permeate the universe. Dōgen's mythopoeic imagination describes it thus:

Where the active Buddha acts, there are sentient beings other than those born of the four forms of life [from eggs, from a womb, from moisture, and from metamorphosis]. There are places which are not the heavenly or human worlds, or the causal, objective world (*hokkai*). Do not use celestial or mortal eyes and do not employ supernal or earthly standards. You should not attempt to discriminate by mustering all of these standards. Even all the bodhisattvas of various stages of perfection do not fully comprehend it, to say nothing of the understanding possible with human and heavenly standards. As human stature is small, what we understand is also slight; as human life is short, what we think is shallow, too. Then how can we measure the majestic movements of the active Buddha?[89]

And:

The august exertions of the active Buddha are free, and absolutely one with Buddha. Because it uses the mud and the water through which it passes, it is unobstructed. In the heavenly world it edifies celestial beings and in the human world, humankind. While it has the efficacy of blooming flowers, it possesses the power of giving birth to the world. Yet there is no hiatus between them [flowers and the world]. . . . In great enlightenment it is equal to it; in great delusion it is identical with it. These constitute just a movement of the active Buddha's toes in the sandals. Sometimes it is the sound of breaking wind, and sometimes it is the smell of urination. Those who have nostrils smell it; those who have ears, body, the will to act, hear it.[90]

The majestic movement of the active Buddha reaches not only the heavenly worlds and beyond, but also the utmost trivia such as breaking wind and urination.

In the foregoing, I have endeavored to show that in Dōgen's thought the historical Buddha and the transcendental Buddha are focalized in the active Buddha and that the latter, in turn, is identified with the historical existence of humanity in absolute freedom in which activity and Buddhahood are undefiled. We see here an extreme similarity between Dōgen and Tantric Buddhism as far as their views of the Buddha-body are concerned.[91] Dōgen restores the fundamental significance of the historical Buddha and provides its existential and religious significance for those who practice zazen-only in the samādhi of self-fulfilling activity (*jijuyū-zammai*). Such is the religious context in which his view of activity is developed.

Thus the fundamental characteristic of Zen as Dōgen sees it consists in the post-enlightenment activity of Buddha (*gyōbutsu*) rather than in the attainment of Buddhahood (*jōbutsu*).

Like expression (*dōtoku*), activity (*gyōji*) is a primitive concept in Dōgen's thought. It is so crucially important that he says that the authenticity or inauthenticity of practice, that is, activity—not the superiority or inferiority of doctrine, nor profundity or shallowness of teaching—is the sine qua non of Buddhist truth.[92] The metaphysical primitiveness of activity is well maintained as follows:

The sun, the moon, and the stars exist by virtue of such creative activities. The earth and the empty sky exist because of activities. Our body-mind and its environment are dependent on activities; so are the four elements and the five skandhas. Although activity is not what worldly people are likely to care for, it is all humans' true refuge. . . . It should be examined and understood thoroughly that functional interdependence (*engi*) is activity, because activity is not functionally interdependent. That activity which realizes those activities—it is our activity now (*wareraga imano gyōji nari*). The now of activity (*gyōji no ima*) is not the self's primordial being, eternal and immutable, nor is it something that enters and leaves the self. The Way, called now, does not precede activity; as activity is realized (*gyōji genjō suru*), it is called now.[93]

As is quite explicit, Dōgen dares to go beyond the traditional Buddhist thought, in construing activity as more primitive than functional interdependence, by saying that functional interdependence is activity but the reverse is not the case. Literally interpreted, this statement may be vulnerable to criticism as a hypostatization of activity as an entity in itself; on the other hand, the statement is too straightforward to be taken as mere rhetorical emphasis on activity. Despite these difficulties in fathoming Dōgen's intention, this statement deepens our understanding of functional interdependence whose conditions and causes are now translated in terms of activities.[94] Thus it points up not the prior existence of independent entities that are functionally interdependent on one another, but precisely the denial of such a view. Activity is the primal property of functional interdependence itself. In brief, this is Dōgen's way of maintaining the emptiness of functional interdependence and the functional interdependence of ‘ emptiness.

The dynamic ongoing movement of activity is envisioned in Dōgen's idea of "perpetuation of the Way through activity" (*gyōji-dōkan*):

The great Way of the Buddhas and ancestors consists always in these supreme activities (*mujō no gyōji*), never interrupted in their continuation: the desire for enlightenment, practice, enlightenment, and nirvāṇa. These four activities never allow even a single interval between them. This is the perpetuation of the Way through activity (*gyōji-dōkan*). Consequently, supreme activity is neither a contrivance of the self nor that of others; it is activity undefiled. The power of such an activity sustains my self and others. Its import is such that all the heavens and the entire earth of the ten quarters enjoy the merit of my activity. Even if neither the self nor others are aware of it, such is the case.[95]

The perpetuation of the Way through activity consists of a succession of "circles" of time, each of which has its circumference ever moving with no limits, its center ever movable in accordance with circumstances, and its advance without ultimate goal or purpose, though it is not without inner reason (*dōri*).

In these ever ongoing endeavors, activity and expression are such that when activity is totally exerted, there is nothing but activity, and similarly, when expression is totally exerted, there is nothing but expression. Thus, "while activity (*gyō*) fathoms the way to be in unison with expression (*setsu*), expression has the path to be attuned with activity."[96] After all, humanity "enacts that which is impossible to enact" (*gyōfutokutei*) and "expresses that which is impossible to express" (*setsufutokutei*).[97]

Creative Expressions

The problem of expression emerges in Dōgen's thought primarily in connection with two different yet mutually related problems: Zen treatment of Buddhist scriptures and the method of kōan meditation. Let us examine them briefly before we get into the problem of expression proper.

As has been previously observed, the principle of "no dependence upon words and letters (*furyū-monji*) should not mean abandoning the use of language, but, rather, using it to our advantage instead of being victimized by it. Dōgen severely criticized those Zen Buddhists who cherished only the records of Zen ancestors at the sacrifice of traditional Buddhist scriptures. Having an over-zealous reaction to the scholastic, doctrinaire tendencies of the school of the Buddha-word (*butsugo-shū*), according to Dōgen, they fell into the dire fallacy of negating language entirely. This Dōgen opposed violently. He writes: "Hearing and seeing (*shōshiki*) should not be regarded as more meritorious than reading sūtras. It is hearing and seeing that delude you, yet you crave and indulge in them. The sūtras do not bewilder you; do not slander [them] in unbelief."[98]

It is we who deceive ourselves; the sūtras do not deceive us. The root of the trouble in dealing with the sūtras consists not so much in the sūtras themselves as in our subjectivity. Hence, Dōgen maintains with Hui-nêng that the mind in delusion is moved by the *Saddharma-puṇḍarīka sūtra,* whereas the mind in enlightenment moves it.[99] The enlightened mind is free to elucidate and appropriate the sūtras.

Sūtras in Dōgen's conception are the entire universe itself. Dōgen expounds this view in a number of places:

What we mean by the sūtras is the entire universe itself. There is no space and no time which is not the sūtras. They use the words and letters of absolute truth or employ the language of relative truth. Sometimes they adopt the symbols of heavenly beings or put to use the expressions of human beings. The words and letters of beasts, those of asuras, or those of hundreds of grasses and thousands of trees are put in action. For this reason, the long, the short, the square, the round, the blue, the yellow, the red, the white—marshalling solemnly in the ten quarters of the universe—are nonetheless the sūtras' language and their face. They are the instruments of the great Way and the scriptures for a Buddhist.[100]

When you devote yourself to the study of the sūtras, they truly come forth. The sūtras in question are the entire universe, mountains and rivers and the great earth, plants and trees; they are the self and others, taking meals and wearing clothes, confusion and dignity. Following each of them and studying them, you will see an infinite number of hitherto unheard-of sūtras appear before you.[101]

Furthermore "boundless words and letters (*kōdai no monji*) permeate the universe with overflowing abundance."[102] The entire spatio-temporal reality constitutes the sūtras, as these quotations amply show. Humanity is born into the sūtras and returns to the sūtras. As soon as one is born into the world, one inescapably meets the sūtras and life thereafter consists in efforts to decipher their meanings: "From aeon to aeon, from day to night, there is not even a single instant when the sūtras are not recited or meditated, even though they are not actually expounded."[103] On the other hand, the sūtras are identical with Dharma in which "eighty-four thousand teachings" are stored and also with the true treasury of the Dharma eye (*shōbōgenzō*).[104]

In his pietistic moments, Dōgen holds that the sūtras are the same as the body-mind of the Buddhas and ancestors:

Therefore the sūtras are the whole body of Tathāgata. To revere the sūtras is to worship Tathāgata, and to meet the sūtras is to greet Tathāgata. The sūtras are Tathāgata's bones; hence the bones are these sūtras. If you know the sūtras are the bones but do not understand the bones are the sūtras, it is not yet the Way. All-things-themselves-are-ultimate-reality (*shohō-jossō*) here and now constitutes the sūtras. The human world and the heavenly world, the oceans and the empty sky, this world and the other world—all are neither more nor less than ultimate reality, sūtras, and bones.[105]

"Now we are born to meet these sūtras," says Dōgen, "how can we fail to rejoice in encountering Śākyamuni Buddha?"[106] It is in this sense that Dōgen admonishes his disciples to study the sūtras assiduously:

An enlightened teacher is always thoroughly versed in the sūtras. "To be thoroughly versed in" means to make the sūtras nations and lands, bodies and minds. The sūtras are made the instruments for liberating others and turned into sitting, resting, walking in meditation. Being thoroughly versed changes the sūtras into parents, children, and grandchildren. Because an enlightened teacher understands the sūtras through practice (*gyōge*), he/she penetrates them deeply.[107]

Thus, the conventional sense of the sūtras is acknowledged for its importance and placed against the cosmic context in which it comprises only a small portion of the whole sūtras. To Dōgen life is an incessant round of hermeneutical activities that try to understand such cosmic sūtras. To be sure, Dōgen often criticizes what he calls the "scholars who count words and letters" and compares them to the "blind guiding the masses of the blind."[108] Furthermore, Dōgen admonishes his disciples that "In the monastics' hall you should not look at words and letters even though they are in Zen books."[109] These typically Zen Buddhistic remarks—not infrequently made by Dōgen—should not obscure Dōgen's real intention concerning language and symbols, which are dynamic and alive in the very core of life.

A brief historical digression may be worthwhile to assess the significance of Dōgen's position in the foregoing matter. When Dōgen speaks of the sūtras, he has in mind a specifically Zen Buddhistic situation in which some maintained the sole legitimacy of the ancestral records as "a special tradition outside the sūtras" (*kyōge-betsuden*)—another Zen principle cognate to "no dependence upon words and letters." This dictum insisted upon this special corpus of ancestral records as opposed to the sūtra tradition of other schools, and in turn rationalized such distinctions as those between Ancestral Zen and Tathāgata Zen, between the school of the Buddha-mind and the school of the Buddha-word, etc. Despite its historical significance in enunciating a distinctively Zen Buddhist identity in its formative period, this principle seems to have been fanatically exaggerated among some Zen Buddhists towards the close of the T'ang period and thereafter throughout the Sung period. Historians today generally think that Lin-chi I-hsüan (d. 850), Tê-shan Hsüan-chien (780–865), and Yang-shan Hui-chi (807–883) were mainly responsible for this extremist predilection within Zen Buddhism.[110] Thus the literalistic, dogmatic interpreters of these two principles went so far as to burn the sūtras and images because they considered them to be altogether harmful spiritually.

This extremist tradition was bequeathed to the so-called Kōan-introspection Zen and Silent-illumination Zen of the Sung period; and, especially during the Southern Sung period when Dōgen studied in China, the sectarian struggle between these two camps seems to have been even more belligerent than during previous generations. The rejection of sūtras notwithstanding, kōan meditation gradually became the Zen equivalent of sūtra studies, as we shall see on later occasion. Hence, we see an intimate relationship between *sūtras* and *kōans*.

The historical connection between Kōan-introspection Zen and kōan itself must be viewed in a proper historical context. Although the origins of kōan in its technical Zen sense are obscure, it appears to have been used first by Mu-chou Tao-tsung (780?–877?, popularly known by his followers as Ch'ên Tsun-su), in the sense of present living and lived realities of life, as the realization of truth itself, in turn used as occasions for enlightenment. This is the kōan realized in life (*genjō-kōan*), which may very well have been what many Zen teachers employed for the guidance of disciples in the T'ang period.[111] Kōan as paradigmatic problems for meditation—neatly packaged in formalized statements—is called the kōan of ancient paradigms (*kosoku-kōan*). This form gradually developed, probably around the end of the tenth century, and the process of fixation seems to have been augmented thereafter by counter attacks from the camps of those who advocated the classical conception of kōan such as Shih-shuang Ch'u-yüan (986–1039), Hsüeh-tou Ch'ung-hsien (980–1052), Wu-tsu Fa-yen (1024?–1104), Yüan-wu K'o-ch'in (1063–1135), and so on. Especially, Yüan-wu emphasized the kōan realized in life, by referring to it frequently, despite his advocacy of the kōan of ancient paradigms. This tradition of the kōan realized in life was also inherited by both Ta-hui Tsung-kao (1089–1163), the foremost leader of Kōan-introspection Zen, and Hung-chih Chêng-chüeh (1091–1157), the celebrated exponent of Silent-illumination Zen, who, though often regarded as fierce enemies, were evidently good friends. They advocated the kōan realized in life and never absolutized either kōan or zazen at the sacrifice of one another.[112] Hence their concern was to remind each other of the dangers of misuses and abuses of these methods which could lead ultimately to dark quietism and deadly intellectualism. The real issue, therefore, was not so much whether or not to use kōan or zazen but how to use them.

Against this historical background, Dōgen emphasized *genjō-kōan* of classical Zen Buddhism and seems to have recognized the limited values of *kosoku-kōan* within that context.[113] Thus, although Dōgen adopted the idea of *genjō-kōan* from the Chinese Zen tradition,[114] he developed the idea further and used it extensively throughout his works.[115] He also used fully the linguistic and symbolic potentialities of the component words "kōan" and "realization" (*genjō*). From Dōgen's standpoint, the traditional kōan of ancient paradigm: (1) was based upon the idea of kōan as a means to the attainment of enlightenment and, consequently, on the idea of enlightenment as realizable in the future (*taigo*), (2) had a strong predilection to an intellectual and intuitive "seeing into one's own nature" (*kenshō*) as if "seeing" and "nature" were two different phenomena, and (3), perhaps most importantly for our purpose in the present context, observed an inherent irrationality in the traditional kōan. In this view, the mind, confronted with kōans, or formulized nonsense, is systematically frustrated in its intellectual functions, and finally deconditioned so as to permit the release of the primitive psychic forces hitherto pent up in it, which is necessary to the experience of enlightenment.[116] Such an instrumental view of kōan is closely related to the corollary view of reason in general and of language and symbols in particular, which is by and large negativistic. Dōgen's method, on the other hand, as is quite evident from his treatment of kōans, is to carefully and compassionately pursue the reason of nonsense, for kōans are not just ordinary nonsense or meaningless expressions, but symbols of life and death, and so reason is not just abnegated but re-constituted in the wider context of enlightenment. To Dōgen, kōans function not only as nonsense which castigates reason, but as parables, allegories, and mysteries which unfold the horizons of existence. In this sense they are realized, though not solved.

The upshot of what we have thus far examined is a strikingly new way of looking at conventional ideas such as sūtras and kōans. In Dōgen they were liberated from narrow confinement in traditional, especially Zen Buddhistic, understanding, which more often than not tended to view them as nothing but instruments or means. This meant that words and letters (i.e., language and symbols)—the common components of sūtras and kōans—were given a positive significance in the total scheme of spiritual things. In short, they were no longer means to an end but, rather, that means which embodies the end within it. Referring to the traditional story that Buddha without a word held up flowers one day before a congregation on Mt. Gṛdhrakūṭa, and Mahākāśyapa alone, laughing, understood it, Dōgen attacks those who regard the absence of the Buddha's utterance as the supreme evidence of the profundity of truth. Then he proposes his own view:

> If Buddha's speech is shallow, his raising flowers without a word must also be superficial. When people say that Buddha's utterance is comprised of mere words (*myōsō*), they do not understand the Buddha-dharma. Although they know that speech consists of words and letters, they do not yet discern that there are no mere words with Buddha. This is due to the deluded state of the ordinary worldy mind. To the Buddhas and ancestors, the whole being of body and mind is cast off and constitutes sermons, discourses through utterances, and the turning of the wheel of Dharma.[117]

Buddha's raising flowers in silence is his "speech," or expression. Thus, the sūtras, words, silence—even an infant's mumblings, the alcoholic's "snakes," and what-not—all these are the possibilities of expression which are in turn the activities of absolute emptiness and Buddha-nature. To study them is to study the "reason of words and letters" (*monji no dōri*). Dōgen's view is neither a derogation nor an idolization of languge, but simply an acknowledgement of the legitimate place of language in the spiritual scheme of things. For this reason Dōgen's emphasis is not on how to transcend language but on how to radically use it.

Language is not that which describes and explains, detached from the subjective operation of the human mind and hence isolatable, at least in principle, from the mind; rather it performs its various functions within the very texture of human subjectivity. It is embedded in the matrix of our experience; as Wittgenstein once said: "the speaking of language is part of an activity, or of a form of life." [118] The range of the functions of language (in its broadest possible sense as Dōgen understood it) becomes coextensive with that of human activities in its broadest possible sense. For Dōgen the false separation of words and activities is closely related to the impoverishment of religion and philosophy; language and activity are inseparably one in his thought, as we shall see.

Dōgen's view of expression (*dōtoku*) points to just this dynamic view of language and symbols. *Dōtoku* consists of two Chinese characters: *dō*, "the Way" and "to say," and *toku*, "to attain" and "to be able." Thus it signifies both actuality and possibility of expression—expression and expressibility. What is expressed intimates what is yet to be expressed—and it is the Way. It also may mean the understanding and grasping of the Way by expression. More importantly, it stresses not what humans express so much as what the Way expresses. These complex, pregnant meanings are implied in the word *dōtoku*. The word is by no means Dōgen's invention—as a matter of fact, it was frequently used, yet perhaps neglected by Zen Buddhists; Dōgen rediscovered it and made it a central concept in his thought. We see here Dōgen's originality with respect to the word *dōtoku*.

Expression does not necessarily mean expression in words: "The wordless (*fugen*) is not the same as the expressionless (*fudō*), for expression (*dōtoku*) is not identical with utterance in words (*gentoku*)." [119] This is the fundamental difference between expression and saying (*gentoku*). Without words and letters we can express ourselves in myriad ways. Comparing the life of the monastic's silent zazen to that of the deaf-mute, Dōgen writes:

Even deaf-mutes have expressions. Do not judge that they cannot possess any expressions. Those who create expressions are not necessarily limited to those who are not deaf-mutes, for deaf-mutes do express themselves. Their voices should be heard and their utterances should be heeded. Unless you identify yourself with them, how can you meet them? How can you talk with them? [120]

From this the following admonition is given: "Do not loathe wordlessness, for it is expression par excellence." [121] Not only those semantic possibilities in metaphors, images, gestures, and moral and aesthetic activities in the human realm, but also those possibilities in the activities of non-human and non-living realms must be taken into

consideration in the problem of expression. Thus, for example, Dōgen says:

The way insentient beings expound Dharma should not be understood to be
necessarily like the way sentient beings expound Dharma. The voices of sentient beings should follow the principle of their discourse on Dharma.

Even so, it is contrary to the Buddha-way to usurp the voices of the living
and conjecture about those of the non-living in terms of them. . . . Even if
human judgment now tries to recognize grasses, trees, and the like, and
fashion them into non-living things, they too cannot be measured by the
ordinary mind.[122]

In this view, all the phenomena of the universe—audible and inaudible, tangible and intangible, conscious and unconscious—are the
self-expressions (*jidōshu*) of Buddha-nature and absolute emptiness.
Nothing is excluded from this.[123]

In order to develop his metaphysic of expression, Dōgen employed
a number of concepts and symbols taken from the repository of Buddhist tradition—some of which were quite ordinary, others which
had been relegated to oblivion, still others which had been deni-
grated—and resuscitated them with a new life, pregnant with aston-
ishingly fresh and revelatory possibilities of meaning. To give some
examples: dreams (*mu*), vines (*kattō*), pictures (*gato*), the sounds of
brooks and the figures of mountains (*keisei-sanshoku*), one luminous
pearl (*ikka-myōju*), the primordial mirror (*kokyō*), sky-flowers (*kūge*),
the infinite light (*kōmyō*), plum blossoms (*baika*), udumbara (*udonge*),
the sound of a flute (*ryūgin*), a particular time (*arutoki*), super-normal
powers (*jinzū*), pilgrimage (*hensan*), charms and spells (*darani*), the
mountains and waters (*sansui*), and so forth. These concepts, metaphors, and images were transfigured and given completely new significations so as to be legitimized as the philosophic and mythopoeic
elements of Dōgen's own thought, as we see, for instance, in the transformation of the "sky-flowers" (which traditionally meant illusory
perceptions) into the "flowers of emptiness." We will examine this
example and others in more detail presently. The point to note at this
juncture is that some such exploration and use of symbols was an integral part of Dōgen's philosophic and religious method. (His versatility and sensitivity in the use of language and expression are well
attested to by many Dōgen students. As we emphasized before, Dōgen's sensibilities were undoubtedly derived from the distinguished
literary tradition of his aristocratic family, but he was more concerned

with philosophic and religious problems than with aesthetic ones, though his poetic and literary excellence was no less distinguished.)

The problem of the symbol and the symbolized is very important in Buddhist thought as in any other philosophical and religious thought. The former in Buddhism is often designated by metaphors (*hiyu*), provisional view (*kesetsu*), provisional name (*kemyō*), and so forth, whereas the latter (the symbolized) is designated by thusness (*shinnyo*), emptiness (*kū*), Buddha-nature (*bussho*), and the like. Metaphors, parables, and names constitute what the Buddhists call means or ways (*upāya; hōben*) which enable sentient beings to cross the river of birth-and-death to the other shore (*pāramitā; higan*) of ultimate reality. This view strongly suggests the instrumentality of symbol which must be transcended in order to attain truth. This view is part of Dōgen's works; he vehemently attacked those who were entrapped and victimized by the words and doctrines they themselves created. Dōgen abhorred a deadly literalism, and attempted to go beyond it. For him symbol was to be realized as an expression of the symbolized. This was possible only when symbol was mediated, liberated, and reinstated by the symbolized, namely, absolute emptiness. Here, we see Dōgen's creative and dynamic interpretation of the Buddhist doctrine of means in which the means in question is not transcendence of duality but realization of it. The means and the end are not obliterated, but remain undefiled. Thus, the motif of realization, rather than that of transcendence, is the strongest motive force in Dōgen's way of thinking about language and symbols, as in other aspects of his thought.[124]

This is clearly shown in Dōgen's analysis of the moon reflected on the water. He has this to say:

Śākyamuni Buddha said: "The true Dharma-body of Buddha is like the empty sky, and it manifests itself according to sentient beings like the moon [reflected] on the water." "Like" in "like the moon [reflected] on the water" should mean the water-moon (*sui-getsu*) [i.e., the nonduality of the moon and the water]. It should be the water-thusness (*sui-nyo*), the moon-thusness (*getsu-nyo*), thusness-on (*nyo-chū*), on-thusness (*chū-nyo*). We are not construing "like" as resemblance: "like" (*nyo*) is "thusness" (*ze*).[125]

Quite an ordinary statement of Buddha's (as translated above in its common-sensical rendering) is transformed suddenly into a profound discourse on the symbol and the symbolized, by again making full use of semantic possibilities of the Chinese characters involved in it. The central character *nyo* means at once "likeness" and "thusness." Similarly *nyo-ze* means "like this" as well as "thusness." Dōgen is astutely utilizing the significant implications of these words. But the deeper underlying motive is through and through religious and philosophical—a profound insight into the metaphysic of symbol. Often the symbol and the symbolized are related to each other in terms of a certain likeness, and the symbol is said to "point to," "represent," or "approximate" the symbolized. Rejecting such a dualism, Dōgen contends that "like this" (*nyoze*) means that both "like" and "this" are emptiness, hence thusness (*nyoze*). Instead of saying, "Thusness is like this," it says: "'Like this' is thusness." "Like this" does not represent or point to thusness but is thusness. Therefore the symbol is the symbolized. In articulating the problem in this manner, Dōgen does not engage in the absolutization of the symbol nor in the relativization of the symbolized, which would be dualistic. What he does in effect is to show how we can use the symbol in such a way that it becomes the total realization (*zenki*) or presence (*genzen*) of the symbolized. Dōgen's view can be best understood in the religious or cultic context of his mystical realism. This is why Dōgen holds: "For Dharma even metaphors (*hiyu*) are ultimate realities (*jissō*)."[126]

The foregoing observations point to the fact that there is no metaphysical or experiential hiatus between the symbol and the symbolized. This becomes clearer when we examine Dōgen's discussion of "intimate words" (*mitsugo*). Employing the combination of the two meanings: "intimacy" and "hiddenness," in the Chinese character *mitsu*, Dōgen advances an ingenious view of mystery. *Mitsugo* is ordinarily understood as "secret words" or "hidden words," the secrecy or hiddenness of which can be removed by extensive learning, supernormal faculties, and the like. In opposition to this interpretation Dōgen says:

The *mitsu* in question means intimacy (*shimmitsu*) and the absence of distance. [When you speak of the Buddhas and ancestors] the Buddhas and ancestors embrace everything; [likewise] you embrace everything; I embrace everything. Practice includes all; a generation includes all; and intimacy includes all.[127]

Intimate words are those words spoken and acted out by us in such a way that there is no hiatus between words and referents, thought and reality, mind and body, expressions and activities. When a symbol is used in such a nondualistic manner, it is totally intimate with and transparent to the symbolized. In a similar fashion, such words as "intimate activities" (*mitsugyō*), "intimate enlightenment" (*misshō*), intimate thought" (*mitsui*), and so on, are used. Mystery, in Dōgen's view, thus consists not in something which is now hidden or unknown in darkness and which will be revealed or made known sometime in the future, but in that absolute intimacy, transparency, and vividness of thusness, for "nothing is concealed throughout the entire universe" (*henkai-fuzōzō*). However, the mystery of emptiness and thusness must go even beyond this: intimacy must be transcended (*tōkamitsu*).[128]

In the same vein, Dōgen holds that "ongoing enlightenment" (*bukkōjōji*)—discussed in connection with Tung-shan Liang-chieh's discourse on ongoing enlightenment and speech—is realized by penetration into the inaudible in speech through practice and understanding.[129] Dōgen observes:

Indeed, you should know that ongoing enlightenment is neither the process of practice nor the result of enlightenment. [It transcends cause and effect.] Nevertheless it is possible to realize and penetrate into the inaudible in speech (*gowaji no fumon*). Unless you attain ongoing enlightenment, you do not experience it; if it is not speech (*gowa*), you do not verify it in your subjectivity. It is neither manifestation nor hiddenness, neither giving nor depriving. Accordingly, when speech is realized, this itself is ongoing enlightenment.[130]

The inaudible in speech transcends the audible (*mon*) and the inaudible (*fumon*) in the conventional sense. The body-mind must adjust itself—by being undefiled—to the inaudible through a new mode of activity. No sooner do we adjust our body-mind totally to a new situation and begin to act in and through the audible than we realize that the inaudible resides in the audible itself. Thus, speech is undefiled by the dualism of the audible and the inaudible. Or to put it differently, speaker and speech are nondualistically one in freedom of activity in ongoing enlightenment.[131] Dōgen goes on:

You must understand clearly the saying of Tung-shan, the founder of the Ts'ao-tung sect, "I await the time of no speech (*fugowa*) and hear immediately." When speech is uttered ordinarily, there is no immediate hearing (*sokumon*) at all. "Hearing-immediately" is realized at the time of "no-speech." But no-speech does not wait for a special occasion. While hearing-immediately, it does not look on speech (*gowa*) [as if speech and no-speech were dualistically separated]. For, where there is a looking-on, there is nothing but the looking-on. In hearing-immediately, speech is not removed from its own place to some remote location. When speech is uttered, hearing-immediately—hitherto hidden intimately in the bosom of speech—does not thunder suddenly. For these reasons, even the monastic [who appears in the story of Tung-shan's discourse] does not hear at the time of speech. Even I hear immediately on the occasion of no-speech. This is [the significance of Tung-shan's] "I understand the meaning of speech a little" and "I realize ongoing enlightenment." In other words, you apprehend hearing-immediately when speech is uttered. Hence, "I await the time of no speech and hear immediately." Even so, ongoing enlightenment is not the remote matter that happened before the Seven Buddhas, but the very ongoing enlightenment of them.[132]

Thus, only in the nondualistic context of "the inaudible in speech" and "the hearing-immediately in no-speech" is speech in the conventional sense liberated, authenticated, and reinstated for use in the enterprise of ongoing enlightenment.

The foregoing observations on intimate words, the inaudible, hearing-immediately, and so forth, indicate that metaphors, images, and symbols chosen from an ordinary context are used and function quite extraordinarily in the realm of enlightenment. Words are no longer just something that the intellect manipulates abstractly and impersonally, but, rather, something that works intimately in the existential metabolism of one who uses them philosophically and religiously in a special manner and with a special attitude. They are no longer mere means or symbols that point to realities other than themselves but are themselves the realities of original enlightenment and Buddha-nature. In this view words and symbols inevitably call for activities so that activity is embedded in expression and expression in activity. In Dōgen, as we have noted previously, expression (*dōtoku*) and activity (*gyōji*) are synonymous.[133]

It is in this context that Dōgen's fresh interpretation of the story of *sendaba (saindhava)* becomes extremely significant. (*Sendaba* means a word having four significations—hence, infinite semantic possibilities.) Dōgen explains the word and comments on it as follows:

The daily language of monastics is [one with] the entire ten quarters of the universe. Their words are upright [in nondualism]. You should clearly understand that, because everyday language (*kajōgo*) is the whole universe, the whole universe is everyday language. . . . It may be compared to the story in which a ruler [using the word *sendaba*] asks for a horse, salt, water, or a bowl, and his subject brings him water, a bowl, salt, or a horse [according to the ruler's wish]. Who knows that enlightened individuals turn their bodies and move their brains in such words? They appropriate words freely in their utterances, making an ocean into a mouth, a mountain into a tongue. This is the daily life of proper language. Therefore, [those who] cover the mouths and close the ears [yet can speak freely and hear everything] are the truly enlightened beings [who understand the truth] of the ten quarters of the universe.[134]

The enlightened person is an adept at appropriating the semantic possibilities of ordinary words to express and act out the extraordinary, and, even the allegedly ineffable, in accordance with the situation. Dōgen's characteristic way of thinking here in connection with the use of language is that the meaning of an ordinary word is totally exerted (*gūjin*) so that there is nothing but that particular meaning throughout the universe at that given moment. This is the idea of the total exertion of a single thing (*ippō-gūjin*) which is central to Dōgen's entire thought. Elsewhere Dōgen presents the view of life as *sendaba:* that is, the world seeks *sendaba* from each of us, and we bring forth whatever we deem to be *sendaba* in life.[135] Our symbolic and expressive activities are inseparably connected with our bringing forth *sendaba* in response to the world's demand. To be sure, the world's search and the self's response are merely two aspects of one and the same reality.

Indeed life is nothing but searching for and acting out the myriad possibilities of meaning with which the self and the world are pregnant, through expressions (*dōtoku*) and activities (*gyōji*). This involves not only the human world but the nonhuman and the nonliving worlds (which will be discussed later in connection with Dōgen's view of nature), and much more. Even dreams, illusions, and imagination are not eliminated from the purview of semantic possibilities, even though we may reject those areas of human experience as illusory or unreal.

Dream is a favorite metaphor in Buddhist tradition and is often used to signify phantasmic and phantasmagoric unrealities. Dreams and realities are sharply differentiated and contrasted, and by and large, the former are conceived in depreciatory terms. In Dōgen's view, however, dreams are as real and legitimate as the so-called realities in that they comprise our incessant efforts to decipher and dramatize the expressive and actional possibilities of existence. Both dreams and realities are ultimately empty, unattainable, and of no self-nature. Going a step further, Dōgen thinks that existence is essentially a discourse on dreams within dreams (*muchū-setsumu*).[136] He writes:

Because this wheel of Dharma has myriad directions and myriad aspects, oceans, Mt. Sumeru, lands, and Buddhas are realized; this is a discourse on dreams within dreams (*muchū-setsumu*) [of the beginningless past] prior to all dreams. Vivid particularities of the entire universe (*henkai no miro*) are dreams; that is, these dreams are comprised of clear and distinct phenomena. . . . As we study them—roots and stems, leaves and branches, flowers and fruits, light and hues—all are equally great dreams. Such should not be mistaken for a dreamy state of mind.

Thus, while encountering this discourse on dreams in dreams, those who try to eschew the Buddha-way think that some nonexistent phantasms are unreasonably believed to exist and that illusions are piled up on top of illusions. This is not true. Even though delusions are multiplied in the midst of delusions, you should certainly ponder upon the path of absolute freedom (*tsūshō no ro*) in which absolute freedom is apprehended as the very consummation of delusions (*madoi no ue no madoi*).[137]

Here, Dōgen's use of the metaphor of dream is so original that dream, as a metaphor of both illusion and reality, and dream, as a metaphor of neither illusion nor reality, entwine exquisitely with each other so as to present a unique metaphysic of dream. If dream is an unreality in the ordinary sense, Dōgen elevates this unreality to the level of cosmic unreality or ultimate unreality in its total exertion (*gūjin*) abiding in the Dharma-position (*jūhōi*). So we read the following:

"As the kōan realized in life, I spare you from thirty blows" [the statement of Ch'ên Tsun-su (780?–877?)]. This is the-discourse-on-dreams-in-dreams of realization (*genjō no muchū-setsumu*).

Therefore, a tree without roots, a land without a sunny or a shady side, a ravine with no echoes all are the-discourse-on-dreams-in-dreams of realization. It belongs neither to the human realm nor to the heavenly; nor is it what the ordinary worldly individual can conjecture. Who can doubt that dream is enlightenment? For it is not something that can be doubted. Who can know it? For it is not the object of knowledge. Because this supreme enlightenment is nothing but supreme enlightenment, dream calls it dream.[138]

The dream of supreme enlightenment and the supreme enlightenment of dream are nondually conjoined in one reality or unreality. Dōgen also calls it "the-discourse-on-dreams-in-dreams of liberation" (*gedatsu no muchū-setsumu*) which is "as though it itself were hanging in the midst of emptiness" (*mizukara kūni kakareru gotoku*) and which lets images, myths, parables, fantasies "play in emptiness" (*kū ni yuke seshimuru*). Thus, Dōgen writes:

Inasmuch as the wondrous Dharma of Buddhas is communicated only between a Buddha and a Buddha (*yuibutsu-yobutsu*), all the phenomena in the
dreaming state as well as in the waking state are equally ultimate realities
(*jissō*). In the waking state are the desire for enlightenment, practice, enlightenment, and nirvāṇa; in the state of dreaming are the desire for enlightenment, practice, enlightenment, and nirvāṇa. Dream and reality—
each is ultimate nature. Neither largeness nor smallness, neither superiority
nor inferiority obtains. . . . Both the dream life and the waking life are
originally one as ultimate reality. For Dharma even metaphors are ultimate
realities. Being no longer metaphors, dream-making (*musa*) constitutes the
heart of Dharma. . . . Although it is in accord with reason that Buddha's
liberating efforts [for sentient beings] continue unceasingly in the waking
life, the truth of the realization of the Buddhas and ancestors consists invariably of dream-making within dreams (*musa-muchū*).[139]

Dreams are thus allowed as legitimate expressions and activities in the
total scheme of things, in which symbols and realities are purified and
reinforced by absolute emptiness so as to work for the liberation of
sentient beings.

So-called illusions are also very carefully considered by Dōgen.
The word *kūge,* as we have mentioned briefly before, originally meant
the "flowers blooming in the sky," that is, flowers which are illusory
owing to our dimmed vision (*eigen*). This term is changed by Dōgen
into the "flowers of emptiness" (the Chinese character *kū* means both
the sky and emptiness)—another example of his ingenious use of the
semantic possibilities of this particular term—which gives a radically
fresh insight into the matter of illusion. Dōgen contends:

There are not yet scholars who grasp this truth [of the flowers of emptiness]
clearly. They fail to understand the flowers of emptiness, because of their
ignorance of emptiness. Owing to their incomprehension of the flowers of
emptiness, they are unacquainted with dim-sighted individuals (*eijin*), do
not see them, do not meet them. They are not blear-eyed individuals. Upon
encountering a blear-eyed person, one can understand and see the flowers of
emptiness. . . . They know only that the sky-flowers exist because of eyes'
dimness, but not the truth that dimness of sight is dependent on the flowers
of emptiness.[140]

Dōgen is vehement in attacking the view that the flowers of emptiness will turn out to be nonexistent when the eyes are cured of disease. To Dōgen, birth-and-death, nirvāṇa, Dharma, original enlightenment—all existences—are the flowers of emptiness. But this is so
precisely because of the universality of "bleary vision." It does not

mean that we see dimly ultimate reality that exists beyond and independent of bleary vision itself. Paradoxically, lucidity and illusoriness
are one here. Dōgen, thus, argues further:

Absurdly construing dimness (*ei*) as unseemly, you should not think there is
truth save this dimness. Such is the view of a small mind. If the flower of
bleariness were untrue, both the subject and the object of the judgment that
misapprehends it to be wrong would be equally so. If all were delusive, there
would be no way of establishing reasonableness (*dōri*). Without reasonableness set up, the idea that the flower of blurry vision is false would not be
permitted. If enlightenment is dimness, all dharmas of enlightenment are
alike the dharmas of solemn dimness (*ei-shōgon*). Inasmuch as delusion is
bleariness, all dharmas of delusion are alike the dharmas of dignified bleariness. Reflect upon this for a minute: Because the blurred vision is nondual
(*byōdō*), the flowers of emptiness are nondual; because the dim-sighted is of
no birth (*mushō*), the flowers of emptiness are of no birth. Just as all things
themselves are ultimate reality (*shohō-jissō*), so are the flowers of dimmed vision. It is not a matter of the past, present, or future; it does not concern
itself with the beginning, middle, or end. Since it is not obstructed by birth-
and-death, it duly allows birth-and-death to be as it is. [Things] arise in
emptiness and perish in it; they come into being in the midst of it; and they
are born in flowers and die in them. So do the rest of all things in time and
space.[141]

The nondualistic oneness of dim vision and flowers of emptiness is
further described as follows:

Vision (*gen*) is realized in and through dimness (*ei*). The flowers of emptiness unfold themselves in vision, vision fulfills itself in the flowers of emptiness. . . . Thus, dimness is totally realized and present (*zenkigen*), vision is
totally realized and present, emptiness is totally realized and present, and
flowers are totally realized and present. . . . Indeed, when and where one
supreme vision is, there are the flowers of emptiness and the flowers of vision. The flowers of vision are called the flowers of emptiness. What they
express is of necessity a disclosure (*kaimei*).[142]

What concerns Dōgen most is not to eliminate illusion as opposed to
reality so much as to see illusion as the total realization—not as one
illusion among others but as the illusion, nothing but the illusion
throughout the universe, in which we can at last find no illusion.
Only if and when we realize the nonduality of illusion and reality in
emptiness can we deal with them wisely and compassionately. Dōgen
writes:

You must surely know emptiness is a perfect grass. This emptiness is bound to bloom, like hundreds of grasses blossoming. . . . Seeing a dazzling variety of the flowers of emptiness, we surmise an infinity of the fruits of emptiness (*kūka*). We observe the bloom and fall of the flowers of emptiness and learn the spring and autumn of them.[143]

Imagination is another area of our consideration. In Zen tradition, the statement "The pictured cakes (*gabyō*) do not satisfy hunger" is often spoken of in relation to the anecdotes of Tê-shan Hsüan-chien (782–865) and Hsiang-yen Chih-hsien, signifying something fantasized and unreal that cannot fill the stomach. Dōgen employs this metaphor and offers quite a positive view of the pictured cakes and of pictures (*gato*) in general.[144] Dōgen writes for example:

The people think that such a view ["The pictured cakes do not satisfy hunger"] tries to say that an unreal thing is really useless, but this is a grave mistake. . . . What we now understand as the pictured cakes are all the paste cakes, vegetable cakes, cheese cakes, toasted cakes, nutritious cakes, and so on—and all are realized out of the pictured cakes. You should note that picture is nondual, cake is nondual, Dharma is nondual. For this reason, all the cakes that are now realized are the pictured cakes as a whole.[145]

Proceeding from this, Dōgen further develops his thesis of picture and imagination:

As you try to paint a landscape, you use paints, strange cliffs and grotesque boulders, the seven rare jems, and the four treasures [a brush, ink, paper, and an ink-stone]. The manner employed to draw cakes is also like this. In order to portray a person, you make use of the four elements and the five skandhas. To delineate Buddha, you utilize not only mud and plaster but the thirty-two distinguishing marks, a stem of grass [from which the golden Buddha-body of one *jō* and six *shaku* is said to be created], the bodhisattva's practice of three asaṃkhyeya-kalpas, one hundred kalpas, and so on. Inasmuch as one draws a scroll-picture of Buddha in such a manner, all the Buddhas are the pictured Buddhas (*gabutsu*); all the pictured Buddhas are all the Buddhas. Examine carefully the pictured Buddhas and the pictured cakes. You should understand thoroughly which is a guardian lion, which is an iron staff, which is form, which is mind. [All are nothing but pictures.] Thus viewed, birth-and-death and coming-and-going are pictures without exception. Supreme enlightenment is nothing but a picture. As a rule, the phenomenal world and the empty sky—there is nothing that is not a picture. . . . If you say that a picture is not real, all things are not real. If all things are not real, Dharma is not real either. If Dharma is real, the pictured cakes should be real.[146]

Picture is reality, reality is picture. The nondual conception of picture and reality is quite evident here. From this Dōgen draws a striking conclusion—entirely contrary to the traditional interpretation—that the pictured cakes alone can satisfy hunger, or to put it differently, unless we eat the pictured cakes, we can never satisfy our hunger. Thus, he writes:

> Therefore, except for the pictured cakes there is no medicine for satisfying hunger. You do not encounter human beings unless [your hunger] is the pictured hunger (*gaki*), nor do you gain energy unless [your satisfaction] is the pictured satisfaction (*gajū*). Indeed, you are filled in hunger and feel satiated in no-hunger; you do not satisfy hunger, nor feel satiated in no-hunger; you do not satisfy hunger, nor do you gratify no-hunger—this truth cannot be understood or spoken of except in terms of the pictured hunger.[147]

As has been abundantly shown by now, Dōgen does not reject creative imaginings and artistic creations as unreal or fictitious any more than he discards the empirical realities of the senses. What is of the utmost importance is not to believe in either imaginings or reality at the expense of one another but to understand and realize both of them undefiled—mediating, purifying, and revitalizing them by absolute emptiness.

The forgotten symbols of dreams, illusions, and pictures are restored from their relegated lowly status in Buddhist thought at large to the foreground of Dōgen's thought, as areas of human experience richly pregnant with valuational possibilities. How and what shall I offer in response to life's demand for *sendaba?* This is everyone's ultimate quest. And dreams, illusions, and imaginings are the rich fountainheads for such a quest. Dōgen's own existential search for *sendaba* extends even to supernormal powers (*jinzū*), charms and spells (*darani*), and so forth, though his interpretations of these symbols are radically different from the traditional ones.[148] His search also extends to many other symbols and metaphors and kōans in which he discovers and rediscovers neglected and unrecognized semantic possibilities through his exceedingly meticulous examination and analysis. Indeed, Dōgen's originality lies primarily in such efforts, which we shall have occasion to mention many times in subsequent chapters.

The foregoing observations should not lead us to think that Dōgen is insensitive to the ineffable in mystical experience. As we have suggested already, quite the opposite is true. He writes, for example:

When this expression is represented, no-expression (*fudōtoku*) is unuttered. If you understand expression in its fullness, yet do not penetrate into the fact that no-expression is left uncommunicated, you are still short of attaining the original face of the Buddhas and ancestors as well as their core.[149]

Dōgen's acknowledgment of no-expression, however, is not a submission to the tyranny of silence but is, instead, a fidelity to the inexhaustible possibilities in the transparency of expressions and activities. Departing radically from the mystic method of *via negativa,* Dōgen is confident in the infinite possibility of what is yet to be expressed, intimated in what has already been expressed, and in what is not expressed or allegedly cannot be expressed. Here he concurs with John Wisdom, who wrote: "Philosophers should be constantly trying to say what cannot be said."[150] Philosophic and religious enterprise consists in fidelity to the inexpressible *and* in the search for expressibility; fundamentally speaking, it is an impossible task,[151] yet it must be carried out, because it is a mode of compassion which Dōgen so eloquently expounded as "loving speech" (*aigo*).[152]

Let us examine the cosmological aspect of expression briefly. Dōgen's metaphysic of expression envisions the universe as a whole to be constituted by dynamic, symbolic activities without interruption. Often we think that humans express something or that the Absolute expresses itself in its self-limiting manifestations, but this still retains some residue of dualistic thinking. Inasmuch as there are only expressions throughout the universe, expressions naturally express themselves in the total exertion of their shared efforts (*jinriki dōtoku surunari; chikara o awasete dōtoku seshimuru*).[153] They are realized neither autonomously nor heteronomously, neither through self-power nor through other-power, yet the Buddhas' and ancestors' practice of the Way and enlightenment are realized in and through expressions. Dōgen then writes:

As seeing-then (*kano toki no kentoku*) was true, it is no doubt expression-now (*ima no dōtoku*). Accordingly, expression-now is endowed with seeing-then, and seeing-then is in possession of expression-now. Thus expression exists now, seeing is now. Expression-now and seeing-then are ever one in their perpetuation. Our efforts now are being sustained by expression and seeing.[154]

Expression at each particular space and time is self-contained and absolutely discrete from preceding and subsequent ones, and each is mutually transcendent as well as inherent. Dōgen uses "seeing" synonymously with expression, rather than with contemplative *theoria*. Expressions, however, must be cast off (*datsuraku*):

As such spiritual efforts are exerted throughout months and years, you further cast off your diligence for years. In the casting-off, the skin-flesh-bones-marrow likewise becomes aware of casting-off. Lands, mountains, and rivers come, together, to an awareness of casting-off. At this time, you hope for and endeavor to attain casting-off as the ultimate model, and such a determination to attain is the presence of realization. So at the time of genuine casting-off, there are expressions being realized unexpectedly. Though neither by the efforts of the mind nor by the strengths of the body, expressions find themselves of their own accord. As they are now fulfilled, they do not show any ostentatiousness or strangeness.[155]

Expressions generate themselves ever anew in incessantly changing particularities in the perpetuation of the Way through activity (*gyōji-dōkan*)—akin to Whitehead's metaphysical vision of "the creative advance of the universe into novelty" from moment to moment.[156] As we shall see in more detail later in conjunction with the examination of Buddha-nature, expressions are, more exactly speaking, self-expressions (*jidōshu*) of Buddha-nature, and hence the Buddha-nature of expression (*setsu-busshō*).

Expressions are compared to "vines" (*kattō*) which attain an entirely new significance in Dōgen's thought. The word "vine" is ordinarily used in derogatory senses such as in reference to doctrinal sophistries and entanglements, attachment to words and letters, theoretical conflicts, and so on. Again we encounter here Dōgen's originality in the positive use of such an ordinary metaphor as this by elevating it to a metaphysical and religious height. In connection with his discussion of vines, Dōgen refers to Bodhidharma's last conversation with his four disciples, Tao-fu, Tsung-chih, Tao-yü, and Hui-k'o, who were said to have attained, by Bodhidharma's acknowledgement, his "skin, flesh, bones, and marrow" (*hi-niku-kotsu-zui*), respectively.[157] The story was apparently designed, according to the conventional interpretation, to justify Hui-k'o's succession to the ancestorship of Bodhidharma on account of his having most deeply understood his teacher's truth—the wisdom of silence, which was thereafter regarded as the hallmark of Zen Buddhism. Speaking of this story, Dōgen admits the existence of differences in the four disciples' interpretations, yet refuses to view them discriminately in terms of superiority and inferiority of views, and instead writes:

It should be noted that the skin, flesh, bones, and marrow of the ancestral way is not a matter of degrees of depth. Even though there are superiority and inferiority of viewpoints, the ancestral way consists solely in the attainment of the whole being [of Bodhidharma]. For the truth of the matter is that the purport of Bodhidharma's saying, whether of the attainment of marrow or of that of bones, is equally to edify individual persons so there is no sufficiency or insufficiency in holding the grass and dropping it [in guiding people according to their abilities and needs]. For example, it is just like Buddha's holding a flower, or like a teacher's imparting the robe to a disciple. What is expounded for the four disciples is the same from the beginning. While the ancestral way is the same, the four interpretations are not necessarily identical. The four views differ in their respective incompleteness, yet the ancestral way is nothing but what it is.

Thus no discord exists between the way [of Bodhidharma] and the understanding [of the four disciples].[158]

Parting from the traditional interpretation, Dōgen here maintains that despite the differences in the disciples' interpretations and responses as "skin, flesh, bones, and marrow," it is also true that each of them, in his or her own way, grasped the teacher's whole being. Hence the following: "The skin, flesh, bones, and marrow partake equally of the first ancestor's body-mind. Marrow is not deepest, skin is not shallowest."[159] Furthermore, there is an infinite progress beyond the marrow.[160] And Dōgen also says:

If there appear hundreds of thousands of disciples after the second ancestor, there will correspondingly be myriad ways of interpretation. There is no limit to them. The number of disciples happened to be four, so there were just four views for the time being. However, many a view is left as yet unexplored and remains to be understood.[161]

The disciples' quests and answers are the skin, flesh, bones, and marrow which cast off the body-mind. Each view is seen in the aspect of its total exertion (*gūjin*) and of abiding in the Dharma-position (*jūhōi*); consequently, it is not an approximation to, nor a self-limiting manifestation of, the Absolute, but a self-activity or a self-expression of Buddha-nature.

In this respect, each person is the second ancestor—the successor to Bodhidharma. However lowly one's symbols and practices as we see in, say, a peasant's religion, one is entitled to enlightenment if and when one uses them authentically. Here is the egalitarian basis for a claim that Dōgen's religion is a religion of the people.

Furthermore, Dōgen provides us with profound insight into the nature of philosophizing activity. To him what matters most is not the relative significance of theoretical formulations but what we do with the ideas and values we have inherited from our past and how we do it—the authenticity of philosophic activity. The issue is not so much whether or not to philosophize as how to philosophize—in absolute freedom with body-mind cast off. The philosophic enterprise is as much the practice of the bodhisattva way as is zazen. And significantly enough, this view implies that metaphysical theory itself is a kōan realized in life.

Different philosophical and religious expressions are vines—conflicts, dilemmas, antinomies which are all too human and real to be brushed away from the texture of existence. The logic of mystical realism impels Dōgen, quite understandably to us by now, to see the heritage and vitality of the Way of the Buddhas and ancestors in the vines themselves, not in an absence of or freedom from vines.[162] Dharma does not and should not avoid intellectual—let alone religious and existential—involvement in conflicts concerning various interpretations and theories. The noncommittal way of life—in this case with respect to conflicts—for which Zen Buddhism has been blamed rightly or wrongly, is absolutely alien to Dōgen's thought. Thus he writes:

By and large, all the sages are commonly concerned with the study of cutting off the root of vines, but do not realize that cutting (*saidan*) consists in severing vines from vines. Nor are they acquainted with entangling vines with vines, let alone with inheriting Dharma in vines and through vines. They rarely know that the inheritance of Dharma resides precisely in vines. There is as yet none who hears about it, none who understands it. Can there be many who experience it?[163]

Each vine grows of its own inner necessity without nullifying other vines:

You should further understand thoroughly that on account of the power to transcend [dualism] a vine seed grows in harmony with branches, leaves, flowers, and fruits that entwine vines, yet its individuality is not lost in others. Hence the Buddhas and ancestors are realized, and kōan is consummated in life.[164]

Each interpretation, though fragmentary and limited, nevertheless exerts itself totally in its Dharma-position, fulfilling its own possibilities and destiny without obstructing others and without being obstructed by others, in absolute freedom. Hence, philosophical and religious unity of expressions and vines is not of entity but of activity—that mode of activity in which "unity" is not contemplated in terms of any metaphysical principle but is, instead, acted out. These entwining vines constitute the living texture of Dōgen's mythopoeic image of a unity that advances infinitely "beyond the marrow" without a *finis,* if not without reason (*dōri*). This is what Dōgen calls the "reason of the skin, flesh, bones, and marrow entwining with each other as vines" (*hiniku-kotsuzui no kattō suru dōri*).[165]

Dōgen interprets the philosophical enterprise as an integral part of the practice of the Way. In contradistinction to cultic and moral activities, philosophy consists predominantly of the activities of intellect which can be no less creative than the former, if and when intellect is purified and reinforced by the samādhi of self-fulfilling activity (*jijuyū-zammai*). Our philosophic and hermeneutical activities are no longer a means to enlightenment but identical with enlightenment, for to be is to understand, that is, one is what one understands. Thus the activity of philosophizing, like any other expressive activity, is restated in the context of our total participation in the self-creative process of Buddha-nature.[166] Dōgen once said in *Tenzo-kyōkun* as I have quoted before: "The monastics of future generations will be able to come to understand a nondiscriminative Zen (*ichimizen*) based on words and letters, if they devote efforts to spiritual practice by seeing the universe through words and letters, and words and letters through the universe." It is small wonder, then, that Dōgen produced a unique style of Zen which fully appreciates our expressive and symbolic activities—including intellectual and philosophic ones—in the context of all beings' soteriological aspirations.

The Actional Understanding

The activity of the body-mind becomes the vehicle of understanding as well as the embodiment of truth: we understand as we act or act as we understand. The fundamental concept, understanding, is activity, in Dōgen's thought. Understanding is indispensably associated with our whole being. Often in conventional thought knowledge and truth are ascribed solely to the functions of sensation and reason, while the functions of feeling and intuition are considered merely subjective. Such an artificial compartmentalization of human activity has resulted in some distorted views of the subject. For Dōgen, the problem of understanding involves invariably the whole being which he calls the "body-mind" (*shinjin*). "Body-mind" is one of Dōgen's favorite phrases, and he often uses the phrase "mustering the body-mind" (*shinjin o koshite*) in order to show the human attempt to understand the self and the world totally.

In Buddhism, as in Hinduism, the human body has traditionally been of crucial religious significance, as Edward Conze rightly emphasizes: "A mindful and disciplined attitude to the body is the very basis of Buddhist training."[167] However, in some aspects of Theravāda Buddhism, an overly analytic and negativistic view of the body cannot be denied. That is, the impurity of the body is assumed, and the realization of its religious implications constitutes one phase of Theravāda meditation.[168] Dōgen discusses this matter in his exposition of the "four applications of mindfulness" (*catvāri smṛty-upasthānāni*; *shinenjū*),[169] and argues with respect to the first application:

The mindfulness of the impurity of body means that a carcass bounded by the skin, upon which you meditate at this moment, is the ten quarters of the universe. Since this is the true body, the mindfulness of the impurity of body leaps and dances in the living path [of nondualism of purity and impurity]. If it does not leap, mindfulness cannot be obtained. It will be like an annihilation of the body. Practice will be impossible, exposition unattainable, and meditation unimaginable.

Mindfulness of the body (*kanshin*) is the body's mindfulness (*shinkan*). It is the body's mindfulness, but no others'. While the body's mindfulness is realized, the mind's mindfulness cannot grasp anything though groping for it, and it is not consummated.[170]

Apparently, Dōgen here uses the Theravāda conception of the body in order to advance his own view without being concerned with the accuracy of his exposition. The human body, in Dōgen's view, is not a hindrance to the realization of enlightenment but the very vehicle through which enlightenment is realized. "By saying that birth-and-death and coming-and-going are the true human body (*shinjitsu-nintai*), I mean that, while an ordinary worldly person wanders about in delusion in the midst of birth-and-death, a great sage is liberated in enlightenment."[171] Dōgen's position on this issue is, as I shall discuss later, a thorough appreciation of the metaphysical and religious significance of the body without monistic and idealistic vestiges that characterized other Mahāyāna schools of Buddhism. Thus, Dōgen states that we quest with the body, practice with the body, attain enlightenment with the body, and understand with the body. All this is epitomized in his statement: "The Way is attained surely with the body." [172] The human body in its utmost particularities and concreteness attains a metaphysico-religious status in Dōgen's thought.

This is due to the body's twofold participation in the self and the world:

(1) The human body is the most primitive matrix from which the human mind evolves and with which the human mind cooperates. In Dōgen's view, both body and mind share their fortune with each other: "because the body necessarily fills the mind and the mind inevitably penetrates the body, we call this the permeation of body-mind. That is to say, this is the entire world and all directions, the whole body and the whole mind. This is none other than joy of a very special kind." [173] Body and mind are so inextricably interwoven that it is impossible to separate them. For Dōgen, the exaltation of the mind at the sacrifice of the body is an enfeebled spirituality. Spirituality must necessarily involve the complex whole of body and mind. [174] The nondual unity of body and mind (*shinjin-ichinyo*) is forcefully brought forth, by Dōgen, in his attack on the Senika heretics who held the view that the self-identical reality of the mind endures throughout the accidental adventures of the body. Dōgen argues:

You should consider carefully that the Buddha-dharma has always maintained the thesis of the nondual oneness of body and mind. Therefore, how can it be possible that while this body is born and dissolves, mind alone departs from body and escapes from arising and perishing? If there is a time when they are one and also another time when they are not, the Buddhist teaching must be false indeed. [175]

It is fundamentally un-Buddhistic in Dōgen's view to treat the body and mind as if they were separable and consequently to regard the former as perishable, changeable, accidental, and the latter as altogether otherwise. The permanence of mind or soul independent of the perishability of body is an illusion. We shall resume this problem in the next chapter.

(2) The body and mind are united with the world as a whole. The body-mind unity at the level of psycho-physical constitution, is now extended to a cosmic dimension which is characterized by such phrases as "the body-mind of Dharma," "the body-mind of the Buddhas and ancestors," "the body-mind of Tathāgata," "the body-mind of the Way," "the body-mind of the three realms and the realms of heavens and humans," and so forth. The body and mind are the entire universe: "The body-mind in the Buddha-way is grass, trees, tiles

and stones; it is wind, rain, water and fire."[176] From this standpoint, Dōgen further writes:

You should see the truth that as all the Buddhas of the past, present, and future are awakened and practice the Way, they do not leave out our bodies and minds.

To doubt this is already to slander them. As we reflect quietly upon this matter, it seems quite reasonable that our bodies and minds enact the Way and our desire for enlightenment is awakened truly with Buddhas of the three periods.[177]

The human body is important as a part of the external world; for although we often think we are separated from the world by our body bounded by skin, it is not always certain where the body ends and where the external world begins, or vice versa. As Whitehead observes, the biological and physiological functions of the human body, such as those of the molecules which constitute it, obscure all the more discontinuity between the human body and its external environment.[178]

Thus, the human body participates in our inner world as well as in our external world, and in turn, both the inner and outer worlds participate in each other through the human body. The mind, body, and nature interpenetrate one another so inseparably that a hard and fast demarcation between them is altogether impossible. In such a view, to cleanse the body is to cleanse the mind; to cleanse the body-mind is to cleanse the entire universe.[179] We shall treat this problem of cleansing in more detail in a different context later.

Now that the mind, body, and nature are inextricably interpenetrated so as to constitute the totality of reality, the act of human understanding (*gakudō*) becomes possible only as we participate in this totality.[180] Dōgen contends: "There are two ways to study the Way: one is to understand it with the mind, the other with the body."[181]

First, understanding with the mind is explained as follows:

Shingakudō is to study [the Way] with all the various aspects of the mind. They are the conscious mind (*citta: sittashin* or *ryochishin*), the cosmic mind (*hṛdaya; karidashin*), the transcendental mind (*iridashin*), and so on. It means also that after having the thought of enlightenment through cosmic resonance (*kannō-dōkō*), you devote yourself to the great Way of the Buddhas and ancestors and acquire the knowledge of the activities of the awakened desire for enlightenment.[182]

It is particularly important for us to note that Dōgen lays a special stress upon the importance, for the attainment of enlightenment, of perception and thought at the conscious level which he calls *sittashin* or *ryochishin:*

Of these aspects of the mind the arising of the thought of enlightenment (*bodaishin*) invariably employs the conscious mind. . . . The aspiration to enlightenment cannot be awakened without this conscious mind. I do not mean to identify this conscious mind directly with the thought of enlightenment, but the latter is engendered by the former.[183]

Despite this emphasis on conscious thought, it constitutes only a portion of Dōgen's conception of mind, as we shall see further in the next chapter. It differs from a narrowly conceived subjectivistic idealism (which Dōgen would consider a form of "naturalistic heresy"); understanding with the mind does not imply, in the least, any subjectivistic and solipsistic predilections. Nor is it a dissolution of the conscious mind as in the case of a certain type of mysticism. The enlightened mind, as is clear from this, is post-critical, though continuous with the pre-critical forces of the body-mind. The critical mind has never been forfeited in this view.

Second, understanding with the body is described:

Shingakudō is to learn the Way with the body—study on the part of the naked bodily whole (*sekinikudan* or *shakunikudan*). The body comes forth from study of the Way, and what originates from investigation of the Way is likewise the body. The entire universe is precisely this very human body (*shinjitsu-nintai*); birth-and-death, coming-and-going are the genuine human body. By moving this body, we shun the Ten Evils, uphold the Eight Precepts, devote ourselves to the Three Treasures, and enter the monastic's life through renunciation. This is the real study of the Way; consequently it is called the authentic human body. A young Buddhist student should never sympathize with any heretical assertions of naturalism.[184]

Again Dōgen is very anxious to remind us of the dangers of naturalistic views. When he speaks of naked bodily existence, he means the true human body that comes forth out of the act of understanding, which is not identical with crude biological instincts and physiological drives. The latter are radically rejected; only thereafter does the "nakedness" of bodily existence, mediated and purified by emptiness, become truly authentic—being free of self-centered orientation. Thus the body comes forth out of understanding; the true human body functions freely and authentically in harmony with the entire universe.

The body-mind totality is at last free from dualistic shackles and hence free for duality—that is, the body-mind is now authentically able to deal with the self and the world. This is the meaning of the body-mind cast off (*shinjin-datsuraku*). Thus, the following famous statement:

To study the Way is to study the self. To study the self is to forget the self. To forget the self is to be enlightened by all things of the universe. To be enlightened by all things of the universe is to cast off the body and mind of the self as well as those of others. Even the traces of enlightenment are wiped out, and life with traceless enlightenment goes on forever and ever.[185]

The self and the world are "cast off" and hence "undefiled" but not dissolved. The inexorable duality of the self and the world—and all the ensuing implications, paradoxes, conflicts—are not dissolved but seen in the light of emptiness and thusness.

The casting-off of the body-mind authenticates "mustering the body-mind" (*shinjin o koshite*), as eloquently stated in the following:

Mustering our bodies and minds (*shinjin o koshite*) we see things, and mustering our bodies and minds we hear sounds, thereby we understand them intimately (*shitashiku*). However, it is not like a reflection dwelling in the mirror, nor is it like the moon and the water. As one side is illumined, the other is darkened (*ippō o shōsuru toki wa ippō wa kurashi*).[186]

Herein is Dōgen's mystical realism epitomized in a nutshell. The Way is "intimately understood" in and through what we express and enact by mustering our body-minds; thus humans and the Way are no longer in a dualistic relation similar to that of the moon and the water, of the mirror and the reflection, or of the knower and the known. Such an intimate understanding is elsewhere likened to forgetting the footsteps of enlightenment.[187] However, Dōgen's nondualistic mystical thinking has an especially realistic thrust, apparent in this quotation, which permeates all aspects of his religion and philosophy. That is to say, nondualism does not primarily signify the transcendence of duality so much as the realization of duality. When one chooses, and commits oneself to, a special course of action, one does so in such a manner that the action is not an action among others but the action—there is nothing but that particular action in the universe so that the whole universe is created in and through that action. And even this action is cast off, leaving absolutely no trace whatsoever of the Way. This is indeed far from being a kind of mysticism which attempts to attain an undifferentiated state of consciousness. Quite the contrary, Dōgen's thought is through and through committal in the dualistic realm—including its empirical as well as rational aspects.

As we try to incorporate these observations on Dōgen's view of the body-mind understanding into what we have previously said about activities and expressions, it is quite evident that for Dōgen, activities, expressions, and understanding are one and the same. It is not that we act first and then attempt to understand, nor is it even that action is a special mode of understanding. For all modes of understanding are necessarily activities and expressions. This is why Dōgen says: "Understanding in faith (*shinge*) is that which we cannot evade."[188] Every activity-expression is a hermeneutical experiment in and through the body-mind. Ontology and epistemology, together, become an ethically, emotionally, and intellectually purified and re-vitalized cognition of life and reality. Thus:

Tathāgata's supernal power, compassion, and everlasting life-energy lead us to understanding in faith by moving our minds and our bodies, the entire universe, the Buddhas and ancestors, and make us believe in faith by setting in motion all things, ultimate reality, the skin-flesh-bones-marrow, birth-and-death, and coming-and-going.[189]

As we have stated before, one is what one understands. Ontology (and soteriology for that matter) is inevitably hermeneutical.

In this chapter we have endeavored to examine how cultic and moral activities (*gyōji*), and mythopoeic and philosophic expressions (*dōtoku*), are differentiated from Dōgen's conception of zazen-only in the samādhi of self-fulfilling activity. The concepts of activity and expression are generally in line with the traditional polar concepts of meditation and wisdom in the Buddhist symbolic model. In Dōgen's thought, however, the philosophy of activity and the activity of philosophy are more radically legitimized in their total scheme without falling into the two poles of "naturalism": one being monistic pantheism and the other, crude secularism (both of which are, according to Dōgen, "naturalistic," because they are dualistic). Hence, ethical and philosophic endeavors in the world of duality are not to be abandoned but to be liberated by the samādhi of self-fulfilling activity in order for humans to act and think authentically; only then can the use of categories and concepts of duality become the co-efficient of our total liberation, a liberation no less creative than other modes of creativity.

Self-understanding of *how* will lead us to the problem of *what*, that is, what to think and act. So far we have been primarily concerned with the how, and shall now turn, in the remaining chapters, to some detailed investigation of what Dōgen thought and did.

FOUR

The Religion
and Metaphysics of
Buddha-Nature

EXPRESSION (*dōtoku*) and activity (*gyōji*) in Dōgen's thought can
be profitably discussed in terms of the religion and metaphysics
of Buddha-nature and the ritual and morality of monastic asceticism.
We will embark on the exposition of these two aspects in the remaining two chapters. As we have observed before, Dōgen's thought was
intimately connected with Japanese Tendai thought and Chinese Zen
tradition. As we probe into close observations of Dōgen's life and
thought, we come to realize that these ideological elements were further transformed by the Japanese ethos of the age in which Dōgen
lived. Two of them stand out most prominently: one is the sentiment
of impermanence (*anitya*; *mujō*) and the other, reason (*yukti*; *dōri*).
Both terms were borrowed from the Buddhist tradition, yet they
had been thoroughly acculturated by the late Heian and the early
Kamakura periods.

As Karaki discusses, there were two major types of conceptions regarding impermanence in the history of Japanese thought.[1] One treats
the actualities of life as evanescent and empty (*hakanashi*). This sentiment was prevalent in the Age of Degenerate Law (*mappō*), in which
hundreds and thousands of sensitive minds turned first from the secular world to established Buddhism, and then turned, in despair and
alienation, from religion to a retreat from everything—to a quiet pursuit of their personal predilections (*suki* or *susabi*). This was essentially a flight from the impermanence of existence by a "sentimen-

talization" of it in melancholic and indifferent fatalism, rather than a
realistic attempt to cope with it. It was a sentiment of impermanence
rather than a metaphysic of impermanence.[2] The other conception
confronted the actualities of impermanence as facts which could not
be escaped and, hence, asked that one attempt to live them and transform them resolutely and heroically. The aesthetic and religious
means of inward fortification which were fashionable at that time
were fatally inadequate because they were merely psychological con-
trivances, and, more importantly, were acts of attachment to the self
which could not change the fact of impermanence. Hence this second
approach concerned itself most with a genuine philosophic understanding and religious transformation of the existential situation.

The leaders of Kamakura Buddhism such as Hōnen, Shinran, Dōgen, and Nichiren shared this latter understanding of the existence
of impermanence, but Dōgen was the first who seriously attempted
to deal with this problem philosophically and religiously, and as a result produced a metaphysic of impermanence.[3] As we recall, impermanence was the alpha and omega of religion for Dōgen: reflection
upon and understanding of the impermanence of existence was tirelessly exhorted throughout his works. His approach was neither emotive nor psychological but instead religious and metaphysical through
and through, as we shall see in more detail in what follows. His view
was alien to the fatalism and escapism that had often been associated
with the sense of impermanence; moreover, he shunned aesthetic indulgence, though he could not help being poetic and eloquent about
impermanence.[4] The crucially important point to note here is the cen-
trality of impermanence and accordingly of death in Dōgen's whole
religious and philosophic thought.

Another important idea that bears deeply upon Dōgen's thought is
the concept of reason, in the sense of the nature or intrinsic logic of
things—not the reasons for, but the principle, meaning, or truth, of
them. The pervasiveness of this concept in medieval Japan has been
well attested by many students of Japanese thought.[5] After the Jōkyū
War (1221) or thereabout an earlier fatalistic view of reason gradually
dwindled in favor of a more positive, realistic understanding of it,
reflecting the fall of the last remnant of Heian aristocracy and the rise
of the military class.[6] In Buddhist tradition, also, the concept of reason was a common subject. Dōgen in particular favored this word,
using it in practically all the subjects with which he dealt.[7] The Buddhist tradition in general has advocated the fourfold reason of the

Saṃdhinirmocana sūtra and the *Yogācāra-bhūmi,* namely, the reason of relation (*kandai-dōri*), the reason of causation (*sayū-dōri*), the reason of recognition (*shōjō-dōri*), and the reason of naturalness (*hōni-dōri*).[8] However, Dōgen's usage seems to be much wider and more comprehensive; in fact, the whole spectrum of his thought and practice is permeated by his search for reason in all aspects of life without exception.[9]

Thus to Dōgen it was imperative, both philosophically and religiously, to understand (*akiramu*) the reason of impermanence and act upon it—this orientation differed fundamentally from the view of being subjugated to and fighting against the intolerable realities of the age. Furthermore, in this pursuit of the reason of impermanence Dōgen in turn probed deeply into the mystery and reason of absolute emptiness.

Two Strands of Mahāyāna Idealism

Buddhism, like other Indian religious and philosophical traditions, approaches the problems of humanity and the world from what we would broadly designate as the "psychological" standpoint.[10] Its methodology assumes that the activities of the mind are the decisive factor in determining our well-being. The opening statements of the *Dhammapada* proclaim that all we are is the result of what we have thought,[11] and the *Ratnamegha sūtra* beautifully describes this:

All phenomena originate in the mind, and when the mind is fully known all phenomena are fully known. . . . Bodhisattvas, thoroughly examining the nature of things, dwell in ever-present mindfulness of the activity of the mind, and so do not fall into the mind's power, but the mind comes under their control. And with the mind under their control all phenomena are under their control.[12]

Nyanaponika Thera summarizes this psychological orientation by saying: "In the Buddhist doctrine, mind is the starting point, the focal point, and also, as the liberated and purified mind of the Saint, the culminating point."[13] Hence, what matters most in liberation (which is, after all, what religion is all about), both individually and collectively, as Buddhism conceives it, is the proper understanding and use of the mind; the way to liberation is founded upon the understanding of our psychic conditions and the moral and religious rectification of them, for all the sufferings of existence arise from what we feel, think, do—and ultimately from the ignorant mind. Careful analysis of the states of consciousness as well as of the unconscious (which was systematized elaborately in the doctrine of consciousness-only of the Vijñānavāda school, as we shall see presently) derives from this methodological orientation. Thus Buddhism has been, from its very beginning, strongly psychological in its outlook and method.[14]

Buddhism has presented, from its earliest phase through Abhidharma and Vijñānavāda Buddhism to the present-day Buddhism, wide-ranging analyses, issues, and theories of the mind such as those of the five aggregates (*goun*); the twelve *nidanas* of functional interdependence (*jūni-innen*); the unity of the six sense-organs (*rokkon*), the six sense-objects (*rokkyō*), and the six consciousnesses (*roku-shiki*); various interpretations of the mind (*citta-manas-vijñāna*; *shin-i-shiki*); various attempts at the classification of mental functions; controversies over the distinction between the mind (*shin'ō* or *shinnō*) and mental functions (*shinjo*) and their relationship; Abhidharmic analysis of dharmas; Vijñānavādin's eight consciousnesses (*hasshiki*) developed from the six consciousnesses; controversies over the original purity of the nature of mind, and so forth. All these are abundantly indicative of the Buddhist's fascination with the human mind as the clue to religious and moral matters.[15]

Buddhist psychology extends beyond conventional concerns to embrace physical, metaphysical, and ethical issues. It deals with the totality of humanity and the world. This will become increasingly clear as we go on in this chapter.

Having observed this, I now wish to review, very briefly, two facets of Mahāyāna Buddhist "idealism" (*citta-mātra*; *yuishin*)[16] as it is broadly interpreted: that is, the tradition of consciousness-only (*vijñāna-mātra* or *vijñapti-mātra*; *yuishiki*) and that of *tathāgata-garbha* (*nyoraizō*).[17] The former has to do with a "substratum" of the mind beyond the six consciousnesses of early Buddhism and Abhidharma philosophy, and the latter pertains to the original nature of the mind, which has been very important throughout the history of Buddhism.

One of the most fascinating aspects of the history of Buddhist thought is the peculiar—almost agonizing—ideological readjustments attempted by various individuals and schools to meet the difficulties posed by the doctrine of no-self (*anātman*; *muga*), which has existed from the very beginning of Buddhism. Abhidharma Buddhism assumed a position which S. Dasgupta calls "pluralistic phenomenalism":[18] the self is viewed as a succession of ever-changing conglomerations of impersonal dharmas—momentary phenomenal forms devoid of ultimate ground or cause. This doctrine of no-self had difficulties explaining to its critics the nature and continuity of a subject who is reborn through a succession of lives, the mechanism of memory and karmic inheritance, the nature of cognition, the locus of moral responsibility, and a legion of other problems. Adherents of this theory searched for some sort of "agent" or "substratum" which could integrate mental functions, transmit karmic effects, and continue the personality through rebirths, but they tried to avoid admitting to any substantialistic self. For example, the idea of "life-force" (*āyus*; *ju* or *jīvitendriya*; *myōkon*) was often referred to in the primitive Buddhism, Abhidharma Buddhism, Vijñānavāda school, and so forth. According to this view, the life-force underlies the six consciousnesses, and its duration and measure are allotted to each person on account of karmic merits; it is said to preserve warmth (*nan*) and consciousness (*shiki*) and is in turn preserved by the latter (although the relation between the life-force, warmth, and consciousness are not always clear). Thus, the life-force is the integrator of the body and mind. These three factors are said to depart from the body at death and to be transmitted to the next life. This idea is only one among many other theoretical concessions such as the "original consciousness" (*kompon-jiki*) of the Mahāsaṃghika school, the "subconscious life-stream" (*bhavaṅga-citta*; *ubun-jiki*) of the Sthavira school, the "person" (*pudgala*; *fudogara*) of the Vatsīputrīya school, and so on.[19]

Let us consider this idealistic line of thought in its historical context. Some rudimentary ideas of consciousness-only appeared in such texts as the *Saṃdhi-nirmocana sūtra*, *Mahāyāna-abhidharma sūtra*, and were later developed by Maitreya (c. 270–350) in the *Yogācāra-bhūmi* (which is traditionally attributed to him), by Asaṅga (c. 310–390) in his *Mahāyāna-saṃgraha*, by Vasubandhu (c. 320–400) in his *Viṃśatikā-vijñapti-mātratā-siddhi*, *Triṃśikā-vijñapti-mātratā-siddhi*, and by Dharmapāla (sixth century) in his *Vijñapti-mātratā-siddhi-śāstra*. The consciousness-only thought reached its highest point in the fourth century and thereafter. Later it was combined, as we see in the *Laṅkāvatāra sūtra* and the *Ta-ch'êng ch'i-hsin-lun* (both of which were presumably fifth-sixth century works), with the tradition of *tathāgata-garbha*, which had been developed independently of the Vijñānavāda tradition. Vijñānavāda thought developed the ideas of manas-consciousness (*manas*; *manashiki*) and store-consciousness (*ālaya-vijñāna*; *arayashiki*) as the seventh and the eighth consciousnesses. Store-consciousness is said to be the psychic repository in which unconscious memories, karmic accumulations, impulses, drives, and so forth are stored in the form of "seeds" (*bīja*; *shūji*). When conditions are right, these seeds produce "manifestations" (*gengyō*) which are taken by the ordinary worldly person to be phenomena of the external world independent of the mind—thus forming a dualistic conception of the mind and the world (*temben*). In this connection, thought-consciousness (*mano-vijñāna*; *ishiki*) and manas-consciousness are primarily responsible for the discrimination and individuation that characterize the empirical world. The manifestations "perfume" (*vāsanā*; *kunjū*) their impressions or energies into the store-consciousness and, thus, form new seeds. This process of seeds-manifestations-perfuming-new seeds takes place constantly, hence, cause and effect occur simultaneously in the present (*sambō-chinden-inga-dōji*); the process repeats itself ad infinitum in a succession of such presents. This is the functional interdependence of phenomena and consciousness (*arayashiki-engi*), in which both subjectivity and objectivity are the products of store-consciousness.

As is clear from these cursory observations, store-consciousness is by far the most sophisticated concept innovated by the Buddhists in response to criticisms of the idea of no-self; indeed, it almost envisions a self-surrogate, yet this differs, or allegedly differs, from any immutable, self-identical substratum of the self.[20] Here we can see the close historical connection between the idea of the self and the idea of the store-consciousness. However, these ideas of store-consciousness, seeds, and so on are sometimes ambiguous and misleading due to the intrinsic connotations of the terms. The store-consciousness often reminds us of a receptacle in which seeds are stored, and, hence, is strongly suggestive of permanence and substance instead of impermanence and nonsubstantiality, that is, the rise and dissolution of store-consciousness from moment to moment in accordance with functional interdependence. Seeds, active in the processes of manifestation and perfuming, are an embryological analogy which strongly suggests the continuity of development, which again is liable to association with the ideas of substratum and immutability.[21] Such a developmental perspective is also reflected in the notion of the "five stages of spiritual discipline" (*goi*) which are necessary in order to realize the so-called "transformation of the eight consciousnesses and the attainment of the four wisdoms" (*tenjiki-tokuchi*). Moreover, the Vijñānavāda school is preeminently psychological and epistemological rather than ontological in that it emphasizes the process of transformation which occurs in store-consciousness, but it does not go so far as to affirm mind-only as the ultimate reality in which the opposites of pure and defiled, good and evil, enlightenment and delusion are resolved in a different way from the process of transformation.[22]

Let us now turn to the *tathāgata-garbha* tradition. This tradition seems to have developed independently along with the Vijñāna-vāda tradition of Buddhism. Its earliest formulations appeared in such sūtras as *Ārya-tathāgata-garbha-namamahāyāna sūtra, Śrīmālādevī-siṃhanāda sūtra,* and many others around the fourth century, and were later developed in such works as the *Laṅkāvatāra sūtra,* the *Ta-ch'êng ch'i-hsin-lun* (popularly known as the *Awakening of Faith*), Vasubandhu's *Buddhatva-śāstra, Ratnagotravibhāga-mahāyānottaratantra-śāstra,* and other treatises in the fifth and sixth centuries. In the history of the evolution of this tradition, the idea of the *tathāgata-garbha* seems to have been acknowledged independently from that of store-consciousness in its earliest stage; next both were acknowledged simultaneously; and, finally, the fusion of the two strands took place as in the *Laṅkāvatāra sūtra* and the *Ta-ch'êng ch'i-hsin-lun.* Especially the latter is said to be the culmination of the *tathāgata-garbha* school of Buddhist thought which influenced practically all the schools and sects of Mahāyāna Buddhism in the East Asian countries.[23]

Although the foregoing observations may give an impression that the tradition of the *tathāgata-garbha* is strictly Mahāyānist, it is actually the result of long developments of Buddhist collective reflections upon the essential nature of the mind—as to whether it is pure or defiled originally, or both, or neither. The issue was debated among the Buddhists in the earliest phase of its history. As Katsumata observes, the primitive Buddhists conceived that the mind is originally pure and illusions are foreign defilements (*shinsho-shōjō; kakujin-bonnō*), and even when some argued for the purity and defilement of the mind, the general tendency was to subscribe to the original purity of the mind and to see the phenomenal nature of the mind as both pure and defiled.[24] In Abhidharma Buddhism the two schools of thought on this issue controverted each other, one maintaining the original purity of the mind (e.g., the Mahāsaṃghika school), the other rejecting it (e.g., the Sarvāstivāda school).[25] What characterizes Mahāyāna Buddhism, on the other hand, is its consistent adherence, throughout its history, to the idea of the original purity of the mind.

Indeed, this is said to be the core of Mahāyāna Buddhism, out of which all the later doctrinal developments are derived, and without which they cannot be adequately understood.[26] In contradistinction to the psychological and ethical approach of early Buddhism and the Abhidharma school, the Mahāyāna approach was predominantly metaphysical with respect to the nature of the enlightened mind and the possibility of Buddhahood, as we see in such concepts as no–mind (*acitta; mushin*), emptiness (*śūnyatā; kū*), *tathāgata-garbha*, Dharma-mind (*dharma-citta; hosshō-shin*), Buddha–nature (*buddhatva; busshō*), thusness (*tathatā; shinnyo*) one mind (*eka-citta; isshin*), original enlightenment (*hongaku*), and so forth.[27] Thus, the crude psychological conception of the original purity of the mind—of early Buddhism—was metaphysically elaborated and refined in various schools of Mahāyāna Buddhism.

Garbha, in *tathāgata-garbha*, refers either to "embryo," which is the potentiality to become Tathāgata, or to "womb," which gives birth to Tathāgata. *Garbha* in the sense of "store" (which is customary in Chinese translations, comparable to the *ālaya* of *ālaya-vijñāna*) may also be interpreted either as the Tathāgata "hidden" in sentient beings or as the Tathāgata which "embraces" sentient beings. In both cases (whose analogies are strikingly similar to those of the Vijñānavāda school at this point), the first meaning seems to have been conceived at the early stages of *tathāgata-garbha* thought.[28] In one case the *tathāgata-garbha* is in us, whereas in the other we are in the *tathāgata-garbha*. In the former, *tathāgata-garbha* is the potentiality to become Buddhas, conceived psychologically and anthropologically; in the latter it is a metaphysical or ontological vision of ultimate reality in which humans are the constituents of the *tathāgata-garbha*. In this latter case we can see the metaphysical possibilities when such an idea is combined with other potent Buddhist ideas such as Buddha-nature, emptiness, mind–only, and so on.

This is precisely what happened in Buddhist idealism around the fifth and sixth centuries when the *Laṅkāvatāra sūtra*, the *Ta-ch'êng ch'i-hsin-lun*, and other sūtras and treatises were produced. It was in these works that the two quite different traditions of store-consciousness and *tathāgata-garbha* were synthesized; yet the synthesis was weighted in favor of the *tathāgata-garbha* orientation, that is, the belief in original purity of the mind. This is especially true of the *Ta-ch'êng ch'i-hsin-lun* which is often said to be the apex of the *tathāgata-garbha* tradition of Buddhist thought.[29] In this work store-consciousness is defined as that in which "neither birth nor death" (nirvāṇa) diffuses harmoniously with "birth and death" (saṃsāra), and yet in which both are neither identical nor different, as well as having the two aspects of enlightenment and nonenlightenment.[30] The Vijñānavādin conception of the significance of store-consciousness is discarded and manas-consciousness, in the scheme of the eight consciousnesses, is dropped, although some basic ideas of the Vijñānavāda school are still utilized. The phenomenal world is construed as arising from the activation of store-consciousness, or thusness, by "basic ignorance" (*kompon-mumyō*), and explained in terms of the three subtle aspects (*sansai*) and the six coarse aspects (*rokuso*),[31] or in terms of the five minds (*goi*).[32] In a symbolic expression, indicative of the mystery of ignorance, this work speaks of ignorance as originating "suddenly."[33] Enlightenment is classified into "original enlightenment" (*hongaku*) and "acquired enlightenment" (*shikaku*), two classifications which became the fundamental concepts in Buddhist thought in its subsequent history.[34] Both enlightenment and nonenlightenment were said to be aspects of the same essence, namely, thusness.[35] The mystery of "perfuming" (*vāsanā; kunjū*)—permeation or suffusion in the Vijñānavāda tradition—is of two kinds: the perfuming of ignorance and the perfuming of thusness. Thus, original enlightenment, ignorance, and the mind in between perfume each other in such a way that one has either a deluded mind or an enlightened mind.[36] Ignorance continues, from the beginningless beginning, perpetually to permeate the mind, until it perishes by the realization of enlightenment, but thusness, or original enlightenment, has no interruption and no ending.[37] Thusness, moreover, has the inner urge to express itself, seeming to suggest that thusness is not only not nothing but not neutral.[38]

These strands of Buddhist idealism are presented here in order to provide the background for our subsequent investigation. Particularly it is noteworthy at this juncture that the oldest idealistic tenet, "The triple world is mind-only" (*sangai-yuishin*), in the *Daśabhūmika sūtra*—which was originally an independent sūtra but later incorporated into the *Avataṃsaka sūtra*—is more closely aligned historically and ideologically with the *tathāgata-garbha* tradition than with the Vijñānavāda tradition, though the latter two provided two different interpretations of the tenet.[39] Indeed, *tathāgata-garbha* thought can be construed as the philosophical-religious explication of the tenet "The triple world is mind-only"; Chinese Hua-yen metaphysics can be regarded as the further development of this interpretation.[40] Further-

more, Zen's relation to these traditions can be conjectured by the legendary association of Bodhidharma with the *Laṅkāvatāra sūtra* and by
the association of Chih-yen (602–668), Ch'eng-kuan (738–840), and
Kuei-fêng Tsung-mi (780–841) with Zen Buddhism. Thus, Hua-
yen metaphysics, the *tathāgata-garbha* tradition, and Zen Buddhism
were intimately related to each other historically and ideologically.
This strand of Buddhist idealism is very important for an understanding of Dōgen's view of mind in general and of Buddha-nature in
particular, to the examination of which we shall now proceed.

Mind: Beyond Monistic Pantheism and Naturalistic Phenomenalism

Dōgen once proclaimed: "Discourse on [the nonduality of] the
mind and its essence (*sesshin-sesshō*) is the great foundation of the
Buddha-way"[41]; he wrote extensively on this subject matter in many
chapters of *Shōbōgenzō*.[42] As shall become increasingly clear in our
subsequent investigations, Dōgen's interpretation of mind inherits the
best elements of Hua-yen, *tathāgata-garbha,* and Zen traditions, yet
overcomes some vulnerabilities inherent in them, and goes beyond
them in being deeply practical and existentialistic.

In general accord with the Mahāyāna Buddhist interpretation of
mind, Dōgen uses this term in various senses.[43] First of all, mind is
the totality of psycho-physical realities. As we have already observed,
Dōgen emphasizes the importance of the conscious mental activities
of intellect, feeling, and will (*ryochi-nenkaku*). However, he also says
that the entire universe of the external world is mind: "The triple
world is mind-only" (*sangai-yuishin*). Thus he equates mind with
"mountains, rivers, and the earth; the sun, the moon, and the stars."[44]
By so doing, Dōgen did not maintain, as some Buddhists would, that
all existence is reducible to mind as ordinarily interpreted by Berke-
leyian subjective idealism. Dōgen discusses the conversations between Saṃghanandi, the seventeenth ancestor of Indian Buddhism,
and his disciple Gayāśata as regards the phenomenon of the tinkle of a
bell—whether what tinkles is the bell, the air, or the mind. Gayāśata's
view, approved by his teacher subsequently, is that the mind—neither
the bell nor the air—tinkles.[45] A subjective idealism in this sense had
also been generally accepted by Zen Buddhists. Dōgen's view, on the
other hand, is, in the final analysis, that inasmuch as these three factors are "quiet" (*jakujō*), that is, empty, the "tinkle of the mind" is
neither the tinkle of the air nor the tinkle of the bell nor the tinkle of

the mind (in its ordinary sense), but, is "the tinkle of the air, the tinkle of the bell, the tinkle of stirring [the air], the tinkle of tinkle (*mei-mei*)"—each abiding in its own Dharma-position as an expression and activity of emptiness and thusness.[46] As already mentioned in this example, Dōgen maintains that mind is not only the totality of the psycho-physical world but also "something" more; accordingly, mind is identified with some important terms such as thusness (*tathatā; shinnyo*), Dharma-nature (*dharmatā; hosshō*), Buddha-nature (*buddhatā* or *buddhatva; busshō*), absolute emptiness, and so forth.

Dōgen writes:

You should note that in the Buddha-dharma the truth of "thusness of mind (*shinshō*) as the all-embracing aspect of the universe" [the *Ta-ch'êng ch'i-hsin-lun*] includes the whole reality; it does not separate reality from appearance, or comment on arising and perishing. Even enlightenment and nirvāṇa are nothing other than mind-thusness. All existences and all phenomena are invariably this one mind—nothing is excluded, all is embraced. All these various teachings are one mind of nonduality (*byōdō-isshin*). To see no particular difference is the way Buddhists have understood the nature of mind.

Such being the case, how can you discriminate between body and mind, dividing birth-and-death and nirvāṇa in this single Dharma? Inasmuch as we are already the children of Buddha, do not listen to those madpeople who speak of heretical views.[47]

It is noteworthy to see here a specific reference to the *Ta-ch'êng ch'i-hsin-lun*'s doctrine of the *tathāgata-garbha* which embraces the Dharma-world (*dharma-dhātu; hokkai*)—indicating the affinity of Dōgen's view of mind to that particular tradition. To Dōgen, thus, mind is at once knowledge and reality, at once the knowing subject and the known object, yet transcends them both at the same time. In this nondualistic conception of mind what one knows is what one is— and ontology, epistemology, and soteriology are inseparably united. This was also his interpretation of the Hua-yen tenet "The triple world is mind-only." From this vantage point, Dōgen guarded himself against the inherent weaknesses of the two strands of Buddhist idealism: the advocacy of mental phenomena (*shinsō*) by the school of consciousness-only, and that of mental essence (*shinshō*) by the school of the *tathāgata-garbha*—both of which are vulnerable to a dualism between phenomena and essence. Thus, philosophically speaking, Dōgen maneuvered between monistic pantheism and naturalistic phenomenalism. In this respect, he sought the middle way in his own manner.

Mind can be posited as the knowing subject in opposition to the known object; the mind in opposition to the body; and the nature or essence of the mind as opposed to the functions of the mind or opposing the mind-body totality. One of the most typical views of mind embraces the first of these three pairs of opposites; another holds only to the second group. Mahāyāna Buddhism, being non-dualistically oriented, by virtue of its two pivotal notions of functional interdependence (*pratītya-samutpāda*; *engi*) and emptiness (*śūnyatā*; *kū*), was ever vigilant against falling into either of these dualistic traps. Nevertheless the dangers of both orientations seem to have existed even at the time of Dōgen. Let us look into this matter a little further.

One of the targets for Dōgen's philosophical attack is the so-called Senika heresy (*senni-gedō*) which held the view of the self-identical reality of mind as opposed to body. Dōgen explains the Senika view as follows:

Speaking of association with non-Buddhist ways, there is a heresy called the Senika in India. Its view is as follows: the great Way resides in our present bodies, and its state can be easily known. That is, it feels pleasure and suffering, is aware of coolness and warmth, and pain and itch. It is neither obstructed by things of the universe nor affected by environments. Although things come and go, and objective realities are born and annihilated, spiritual intelligence (*reichi*) endures, being immutable forever. This spiritual intelligence permeates everything, making no discrimination between ordinary worldly persons, saints, and other sentient beings. Even though it harbors the illusory flowers of false Dharma temporarily, as wisdom appears in accord with a single thought and as things are dissolved and environs annihilated, the original nature of spiritual intelligence alone remains serenely changeless. If bodily characteristics disintegrate, spiritual intelligence emerges intact. It can be compared to the owner of a house coming forth from his/her burning house. On account of its vividness and mysteriousness, it is called the essence of the enlightened and the wise. This is also called Buddha or enlightenment. It possesses both the self and others, and penetrates delusion as well as enlightenment. Whatever things and realities may be, spiritual intelligence does not partake of environs, nor is it the same as objects. It is eternally changeless. All phenomena now existing may be regarded as real by virtue of their being the locus of spiritual intelligence. They are true dharmas, because they are derived from the original essence. Even so, they are not permanent like spiritual intelligence, for they arise and perish. Because [spiritual intelligence] does not concern itself with light and darkness, yet mysteriously knows, it is called mysterious intelligence. In addition, it is variously called the true ātman, the ground of enlightenment, original nature, or noumenon. To realize such an original nature is said to be a homecoming to eternity or a great sage who returns to truth. After this, one no longer suffers in the cycles of birth-and-death, and enters into the transcendent sea of no birth and no death. Anything other than this is not true. The more such an essence is obscured, the more the three realms and the six worlds vie with one another for emergence. Such is the view of the Senika heresy.[48]

The Senika is quite clear from Dōgen's own exposition. The spiritual intelligence is serenely unaffected by the vicissitudes of the bodily existence and, even after the latter's dissolution, retains its self-identical existence. The idealistic orientation of Buddhist thought in general left many susceptible to the Senika heresy, and Dōgen wrote frequently in his works to warn his fellow Buddhists against allowing variously disguised versions of this same heretical view to creep into their thoughts. Dōgen writes for example: "Hearing the word Buddha-nature, many scholars erroneously take it for the ātman of the Senika heresy."[49] Thus Dōgen's critique of the mistaken view of the eternity of mind and the perishability of body (*shinjō-sōmetsu no jaken*) is vehement and relentless in its tone:

You should understand this: Both in India and in China it is well known that the Buddha-dharma from the very beginning has maintained the unity of body and mind and the nonduality of reality and appearance. You must not dare doubt it. Accordingly, from the standpoint of changelessness (*jōjū*), all things are changeless without exception, for body and mind are not separated. From the viewpoint of unconditionedness (*jakumetsu*), all existences are equally unconditioned, for reality and appearance are not discriminated. Therefore, is it not against reasonableness for some to assert that while body perishes mind perpetuates? What is more, it should be realized that the very birth-and-death itself is nirvāṇa; nobody can speak of nirvāṇa independent of birth-and-death. Indeed, even if you intellectually apprehend the eternity of mind that is separated from body, and thereby deceive yourself into construing it as the Buddha-wisdom estranged from birth-and-death, this mind of your abstract understanding and discriminative perception is still subject to birth and annihilation, and it is by no means timeless. Is this not pitiful?[50]

Dōgen's worry is quite justifiable since it is an ever-recurring philosophical temptation to corrupt the ideas of functional interdependence and absolute emptiness—the lasting Buddhist contribution to the philosophical and religious heritage of the world. The real purpose of Dōgen's critique of the Senika heresy, thus, is to warn those

Buddhists who unwittingly accept the Senika presuppositions and, consequently, demolish the Buddhist metaphysical foundation.[51]

Another frequent target of Dōgen's vehement attack is Ta-hui Tsung-kao (1089–1163), the foremost leader of the Lin-chi (Rinzai) sect of Chinese Zen Buddhism, who advocated a view different from that of the Senika heretics. Dōgen writes:

Zen Teacher Ta-hui Tsung-kao of Ching-shan appeared and said: "Buddhists today are fond of arguing the problem of mind and its nature, and like to talk about its mystery and subtlety; consequently, they are slow in the attainment of the Way. When we resolutely discard both mind and its essence, and forget its mystery as well as its subtlety (these two aspects are of no-birth)—only then do we attain enlightenment."

Such a view does not yet understand the fine writings of the Buddhas and ancestors, nor does it hear about the splendor of their gems.[52]

We are told then that Tsung-kao is asserting a kind of negativistic mysticism which totally obliterates any mental activities. This is clearly stated in the following interpretation, by Dōgen, of Tsung-kao's view:

Accordingly, he holds such a view because he conceives mind to be nothing but intellect and perception, but fails to learn that intellect and perception are also [an integral part] of mind. His view unwarrantedly regards the essence of mind as serene and calm exclusively, but does not understand the existence and nonexistence of Buddha-nature or Dharma-nature; it has never even dreamt of the nature of thusness (*nyozeshō*), hence it distorts the Buddha-dharma in this way.[53]

While I have some reservations about Dōgen's interpretation at this point, in light of his frequently sectarian attitude toward his rival sect (to which Tsung-kao belonged), despite his catholic view of Buddhism as a whole, we must appreciate Dōgen's attack on the negativistic predilection of Tsung-kao's thought. Thus, in contrast to the Senika heretic who held the eternity of the spiritual intelligence, Tsung-kao maintained the dissolution of any discriminative activities of consciousness—a state of unconsciousness. As Dōgen further argues, "discarding both mind and its essence" itself is the very act of mind; likewise, "forgetting its mystery as well as subtlety" itself is an expression of the profound mystery of mind—hence there is no escape from mind.[54] So, enlightenment would not be a static unconsciousness but a dynamically heightened awareness. Going a step further, Dōgen detects in Tsung-kao a dualistic presupposition con-

cerning the "serene and calm" essence of mind (*shō*), and the phenomenal functions of mind (*shin*), in the former of which, alone,
Tsung-kao thinks enlightenment lies. Perhaps this criticism bears
closely upon Dōgen's unusually severe criticism (as we have seen previously) of the phrase "seeing into one's nature" (*kenshō*), in Hui-
nêng's *Platform Sūtra,* as inauthentic. Dōgen seems to have sensed in it
a hint of a substantialistic way of thinking.[55] His view is in support of
the nonduality of mind and its essence, said to be "the great foundation of the Buddha-way."[56] In any event Tsung-kao and the Senika
heretic are not far apart from one another at their deeper level—there
is only the difference of the substantialization of mind in opposition
to body in one case, and that of mental essence as opposed to mental
functions in the other.[57]

It is patent in the foregoing observations that in whatever way we
may interpret mind—as the knowing subject, the mind, or the spiritual essence in relation to the known object, the body, or the mental
functions, respectively—its elevation to any metaphysical preemi-
nence is radically repudiated by Dōgen once and for all. Hence, mind
in Dōgen's thought is not an all-embracing and all-pervasive metaphysical principle (such as the Absolute, the ground of being, etc.),[58]
nor is it a cosmic extension of the ordinary mind (such as Spirit, Cosmic Consciousness, etc.).

Mind comes into and out of being with the psycho-physical activities of the mind and the creative activities of the physical universe. Yet
it is not just coextensive with them nor in proportion to them, but
transcends the sum total of them, as we shall see later in connection
with Buddha-nature. Hence, the depths and mysteries of mind cannot be fathomed by what Dōgen calls "naturalistic heresy" (*jinen-
gedō*), from which Dōgen equally vehemently dissociates himself.
Naturalistic heresy is the reductionistic view of mind as nothing but
the product of some materialistic, organismic, or phenomenalistic
conditions (the second of our three pairs of opposites, referred to previously). Perhaps the dangers of naturalistic heresy might have been
less conspicuous in Dōgen's time than today in this age of secularization; nonetheless, his frequent mention of it is evidenced, implicitly
or explicitly, throughout his works. In his criticism of Tsung-kao,
which we quoted a moment ago, Dōgen charged him with subscribing to what essentially amounted to a naturalistic view of mind, as
solely the activities of sensation and intellect, but not as something of
which the activities of sensation and intellect are an integral part. In

his discourse on "this mind itself is Buddha" (*sokushin-zebutsu*), the Zen equivalent of the esoteric Buddhist principle "this body itself is Buddha" (*sokushin-jōbutsu*), Dōgen points out the mistake of naively identifying the discriminating and individuating activities of mind with Buddha.[59] For they must be purified and reinforced by enlightenment; the mind must be redeemed by the mind that is Buddha in order to be able to say that it is "mountains, rivers, and the earth; the sun, the moon, and the stars." This is the true meaning of the principle "this mind itself is Buddha."

Thus, Dōgen's position adroitly avoids any monistic and reductionistic pitfalls and abides, remarkably consistently, with the nondualism of mind and matter, mind and body, spirit and mind, and so on. He writes:

This mind [the thought of enlightenment (*bodaishin*)] does not exist independently or rise suddenly now in a vacuum. It is neither one nor many, neither spontaneous nor accomplished. [This mind] is not in my body, and my body is not in the mind. This mind is not all-pervasive throughout the entire world. Neither before nor after, neither existent nor nonexistent does it obtain. It bears not upon self-nature or other-nature, upon common nature or causeless nature. Despite all this, the arising of the thought of enlightenment occurs where cosmic resonance (*kannō-dōkō*) presents itself. It is neither furnished by the Buddhas and bodhisattvas, nor is it one's own effort. Because the thought of enlightenment is awakened through cosmic resonance, it is not natural.[60]

Things, events, and beings of the universe are the expressions (*setsu*) of mind, without exception.[61]

Dōgen discusses the classical Buddhist statement: "The triple world is mind-only; there is no dharma other than the mind. Mind, Buddha, and sentient beings—these three are no different from one another." He argues that we do not say that "the triple world is mind-only," as if there were two separate entities, "the triple world" and "mind-only"; rather we say the triple world of mind-only and the mind-only of the triple world.[62] It is said to be the "total realization of the total Tathāgata" (*zen-nyorai no zen-genjō*) other than which there is no world whatsoever; there is nothing outside the triple world (*sangai wa muge nari*) any more than there are any beings other than "sentient beings" (*shujō*) which for Dōgen means all beings—sentient and insentient. The triple world is to be seen not as a subjective creation but as the "given" (*sangai no shoken*): Dōgen writes:

The triple world is not the primordial being, nor the present being. The triple world is neither newly formed, nor born by way of causation. It is not circumscribed by the beginning, the middle, and the end [of the time scheme]. There is the triple realm we transcend, and there is the triple world we live in here and now. Thus activities meet one another, conflicts grow with one another [in absolute freedom]. The triple world of here-and-now is the triple world that beholds. Beholding means to see from [the standpoint of] the triple world. This in turn is the realization of the three realms, and the three realms of realization—the consummation of kōan in life (*genjō-kōan*).[63]

Mind-only is explained as follows:

Mind-only is not one or two. It neither is the triple world nor overpasses it—perfect as it is in nonduality. It is at once the conscious mind and the nonconscious mind. It is walls and tiles, mountains, rivers, and the great earth. Mind is the "skin-flesh-bones-marrow" and the "raising-a-flower-and-bursting-into-laughter." There are: the mind of being and the mind of nonbeing; the mind of body and the mind of nonbody; the mind prior to the physical formation and the mind posterior to it. The body is variously begotten from a womb, eggs, moisture, or metamorphosis; the mind is differently created through a womb, eggs, moisture, or metamorphosis. Blue, yellow, red, white—these are mind; long, short, square, round—these are mind. Birth and death, coming and going constitute this mind, and years, months, days, hours form this mind. Dreams, visions, and the illusory flowers in the sky are mind; bubbles and flames are mind. The spring flowers and the autumn moon are mind, and rush and confusion are mind. Despite all this, mind should not be abandoned. For the aforementioned reasons, it is the mind in which all things themselves are ultimate reality (*shohō-jissō-shin*), and the mind which communicates between a Buddha and a Buddha (*yuibutsu-yobutsu-shin*).[64]

What emerges from these observations is that the triple world and mind-only are not the two polar concepts of an epistemologically oriented idealism nor of a cosmological explanation. As we have alluded to earlier in this chapter and shall make clearer later, any embryological, genetic, cosmological, emanationistic, or causal outlooks are alien to the basic religious and philosophical insight of Buddhism, and particularly to Dōgen's thought. In his exposition of the idea of functional interdependence, Ui is emphatic in pointing out that the original intention of functional interdependence was not to probe into the process or causation of origination so much as to envision the state or fact of functional interdependence of the conditions and forces of the world. The idea of functional interdependence was not a theoretical explanation but an ontological fact.[65] Thus, combined with the idea of functional interdependence and its twin idea of absolute emptiness, Dōgen's "idealism" of mind-only provides us a unique vision of reality in which mind-only is the one and only reality that is both subject and object (the triple world) and their (its) ground. This is why "the triple world is mind-only" is also equated with "all things themselves are ultimate reality" (*shohō-jissō*), "the kōan realized in life" (*genjō-kōan*), and so forth.

At this juncture we must still probe further into Dōgen's view of mind as unattainable (*anupalambha*; *fukatoku*), which is often associated with the negative aspects of emptiness such as: its being unobtainable; nothingness; an innate endowment; and so on. However, Dōgen is openly critical of such a view.[66] In the context of his discussion of extensive pilgrimages (*hensan*), which to Dōgen were not so much physical travelling or visiting Zen teachers in the spatio-temporal realm, as "nondual participation" (*dōsan*) in the enlightenment of the Buddhas and ancestors, Dōgen has this to say:

As extensive pilgrimages are already totally exerted, so are they cast off. [It is just like] the sea which is dried up, yet does not show its bed, or the one who dies and does not retain mind. "The sea is dried up" means the total sea is totally parched dry. Nevertheless, when the sea runs dry, the bed is not seen [because it is of no-bed, empty, and unattainable]. Analogously, the nonretaining and the total retaining [of mind]—both are our mind. When we die, mind is not maintained [i.e., mind dies]. Because dying is exerted, mind is not left behind. Thus, you ought to know that the total human is mind and the total mind is human. In such a manner we understand both sides of a matter.[67]

Here, we have the application of Dōgen's fundamental idea of "the total exertion of a single thing" (*ippō-gūjin*) to the theme of pilgrimage. Unattainability, in Dōgen's thought, is maintained less in the static and transcendent mode of emptiness than in the dynamic and creative mode in which any single act (dying, eating, or what-not) is totally exerted contemporaneously, coextensively, coessentially with the total mind—not with a fragment of that mind. Thus in this moment, this single act alone is the mind-only of the triple world, excluding all other acts or things. This is Dōgen's metaphysics of "mystical realism," epitomized in the statements "when one side is illumined, the other is darkened" (*ippō o shōsuru toki wa ippō wa kurashi*) and "the total experience of a single thing is one with that of all things" (*ippōtsū kore mambōtsū nari*). This is also what Dōgen means by "abiding in a Dharma-position" (*jū-hōi*). Thus viewed, Dōgen's theory of mind is far from being a dry, impersonal theoretical pursuit of the nature of mind but a profoundly personal and existential concern with the self, as quoted previously:

To study the Way is to study the self. To study the self is to forget the self. To forget the self is to be enlightened by all things of the universe. To be enlightened by all things of the universe is to cast off the body and mind of the self as well as those of others. Even the traces of enlightenment are wiped out, and life with traceless enlightenment goes on forever and ever.[68]

This is Dōgen's answer to the dictum "Know thyself" (the common heritage of Greek and Buddhist philosophy).[69] The net result of this approach to the self and the world is Dōgen's preeminent emphasis on a choice or commitment—in creative activities (*gyōji*) and creative expressions (*dōtoku*)—to live duality in the manner of "abiding in a Dharma-position" and of "the total exertion of a single thing" rather than a flight from or an obfuscation of it. In this view what duality implies is not necessary evil but the necessary (and the only) habitat in which we live and are enlightened. We are now prepared to proceed to the pivot of Dōgen's thought: Buddha-nature.

Buddha-Nature

Dōgen's analysis of Buddha-nature (*buddhatā* or *buddhatva*; *busshō*) starts with his own unique interpretation of a passage taken from the *Mahāpari-nirvāṇa sūtra*, which reads: "All sentient beings possess Buddha-nature without exception" (*issai no shujō wa kotogotoku busshō o yūsu*). However, the same Chinese sentence can also read as Dōgen reads it, "All existence (i.e., all sentient beings) is Buddha-nature" (*issai-shujō shitsuu-busshō*),[70] and thus have its meaning dramatically transformed. In his reading of this classic passage, in a manner which reveals his ingenuity and versatility in interpreting scriptural passages, Dōgen modifies the conception of Buddha-nature and the conception of sentient beings. He accomplishes the first by his equation of all existence with Buddha-nature; the second by his equation of all existence and sentient beings. In both cases of the transformation, both Buddha-nature and sentient beings are liberated from anthropocentric and biocentric perspectives; as a consequence, they acquire new scope and new depth. Let us examine them in some detail in what follows.

As is clear from the history of Buddhist thought, Buddha-nature is intimately related to the *tathāgata-garbha* strand of the Buddhist idealist tradition which pursued, as we have seen before, the problem of the original purity of the mind. It is also well known that this tradition employs misleading metaphors such as seed, embryo, womb, *gotra,* and so forth. Thus Buddha-nature is construed, more often than not, as the innate potentiality of Buddhahood. Whether this potentiality should be attributed to all sentient beings without discrimination or only to certain types of beings was hotly debated by the Buddhists, producing two schools of thought on the matter: one which advocates the universality of the Buddha-nature in all sentient beings (the *tathāgata-garbha* tradition); and the other which, as in the consciousness-only sect, holds that there are the so-called "five groups" (*goshō*) of sentient beings, classified according to their "inherently existing seeds" (*honnu-shūji*) and thus rigidly predetermined as regards their spiritual destinies. For example, the *icchantika* group (*issendai*) of sentient beings are said to lack undefiled seeds (*muro-shūji*) in store-consciousness and are hence doomed to eternal wandering through rebirths. The *śrāvaka* group (*shōmon-jōshō*) and the *pratyekabuddha* group (*engaku-jōshō*), though far better than the *icchantika* group, in the sense that they may be able to attain the arhatship and the pratyekabuddhahood respectively, were eternally precluded from the possibility of attaining Buddhahood owing to the lack of undefiled seeds. Thus, only the bodhisattva group (*bosatsu-jōshō*) and some from the indeterminate group (*fujōshō*) could entertain hope for the enlightenment of Buddha. In this manner sentient beings are graduated in accordance with the nature of inherently existing seeds and the possession and nonpossession of undefiled seeds; in consequence, certain groups of sentient beings are branded as possessing no Buddha-nature.[71] It goes without saying that Dōgen sides, as other Mahāyānists would, with the universalism of the *tathāgata-garbha* tradition in advocating the theory of one group or nature— Buddha-nature possessed by *all* sentient beings. However, the theory still has disturbing implications: the Buddha-nature is strictly confined to sentient beings, not including insentient beings; and Buddha-nature is the native endowment or potentiality possessed by sentient

beings. That is to say, its "universalism" is still restrictive and conceived in a highly anthropocentric or biocentric manner. Dōgen revolts against these implications of the traditional theory.

Thus, Dōgen declares the absolute inclusiveness of Buddha-nature
within which sentient as well as insentient beings are equally subsumed. This is what Dōgen means by "all existence." He writes:

Therefore, these mountains, rivers, and the earth—all constitute the sea
of Buddha-nature. "All are created by Buddha-nature" (*kaie-konryū*) [in
Aśvaghoṣa's saying previously quoted] means that at the very moment of
creation it is mountains, rivers, and the earth. As we have already said "all
are created by Buddha-nature," we must know that such is characteristic of
the sea of Buddha-nature. It has absolutely nothing to do with the inside or
the outside, or the center of the universe. Thus, to see mountains and rivers
is tantamount to experiencing Buddha-nature. To behold Buddha-nature is
to observe a donkey's jaw and a horse's mouth [which are nothing particular
in our ordinary experience]. By the dependence of all (*kaie*) we understand
all is Buddha-nature (*zen'e*) and Buddha-nature is all (*ezen*), and transcend
even this understanding.[72]

The self-creation of Buddha-nature itself constitutes all the phenomena of the universe. In a spirit similar to that of Meister Eckhart,
Dōgen would say that Buddha-nature "abhors an empty space."

Dōgen further elaborates on "all existence" as follows:

Note the following: Existence completely embraced now by Buddha-nature
is not that being which is in opposition to nonbeing. All existence is the
words of Buddhas, their tongues, the eyeballs of the Buddhas and ancestors,
and monastics' nostrils. It goes without saying that the word "all existence"
is not the existence with a beginning in time (*shiu*), or the existence innate in
things (*honnu*), or the mysterious and subtle existence (*myōu*)—much less
the existence in causation (*en'u*) or the existence caused by ignorance (*mōu*).
It cannot be labeled by such words as subject or object, noumenon or phenomenon. . . . In the entire universe there is not even a single object alien to
Buddha-nature, nor is there any second existence other than this universe
here and now.[73]

Dōgen is emphatic in rejecting all existence as the result of karmic
forces (*gō-zōjōriki*), functional interdependence in delusion (*mō-engi*),
naturalness (*hōni*), or a miraculous formation (*jinzū-shushō*).[74] Not
only is Buddha-nature not existence with a beginning, as we have
seen, but not existence with no beginning (*mushiu*).[75]

It is evident in these observations that by declaring "all existence is

Buddha-nature" Dōgen presents a new theory of Buddha-nature consistent with his general theory of mind. To put it differently, Dōgen radically transforms the predominantly psychological conception of Buddha-nature into a predominantly ontological one whereby it is equated with, and hence used synonymously with, thusness (*tathatā*; *shinnyo*) and the Dharma-nature (*dharmatā*; *hosshō*), which in Buddhist thought refer to the impersonal ground of being or ultimate reality. Buddha-nature, in Dōgen's view, is at once beings and being itself.[76]

Buddha-nature is all existence which includes sentient and insentient beings, and is no longer the possession of these beings. As a result, the absolute inclusiveness of Buddha-nature does not mean that Buddha-nature is immanent in all existences but that all existence is immanent in Buddha-nature. As we compare this with what we are told by Dōgen to be the traditional psychologically minded view of Buddha-nature, we can easily see the revolutionary nature of his reconception of this notion. Obviously "all existence is Buddha-nature" should not be construed as a mere formal identity. The mysterious relationship between Buddha-nature and all existence is expressed in a slightly different context as follows: "Though not identical, they are not different; though not different, they are not one; though not one, they are not many."[77] This is Dōgen's (hence Buddhism's) way of expressing the nondualism of beings and being itself, in terms of "neither identical nor different" or "neither one nor many" (*fuitsu-fui* or *fusoku-furi*), or the Hua-yen principle "mutual identity and mutual penetration" (*sōsoku-sōnyū*). Thus, it is a gross mistake for us to equate his thought with pantheism, for Buddha-nature is more than the de facto sum of all beings and more than the naive identity of the Absolute and the relative, of the necessary and the contingent.[78]

Since we have considered thus far the proposition "all existence is Buddha-nature," we shall examine now Dōgen's equation of all existence with all sentient beings. Along with his extension of the meaning of Buddha-nature, Dōgen also extends the meaning of sentient beings (*shujō*). He argues:

We use such names as *shujō, ujō, gunjō,* or *gunrui.* The expression "all existence" refers to sentient beings or to all things. That is, all existence is Buddha-nature, and the totality of all existence is called sentient beings. Its truth is such that all beings of Buddha-nature exist both inside and outside [the minds of] sentient beings.[79]

Furthermore, Dōgen states: "Just as no realm exists outside the triple world, so there exists no being other than the sentient."[80] While the words "sentient beings" (*sattva; shujō*) ordinarily referred to all living beings who transmigrate in the six realms of life (the worlds of hell, hungry spirits, animals, *asuras,* humans, and gods), in the Buddhist scheme, it may have originally meant whatever was generated by the functional interdependence of conditions and forces of the universe; accordingly, the words may have included not only sentient beings but also insentient beings.[81] Dōgen seems to have been aware of this wider sense when he wrote: "Sentient beings are the true body of the entire universe. For the reason that each sentient being comes into existence through [the co-creation of] myriad things, it is called 'sentient being'."[82] Thus Dōgen seems to be proposing here that Buddhism adopt the original (indeed the widest possible) sense of the words.

However, deeper than this etymological awareness is the demand made by the logic of his thought, especially regarding his view of mind. Dōgen's reasoning on this point is clearly stated as follows:

"All sentient beings," discussed now in Buddhism, means all those possessing mind, for mind is sentient beings. Those possessing no-mind (*mushinsha*) should be equally sentient beings, for sentient beings are mind. Therefore, mind is invariably sentient beings; sentient beings are necessarily the Buddha-nature of existence (*u-busshō*). Grasses, trees, and the earth are mind. They are sentient beings by virtue of being mind, and the Buddha-nature of existence on account of being sentient beings. The sun, the moon, and the stars—all are mind. They are sentient beings by reason of being mind, and are the Buddha-nature of existence because of being sentient beings.[83]

By defining sentient beings thus, Dōgen presents the two propositions: all existence is sentient beings; and sentient beings are Buddha-nature. Thus the nondual oneness of all existence, sentient beings, and Buddha-nature is completed. This is neither a merely arbitrary redefinition of the words, nor a mere conformity to the original senses of them; it is rather the result of the logical demand made by his thought, deeply rooted in his radical reconception of mind, and of Buddha-nature as well. It is important to note here Dōgen's vehement de-anthropocentricization and de-biocentricization of the originally anthropocentric and biocentric notion of sentient beings.[84] We might call this Dōgen's way of demythologizing, in which we cannot fail to note his rigorous exercise of logic and reason (*dōri*), if in a uniquely Buddhist way.

It is evident through the foregoing observations of Dōgen's fundamental proposition, "all existence (i.e., all sentient beings) is Buddha-nature" that not only is Buddha-nature not an embryo or a seed, but it is not a Platonic "receptacle" or a Newtonian "absolute space" (the *tathāgata-garbha* itself was highly vulnerable to such interpretations). Buddha-nature has no wall, no circumference, no compartment, so to speak, in which all existence, or sentient beings, is "contained."[85] As the proposition says, all existence is Buddha-nature itself, although there is some distinction between them. This nondual "oneness" is generally expressed within Buddhism, as we have noted already, in terms of "neither identical nor different"; the structure of this nondual relation in Dōgen's own thought will become clearer in subsequent pages. Having set forth these preliminary remarks, we now proceed to a detailed analysis of Dōgen's theory of Buddha-nature.

All existence and phenomena are the activities (*gyōji*) and expressions (*dōtoku*)—respectively, the self-activities and the self-expressions—of Buddha-nature. These self-activities and self-expressions, however, must be understood in the context of Dōgen's own conceptions of "all things themselves are ultimate reality" (*shohō-jissō*) and "the kōan realized in life" (*genjō-kōan*), which we have touched on in connection with his theory of mind, that is, they are not emanationistic manifestations, or cosmological processes, or the like, but are, rather, the ontological realization of things as they are in thusness. Addressing himself to the embryological argument concerning Buddha-nature, Dōgen writes:

A certain group of Buddhists think that Buddha-nature is like the seed of plants or trees. When the rain moistens it generously, buds and stems grow, branches, leaves, and fruits become dense, and eventually the fruits bear seeds. Such a view is what an ordinary worldly person imagines. Supposing that you understand the matter in this way, you should realize that the seeds, the flowers, the fruits are each the absolute actualization of Buddha-nature (*jōjō no sekishin*). A seed in a fruit, though unseen, grows roots and stems and, though not assorted, flourishes with a thick trunk and big branches. Although not a matter of inside or outside, this is true through the ages. For this reason, even if an ordinary worldly person's approach is granted [for the sake of the argument], roots, stems, branches, and leaves are all born in the same manner and all die in the same way. [They are] equally one and the same Buddha-nature of all existence.[86]

Perhaps the full implications of this thesis can be understood adequately once we examine Dōgen's view of existence and time (*uji*) later in this chapter. Suffice it to say that the self-realization of Buddha-nature in its myriad forms of existence defies the model of processes, degrees, and levels from potentiality to actuality, from the hidden to the manifest, from the lower to the higher, from the imperfect to the perfect; quite the contrary, it is the realization that each form of existence is perfect and self-sufficient in its "total exertion" (*gūjin*) in the Dharma-position (*hōi*), amounting to the total actualization of Buddha-nature. Hence, processes, degrees, and levels are those actualities which are arranged conveniently in a linear fashion. This is why Dōgen says, in reference to Bodhidharma's "skin, flesh, bones, and marrow" (*hiniku-kotsuzui*), that "Marrow is not deepest, skin is not shallowest."[87] Or to put it differently, Dōgen's concern here is not with how and why all existence is as it is but simply that all existence exists in thusness—in this simple fact does he find Buddha-nature. It is in this sense that Dōgen uses "the Buddha-nature of existence" (*u-busshō*) by which he means that Buddha-nature is always and necessarily particularized in concrete existence. Without understanding this aspect of Buddha-nature, the study of the Way is not complete.[88]

All existence as particularities is necessarily limited and circumscribed, hence vulnerable to similar dangers inherent in all forms of phenomenalistic thought. Dōgen warns thus:

We do not say "all sentient beings are Buddha-nature" (*issai-shujō soku busshō*) [for even "are" smacks of dualistic thinking], but instead "all-sentient-beings-the-Buddha-nature-of-existence" (*issai-shujō-u-busshō*). This should be considered carefully. "Existence" of the Buddha-nature of existence should indeed be cast off. Casting off signifies absolute freedom, and absolute freedom means [leaving no traces like] a bird's path. Therefore, [it is to be expressed as] "all-Buddha-nature-existence-sentient-beings" (*issai-busshō-u-shujō*). The truth of the matter is that you elucidate and transcend not only sentient beings but also Buddha-nature.[89]

Here, clearly, Dōgen recommends transcending the ordinary dualistic mode of existence. Buddha-nature has an aspect called the Buddha-nature of nonexistence (*mu-busshō*) which negates and transcends concrete realities. *Mu-busshō* was traditionally understood in

Buddhism to signify the absence of Buddha-nature, analogous to a nonbeing which is antithetical to being. But, inasmuch as all existence is Buddha-nature, the nonexistence in question cannot and should not mean the absence of Buddha-nature. The Buddha-nature of nonexistence means, rather, the liberating and transcending powers inherent in Buddha-nature which liberate us from fixation on the particularities of existence. In thus transforming the traditional Buddhist terms in a manner consistent with his thought, Dōgen shifts the direction of the issue from whether or not any existence has Buddha-nature to how it can use (*shitoku suru*) Buddha-nature in the midst of its presence. Thus, Dōgen devotes a great deal of effort to clarification of the Buddha-nature of nonexistence, without the study of which he contends the Way cannot be fully understood.[90]

The inner structure of Buddha-nature has the element of nonexistence, not as a dualistic antithesis to existence, but as one of the poles in the nondualistic structure. This view is unmistakably evidenced in the kōan in which Chao-chou Ts'ung-shên (778–897) answered both yes and no on different occasions to a well-known question concerning whether the dog has Buddha-nature. The story goes something like this: A monastic in one case asks, in response to Chao-chou's "No," "All sentient beings have Buddha-nature, but why doesn't the dog have Buddha-nature?," and Chao-chou answers, "Because the dog has karmic consciousness." In another case a monastic asks, in response to Chao-chou's "Yes," "If Buddha-nature already exists, why did Buddha-nature enter this skin-bag?" and Chao-chou answers: "Because the dog commits evils knowingly and purposely."[91] Dōgen's comments on the kōan repudiate every possible implication derived from the literal and dualistic interpretation of Chao-chou's answers and hold in effect that the dog's karmic existence and its committing evils knowingly and purposely are, paradoxically enough, themselves the absolute thusness of Buddha-nature, for the *because* in Chao-chou's answers does not signify, according to Dōgen's interpretation, the causal relationship as ordinarily interpreted. The problem, therefore, is not whether the dog has Buddha-nature or not (which was the assumption of this kōan as conventionally interpreted); both *yes* and *no*, or existence and nonexistence, are construed as nondual structural elements of Buddha-nature. Each has absolute significance and value in Buddha-nature.[92]

It is in this vein that Dōgen says:

Should the existence (*u*) of "all existence is Buddha-nature" not inherit the nonexistence (*mu*) of all nonexistence (*mumu*)? . . . Setting aside nonexistence in the issue of the existence or nonexistence [of Buddha-nature] for a while, ask instead how Buddha-nature is and what Buddha-nature is. When some people nowadays hear about Buddha-nature, they do not further inquire about what Buddha-nature itself is but, appear to be preoccupied with its existence or nonexistence. This is heedless, indeed. Therefore, nonexistence in its various forms should be interpreted in terms of the Buddha-nature of nonexistence.[93]

What Dōgen tries to emphasize with the term Buddha-nature of nonexistence is the emptiness of Buddha-nature, or the Buddha-nature of emptiness (*kū-busshō*), which at once subsumes and transcends existence and nonexistence. In his discourse on Buddha-nature, nonexistence (*mu*) and emptiness (*kū*) go hand in hand, and the former is always spoken of in terms of the latter.

When speaking of emptiness, Dōgen emphasizes, as I have pointed out elsewhere, the dynamic and creative aspect, rather than the static and transcendent aspect, of this cardinal idea, along with the idea in Mahāyāna Buddhism of functional interdependence: that existence which is mediated, purified, and authenticated by emptiness and hence called wondrous existence (*shinkū-myōu*). Dōgen's view of emptiness pursues this direction rigorously.[94] Just one example will suffice. There is a Zen story involving two Zen teachers, Shih-kung Hui-tsang and Hsi-t'ang Chih-tsang, both of whom were the disciples of Ma-tsu Tao-i (709–788). One day Shih-kung asked Hsi-t'ang: "Can you grasp emptiness?" Hsi-t'ang replied: "Yes, I think I can." Shih-kung continued: "How would you grasp emptiness?" Using his hand, Hsi-t'ang then grasped at empty space. Shih-kung replied: "You don't understand how to hold emptiness." "How do you grasp it, then?" asked Hsi-t'ang. Shih-kung seized Hsi-t'ang's nose and pulled it. Hsi-t'ang exclaimed: "Ouch! Ouch! You are going to pull off my nose!" Shih-kung said: "You can grasp emptiness only in this way."[95] Commenting on this kōan, Dōgen observed at one point that that which grasps and that which is grasped are, after all, one and the same emptiness—emptiness grasps emptiness. Thus Dōgen asserts that it might have been more appropriate if Shih-kung had grasped his own nose. Despite this, Dōgen praises Shih-kung for his understanding of the mystery of emptiness and admonishes his disciples as follows: "Even if you are adept at grasping emptiness, you should study its inside and out, investigate its life and death, and appreciate its weight."[96]

Let us pursue Dōgen's view of Buddha-nature as emptiness a little further in this vein. Dōgen, like other Zen Buddhists, was fond of using such interrogative pronouns as "what," "how," "which," etc. (*nani, ga, ka, nanimono, shimo, somo, immo,* etc.) in order to denote the ultimate truth of thusness and emptiness. For example:

Teacher Ta-chien [Hui-nêng] of Mt. Ts'ao-ch'i once asked Nan-yüeh Ta-hui: "What is this that comes thus?"
    This saying [containing] "thus" is not actually an interrogation, because it transcends human understanding. We should investigate thoroughly that, because "this" [particularity] is the "What," all things are always the "What," and each and every thing is always the "What." The "What" is not an interrogative; it is the "coming of thusness."[97]

In asking the question "What is this that comes thus?," we already know that the answer to "What" is "this that comes thus." In this respect, to quest is to know, because "What" is "thusness" (*monsho no dōtoku*). To put it differently, the What is the eternal kōan realized in life (*genjō-kōan*); this theme is expanded and elaborated upon in Dōgen's discourse on Buddha-nature when he takes up the conversation between Ta-i Tao-hsin (580–651), the fourth ancestor of Chinese Zen Buddhism, and Ta-man Hung-jên (601–674), the fifth ancestor, which runs as follows: On the way to Mt. Huang-mêi, Hung-jên met Tao-hsin, and the latter asked: "What is your name?" Hung-jên replied: "Although I have a name, it is not an ordinary one." "What is it?" further asked the teacher. "It is Buddha-nature" came the answer. Then Tao-hsin said: "You do not have Buddha-nature." Hung-jên responded thus: "Because Buddha-nature is empty (*kū*), it is called nonexistence (*mu*)."[98] Once again Dōgen probes deeply into Buddha-nature by giving an extraordinary interpretation of this story. Dōgen explains:

Thus as we examine the story of the two ancestors, there is profound meaning in the fourth ancestor's question, "What is your name?" In ancient times there were persons from the country of Ho as well as persons with the surname of Ho. [So the real purport of this interrogative statement is an affirmative statement, and thus] to say "You name is Ho" is just like saying that I too am thusness, and you are thusness, also. [You and I belong to the same family of Buddha.][99]

Since the Chinese character *ho* (the Japanese rendering: *nani* or *ka*) has the meaning of "what," "your name is Ho" means "your name is What." Thus, according to Dōgen's interpretation, Tao-hsin's statement reveals his profound understanding of the nature of one's "name" (*shō*)—an eternal question mark of What—which is at the same time one's "nature" (*shō*), that is, Buddha-nature (*busshō*). In a very special sense name is nature. All existence has the same family name of Ho or What, which is the essence of Buddha-nature. (This becomes more significant in view of the fact that Hung-jên's real surname was Chou.) From this vantage point Dōgen develops his remarkable interpretation of emptiness in relation to name: "The fifth ancestor said: ['Although I have a name, it is not an ordinary one,' which means:] 'Name' is 'existence-itself,' 'not-this,' and 'ordinary-name-as-permanent-nature.' Its import is: 'Existence as name-nature' is not an 'ordinary name'; an 'ordinary name' is not adequate to this 'existence-itself'." [100]

This is not to deny the significance of an ordinary name. On the contrary, name as an ordinary name becomes an extraordinary one only when it is mediated and authenticated by Buddha-nature. It is in this sense that the name of Chou—the real surname of the fifth ancestor—"cannot be understood as having been bequeathed by father or by ancestors, or as the name of mother, let alone as having originated with the onlooker." [101] Dōgen further develops his view in a truly extraordinary manner:

The fourth ancestor said: ["What (name) is it?" which means:] "'This' (*ze*) is the 'name-nature' (*shō*) of 'What' (*ka*)." "What" is "this," and it has been exerting "this" as "What" (*ze o kashi kitareri*): such is "name-nature." That which makes "What" what it is does so by virtue of "this"; that which makes "this" what it is is the power of "What"; and "name-nature" is "this" and "What" at once. We brew herbal tea with this [realization]; so do we ordinary tea. We also make [this realization] our everyday meal. The fifth ancestor said: "It (or this) is Buddha-nature," in which "this" is in itself "Buddha-nature." Because of "What," it is "Buddha." Yet, can we profoundly grasp "this" by "What" and "name-nature" alone? When "this" is unmistakably "not-this," it is "Buddha-nature." Such being the case, "this" is "What" and "Buddha"; nevertheless, once it has cast off and liberated itself, it is bound to be "name." [In the case of the fifth ancestor] that name was Chou. [102]

Dōgen lifts "what," "this," and "name" out of the quite ordinary context of the two ancestors' dialogues and elevates them to the height of philosophical analysis of and insight into Buddha-nature. He does so not in a speculative spirit but in a deeply personal, existential, and practical mode of thought. Thus, the dynamic creativity of the Buddha-nature of emptiness is ingeniously characterized in the context of "What"—the eternal quest, or kōan realized in life, which shows us abysmal depths and mysteries of existence with infinite possibilities; "this"—the particular concretization of existence in thusness in which "What" unfolds ever afresh; and "name"—the linguistic and symbolic mediation by virtue of which "What" is "this" and "this" is "What." "What," "this," and "name" are each the total exertion (*gūjin*) of the Buddha-nature of emptiness in the Dharma-position. Dōgen observes:

The emptiness in question is not that emptiness which is spoken of in "form is emptiness" (*shikisoku-zekū*). Speaking of "form is emptiness," you do not artificially designate form as emptiness, nor do you construct form by dividing emptiness. [What I mean] is emptiness in "emptiness is emptiness" (*kū-ze-kū*). The emptiness of "emptiness is emptiness" means that in the realization of emptiness there is nothing but emptiness.[103]

When emptiness is totally exerted, there is emptiness only; when form is totally exerted, there is form only.[104] In this manner the principle of the "total exertion of a single thing" (*ippō-gūjin*) applies to everything—eating, sleeping, laughing, and what-not. The wondrous existence of this emptiness (*shinkū-myōu*) we referred to means, for Dōgen, precisely this total exertion of a single thing which abides in the Dharma-position.

"Nothing but," in this context, does not imply, by any means, a reductionistic mode of thinking; on the contrary, herein lies the crux of Dōgen's mystical realism—his solution to the perennial metaphysical problem of the relation between Buddha-nature and all existence, or between one and many, or between the Absolute and the relative, in general philosophical terms. Buddhism generally defies the view that Buddha-nature is identical with, or in proportion to, or nothing but, all existence, as well as the view that Buddha-nature is something other than, or transcendent to, or inclusive of, all existence; instead it takes recourse to the mystery of emptiness, making reference to "neither identical nor different," "neither one nor many," and so forth. This is not a flight from linguistic commitment, but the awareness of the nature and limits of it, which frees and authenticates the use of it. From Dōgen's standpoint, however, these dicta still

smack of an abstract formalism. The mystery or paradox of "all existence is Buddha-nature" (or of one and many) is experientially and
practically verified and enacted, though it still remains unresolved
(and perhaps never will be resolved), theoretically. Once again, this
does not mean that Dōgen went as far as he could intellectually, let-
ting experience take over for the remainder, for intellect does not
leave room for intuition or faith. At each moment of existence, reason
(*dōri*) goes hand in hand with expressions and activities so as to exert
totally. Thus, in the realization of life there is nothing but life; in the
realization of death there is nothing but death. When there is nothing
but life, life becomes meaningless, because it is meaningful only
in view of death. By the same token, when there is nothing but
Buddha-nature, it is nil, empty, and meaningless. In this total meaninglessness, Dōgen found the reason and logic of "all existence is
Buddha-nature."[105]

Thus far we have examined the Buddha-nature of existence, the
Buddha-nature of nonexistence, and the Buddha-nature of emptiness, and thereby gained a glimpse of Dōgen's view of Buddha-
nature, which is the core of his philosophical and religious thought.
Dōgen's analysis of the matter, however, does not stop at this. The
creative dynamism of Buddha-nature must further be probed in
connection with the Buddha-nature of expression (*setsu-busshō*), the
Buddha-nature of activity (*gyō-busshō*), the Buddha-nature of impermanence (*mujō-busshō*), and the Buddha-nature of time (*ji-busshō*).[106]
As we have noted, all existence is the expressions (*dōtoku*) and activities (*gyōji*) of Buddha-nature. The expressions and activities of
Buddha-nature incessantly arise and perish moment by moment.
Being impermanent, existence is necessarily temporal. The hallmark
of Dōgen's thought, at its core, can be reached by reviewing these as-
pects of Buddha-nature. We shall devote a separate section to the
Buddha-nature of time.

In a slightly different context, in which the problem of mind is discussed, Dōgen has this to say: "There is yet no expression (*setsu*) that
is not essence (*shō*); there is as yet no mind (*shin*) that is not expression."[107] Quite understandably, the usual distinction between the
mind and its essence or between essence (*shō*) and attributes (*sō*)—
along with the presupposition that one is eternal and unchangeable
while the other is phenomenal and changeable—is challenged here.
However, more importantly, with regard to the present subject matter, both mind and its essence are invariably the expression, or more
precisely the self-expression (*jidōshu*) of Buddha-nature. In short,

there is no expression that is not Buddha-nature, and vice versa. As we have emphasized earlier in this work, expression is ultimately the impossible task made possible. This paradoxical situation, with which every possible expression is confronted, is well stated in the following quotation. Dōgen refers to Po-chang Huai-hai's statement, "If you say sentient beings have Buddha-nature, you slander the Buddha, Dharma, and Saṃgha; if you say sentient beings do not, you defame the Buddha, Dharma, and Saṃgha."

Therefore, the Buddha-nature of existence and the Buddha-nature of non-existence—both are equally disparagements. Although they are vilifications, you cannot but express them somehow. . . . Indeed, slanderous utterances are made, but did you or did you not express Buddha-nature therewith? If you did, your expression is Buddha-nature. Where there is one who speaks, there is one who hears. [Both the speaker and the hearer are of Buddha-nature.][108]

Language and symbols are not always necessary evils (as "slanderous utterances" may well suggest), but can be used in such a way that they are expressions of Buddha-nature. Giving positive significance to expressions, Dōgen also contends, in reference to Nāgārjuna's discourse on Buddha-nature and Kāṇadeva's interpretation of it, that Buddha-nature beyond forms, qualities, and measures is realized in and through bodily activities and expressions. This is called the bodily realization of Buddha-nature (*shingen*) which is boundless (*kakunen*) and transparent (*kōmei*), as characterized by Kāṇadeva.[109] Language and symbols are inseparably intertwined with bodily expressions, and together constitute the realization of Buddha-nature, in the sense that a particular concretization of expression is not one being among many others but the being, as the absolute presence of Buddha-nature symbolized in the metaphor of the full moon—a symbol of enlightenment.[110]

Expression is necessarily activity and activity is necessarily expression. For an expression is not a theory or an abstraction but an activity: to see, understand, and express Buddha-nature is tantamount to acting out Buddha-nature. Thus, we see the necessary connection between the Buddha-nature of expression and the Buddha-nature of activity. With the following statement Dōgen begins his exposition on time and existence:

A Buddha said: "If you want to know the meaning of Buddha-nature, you should surely reflect upon the reason of time (*jisetsu no innen*). If time arrives, Buddha-nature will be realized."

"If you want to know the meaning of Buddha-nature" does not imply solely intellectualization. You can say also: "If you want to act," "if you want to experience," "if you want to elucidate," "if you want to forget," and so on.[111]

Another of Dōgen's remarks is pertinent to our discussion:

To say "if time arrives" is tantamount to declaring that time has already arrived; how can you doubt this? You may entertain a doubt about time. Be that as it may, restore Buddha-nature to yourself. You should know that [as we understand it] "if time arrives" [in this manner], every moment of twenty-four hours does not pass by vainly. The "if-arrives" (*nyakushi*) is construed as the "already-arrived" (*kishi*). [Otherwise] "if time arrives" means "Buddha-nature never arrives." For this reason, as time has already arrived, Buddha-nature is unmistakably present here and now.[112]

If we consider this statement, along with the seed analogy we have touched upon before, Dōgen's position is evident. Buddha-nature actualizes itself not in such ways as: from potentiality to actuality; from the not-yet to the already; from the lower to the higher; from the hidden to the manifest; but coeval and coessential with what we act out in our activities and expressions. Thus Dōgen's paradoxical statement, quoted earlier: "The logic of Buddha-nature is such that it is provided not before becoming a Buddha, but afterwards. Buddha-nature and becoming a Buddha always occur simultaneously."[113] *Being* Buddha and *becoming* Buddha, or original enlightenment and acquired enlightenment, though distinct, occur simultaneously. To the extent that we take risks when we choose to act, Buddha-nature becomes visible, audible, tangible. Prior to this, Buddha-nature cannot be said to exist or subsist in such forms as potentialities, innate ideas, eidetic forms, and the like.

The Buddha-nature of expression and the Buddha-nature of activity are inevitably impermanent and temporal, ultimately leading to death. There is no way out of this ultimate limitation. Thus Dōgen expounds the Buddha-nature of impermanence (*mujō-busshō*). If the world is as fleeting and transient as a dewdrop of the morning, and this not a mere sentiment but a fact of life, then how can I commit myself to specific expressions and activities, so that they are at once my self-realization and the self-expression of Buddha-nature? This was the ultimate question with which Dōgen was concerned throughout his lifetime, as has been pointed out so often in this work. For Dōgen, it was not a matter of whether to commit, but how to commit—a specific commitment in absolute freedom. In his analysis of the Buddha-nature of impermanence, Dōgen revolts against the conventional idea that Buddha-nature is permanent (*ujō*), and that religiosity consists in seeking and attaining such a permanence by departing from impermanence; consequently, he asserts that impermanence is Buddha-nature, and vice versa. Referring to Hui-nêng's saying, Dōgen observes:

The sixth patriarch [Hui-nêng] once said to his disciple, Hsing-ch'ang: "Impermanence is Buddha-nature. Permanence is the mind that discriminates between good and evil and all existence."

Hui-nêng's conception of impermanence is far from those grasped by heretics and Hīnayānists. Even if their founders and followers speak of impermanence, they do not penetrate it deeply. Thus, impermanence expounds itself, enacts itself, and enlightens itself—all these are [expressions of] impermanence. Those of us who now particularize ourselves in myriad forms and thereby liberate ourselves—we expound Dharma through our particularizations. Such is Buddha-nature. It sometimes discloses itself in a long Dharma-body, sometimes in a short Dharma-body. A sage who is thought to be permanently enlightened is impermanent; an ordinary worldly person, though appearing to be constantly deluded, is momentary. The unchangingness of both the sage and the worldly should not be identified with Buddha-nature.[114]

Hui-nêng's statement is not only apparently in opposition to the conventional view of Buddha-nature as permanent and the discriminating mind as impermanent, but might well be interpreted as saying that permanence and impermanence are mutually exclusive. Dōgen, however, interprets it as saying that permanence and impermanence are equally Buddha-nature, for "permanence," according to him, is the state of "nonturning" (*miten*) or nondualism. "Nonturning means that whether we overcome delusions or are conditioned by them, we are never attached to the traces of their coming and going. Hence, this is called permanence."[115] Thus, Dōgen accepts Hui-nêng's notion that Buddha-nature is impermanent, but also reconciles permanence and impermanence, and Buddha-nature and the discriminating mind. The following, then, can be understood in this context in which impermanence and nonduality are fused:

On this account, plants, trees, and woods are impermanent, hence Buddha-nature. Human bodies and minds are transient, thus Buddha-nature. Countries, mountains, and rivers are evanescent, because they are Buddha-nature. Since supreme enlightenment is Buddha-nature, it is impermanent. The perfect quietude of nirvāṇa is momentary and thereby Buddha-nature.[116]

"Everything perishes as soon as it arises" (*setsuna-shōmetsu*) is a well known assertion in Buddhism. The corollary is that nothing in the universe remains unchanged and unchangeable. Despite this metaphysical insight into the scheme of things, Buddhists, more often than not, have betrayed it by excepting ultimate reality from this principle. It seems to be an almost universal (both Eastern and Western) philosophical temptation to revere being by degrading becoming. For Dōgen's part, he refuses to exempt Buddha-nature. The universality of the momentariness of arising and perishing must be applied to Buddha-nature as well. Hence, Buddha-nature is impermanent.

This thought is vividly expressed in terms of the metaphors "the blue mountain always walks" (*seizan jō-umpo*) and "the eastern mountain floats on the water" (*tōzan suijō-kō*).[117] The mountain—regarded as immovable—is said here to be walking and floating, thus alluding to the fact that nothing in the universe is static and immutable. The universe is not fixed and immovable; it is becoming in time.[118] Thus, the impermanence of Buddha-nature is that aspect of Buddha-nature which eternally comes into being and out of being with the universe—all existence. It pulsates with the arising and perishing of the universe, at any given moment, in accordance with the infinitely intricate functional interdependence of its constituents. Buddha-nature gives birth to a new creation from moment to moment, sharing the fate of the universe. Being and becoming are not two separate metaphysical realities but one and the same in the process of impermanence. The religious and philosophical significance of impermanence is the infinite versatility and dynamism of Buddha-nature in its ever-changing and ever-becoming character.[119]

Dōgen's primary concern was with the religious implications of the Buddha-nature of impermanence. As he probed into the ethos of impermanence, thoroughly indigenized by the medieval Japanese mind, Dōgen did not indulge in aesthetic dilettantism and sentimentalism as a way to escape from the fleeting fates of life but, instead, examined the nature of impermanence and its ultimate companion, death, unflinchingly, attempting to realize liberation in and through this inexorable scheme of things. In his view, things, events, relations were not the given (entities), but were possibilities, projects, and tasks that could be lived out, expressed, and understood as self-expressions and self-activities of Buddha-nature. This did not imply a complacent acceptance of the given situation, but required our strenuous efforts to transform and transfigure it. Dōgen's thought involved this element

of transformation, which has been more often than not grossly neglected or dismissed by Dōgen students.[120] To put it differently, his
search for the reason of impermanence impelled him to live duality
(of impermanence and temporality) radically by being liberated for
duality. Dōgen's entire philosophical and religious work is the testi-
monial of his passionate search for those possibilities and tasks, in his
own time, through symbols, rites, and concepts, available at hand in
his inherited Buddhist tradition.

Moreover, he composed his abstruse philosophical prose in the
medieval Japanese style, only occasionally using the classic Chinese
style. This fact alone places Dōgen in a unique position in the history
of Japanese thought. He sought the reason of impermanence, with
the Japanese language, in the Japanese manner.[121]

The analysis of impermanence, however, must still go on, delving
into the problem of temporality—the culmination of Dōgen's metaphysics and religion of Buddha-nature.

Existence and Time

Buddhism has maintained throughout its history that everything
in the universe is born, changes, and perishes, and that there is nothing
which is not subject to impermanence and death. An ardent Buddhist,
Dōgen inherited this sense of the impermanence of existence, but the
quality of his awareness was medieval Japanese to the core in its intensity and content. The age was deeply troubled, dark, and hopeless,
characterized as the Age of Degenerate Law; the people despaired of
the world and life and retreated into their own egotistic shells in the
pursuit of various diversions. Life was nothing but fleeting, weari-
some, and empty (*hakanaki* or *hakanashi*). These psychological states
are said to have resulted from an inner failure to cope with the pace of
rapidly changing world. The sense of despair and emptiness was the
internalization of this failure.[122] Dōgen rejected this psychological or
subjectivized view of impermanence (which was, after all, dualistic),
seeing, instead, that impermanence was structurally inherent in the self
and the world and, hence, should be taken seriously, metaphysically
as well as religiously; only then was one assured of understanding and
living the reality of impermanence.[123]

At this point in our investigation, we digress for a while to review
the development of some salient aspects of the problem of time in the
history of Buddhist thought. The problem of time has been an essen-

tial part of Buddhist thought from its very inception, as we see in the doctrine of the impermanence or momentariness of all things, as one of the three characteristics of existence (the other two being suffering and nonsubstantiality), as well as in the doctrine of moral causation and rebirth in the three periods of past, present, and future.[124] The fundamental assumptions running through the history of the mainstream of Buddhist thought in relation to the problem of time are twofold: one is characterized by the proposition: "Time has no independent existence but is dependent on dharmas" (*jimubettai-ehōjiryū*); the other is related to the mutual implication of space and time—the flow of events and vicissitude of things as they occur in the world—clearly indicated by the word "se" (used in, e.g., *sanze*, "three periods") which means both "period" and "world."[125] It goes without saying that these two assumptions are deeply rooted in the doctrines of nonsubstantiality and of functional interdependence. Thus, time is not considered a self-same entity but is construed invariably as the bearer of events of the self and the world; in brief, events do not move in time but are time.[126]

Various formulations and issues regarding time evolved with the history of Buddhism. One of the most prominent controversies in early Buddhism can be noted by contrasting the views of the Sarvāstivādin and the Sautrāntika. The former believed that the three periods (of the past, present, and future) are realities and that dharmas do not change, whereas the latter held that the past and the future are not realities—only the present is real—and that, although past is that which once existed and future that which does not yet exist, the present contains the past and the future in some way. Both schools concurred on the reality of the present but differed on the nature of the reality of the past and future in relation to the present.[127] The Vijñānavādin's view consisted of the thesis that the manifestation (*abhisaṃskāra*; *gengyō*) arising from an original seed (*bīja*; *shūji*) in store-consciousness (*ālaya-vijñāna*; *arayashiki*), and the "perfuming" (*vāsanā*; *kunjū*), or projection of a new seed into store-consciousness, take place simultaneously. Thus, this view held that the "causal" relationship between the processes of the original seed producing its manifestation and of the manifestation perfuming the new seed is simultaneous in the present; that is to say, cause-effect is born and perishes in the same moment of the present; the process repeats itself ad infinitum in a succession of such presents. In this respect, each present embraces the past and future in the form of seeds in store-consciousness.[128] The Mādhyamika philosophy of Nāgārjuna viewed dharmas as empty and unobtainable, hence the so-called three periods as having no existence of their own. Time is but a mental construction, the fact of which should not lead us to bondage in it.[129]

The foregoing observations point to a gradual evolution of Buddhist consciousness, probing into the structure of a present, in which the essence of time lies and in which the past and the future are somehow contained. Both the Sarvāstivādin and the Sautrāntika analyzed the three periods but did not clarify the nature of the present sufficiently. The Vijñānavāda view provided a psychological solution, offering profound insights into the mystery of our unconscious strivings and aspirations, both personal and collective. Yet it remained idealistic, neglecting the significance of the world in the structure of present. The Mādhyamika view radically rejected time as nothing but absurd. This negativism, however, should not obscure the other side of the Buddhist idea of emptiness, namely, the creative and dynamic aspect.

The implications of this are developed in Hua-yen philosophy, along with other insights of various schools of Buddhism. In Hua-yen Buddhism we see philosophical and religious efforts to take into account both the self and the world in the consideration of time. Hua-yen Buddhism uniquely interprets the Dharma-realm (*dharma-dhātu*; *hokkai*) in terms of the principle of the nonobstruction of phenomena in opposition to phenomena (*shih-shih wu-ai*; *jiji-muge*).[130] The entire universe consists of creative processes in which the multiplicity of things and events interact with and interpenetrate one another without obstruction. Particularities are not obliterated or deficient in any way, yet are unhindered in the perfect harmony of the total Dharma-realm. This nonobstruction (*muge*) is possible through the mediation of emptiness. This grand cosmic process of interaction, interpenetration, and integration in all realms, dimensions, perspectives of the self and the world goes on ad infinitum (*jūju-mujin*).[131]

This ontology obviously avoids the reductionism of phenomena as well as the reductionism of principles. Moreover, it regards even the perfect harmony of principles and phenomena as merely an expediency for the final envisionment of the Dharma-realm of the nonobstruction of phenomena in oppostion to phenomena, in which the absolute lucidity and freedom of particularities in the transparent transcendence of emptiness is realized.

The fundamental logic underlying the principle of the nonobstruction of phenomena in opposition to phenomena, is the principle of mutual identity and mutual penetration (*sōsoku-sōnyū*). Mutual identity refers to the nondifferentiated state in which antitheses such as one and many, absolute and relative, being and nonbeing, and so forth, co-exist in oneness and interfusion.[132] Mutual penetration refers to the simultaneous origination of all things and events interpenetrating one another in their myriad realms and dimensions. As Chang explains, different "entities" of different realms (e.g., water as a liquid, H_2O, an aggregate of molecules, etc.) penetrate into and contain one another without the slightest hindrance and, thus, arise simultaneously.[133] From this underlying logical basis, traditional Hua-yen philosophy extends its ontology in terms of the "principles of the ten mysteries" (*jūgemmon*).[134] The first and ninth principles are crucially important for our examination of the problem of time.[135] The first is the "principle of simultaneous completion and co-existence" (*dōji-gusoku-sōō-mon*) and the ninth the "principle of the various formations of the discrete events of the ten periods" (*jisse-kyakuhō-ijō-mon*). The first is usually regarded as the general principle, because it is basic to all the other principles: All things and events of the universe originate, co-exist, and integrate simultaneously, being co-related not only in reference to space but also to time. Hence, the fundamental idea is simultaneity (*dōji*). As fundamentally contradictory and incompatible as one and many, or nondifferentiation and differentiation, may be, the former does not come after the latter or vice versa; on the contrary, these pairs of antitheses exist simultaneously. Thus, all the principles of the ten mysteries presuppose this notion of simultaneity—the simultaneous completion of all things and events in space and time. Furthermore, this simultaneity is experienced most concretely and vividly in the present moment of a single thought of one's lived experience. These two characteristics constitute the unique conception of time that underlies all the principles of the ten mysteries.[136]

The principle of mutual identity and mutual penetration is applied more specifically to time in the ninth principle of various formations of the discrete events of the ten periods. The "ten periods" here means the past, present, and future, each containing three periods, by virtue of the principle of mutual identity and mutual penetration, thus comprising nine periods altogether, which in turn form one period—amounting to a total of ten periods. Each of these ten periods is fulfilled in the present moment of a single thought.[137] The corollary to this follows easily: the great aeons are one moment and one moment is the great aeons. The thesis that all the aeons and *kalpas* are contained and fused in the present moment of a single thought does not obliterate the distinctions of the three periods and the triple divisions within each of the them. The present is distinct and separated from the past and the future: they are discrete events (*kyakuhō*). Nevertheless, these mutually exclusive and discontinuous times or periods are "variously formed" (*ijō*). The various formations of discrete events, thus, take place in the matrix of the present moment. This accounts for the fundamental structure of time in which the three periods or nine periods are simultaneously, yet variously, realized in each moment—one-in-many or many-in-one in the present.[138] Another important implication of this concept of the various formations of discrete events concerns that succession of self-contained present moments which we call the flow of time. The present moment, absolutely discrete from those before and after it, proceeds to another, and another, thus, forming the succession of presents, in each of which the various formations of discrete events are executed in a unique way.[139] When we consider the first and the ninth principles together, one important implication becomes immediately clear: the present moment of a single thought is not only temporal but spatial in that it contains at once the ten periods and the ten quarters. The mutual identity and mutual penetration of space and time can be seen clearly in this juxtaposition of the two principles.[140] Fa-tsang (643–712) described this as follows:

Since a single moment has no substance of its own, it becomes interchangeable with the great aeons. Because the great aeons have no substance, they also embrace the single moment. Since both the single moment and the great aeons have no substance, all the marks of the long and the short are merged into [a great harmony], hence all the universes that are far away or near by, all the Buddhas and sentient beings, and all things and events in the past, present, and future come into view simultaneously. . . . [Since time is inseparable from events,] if one moment becomes nonobstructive, all dharmas will [automatically] become harmoniously merged. This is why all things and events in the three times vividly appear within one moment.[141]

We have examined some salient features of the Hua-yen philosophy of time briefly in the foregoing. The basic Buddhist assumptions were retained, yet greatly extended and deepened as Hua-yen probed into the structure of the present moment from the standpoint of its totalistic ontology. However, the Hua-yen school was conspicuously speculative; consequently, its profound insight into the nature of time remained largely submerged in the abstract discourse of a grand ontology.

As we turn to Dōgen's view of time, we must, at the outset, note the fact that although the problem of time was an integral part of Buddhist thought, it had never been treated as central, but was instead subordinated to such issues as nonsubstantiality, causation, emptiness, Buddha-nature, and so forth. Perhaps the unique significance of Dōgen, in this regard, consists in his attribution of central importance to this problem.[142] Dōgen picks the problem of time out of its obscurity and places it in relief, in the total context of his thought. This is done not from any speculative interests, which he vehemently disdained, but out of existential concerns with the impermanence of life and its limit situation, namely, death. Thus, his analysis of time, as we shall see presently, is deeply personal, existential, and practical.[143]

In his exposition of time, Dōgen recommends that one consider the common-sense view that a day is divided and subdivided in some measurable units or quanta—a view which presupposes that time *flows* uniformly in an infinite series of homogeneous temporal units from the past through the present to the future. In short, according to this view, time is akin to what Bergson designates as "spatial time," which is time organized spatially or segmentally. Dōgen urges his disciples to examine such a presupposition carefully.

Study the twenty-four hours [we use] nowadays. A devil with three heads and eight arms is time. [Even such an angry devil is no exception to the fact that all existence is time.] Because it is time, it is no different from the present time of twenty-four hours. Although people do not yet measure time, when they speak of it as long or far, short or close, they are speaking of the time of twenty-four hours. The directions and traces of its coming and going [such as four seasons] are so obvious that people never bother to doubt it. This, however, does not mean that they understand [time].[144]

The so-called "coming and going" (*korai*) of time is so deeply and naturally ingrained in the ordinary mind that its nature is never questioned or analyzed. The twelve horary divisions of time are a part of this conventional view of time, undoubtedly useful for daily living, but they should not delude us into thinking that they constitute the structure of time. Yet such a view may be worth examining as an initial step into the mystery of time. For in one sense time "flows," and "comes and goes"; accordingly, we must examine what we mean by that.

When we use such expressions as "time flows," "time flies," and so forth, two different situations are implied: time is a kind of entity, or a thing in itself, which moves, apart from and independent of, the flow of events and vicissitudes of life in the world; and the things and events of the world move against the background of time. If we use the familiar analogy of a fruit in a pot, with the pot representing time, the former case is analogous to the situation in which the pot is moving but the fruit is still, the latter to the reverse. Regardless of these differences, the two scenarios are actually speaking of one and the same thing: the fundamental assumption, quite familiar to us by now, of the dualism of time and event. Thus, temporal units are represented only quantitatively, abstracted from their experiential contact with felt qualities of life; events are but episodes or appearances on the stage of the impersonal passage or duration of time. Time and event are divorced from one another. Such a dualistic assumption is deeply rooted in the conventional view of time. This is why Dōgen says: "According to an ordinary worldy person's view of existence-time, even enlightenment and nirvāṇa are merely the appearance of its coming and going." [145] Thus, Dōgen admonishes us as follows:

Do not think that time only flies away. You should not regard time's flying as its sole activity. If time were exclusively dependent on flying, there would be an interval (*kenkyaku*) [between time and the experiencing self]. People do not listen to the truth of existence-time, because they conceive it to be only passing away. [146]

As is clear from this statement (and from other passages of *Shōbō-genzō*), Dōgen is not rejecting the common sense view as totally irrelevant or false. There is a grain of truth in the statement "time flows." Dōgen's task then lies in explicating this truth as much as possible while probing into and clarifying its misleading and falsifying aspects. This is the meaning of his admonition, "Study the twenty-four hours [we use] nowadays."

Dōgen thus proclaims: "The existence-time in question means that time is already existence and existence is necessarily time." [147] He quotes the statement of Yüeh-shan Wêi-yen (745–828), but modifies it in such a way that "a particular time" (*arutoki*), of Yüeh-shan's original, is interpreted now as "existence-time" (*ujī*). Dōgen's own modified version reads:

Standing on the peak of a high mountain is existence-time. Diving to the bottom of the deep ocean is existence-time. An angry devil with three heads and eight arms is existence-time. The Buddha [with the magnificent body] of one *jō* and six *shaku* is existence-time. A staff and a wand are existence-time. A pillar and a lantern are existence-time. You and friends in the neighborhood are existence and time. The great earth and the empty sky are existence-time.[148]

Also he states:

Mountains are also time, oceans are time as well. If they were not, there would be neither mountains nor oceans. Do not say that the absolute now (*nikon*) of mountains and oceans does not bear upon time. If time perishes, mountains and oceans will vanish as well; if time does not, then neither will they. In and through this truth was Buddha's enlightenment unfolded, Tathāgata originated, the eye-balls proclaimed, and Buddha's holding a flower manifested. Such is time. Were that not the case, they would not be possible.[149]

Likewise, "a pine tree is time; a bamboo is time." Time even has colors: "Various times have such colors as blue, yellow, red, white, and so on."[150] If time is existence and vice versa, it is not surprising to see that time has shapes, colors, smells, sounds, and so on. Moreover, "good and evil are time; time is neither good nor evil."[151] All in all, the things and events of the entire universe are invariably time, hence existence-time.

Dōgen's position is quite consistent with the traditional Buddhist position that time has no independent existence but is dependent on dharmas. The particularities of the world and the particularities of time are not two different sets of realities but one and the same. The common-sense view, on the other hand, tends, as we have seen before, to regard time as something that proceeds endlessly, uniformly, and unilinearly from the unknown past to the unknown future irrespective of the actualities of reality and life. The actualities of the world, in this dualistic view of existence and time, become merely the arising and dissolving or coming and going, or "appearances" in a temporal succession. Dōgen vehemently rejects such a view.

Time as existence-time is at once temporal and spatial. Again, consistent with Buddhist tradition, particularly the Hua-yen metaphysics of time, Dōgen observes:

You should examine the fact that all things and events of this entire universe are temporal particularities (*jiji*). . . . existence-time invariably means all

times. Every particular phenomenon and every particular form are likewise
time. All existence and all worlds are contained in a temporal particularity.
Just meditate on this for a moment: Is any existence or any world excluded
from this present moment?[152]

Dōgen's whole thesis in this regard is crystallized in the following:
"As we totally realize with the utmost effort that all times (*jinji*)
are all existence (*jin'u*), absolutely no dharma remains."[153] In other
words, existence-time subsumes space and time exhaustively. At this
point the following observations should be made. First, space and
time are so inseparably interpenetrated, in Dōgen's view, that to see
one without the other destroys the fundamental understanding of his
thought, particularly of his thought about Buddha-nature. Thus,
spatiality and temporality are equally crucial to existence and, hence,
to Buddha-nature.[154] In this connection Dōgen's view of "all times"
and "all existence" should not be construed as comparable to "absolute time" and "absolute space" or to such mythopoeic metaphors as
"cosmic womb," "cosmic receptacle," and the like, as we shall see in
more detail later. Secondly, related to this last remark is the fact that
temporality, for Dōgen, is not a manifestation of a timeless eternity in
which a metaphysically inferior status is attributed to the former. A
dualistic—transcendental and static—view of eternity in contradistinction to time is alien to Dōgen's thought. A hasty association of
"all times," with a dualistic conception of eternity (or any other notions of "everlastingness" and "timelessness," for that matter), should
be avoided.[155]

While following the traditional Buddhist conception of time fairly
closely, Dōgen parts with it in his highly personal and existential emphasis. This is especially notable in his search for the "reason of the
time of my self" (*jiko no toki naru dōri*):

My self unfolds itself throughout the entire world (*ware o hairetsu shi-okite
jinkai to seri*). You should examine the fact that all things and events of this
entire universe are temporal particularities. Just as particular times are unobstructed by one another, so are things and events unobstructed. Therefore,
while desire for enlightenment [of the self and the world] is awakened simultaneously, time is aroused by one and the same enlightenment. This holds
true of practice and enlightenment.

My self particularizes itself in space and time, and beholds it. Such is the
reason of the time of my self.[156]

Quite obviously, my self is not merely the psycho-physical ego but
that self which is one with the world—both the self and the world

being the self-expressions (*jidōshu*) of emptiness. Yet this self is my self with an individual's own unique doubts, fears, hopes, agonies, and aspirations.[157] Hence, it is neither an abstract speculation about the self in relation to the world (as is often the case with the traditional Buddhism of, say, Hua-yen metaphysics), nor a subjectivistic involvement with the empirical "I" (as we see in some schools of existentialism). While employing the traditional categories, such as the self, mind, time, the world, and so forth, Dōgen's use of them is imbued with his personal experience, as well as with the ethos of medieval Japan. This is clearly expressed in the following:

Nevertheless, ordinary worldly people, being untutored in the Buddha-dharma, have their own view of time, and, by hearing the word *uji,* think as follows: "At one time it became an angry devil with three heads and eight arms, at another the magnificent Buddha of one *jō* and six *shaku.* For example, it is like [a self-same I's] crossing rivers and climbing mountains. Although they currently remain behind, I have passed through them, and now dwell in a grand palace. Thus, the mountains and the rivers are as far separated from me as heavens from the earth." [In this view the self-identical I is presupposed in contrast to physical environments.] Such a view, however, does not tell the whole truth of time. When I waded rivers and ascended mountains, I was there. To [that particular] me belongs a particular time. As I am already here and now, time should not depart from me. If time does not have the quality of coming and going, the occasion of mountaineering is the absolute now of [my] existence-time. If time does come and go, the absolute now of existence-time is [still] mine. [Existence-time is invariably a personal time, irrespective of whether time comes and goes.] This is the meaning of existence-time. Doesn't that time of climbing and fording swallow this time of dwelling in the grand palace? And doesn't this eject that? [There is nothing but the absolute present of climbing and fording, or that of dwelling in the palace.] The angry devil with three heads and eight arms is yesterday's time; the Buddha of one *jō* and six *shaku* is today's time. But the truth of yesterday and today is [comparable to] that moment which enters into mountains and looks around tens of thousands of peaks at a glance. [Yesterday and today, and all times for that matter, are seen simultaneously.] Time does not pass. The particular time of the angry devil [of yesterday] is also experienced precisely as my existence-time; though it appears to be in the distance, it is the absolute now. The particular time of the magnificent Buddha [of today], too, is realized as nothing but my existence-time; seeming to be far away, it is the absolute now. [Both are here and now in the absolute now of my self.][158]

Although the foregoing passage has many important elements on which we should comment, suffice it to say, for the moment, that

Dōgen has sufficiently shown his existential tenor, in his treatment of existence and time—radically concretized by his concept of self. In other words, Dōgen's concept of time fully incorporates into itself the self and the world—traditional bipolar concepts of Buddhism—yet deepens the whole character of the problem, by this concept of self based on his own personal experience as well as on the cultural ethos of Japan. In this respect Dōgen's view of time is extremely similar to Heidegger's in its vehement insistence on the "mineness" of temporality as regards death.

Thus, Dōgen writes:

Indeed, existence-time is realized free from bonds and delusions. Heavenly rulers and celestial beings, now actualized here and manifested there, are existence-time which is one with exertions I still make. In addition to these beings, myriad forms of existence-time, in water and on land, are fulfilled through my efforts now. All kinds of beings that constitute existence-time, in the invisible world as well as in the visible, are the embodiments of my endeavors without exception. Exertions move in time (*jinriki kyōryaku nari*). You should learn that unless my self puts forth the utmost exertion and lives time now (*waga ima jinriki kyōryaku ni arazareba*), not a single thing will be realized, nor will it ever live time.[159]

This last sentence well summarizes Dōgen's view of "my self" in connection with the problem of time. In this passage and others to which we have already referred, the problems of the absolute now (*nikon*), and of continuity (*kyōryaku*), stand out as particularly important in Dōgen's thought. Thus, we will now examine them one by one.

Existence-time is realized in the present. Its concrete realization takes place in the present moment; hence, an analysis of this is fundamental to all other aspects of the problem of time. As Dōgen asks: "Is any existence or any world excluded from this present moment?" (as we quoted earlier in this section). He also writes:

The present time (*konji*) under consideration is each individual's absolute now (*ninnin no nikon*). I think of the past, present, and future, and no matter how many periods—even tens of thousands of them—I may think of, they are the present moment, the absolute now. A person's destiny (*ninnin no bunjō*) lies necessarily in the present. In other words, the eyeballs are now, the nostrils are now.[160]

It is also at this point that Dōgen's critique of the common sense view of time as flowing, "coming and going" (*korai*), uniformly and one-directionally, becomes most severe. The first step toward the analysis of time is to understand the traditional Buddhist dictum: "Everything perishes as soon as it arises" (*setsuna-shōmetsu*). However, the ordinary worldly person is not aware of this truth, according to Dōgen. Hence:

You should take note that the human body in this life is formed temporarily as a result of the combination of the four elements and the five skandhas. There are always the eight kinds of suffering [birth, old age, sickness, death, separation from the beloved, togetherness with the hated, frustrations, and those sufferings caused by clinging to the five skandhas], not to mention the fact that life arises and perishes instantaneously from moment to moment, and does not abide at all, or the fact that there are sixty-five *setsunas* being born and annihilated in one *tanji*, yet ordinary worldly persons do not yet realize this owing to their own ignorance. Although one day and one night is comprised by 6,400,099,980 *setsunas*, and the five skandhas appear and disappear, they do not know it. Pity those who are altogether unaware of their own births and deaths! [161]

Thus, to probe into this aspect of impermanence is crucially important, philosophically and religiously. In short, the tenet, "Everything perishes as soon as it arises," denies duration: the ultimate limit of momentariness is lack of duration, and absence of coming and going as well. The common-sense view fails to see this.

Dōgen analyzes this problem as follows:

When firewood becomes ash, it can no longer revert to firewood. Hence, you should not regard ash as following and firewood as preceding [as if they formed the continuous process of becoming of a self-identical entity]. Take note that firewood abides in its own Dharma-position (*hōi*), having both before and after. Although there are before and after, they are cut off (*zengo saidan seri*) [so that there remains only middle or present, i.e., the Dharma-position of firewood]. Likewise, ash resides in its own Dharma-position, possessing both before and after. Just as firewood does not revert to firewood again after having been burnt to ash, so death is not transformed into birth after the individual is dead. Thus, you do not hold that birth becomes death; this is generally accepted in the Buddha-dharma. On this account, it is called non-birth (*fushō*). Buddhist teachings proclaim that death does not change to birth; accordingly, it is called non-death (*fumetsu*). Birth is a position of total time, death is a position of total time as well. They are likened to winter and spring. We do not think that winter turns into spring, or say that spring becomes summer. [162]

Thus firewood and ash, birth and death, winter and spring—all have their own Dharma-positions which are absolutely discrete and discontinuous. Each has its before and after but is cut off from those Dharma-positions preceding and following. Because of its central importance to an understanding of Dōgen's mystical realism, we shall attempt to delve into the problem of abiding in the Dharma-position (*jū-hōi*) in some detail here.

First, a Dharma-position is comprised of a particular here and a particular now (a spatio-temporal existence in the world), hence, it is inevitably comprised of the existential particularities—biological, psychological, moral, philosophical, religious, and so forth—which are observed, compared, judged, and chosen in the dualistic scheme of things. That is to say, the existential particularities of a given moment constitute a particular position of time which in turn is a Dharma-position. What makes a particular position of time a Dharma-position is the appropriation of these particularities in such a manner that they are now seen nondualistically in and through the mediation of absolute emptiness. The significance of the existential qualities and phenomenalities of things and events is by no means minimized; on the contrary, they are reconstituted, without being naively phenomenalistic, in their true aspect of thusness. "Dharma abides in a Dharma-position" (*hō wa hōi ni jūsuru nari*), therefore, does not imply that the Dharma-position is in any way a self-limiting manifestation or a temporal instance of eternity. To abide in a Dharma-position, therefore, should not be construed as instrumental and subsidiary to some idea of eternity, but, rather, as an end in itself—as eternity in itself. Thus the act of eating, for example, is viewed as the absolute given, self-sufficient in itself; it is the kōan realized in life (*genjō-kōan*).

Second, such a particular here-and-now is also the bearer of the total situation in which it is lived. Dōgen frequently uses the expression he is so fond of, "the total exertion of a single thing" (*ippō-gūjin*)—or simply "the total exertion" (*gūjin*). He writes, for example:

Those who know a single object comprehend the entire universe; those who penetrate a single dharma exhaust all dharmas. Unless we understand all dharmas thoroughly, we do not apprehend a dharma. When one understands the meaning of thoroughness (*tsū*) and thereby penetrates thoroughly, one discerns all dharmas as well as a single dharma. For this reason, while one studies a single object, one learns the whole universe without fail.[163]

Elsewhere, related to the idea of the total exertion of a single thing, Dōgen has this to say: "When one side is illumined, the other is darkened" (*ippō o shōsuru toki wa ippō wa kurashi*).[164] As we have noted in the foregoing, when one eats, eating is the total activity at that particular moment, and nothing else. All other things remain in darkness, so to speak. This does not mean, however, that this affirmation of eating is achieved through the negation of the existence of the "hidden"; such would be dualistic. On the contrary, eating is enacted in such a way that it embodies, nondually and undefiledly, both the disclosed and the concealed, the part and the whole, microcosm and macrocosm; the activity of eating is, according to Dōgen's favorite expression, "the whole being of emptiness leaping out of itself" (*konshin-chōshutsu*). When part and whole are simultaneously and unobstructedly realized in the act of eating, it is the moment when the whole being of emptiness leaps out of itself "mustering the whole body-mind" (*shinjin o koshite*)—another favorite expression of Dōgen's. This is precisely what Dōgen meant by "total realization" or "total function" (*zenki*). As I intend to consider this matter in a different context later, I shall quote just one passage in this connection:

Life is, for example, like people sailing in a boat. Although we set a sail, steer our course, and pole the boat along, the boat carries us and we do not exist apart from the boat. By sailing in the boat, we make the boat what it is. Study assiduously this very time. At such a time, there is nothing but the world of the boat. The heavens, the water, and the shore—all become the boat's time (*fune no jisetsu*); they are not the same as the time that is not the boat. Hence, I make life what it is; life makes me what I am. In riding the boat, one's body and mind, the self and the world are together the dynamic function of the boat (*fune no kikan*). The entire earth and the whole empty sky are in company with the boat's vigorous exertion. Such is the I that is life, the life that is I.[165]

Third, a Dharma-position does not come and go, or pass, or flow as the common sense view of time would assume. This is a radical rejection of the flow of time, or the stream of consciousness, or any other conceptions of time based on the idea of continuity and duration. That is, time is absolutely discrete and discontinuous. This characteristic is primary in Dōgen's thought.[166] Dōgen's thesis, however, is not based on any quantitative and atomistic consideration of time, that is, not on a theoretical concern, but rather on the qualitative and practical reflection on his existential and religious experience of the present. As he probed into the "reason of the total exertion" (*gūjin no ri*), he could not but come to this idea of the absolute discontinuity of the present.

The ideas of abiding in the Dharma-position and of the total exertion of a single thing, though the expressions themselves are by no means Dōgen's own invention, bear, nevertheless, the imprints of typically Dōgen-like mystical realism, epitomized in the statement (the English translation of which can hardly do any justice to the spirit, eloquence and force of the original Japanese): "Obstruction hinders obstruction, thereby obstruction realizes itself (*ge wa ge o sae, ge o miru*); obstruction obstructs obstruction (*ge wa ge o gesuru nari*)— such is time."[167] As Dōgen explains immediately after this passage, "obstruction" (*ge*, a shortened expression of *keige*) is used not in the ordinary sense of the word but in the sense of "self-obstruction" while abiding in a Dharma-position—a thing is obstructed by itself, nothing else, that is, it exerts itself in absolute freedom.[168] Dōgen's purport is to express the realistic aspect of thusness, which entails neither a monistic nor a naturalistic reductionism. Accordingly we might legitimately translate the above passage as: "Thusness thus-es thusness, thereby thusness realizes itself. . . ." Analogously, "a mountain mountain-s a mountain, thereby a mountain realizes itself. . . ." and so on in the manner of total exertion.[169]

So much for the idea of abiding in the Dharma-position. It was my intention to establish the necessary relation between this and the idea of the absolute now in Dōgen's thought. For Dōgen declares: "Living vigorously in a Dharma-position—such is existence-time."[170] We can now fully understand the statement to which I referred earlier:

The angry devil with three heads and eight arms is yesterday's time; the Buddha of one *jō* and six *shaku* is today's time. But the truth of yesterday and today is [comparable to] that moment which enters into mountains and looks around tens of thousands of peaks at a glance. Time does not pass. The particular time of the angry devil [of yesterday] is also experienced precisely as my existence-time; though it appears to be in the distance, it is the absolute now. The particular time of the magnificent Buddha [of today], too, is realized as nothing but my existence-time; seeming to be far away, it is the absolute now.[171]

The present moment of a single thought (regardless of its length from the theoretical standpoint) is the subjectively appropriated, absolute, completed, and realized existence-time. It clearly entails a denial of the present as an instance of the linear conception of time. Instead, the motif of simultaneity we have examined in connection with the Hua-yen metaphysics of time is strong and pervasive in Dōgen's concept of time.[172] In this framework such statements as the following can be properly understood:

You should understand that even though there was a moon last night, the moon you see tonight is not last night's moon. Tonight's moon, whether of the earlier, the middle, or the later phase, is equally nothing but the moon of tonight. Although the moon is there, it is not a matter of new or old, because the moon inherits the moon.[173]

Analogously, the present can be divided into earlier, middle, and later phases, or into new and old, or into past, present, and future. The present, however, is not divided in the actuality of human subjectivity. This view is strikingly similar to what Whitehead conceived in his "epochal theory of time" in which the epochal quantum of becoming is said to be divisible but not divided.[174] Thus each absolute now constitutes a unique whole of actuality.

Furthermore, the structure of the absolute now is such that the past, present, and future, in an epochal whole (to use Whitehead's term here for convenience's sake), are not arranged in a linear fashion but realized simultaneously in the manner of mutual identity and mutual penetration (*sōsoku-sōnyū*). This refutes the ordinary ways of defining these three periods:

[A common belief] says that the past life has already perished, the future is yet to come, and the present does not stay. The past did not necessarily already perish, the future is not inevitably yet to come, and the present is not inexorably impermanent. If you learn the not-staying, the not-yet, and the no-longer as present, future, and past, respectively, you should certainly understand the reason that the not-yet is the past, present, and future. [The same holds true of the no-longer and the not-staying.][175]

What is said here indicates, in the final analysis, that the manner in which an epochal whole of the present incorporates into itself the selective memory of the past, as well as the projected anticipation of the future, is far more complex than the conventional definitions of the past, present, and future, in terms of the no-longer, not-staying, and not-yet, would assume it to be. The very complexity of this problem, in turn, is an indication of various possibilities of freedom in this subjective appropriation of the three periods in the absolute now, in which Buddha-nature is realized (*ji-busshō*). We come now to the problem of continuity (*kyōryaku*) in Dōgen's view of time.

As we embark on an examination of Dōgen's view of continuity, several prevalent views must be cleared from our path at the outset. First, as is apparent from the general characteristics of his metaphysics, Dōgen would reject any supernaturalistic agent who governs a providential continuity or a sacred history, independent of the ever-changing flux of existence and time. Any other all-embracing principle of eternity or timelessness, or any evolutionary scheme of history, is also alien to Dōgen's thought. Secondly, Dōgen's analogy of firewood and ash indicates that the continuity of becoming from firewood to ash is an illusion which presupposes some changeless substratum which endures throughout the accidental changes of the burning firewood till the time of its reduction to ash. Certainly, a uniformly flowing and uniformly measurable time, in an infinite continuum, assumes such a presupposition. The drawbacks of these two views are fairly easy to detect. On the other hand, the third view of continuity as a process from potentiality to actuality is subtler than the other two; so much so that Dōgen undertakes his analyses with great care, repudiating it once and for all.

Let us examine this last view a little more closely. Dōgen presents a metaphor strikingly similar to Aristotle's acorn and oak:

A certain group of Buddhists think that Buddha-nature is like the seed of plants or trees. When the rain moistens it generously, buds and stems grow, branches, leaves, and fruits become dense, and eventually the fruits bear seeds. Such a view is what an ordinary worldly person imagines. Supposing that you understand the matter in this way, you should realize that the seeds, the flowers, the fruits—each is the absolute actualization of Buddha-nature (*jōjō no sekishin*). A seed in a fruit, though unseen, grows roots and stems and, though not assorted, flourishes with a thick trunk and big branches. Although not a matter of inside or outside, this is true through the ages. For this reason, even if an ordinary worldly person's approach is granted [for the sake of the argument], roots, stems, branches, and leaves are all born in the same manner and all die in the same way. [They are] equally one and the same Buddha-nature of all existence.[176]

Buddha-nature is not something that will be realized in some future if and when a right season arrives, as is the case with a seed that grows into a plant and bears fruit. That is, Buddha-nature is not a potentiality to be actualized some time in the future, but is an actuality in the present. Dōgen contends:

Some people, ancient and modern, often think that the Buddhist saying "if time arrives" means waiting for some time in the future when Buddha-nature is realized, and that, as they practice the Way in this manner, they meet such a time of realization naturally. But unless time comes, it never presents itself, even though they visit teachers and inquire about Dharma and endeavor to study the Way. Thinking this way, they are aimlessly enmeshed in the whirlwind of worldly dusts and observe the Milky Way vainly. Such people belong perhaps to a kind of naturalistic heresy.[177]

Dōgen then expounds his view as follows:

To want to know the meaning of Buddha-nature, as we see it, is, to really know it. To reflect upon the reason of time is to actually know it. If you wish to know Buddha-nature, you must know the reason of time this way. To say "if time arrives" is tantamount to declaring that time has already arrived; how can you doubt this? You may entertain a doubt about time. Be that as it may, restore Buddha-nature to yourself. You should know that [as we understand it] "if time arrives" [in this manner], every moment of twenty-four hours does not pass by vainly. The "if-arrives" (*nyakushi*) is construed as the "already-arrived" (*kishi*). [Otherwise] "if time arrives" means "Buddha-nature never arrives." For this reason, as time has already arrived, Buddha-nature is unmistakably present here and now. The reason of Buddha-nature discloses itself. There is absolutely no time which has not yet arrived [according to our interpretation of "if time arrives"]; there is no Buddha-nature which is not yet realized.[178]

We see here Dōgen's emphatic repudiation of continuity as the process from potentiality to actuality. If we seek a kind of continuity in Dōgen's thought, we should do so without doing injustice to what Dōgen has to say with respect to the discontinuity of actualities. In any event this much is clear: The concept of continuity in Dōgen's thought does not refer to a process of evolutionary becoming, from the inferior to the superior, from the imperfect to the perfect, from the incomplete to the complete, or from the hidden to the revealed, which is invariably associated with the image of the linear flow of time. Realization (*genjō*) in Dōgen's thought rejects such a process of evolutionary becoming, or "coming and going," and "arising and perishing," for that matter. Rather, it means that reality, as it is here and now, is a completed, absolute reality. (Obviously, this is not a naive phenomenalism that affirms the empirical reality at its face-value. We shall have occasion to say more about this later.)[179]

Dōgen writes:

Existence-time has the characteristic of passage (*kyōryaku*): it moves from today to tomorrow, passes from today to yesterday, shifts from yesterday to today, runs from today to today, flows from tomorrow to tomorrow [in the consciousness of my absolute now]; for dynamism (*kyōryaku*) is the characteristic of time. While the times of ancient and modern do not pile up, nor do they line up [they are mutually identical and mutually interpenetrated], Ch'ing-yüan [Hsing-ssŭ] is also time, Huang-po [Hsi-yün] is also time, [Ma-tsu tao-i of] Chiang-hsi and Shih-t'ou [Hsi-ch'ien] are times as well. Because the self and others are already times [discrete from each other], practice and enlightenment are different times. Also, to enter the mire and go into the water [to guide sentient beings] is likewise time.[180]

Continuity or passage, in this view, is not so much a matter of a succession or contiguity of inter-epochal wholes, as that of the dynamic experience of an intra-epochal whole of the absolute now in which the selective memory of the past and the projected anticipation of the future are subjectively appropriated in a unique manner. In brief, continuity in Dōgen's context means dynamism. (In this sense alone Dōgen allowed the notion of "flow" in time.) This is in accord with what we have seen previously in connection with the Hua-yen "principle of the various formations of the discrete events of the ten periods" (*jisse-kyakuhō-ijō-mon*). In the absolute now, the discrete events of past, present, and future are variously formed at a given moment. The dynamic structure of the absolute now, and its manner of appropriating these three periods, are extremely complex and defy any simplistic characterization from the linear perspective alone.

If we take the linear or directional metaphor advisedly, as Dōgen did (as we see in the idea of continuity), time may be said to be multidirectional and multi-dimensional: as we have already quoted, it moves from today to yesterday, from tomorrow to tomorrow, from yesterday to today, and so forth; not only that, but it moves "vertically." Dōgen writes:

The hour of the horse [11 A.M.–1 P.M.] and the hour of the sheep [1–3 P.M.], in relation to things arranged in the world now, are as they are by virtue of their abiding in the Dharma-positions, ascending and descending, up and down.[181]

Thus, continuity in the intra-epochal whole of an absolute now, as Dōgen sees it, is perhaps best described in terms of the Hua-yen philosophy of simultaneity. Dōgen says:

You should not construe passage (*kyōryaku*) as something like a storm passing from east to west. The world is neither motionless and changeless, nor without advance and retreat: it is passage. Passage is, then, like spring. Myriad events take place in the spring, and they are called passage. It should be noted that [spring] passes without anything outside itself [such as winter or summer]. For example, the passage of spring always passes through spring itself. [There is nothing but the dynamism of spring.] Although passage is not confined to spring alone, it is now realized at this particular time of spring, because it is the dynamism of spring. This should be understood carefully. Speaking of passage, ordinary people think that the objective environment exists independently, while the subject of passage (*nōkyōryaku no hō*) traverses eastward through hundreds of thousands of worlds and aeons. However, the study of Buddha-way is not devoted to this one thing alone.[182]

As we recall, Dōgen said: "Unless my self puts forth the utmost exertion and lives time now, not a single thing will be realized, nor will it ever live time." Herein lies Dōgen's existential solution to the problem of one and many.

The foregoing examples illustrate Dōgen's existential and religious concerns with the "intra-subjective" reality of the absolute now as well as with continuity. The deepest motive behind Dōgen's metaphysic of time was not a theoretical, but, rather, a practical interest, consisting in the activity of philosophizing, which for Dōgen was none other than the practice of the Way (*bendō*). Thus, humans are neither enslaved by time, nor do we have to "kill time"; instead, we now use time freely and creatively.[183]

My observations thus far concerning the self, the absolute now, continuity, and so on, which constitute existence-time, might have given an impression that Dōgen's view of time is nothing but an affirmation of reality as it is here and now as the absolute given, that is, a completed reality. We have seen references to this aspect of realization (*genjō*) previously, and this impression seems to be quite justified. We are led to ask: Isn't Dōgen's metaphysic of time all but static? Can we find any dynamic elements of transformation and progression in Dōgen? Such questions lead to another aspect of fundamental importance in Dōgen's view of time: his notion of the "perpetuation of the Way through activity" (*gyōji-dōkan*), which we have had occasion to touch on previously.[184] The key passage runs as follows:

The great Way of the Buddhas and ancestors consists always in these supreme activities (*mujō no gyōji*), never interrupted in their continuation: the desire for enlightenment, practice, enlightenment, and nirvāṇa. These four activities never allow even a single interval between them. This is the perpetuation of the Way through activity (*gyōji-dōkan*). Consequently, supreme activity is neither a contrivance of the self nor that of others; it is activity undefiled. The power of such an activity sustains my self and others. Its import is such that all the heavens and the entire earth of the ten quarters enjoy the merit of my activity. Even if neither the self nor others are aware of it, such is the case.[185]

The merit, or power, of the progression of creative activity is here clearly set forth. As we have seen, creative activity is metaphysically primitive to such an extent that we may rightly claim: In the beginning was activity. This conveys well what Dōgen meant by the following:

The sun, the moon, and the stars exist by virtue of such creative activities. The earth and the empty sky exist because of activities. Our body-mind and its environment are dependent on activities; so are the four elements and the five skandhas. Although activity is not what worldly people are likely to care for, it is all humans' true refuge. . . . It should be examined and understood thoroughly that functional interdependence (*engi*) is activity, because activity is not functionally interdependent.[186]

Dōgen goes beyond the conventional way of thinking evidenced in the Buddhist philosophy, by asserting that activity is more primitive than functional interdependence. This is not to deny the significance of the latter, but to probe into the nature of its conditions and causes— all things of the universe—in order to deepen our understanding of them as activities.[187] The crux of the matter is succinctly stated in the following manner:

That activity which realizes those activities—it is our activity now (*wareraga imano gyōji nari*). The now of activity (*gyōji no ima*) is not the self's primordial being, eternal and immutable, nor is it something that enters and leaves the self. The Way, called now, does not precede activity; as activity is realized (*gyōji genjō suru*), it is called now.[188]

It is evident that now is realized contemporaneously with activity. Or to put it another way, time is activity, and activity is time. The absolute now consists, not in a static timelessness that enables us to accept the given reality as it is, but, rather, in a dynamic activity that involves us intimately in time, hence, transforming our deeds, speech, and thought. The realization of activity (*gyōji-genjō*) signals this element of transformation. But this element is in turn inseparably connected with the perpetuation of the Way (*dōkan*), comparable to the foreward revolution of the wheel of Dharma—it advances in history, but note that this is an advance in enlightenment (*bukkōjōji*). Thus, if we construe these observations as indicating the process of evolutionary becoming (as in a Hegelian dialectical development, proposed by some philosophically oriented students of Dōgen), our previous effort toward establishing the primacy of discontinuity will end in failure at this very point. For nowhere does Dōgen advocate any evolutionary theory of time, as we have emphasized. Hence, even when we appreciate the significance of transformation and progression in Dōgen's thought, we should do so in the context of the ultimacy of discontinuity.

Religious Life and Buddha-Nature

As I have shown in the foregoing, Dōgen's thought has a specifically philosophical import and relevance even today, which has been often pointed out by many students of Dōgen. This does not mean, however, that he endeavored to construct any philosophical system; such was alien to his orientation. Dōgen was engaged in all the apparently philosophical analyses, comments, and expositions, due to the existential and religious exigency he was confronted with in the particular situation of his time. Thus, he was primarily a religious thinker who regarded the act of philosophizing as an essential element of his religiousness. This can be shown, for example, by the fact that while Dōgen used such traditional Buddhist terms as mind-only, Dharma-nature, thusness, and Buddha-nature synonymously throughout his works, he regarded Buddha-nature as particularly fitting and as central—perhaps for the reason that the term retained more personal, affective, and existential connotations when compared with the impersonal, speculative, and transcendental connotations of the other terms. This affective strand in his personality is as strong as his cerebral disposition and cultic rigorism—and might have been engendered by his mother's tender religious piety. In this respect, Buddha-nature becomes Dōgen's own mythopoeic vision—no longer a cold metaphysical concept—in its religious intention only loosely comparable to, yet in its emotive tones strikingly similar to, the Amitābha or Amida faith of Pure Realm Buddhism. Zen Buddhism is, after all, a religion, not a philosophy alone. Dōgen proves this abundantly.[189]

As we have reminded ourselves so often, Dōgen's philosophical and religious thought revolved around his search for the meaning and reason (*dōri*) of existence, specifically of human existence in the context of impermanence and ultimately of death. Dōgen writes:

To understand birth-and-death lucidly is the matter of the greatest importance for a Buddhist.

An old sage [Śākyamuni Buddha] said: "When you are first born into the world, you are provided with the ability to expound Dharma." The ability to expound Dharma is the power of Tathāgata's great discourse, or the great discourse itself.[190]

His seriousness concerning the problem is well testified to by these remarks: "We are born in the world without knowing our beginning and end. Although we do not know the bounds of the world, we do look hard at this place and do tread in this place."[191] And:

If someone seeks Buddha outside birth-and-death, it is like orienting a cart toward the north in order to head for the province of Yüeh, or like facing toward the south in order to gaze up at Charles' Wain. The more we collect the conditions of birth-and-death, the further we go astray in finding the way of liberation. We understand that birth-and-death itself is nirvāṇa; thus we neither loathe birth-and-death nor long for nirvāṇa. Then, for the first time, we are free in birth-and-death.[192]

The meaning of impermanence is not prior to, nor independent of, the fact of impermanence. They are mutually identical and mutually interdependent. Or to put it somewhat differently, myth is reality, and reality is myth. Dōgen does not believe, as the modern world does, in a dualism between reality and myth in which reality is construed as isolatable from myth so as to attain a progressively greater degree of objectivity; rather, his purport is to clarify, purify, and reinforce myth—that is, Buddha-nature—in order to see and touch reality as it is. What the mythopoeic vision of Buddha-nature produces is not beclouded feelings and emotions that coat, or hide, or soothe, the inexorable reality of impermanence and death, but those feelings and emotions cleansed in thusness, that are embedded in and transparent to that reality.

Let us then see Dōgen's criticism of the Senika view of the immortality and eternity of soul. Dōgen's disciples ask:

Some people say: "We must not grieve over birth-and-death, for there is a very easy way to liberate ourselves from it, namely, to know the immortality of mind's essence (*shinshō no jōjū*). Its tenet is as follows: While this body, having already been born, shall be transferred, of necessity, to death, this mind never perishes. Knowing that mind's essence is not affected by birth-and-death but resides in the body, one construes it as the original being; accordingly, the body is a temporary carcass that suffers an endless series of birth-and-death. Mind is permanent and changeless throughout the past, present, and future. To understand in this way constitutes liberation from birth-and-death. Those who know this truth endure the present life and, as our bodies dissolve, enter the realm of essence. As we merge into the realm of essence, we will be endowed with wondrous virtues like Buddhas and Tathāgatas. Even if we know this truth in the present life, we are not equal to these sages, because of our bodily existences with their attendant karmic effects from previous lives. Those who do not know this tenet as yet shall ever wander in the cycles of birth-and-death. Therefore, you must understand, without losing a moment, the truth of the immortality of mind-essence. What do you expect to happen if you pass your life wastefully in idle sitting?" Is or is not such a view truly in accord with the Way of the Buddhas and ancestors?[193]

The temporariness and temporality of bodily and phenomenal existence, in this view, are forfeited for the sake of an after-life in the ocean realm of essence. Against this Senika view, Dōgen submits his own case for the radical affirmation of human existence:

Nevertheless, to equate such an opinion with the Buddha-dharma is more foolish than grasping tiles and pebbles and believing they are golden treasures. Such a delusion is shameful. National Teacher Hui-chung (?–775), of the great T'ang dynasty, strongly warned against such a view. Aren't they most despicable and pitiful who currently contrive an erroneous doctrine of the immortality of mind and perishability of phenomena, identifying it with Buddhas' wondrous Dharma, and thinking themselves to be liberated from birth-and-death, while creating the root cause of suffering in birth-and-death? . . . From the standpoint of changelessness, all things are changeless without exception, for body and mind are not separated. From the viewpoint of unconditionedness, all existences are equally unconditioned, for reality and appearance are not discriminated. Therefore, is it not against reasonableness for some to assert that while body perishes mind endures? What is more, it should be realized that this very birth-and-death itself is nirvāṇa: nobody can speak of nirvāṇa independent of birth-and-death.[194]

What matters most in religion, as Dōgen sees it, is not a deferred realization of immortality in an after-life, nor an eternal recurrence of rebirths, but, rather, the realization of enlightenment here and now. Hence, this present birth-and-death is the only absolute locus—discrete from before and after—in which, alone, we can speak of religion, that is, our liberation. In short, birth-and-death is the very locus in which the two possibilities of enlightenment and delusion are offered to every one of us. Thus, " . . . while an ordinary worldly person wanders about in delusion in the midst of birth-and-death, a great sage is liberated in elightenment."[195] Life can be either a blessing or a curse; hence, we must choose either enlightenment or delusion, not both. Dōgen's view of religious life bears strictly on this life—no more, no less.

The meaning and reason of human existence cannot be adequately considered in isolation from all nonhuman existence in its functional interdependence. Precious though it is, human existence can be adequately understood only in its cosmic context. To be sure, in any ontology, human existence may have a favorable status as a point of departure, at least from the human standpoint. However, this should not imply or lead to an exaggeration of the value of human existence in the total context. This cosmic orientation is apparent in the following:

The mind of a sentient being is destined to desire to know its own self. However, those whose eyes see their true selves are exceedingly rare indeed; Buddha alone sees it. All other heretics vainly opine for that which is not the self. What Buddha means by the self is precisely the entire universe (*jindaichi*). Thus, whether one is aware of it or not, there is no universe that is not this self. . . .

An ancient Buddha says that mountains, rivers, the earth, and humans are born together; likewise, the Buddhas of the three periods and humans have been endeavoring together.

On this account, as I see mountains, rivers, and the earth at the time when humans are born, it does not appear that they come into being as additional elements piled upon those mountains, rivers, and the great earth which have existed since before human births. . . . We are born in the world without knowing our beginning or our end. Although we do not know the bounds of the world, we do look hard here and do tread in this place. Do not hold a grudge against the mountains, the rivers, and the earth, because they are not like human life. You should understand clearly that [the above saying] shows the oneness of the universe and my existence. Furthermore, the Buddhas of the three periods already exerted themselves to perfect the Way and realize enlightenment. How should we understand this oneness of Buddha and the self? Observe the activities of Buddha for a while. Buddha's activities take place with the entire earth and with all sentient beings. If they are not with all existence, they are not yet the activities of Buddha.

Hence from the arising of the desire for enlightenment to the attainment of enlightenment, Buddha is enlightened and conducts himself/herself always with the whole world and with all sentient beings.[196]

"To study the Way is to study the self. To study the self is to forget the self. To forget the self is to be enlightened by all things of the universe."[197] Furthermore: "We practice and experience all things by bringing our selves forward—this is delusion; as all things advance forward and practice and verify the self, we are enlightened."[198] While Dōgen conceives of human existence in the context of the world, and as does Heidegger, in terms of "a being-in-the-world," he never asserts an excessive "mineness," as Heidegger does, at the expense of cosmic concern.[199] In Dōgen, the self and the world, anthropology and cosmology, are inseparably interpenetrated in the total context of his ontology. Both the self and the world arise and perish together in the simultaneous realization of Buddhahood (*dōji-jōdō*).

It is against this general background that we must understand Dōgen's most pietistic statements, such as the following, which is well-nigh indistinguishable from sentiments of Pure Realm Buddhism:

This birth-and-death itself is the life of Buddha. If you loathe and abandon it, you will lose Buddha as well; if you cling to birth-and-death by being confined to it, this too will result in missing Buddha's life—leaving the appearance of Buddha behind. When you neither loathe nor crave it, only then do you enter the heart of Buddha for the first time. But do not calculate it with your mind or explain it in words. When you cast off and forget your body and mind and plunge into the abode of Buddha so that Buddha may act upon you and you may be faithful to it, you become Buddha liberated from the sufferings of birth-and-death, without effort and anxiety.[200]

It is noteworthy at this point that despite these pious statements Dōgen's religiousness is radically different from Shinran's, primarily because of differences in the two thinkers' perceptions of human existence. Dōgen views it in the light of radical impermanence, whereas Shinran views it in the light of radical sinfulness. To be sure, Dōgen did not lack an awareness of sinfulness, as we shall see in the next chapter in connection with confession, any more than Shinran lacked an awareness of impermanence, inasmuch as he lived in medieval Japan, which was thoroughly saturated with it. Nevertheless, no one can legitimately challenge the general validity of the above observation. Thus, death is viewed, in the case of Dōgen, from the standpoint of impermanence, and in the case of Shinran, from the standpoint of sinfulness. Moreover, for Shinran, there is an unbridgeable gap between Amida and the common mortals, at least existentially, because of our moral wretchedness and utter incapacity to save ourselves except by the power of Amida's original vow (*hongan*). This view may have appeared to Dōgen as an exaggerated, rather than an accurate, description of the human condition. For both Dōgen and Shinran, our most serious limitation is not a lack of intuitive insight into our nature, but has to do with our acts. Thus, for Dōgen, it is the failure to act, whereas, for Shinran, it is the incapacity to act. It has been fashionable to speak of the dichotomies of faith and enlightenment, as well as of other-power (*tariki*) and self-power (*jiriki*), which are applied too hastily to an understanding of the Pure Realm tradition and the Zen tradition in Buddhism. It seems to me that these distinctions turn out to be irrelevant and fruitless at a deeper level within the two traditions, despite their having a certain amount of usefulness. This is most strongly substantiated by the two thinkers' writings concerning nondualistic freedom and liberation—in the samadhi of self-fulfilling activity (*jijuyū-zammai*) for Dōgen, and in naturalness (*jinen-hōni*) for Shinran. Nevertheless, we should not obscure or minimize the fundamental differences at a deeper level, some of which we have pointed out here briefly.[201] Thus, Dōgen's occasional outpouring of pious sentiments should be understood in the context of his mythopoeic vision of Buddha-nature, which is significantly similar to, as well as significantly different from, that of Amida of Pure Realm Buddhism.

In the course of his discourse on Buddha-nature, Dōgen writes:

In exerting life you are not blocked by life; in making use of death you are not obstructed by death. You should not be attached to life aimlessly, or be afraid of death unreasonably. [The body of the five skandhas] is already the locus of Buddha-nature, and both perturbation [in one's lust for life] and abomination [of death] are un-Buddhistic. As you understand that [the body of the five skandhas] is formed by various conditions at hand, you are able to exert it unobstructedly. This is the supreme Buddha. The abode of this supreme Buddha itself is the wondrous Pure Land.[202]

The logic of exerting (*shitoku suru*) birth-and-death is such that, as life is exerted totally, there is nothing but life in the entire universe, and, when this happens, life becomes no-life, negating itself (i.e., mentioning life is meaningless in the situation where there is nothing but life). This is the logic of total exertion, to which we have referred frequently, and also the logic of "total dynamism" (*zenki*) of the entire universe and of Buddha-nature.[203] Total realization is equivalent to the principle of the total exertion of a single thing, with the only difference being that it is now applied to the entire universe and Buddha-nature. When a single thing, say, the sound of flowing water, is totally exerted, the total realization of Buddha-nature is present in that single phenomenon. Thus, the principles of total exertion and total dynamism are two aspects of one and the same reality of subjectivity in Dōgen's metaphysical realism. Loosely speaking, the former (total exertion) addresses itself primarily to the self, whereas the latter (total dynamism) speaks to the world. Both refer to the undefiled freedom and liberation of the self and the world as the self-expression of Buddha-nature.

We are now in a position to examine Dōgen's idea of total dynamism in a little more detail. Dōgen writes:

As it works consummately, the great Way of all Buddhas is transparency (*tōdatsu*) and realization (*genjō*). Transparency means that life becomes transparent to life itself and death becomes transparent to death itself. Thus, there is liberation from birth-and-death as well as involvement in birth-and-death: both are the great Way of total exertion (*gūjin no daidō*). There is discarding of birth-and-death, and there is crossing of birth-and-death: they are equally the great Way of total exertion. Realization is life; life is realization. In such realization, life cannot be other than its total realization, death is nothing but its total realization. This dynamic function (*kikan*) lends itself to life as well as to death. At the very time when this dynamic function is culminated, it is not necessarily large, nor is it necessarily small; it is neither infinite nor finite, neither long and far nor short and near. Life now is in this dynamic function, and this dynamic function is in life now. Life is not coming, life is not going. Life is not manifestation, life is not formation. Nevertheless, life is the presence of total realization, death is the presence of total realization. You should take note that among an infinite number of dharmas that constitute the self, there is birth and there is death.

Reflect quietly upon the following: This present life and all things co-existent therewith—do they or do they not share a common destiny? Not a single moment, not a single thing exists that does not co-work with life; not a single event, not a single mind exists that does not take part in life.[204]

In what the existentialist deems to be my existence, Dōgen would see the total activity of the universe engaged in the common endeavor of creation. The entire universe suffers the pangs of a new creation in and through my existence.[205] Dōgen's existential concern, as we have noted before, has never gone astray in an excessive assertion of personal concern, as such; instead, both the self and the world share their common destiny as the self-activities and self-expressions of Buddha-nature.

The same thesis is explicated in Dōgen's parable of a boat as quoted before:

Life is, for example, like people sailing in a boat. Although we set a sail, steer our course, and pole the boat along, the boat carries us, and we do not exist apart from the boat. By sailing in the boat, we make the boat what it is. Study assiduously this very time. At such a time, there is nothing but the world of the boat. The heavens, the water, and the shore—all become the boat's time; they are not the same as the time that is not the boat. Hence, I make life what it is; life makes me what I am. In riding the boat, one's body and mind, the self and the world are, together, the dynamic function of the boat. The entire earth and the whole empty sky are in company with the boat's vigorous exertion. Such is the I that is life, the life that is I.[206]

Dōgen asserts the following immediately after the above parable:

Teacher Yüan-we K'o-ch'in [1063–1135] once said: "Life is the realization of total dynamism; death is the realization of total dynamism."

You should elucidate and penetrate this statement deeply. You may penetrate it deeply in such a way that although the verity of "life is the realization of total dynamism," with no bearing on a beginning or an end, involves the whole earth and the whole sky, not only does it not obstruct life as the presence of total working, it does not even hinder "death is the realization of total dynamism." Even though when death is total function's consummation it embraces the entire great earth and the entire empty sky, it does not hinder death as the consummation of total function, nor does it hinder life as the consummation of total function. Therefore, life does not obstruct death, death does not obstruct life. The entire earth and the entire sky are involved equally in life as well as in death. This does not mean, however, that any single [fixed] earth or any single [self-same] sky is totally working in life or in death. Though not identical, they are not different; though not different, they are not one; though not one, they are not many. Accordingly, in life are multitudinous things that realize themselves in total function; in death are countless dharmas that actualize themselves in total dynamism. The realization of total dynamism exists even in what is neither life nor death. In the presence of total working, there is life, and there is death.[207]

The total realization of Buddha-nature does not obliterate the individual particularities and identities of events and things as though they are dissolved in an undifferentiated realm. True to the Hua-yen metaphysics of the "nonobstruction of phenomena in opposition to phenomena (*jiji-muge*), based on the principle of "mutual identity and mutual penetration" (*sōsoku-sōnyū*), Dōgen does maintain that the concrete particularities of things, absolutely discrete spatially and temporally, are mutually interpenetrated and unobstructed—each exerting total realization in its own right. Furthermore, in effect: "Though not identical, they are not different; though not different, they are not one; though not one, they are not many." The particularities in question are not dissolved or fused in Buddha-nature. The all-inclusiveness of Dōgen's mythopoeic vision should be understood in this manner. On the other hand, Dōgen's vision is exclusionary in that when life is totally exerted and realized, there is nothing but life, excluding everything else, and ultimately life itself becomes "meaningless"—the stage in which the distinction between symbol and reality becomes liberatingly irrelevant. This exclusionary aspect of the mythopoeic vision of Buddha-nature demands that we commit ourselves to, and choose, a definite course of action at each moment—

whatever that may be. Such an orientation is far from noncommittal, as Zen Buddhism is so often misunderstood as being. A definite philosophic and moral commitment or choice, however, must be "undefiled" (*fuzenna*), totally exerted as the self-creation of Buddha-nature in the absolute freedom of the samādhi of self-fulfilling activity. These two characteristics, inclusionary and exclusionary, are unobstructedly and nondualistically envisioned in Dōgen's mythopoeic vision of Buddha-nature.

At this point we must take into account the problem of time. The analogy of firewood and ash, which we have discussed previously, can be applied to the problem of birth-and-death. Dōgen repudiates the popular conception of death as the termination of life, as if life becomes or changes into death. "It is a mistake to think that there is a transition from life to death."[208] For Dōgen, the continuity of becoming, between birth and death, obscures the real crux of the problem, for birth and death are two discrete "positions of time." He writes:

Thus, you do not hold that birth becomes death; this is generally accepted in the Buddha-dharma. On this account, it is called nonbirth. Buddhist teachings proclaim that death does not change to birth; accordingly, it is called nondeath. Birth is a position of total time, death is a position of total time as well.[209]

The same thesis is stated in another place:

Birth is a position of total time (*hitotoki*), having both before and after. Accordingly, in the Buddha-dharma, birth itself is said to be nonbirth. Likewise, extinction is a position of total time, possessing before and after. Hence, extinction itself is said to be nonextinction. When you speak of birth, there is nothing but birth; when you speak of death, there is nothing but death. For this reason, when birth comes, you should surrender yourself solely to birth; when death comes, you should be devoted just to death. Do not hate them. Do not desire them.[210]

When death is chosen totally by abiding in its Dharma-position, it is not a death among other innumerable deaths, or death as opposed to life, but the death which is paradoxically nondeath, yet at the same time supremely a death which nothing can replace.

With Heidegger, who has characterized human existence as the "being-toward-death," Dōgen maintains that death is not some external power which visits at the close of human life, and, consequently, can be dealt with somehow indifferently, but something copresent with our life: life and death interpenetrate one another in the structural whole of human existence. Dōgen writes: "Although we have not yet left life, we already see death. Although we have not yet discarded death, we already meet life. Life does not obstruct death, death does not obstruct life."[211] Elsewhere he has this to say: "There is life in death, and there is death in life. There is death that is constantly in death; there is life that is always in life. This is not contrived by us willfully, but acted by Dharma naturally."[212]

Dōgen develops the notions of the use of birth-and-death, and of the surrender of birth-and-death to birth-and-death, as follows:

You should know this: Birth-and-death is the living of the Way; birth-and-death is the instrument for a Buddhist. If you wish to use it, you should use it; if you desire to clarify it, it shall be clarified. Thus Buddhas understand clearly its various conditions and are skillful in using it freely. If you are uninformed of conditions of this birth-and-death, who would address himself/herself to you as [the authentic] you? Who would call you a person who understands life lucidly and penetrates death thoroughly (*ryōshō-tasshi no kan*)? [Thus the following admonitions:] Do not listen to the view that human beings are ruined in life's wretchedness; do not think we find ourselves in birth-and-death; do not fail to understand [birth-and-death]; do not fail to discern [birth-and-death]. . . .

The great Way to understand life lucidly and penetrate death thoroughly, though it has been already well understood, has [further] a time-honored adage: The great sage surrenders (*makasu*) birth-and-death to the mind, surrenders birth-and-death to the body, surrenders birth-and-death to the Way, and surrenders birth-and-death to birth-and-death.[213]

To use freely and exert totally birth-and-death is the only way to penetrate it thoroughly and radically. Dōgen contends that there is no other way than "grasping it by practice" (*gyōshu*) in the spirit of surrender. In short, to use and to surrender (or we might say, self-power and other-power) are one and the same. This is the "reason of total surrender" (*ninnin no dōri*) which enables us to grasp by practice "our own home" (*jiko no kakyō*)—the nirvāṇa of birth-and-death.[214]

FIVE

Monastic Asceticism: The Way of Ritual and Morality

CULTIC and moral endeavors constitute one of the two foci of Dōgen's zazen-only (*shikan-taza*), the other being the philosophic and mythopoeic ones which we have considered in the preceding chapter. Dōgen, in the latter part of his life, seems to have become more and more involved with the former orientation, through the establishment of a monastic community, as well as the education of monastics by the passionate pursuit of a very rigorous and "puritanic" monastic asceticism.

When Dōgen returned from China in 1227, he immediately wrote *Fukan-zazengi*, in which he attempted to correct the errors and shortcomings of Tsung-che in his *Ch'an-yüan ch'ing-kuei*, and, thereby to restore the spirit of the monastic ideal envisioned by Po-chang Huai-hai. Here, once again, we see Dōgen's fascination with, and aspiration to, the classical period of Zen history. He finally retreated from Kyōto to Echizen in 1243 and embarked upon the ambitious enterprise of establishing an ideal monastic community of the Eiheiji temple in this remote region.

A deep love for the ascetic life unified these two periods in Dōgen's life. The second, the Echizen period, was marked by a more intensive and full-fledged monastic asceticism; the emotion and philosophy which motivated Dōgen at this time were fundamentally the same. For this reason, this period can be seen as a total retreat from the world, only in the most superficial sense; actually, it was Dōgen's method of coping with his sense of pessimism as regards the practicability of universal monasticism in the intractable secular context. He became entirely concerned with the education of a select few in order to exemplify his vision of an ideal community as a challenge to the world. In this regard, his and his followers' ascetic endeavors were as intensely and passionately social as they were personal. Indeed they were intended to transform the world as well as the self.

Background of Zen Monasticism

The origins of Zen monasticism in China are rather obscure at the present state of our knowledge in this area. According to a very reliable reconstruction,[1] there was no formation of a communal life among the Zen followers of Bodhidharma (d. 532)—the last of twenty-eight Indian ancestors and the first ancestor of Chinese Zen, according to the official Zen account—up until the third ancestor Sêng-ts'an (d. 606). Zen teachers themselves engaged in the ascetic practices of the mendicant's life and had no fixed place where they could gather for a corporate life with their disciples. However, the situation was significantly changed at the time of Tao-hsin (580–651) and Hung-jên (601–674), the fourth and fifth ancestors, respectively, each of whom settled at a fixed place and established a monastic community having economic self-sufficiency. Each of them is said to have had some five hundred disciples who cooperated in the maintenance of their communal life. In those days governmental aids were not available, lay believers' contributions were scarce, and the mendicant's life impracticable, if not impossible, in the Chinese environment. These special circumstances led Zen Buddhists to self-supporting activities such as the cultivation of land for growing grains and vegetables, woodcutting, water-carrying, and so forth. Such a life was evidently a violation of the Buddhist vinaya, yet this was the beginning of sinicization of monastic life.[2] Thus various observances, rules, and regulations were established for the maintenance of a corporate life. Such a practical change also led the monastics to regard manual labor as spiritual discipline; Zen was now equated with every aspect of daily living. The scriptural teachings were interpreted according to the spirit rather than the letter. In addition, Zen was opened up to the laity in general.[3]

Po-chang Huai-hai, though often said to be the originator of Zen monasticism (*sōrin kaibyaku no so*), was not in fact the originator, as the foregoing cursory observations reveal, but, rather, the sys-tematizer of the rules and practices of Zen monasteries started by Tao-hsin. Not until Po-chang, however, was the sinicization and in-stitutional independence of Zen completed, along with Hui-nêng's doctrinal revolution of Zen thought; prior to that time Zen had re-mained tied to the vinaya monasteries, and, hence, its identity had been rather ambiguous. Po-chang's originality was, thus, not doc-trinal so much as institutional. He succeeded in synthesizing the Hīnayāna vinaya as well as the Mahāyāna vinaya, and in going beyond them to produce a uniquely Chinese Zen monasticism.[4]

Unlike the customary way of building a Buddha hall, Po-chang built a Dharma hall where the monastic head delivered lectures and sermons before the congregation. The Dharma hall was greatly em-phasized here. In addition, there were the monastic head's living quarters, the monastics' hall where trainees carried out their medita-tion, eating, and sleeping, and an administrative building. In the morning the monastics had individual interviews with their teacher for spiritual counseling and in the evening the monastic head gave lectures before the assembly in the Dharma hall. Along with medita-tional sessions they engaged in manual labor (*tso-wu*; *samu*) for the maintenance of economic sufficiency. A famous saying of Po-chang's states, "a day without work—a day without eating"; he himself abided by it rigorously. Po-chang appointed ten monastic officers and had them oversee the monastic affairs through regulations. Strict punish-ments were instituted for those who disturbed the harmony and peace of the monastery or violated its rules. These regulations were codified by Po-chang for the first time in the history of Chinese Zen. These were some characteristics of Po-chang's envisionment of the monastic community which distinguished Zen thereafter from all other schools and sects of Buddhism in China. Po-chang's greatest contribution was his articulation of the Zen spirit in and through moral disciplines and spiritual practices (*ch'ing-kuei*; *shingi*).[5]

The streak of classicism in Dōgen's thought is evident in his enthu-siasm and admiration for Po-chang's monastic ideal. Dōgen admon-ished the students of Buddhism to observe the regulations and pre-cepts of Po-chang with great diligence: "The Buddhist student should observe Po-chang's monastic rules with the utmost care."[6] As we have noted before and will see again presently, Dōgen aspired to the realization of this monastic ideal on Japanese soil, and was the first, in the history of Japanese Zen Buddhism, to succeed in this. The Kōshō-hōrinji temple, founded by Dōgen in 1233, thus, had historic significance in that it was the first attempt ever made by the Japanese to establish "pure Zen" (*junsui-zen*) clearly distinguished, not only from other non-Zen schools of Buddhism, but from "mixed Zen" (*kenju-zen*) the most common Japanese Zen in those days.[7] One example of mixed Zen was Eisai, the founder of the Kenninji temple. Despite Dōgen's insistence on pure Zen, he conceived it in a particularly Japanese context, and wherever and whenever necessary, did not hesitate to modify it. For example, when someone asked him whether a monastic should beg for alms or not, Dōgen replied:

Yes, you should. The resolution of this matter, however, must take into consideration the climate and customs [of a country]. In any event, you should espouse the extension of other beings' benefits and the development of your own practice. If you walk wearing the robe along roads that are soiled, such a practice is bound to make your robe dirty. Moreover, because of the poverty of the people, the prescribed way of begging [at seven houses] may not be practicable. Accordingly, your practice of the Way may retrograde, and benefits to others may be impeded. If you observe the customs of the country and practice the Way in a proper manner, people in all walks of life will offer alms unassumingly, and, hence, the well-being of the self and others will be realized. As regards problems like this, while you are confronted with particular occasions and circumstances, you should ponder upon reasonableness, disregard what others may think of you, forget about your own gains, and endeavor in whatever way to serve the Way as well as the good of all sentient beings.[8]

As I have previously noted, Dōgen's treatment of Tsung-che's *Ch'an-yüan ch'ing-kuei* reflects a similar critical attitude. Mention of other examples will be made later as our investigation proceeds.

At this juncture it is worthwhile for us to recall some of the historical circumstances under which Dōgen's thought, especially his monastic rigorism, developed. Dōgen's original question on Mt. Hiei, as we saw before, was concerned with the doctrines of original enlightenment and of this-body-itself-is-Buddha, which became the ideological foundation of the moral and religious crisis of the time. Coupled with the general ethos of the Age of Degenerate Law, these doctrines led too readily to the absolutization of the given, the pervasive sense of cynicism and fatalism, and moral complacency. Thus the late Heian and early Kamakura periods abounded with such examples as: the accumulation of wealth and properties by powerful monastics; the establishment by aristocrats of private temples for their personal and familial benefits; the degeneration into magic of esoteric Buddhism; fashionable trend of aristocrats becoming monastics (ironically enough) in order to secure worldly success; the institution of armed monastics contrary to the pacifist spirit of Buddhism; and indulgence in aesthetic hedonism, to mention only a few.

Under these circumstances there emerged two different schools of thought concerning Buddhist precepts (*kairitsu*) in the Kamakura period. One advocated the observance of the precepts as primary in Buddhism, whereas the other school repudiated this, or at best regarded observance of the precepts as secondary to the supremacy of faith. Roughly speaking, the former school of thought was associated with Zen Buddhism, the latter with Pure Realm Buddhism. These two trends existed side by side in Kamakura Buddhism.[9] Needless to say, Dōgen belonged to the former tradition, as did Myōan Eisai, who was equally eager to restore unremitting observance of the precepts—in his case both the Mahāyāna and Hīnayāna precepts.[10] As a matter of fact, the hallmark of Kamakura Zen was the advocacy of the "primacy of precepts" (*kairitsu-isen*) as well as of the "unity of meditation and precepts" (*zenkai-itchi*). Both Eisai and Dōgen concurred on this fundamental point of Zen Buddhism. Nevertheless, there were significant differences between them in several respects.[11] Very briefly stated, they were: (1) Dōgen advocated pure Zen, while Eisai advocated mixed Zen combined with the esoteric Buddhism of the time;[12] (2) Dōgen was more intent on the codification of the monastic rules and regulations than Eisai; (3) Dōgen interpreted the precepts in the context of his conception of zazen-only and subsumed them in it; hence, he was critical of both Eisai's view of the precepts and the vinaya Buddhist view of the precepts, both of which regarded them as more or less independent of zazen; (4) Dōgen adopted only the bodhisattva (Mahāyāna) precepts as necessary and sufficient, whereas Eisai advocated both the bodhisattva precepts and the Hīnayāna precepts; and (5) the two conceived of the relationship between the bodhisattva precepts and the monastic rules differently: while Dōgen tried to implement the precepts in the rules by codifying the details of the monastics' daily behaviors, Eisai did not.

The last statement is particularly significant for the purpose of our investigation, because it refers to the heart of Dōgen's thought: the ritualization of morality. A prime characteristic of Dōgen's thought lies in his passionate search for the translation of moral visions— hence spiritual visions—into the daily activities of monastic life, as we shall see presently in what follows. How he differs from his Chinese as well as Japanese predecessors and contemporaries bears upon this fact—moral visions made concrete and routine in the daily behavior and activities of the monastics. Scrupulous instructions, exhortations, and admonitions with respect to rules, manners, virtues, and behavior, are not codes that bind the monastics' outward movements, but are ritualized expressions and activities of Buddha-nature and absolute emptiness. Here we see the fundamental character of Dōgen's mystical realism far from any kind of pedantic moralism.

Purity and Purification

The themes of purity and purification occupy a vitally important place in Dōgen's thought. In two major chapters of *Shōbōgenzō*, namely, "Semmen" and "Senjō," Dōgen expounds, admonishes, and elaborates, meticulously and fastidiously, the rules, prescriptions, and instructions concerning washing the face, bathing the body, using the latrine, washing the robes and bowls, cleansing the mouth and the teeth and the tongue, taking care of fingernails and toes and hair, and even the acts of urination and excretion. All these cleansing activities—undoubtedly some may be prone to view this as an obsession with cleanliness—constitute an integral part of the right Dharma of the Buddhas and ancestors:

In the Buddha-dharma the principles of cleansing with water are always prescribed. To wash the body, to wash the mind, to wash the feet, to wash the face, to wash the eyes, to wash the mouth, to wash after the two acts of urination and excretion, to wash hands, to wash a bowl, to wash a robe, or to wash the head—all these acts comprise the right Dharma of the Buddhas and ancestors of the three periods.[13]

Instead of going into all the details of these prescriptions, I wish to illustrate with just a few examples. Dōgen enjoins monastics to follow Buddha's advice (though the source is not clear) for bathing and incense burning. Monastics bathe their whole bodies in water, wear clothes as usual after the bathing, kindle incense in small incense burner and fumigate their bosoms, the robes, the seats, and so forth. This cycle of bathing and fumigation is repeated three times, and it is followed by obeisance to Buddha, silent sūtra reading, zazen, and walking after zazen. Before they resume zazen, the monastics should wash their feet.[14] Dōgen was very proud of adding the washroom (*goka*) to the monastics' hall for the purpose of washing the face, and especially for cleaning the teeth, which he greatly stressed. Dōgen writes on this matter:

Although in the Zen monasteries of great Sung nowadays the use of the wooden tooth cleaner has gone out of fashion and has not been transmitted for a long time, and, hence, no place for it is provided, there is now a place for the use of the wooden tooth cleaner here at the Eiheiji temple on Mt. Kichijō. This is my new idea.[15]

Dōgen's enthusiasm about this matter, perhaps in direct proportion to his disappointment in China, which was strongly expressed, is such that he traces the use of the wooden tooth cleaner (*yōji* or *shimoku*) to the *Brahmajāla sūtra* where it is one of the eighteen belongings (*jūhachi-motsu*) of a Mahāyāna monastic, declaring that "those who understand the meaning of the use or nonuse of this tooth cleaner are the bodhisattvas who understand the Buddha-dharma."[16] When monastics use the tooth cleaner, they should recite the following gāthās:

> Holding the wooden tooth cleaner,
> May I vow with sentient beings,
> To attain the right Dharma
> And purity spontaneously.

And then:

> Using the wooden tooth cleaner every morning,
> May I vow with sentient beings,
> To attain teeth strong enough
> To gnaw away all illusions.[17]

Dōgen also underscores the importance of not growing long hair or long fingernails and toenails. Here again, Dōgen recounts his experience with the widespread practice of monastics in China to grow long hair and long fingernails, and denounces them as heretics.[18] Manners in the latrine (*tōsu*) are also minutely specified. Monastics are instructed to keep the latrine clean and tidy, to be silent, abstaining from singing songs or conversing with the person next to them, to be reverential and courteous to others waiting for their turns, and so on. Dōgen's instructions are lengthy and scrupulous, yet we cannot fail to appreciate his compassionate concern for the harmony and peace of the monastic community and the mutual benefits of its members, and thereby for the sacredness of admittedly insignificant and ignoble activities in the latrine. Dōgen says that those with little learning in Buddhism think that activities in the latrine are not and cannot be the "majestic activities of the Buddhas and ancestors" (*busso no igi*), but this is wrong, says he, because their observation is based on the assumption that the defiled land (*edo*) of this world is not like the Pure Land (*jōdō*)—hence on a dualism. Dōgen compares the Pure Land with the defiled land of delusions and passions. This distinction, however, does not apply to the majestic activities of the Buddhas and ancestors.[19] Thus Dōgen boldly proclaims: "Buddha finds an opportunity to turn the wheel of the Dharma in the latrine."[20] I could go on enumerating the apparent excesses of minutiae almost indefinitely.

The foregoing observations on cleansing can be adequately understood only in the context of Dōgen's "metaphysic of purification" which is consistent with his general thought pattern. He opens the subject of cleansing with reference to the undefiled unity of enlightenment and practice. He writes:

Although the body and mind are undefiled, there is the truth of cleansing the body, and there is the truth of cleansing the mind. Not only do they purify the body-mind, but they purify even lands and trees. The lands never have been covered with dust and dirt, yet it is the desire of Buddhas to cleanse them. Attaining the fruit of enlightenment, they still do not retreat nor abandon. Such a supreme principle (*shūshi*) is difficult to comprehend. Ritual conduct (*sahō*) is the supreme principle; the realization of the Way is ritual conduct.[21]

Also he says:

In what we deem to be the genuine Dharma transmitted authentically through the Buddhas and ancestors, bathing the body, as it is put into action, cleanses instantly: both the inside and outside of the body-mind; the viscera; the personal and environmental rewards of karma; the inside, outside, and middle of the entire reality and the entire space. When you purify yourself by incense and flowers, the past, present, and future, all the karmic conditions, and all the activities of existence will be purified instantaneously.[22]

In the same vein Dōgen argues elsewhere:

As you bathe, even the four elements, even the five skandhas, and even the indestructible Dharma-nature can be clean and pure without exception. This should not be understood only to mean that undefiledness is attained after you cleanse the body with water. How can water be originally pure or originally impure? Even if it is originally pure or impure, you do not say it can make clean or unclean the place to which water eventually flows. Only when practice and enlightenment of the Buddhas and ancestors are maintained, has the Buddha-dharma of washing and bathing been imparted. As you practice and confirm bathing, according to this principle, you transcend purity, surpass impurity, and cast off neither undefilement nor defilement.

Thus in spite of being not yet defiled, you bathe your body; although you are already supremely pure, you cleanse yourself. This truth is preserved only in the Way of the Buddhas and ancestors. None of the heretics knows it.[23]

This amounts, in the final analysis, to saying: "By way of using emptiness, you cleanse emptiness; by way of moving emptiness, you bathe your body-mind."[24] Every act of cleansing and washing is not only ritualized, sacramentalized, and sanctified, but philosophized and rationalized in the unique logic of emptiness.

Purification is not an attempt to be liberated from pollutions, sins, or guilts, whether physical, moral, or spiritual, but the self-affirmation of original purity or emptiness undefiled by dualism. For it is neither removal of impurity nor seeking for purity—which means that one is defiled only by a belief in the dichotomous existence of purity and impurity. Thus, the act of purification is fundamentally based on original purity, being the self-enactment of the latter. Only when this is realized do the rites of purification embody the undefiled unity of enlightenment and practice.[25] This is why Dōgen says: "What is significant in this [cleansing] is not cleaning one's body with water so much as preserving the Buddha-dharma by the Buddha-dharma itself. This is called washing."[26] The body, the act of cleansing, and water comprise Dharma itself.

It is small wonder that Dōgen regards the rites of purification with the utmost seriousness. He warns his disciples against the common-sense view that bathing is nothing but the cleansing of the bodily surface; on the contrary, it is a rite in and through which the three periods and the ten quarters of the universe, the Buddhas and ancestors, the interior and the exterior of the body-mind, the vital organs, all existences—spiritual and temporal, and even beyond space and time—are purified. For this reason, the Pure Land, the sublime Buddha-land, is actualized here and now on this earth.[27] Dōgen's seriousness about this subject is well reflected in the fact that he presented and explicated the "Semmen" chapter of *Shōbōgenzō* on three different occasions—an emphasis unique to that particular chapter of his book.[28]

The activities revolving around food, whether preparing meals or eating, are an integral part of the monastic life. The sanctity of these activities, manners, and attitudes with respect to preparing and taking the meals is well testified to in Dōgen's works. The monastic community has two main meals a day, the morning meal of gruel and the midday meal of cooked rice, with abstention from eating between midday and the following morning, though this is only in principle.[29] All the foods, prepared or taken, must be pure. Dōgen's concern with absolute poverty is reflected in this case as well. He says:

Three types of food—the fruits of trees and plants, food obtained from begging, and food donated by the devotees—all these are pure foods (*shōjō-jiki*). The four types of food obtained through the occupations of farmers, merchants, warriors and artisans are without exception impure foods (*fujō-jamyō no jiki*), not the monastics' foods.[30]

Dōgen also writes:

You should not arrange in advance for the supply of your clothing and food.

Even as regards the places of alms begging, to plan beforehand to beg at certain places or ask certain persons in case you should run out of food is tantamount to storing up provisions, and amounts to the defiled livelihood. Monastics are like the clouds and have no fixed abode; like flowing water, they have nothing to depend on—hence they are called monastics. Even if they possess nothing other than a bowl and a robe, to rely upon even one supporter or to have in mind even one household of relatives is neither more nor less than a bondage for the self and others alike; hence the food is impure.

If one whose body and mind are nourished by such unclean livelihood desires to attain and understand the great Dharma of Buddhas' purity, it is altogether impossible.[31]

It is not known how consistently Dōgen maintained his alleged economic independence or his interpretation of pure food with the ever-growing number of monastics in the Eiheiji temple. Nevertheless, I see Dōgen's absolute poverty as an ideal with respect to the problem of food and livelihood.[32]

In *Tenzo-kyōkun*, Dōgen takes this matter very seriously and gives minute instructions for his disciples, especially for the chief cook of the monastery. This is in line with his ideal of restoring the monastic vision of Po-chang Huai-hai in Japan, as we have noted on several occasions. Dōgen frequently refers to and quotes from Ch'ang-lu Tsung-che's *Ch'an-yüan ch'ing-kuei* for his guidance and inspiration, and also makes reference to Kuei-shan Ling-yu (771–853), Tung-shan

Shou-ch'u (?–990), and Hsüeh-fêng I-ts'un (822–908), who are said to have been chief cooks for some time. Following the Chinese monastic practice of the Sung period, Dōgen regarded the chief cook as one of the six highest officers (*chiji*) in the monastery; this was unheard of in Japan at that time.[33]

Drawing upon the *Ch'an-yüan ch'ing-kuei*, Dōgen sets forth the functions and responsibilities of chief cooks. First and foremost they are to nurture monastics and ensure their well-being and peace (*anraku*). Elsewhere, Dōgen uses the phrase the "act of nourishing the seeds of Buddha" (*shōtai chōyō no gō*). Chief cooks bear the full responsibility on their shoulders for nourishing monastics not only physically but also morally and spiritually. They are not just cooks or dieticians in the modern sense, but truly religious leaders. Every act of their duty is performed with the aspiration of enlightening and benefiting others (*dōshin*). This means, in the final analysis, that the monastic meals are not merely means to physical sustenance, or even to spiritual sustenance for that matter, but daily communal feasts that celebrate the enactment of the body-mind cast off and undefiled. Eating itself is a spiritual matter.[34]

Some significant highlights of the cook's responsibility may be illustrated: (1) Handling and cooking of grains and vegetables must be done with the utmost care and reverence: for example, the white water after washing rice should not wastefully be thrown away. The chief cook should inspect every minute process of food preparation with vigilance, sincerity, and diligence. Thus the chief cook must be adept in distinguishing the six kinds of taste (bitter, sour, sweet, hot, salty, and insipid) and possess the three virtues of cookery (mildness, cleanliness, and courteousness). Moreover, the chief cook must cultivate the joyous mind (*kishin*), joyous at the opportunity of human existence; the solicitous mind (*rōshin*), likened to the disposition of parents taking care of their children; and the magnanimous mind (*daishin*), unbiased and fair to all beings. (2) Immediately after the midday meal, the chief cook should consult with all other officers as to the menus and provisions for the next day, and announce the result on the bulletin boards in the monastic head's quarters and in the library. The implication is, obviously, that eating is the business of the entire commune. (3) The chief cook must live in the spirit of absolute poverty—absolute nonpossession—regardless of quality and quantity of food materials. "Day and night, things [grains, vegetables, etc.] come and live in the mind, and the mind returns to the things and dwells in them. Without discrimination both practice the Way together assiduously."[35] Richness is unlimited in such an absolute poverty. (4) When foods are prepared, the chief cook places them on the table in the kitchen, wears the surplice, spreads a rug on the ground, faces toward the monastics' hall (*sōdō*), burns incense and bows nine times. Only after this observance are foods carried to the monastics' hall for consumption. (5) In preparing a meal, the chief cook should not be concerned with delicacy but with dispositions of mind, no matter what materials are used. Dōgen writes:

It is not necessarily superior to prepare refined milk, so-called, of exquisite taste (*daigomi*), nor is it invariably inferior to cook a plain vegetable soup (*fusaikō*). When you pick up and choose a plain vegetable, do so with the mind of fidelity, sincerity, and purity, just as in the case of cooking the finest refined milk. The reason for this is that, just as hundreds of rivers run into an ocean, congregations in the great ocean of Dharma's purity neither see the taste of refined milk nor concern themselves with the taste of vegetable soup, but only with the taste of a single great ocean. In addition, in nourishing the buds of the Way (*dōge*) and nurturing the seeds of Buddha (*shōtai*), the refined milk and the plain vegetable are one thusness, not two. There is an ancient saying: "The mouth of a monastic is just like a furnace." You should keep this in mind. Reflect upon this: The plain vegetable feeds the seeds of Buddha and sustains the buds of the Way. You should not disdain or make light of it. Indeed, a spiritual leader of the heavenly worlds and of the human world is the one who is to execute the transforming efficacy [for sentient beings] of the plain vegetable.[36]

This transforming efficacy may be likened to "build[ing] a great temple by making use of grass, and turn[ing] the great wheel of Dharma by entering into a particle of dust." Dōgen further writes: "You hold a vegetable and change it into Buddha's body of one *jō* and six *shaku*, and invite Buddha and alter him into a vegetable. [The chief cook is] the one who brings forth miraculous powers and transformations, promoting Buddha's affairs and sentient beings' welfare."[37] This is precisely the religious-metaphysical significance of cookery as Dōgen conceived it. Lastly, (6) the monastic kitchen is often called "the department of fragrance" (*kōshakukyoku* or *kōjakukyoku*) in the Zen tradition; this reference is derived from the "Buddha-land of fragrance" where Tathāgata Kōjaku is said to reside. Dōgen admonishes his disciples to exercise the utmost reverence and the most courteous language in relation to food. Decorum and speech worthy of the department of fragrance are strongly recommended. Thus Dōgen urges monastics to use honorific expressions such as *on-kayu, on-toki, on-shiru,* and so forth, when speaking of gruel (*kayu*), cooked rice (*toki*) and soup (*shiru*), for example. The kitchen utensils must be handled respectfully. While preparing a meal, the monastic should recite scriptural passages or sayings of the ancestors, instead of worldly gossip.[38]

Receiving and taking a meal in the monastic's bowl (*gyōhatsu*) is a solemn and joyous occasion in monastic life. Monastics reflect upon the "gāthās of five meditations" (*gokan no ge*) which are: (1) indebtedness to the pains of the people who provide food, (2) consideration of whether the monastics deserve to receive the food, (3) restraint from greed and excessive eating, (4) conception of food as medicine to heal hunger and thirst and nourish the body, and (5) conception of food as taken for the sake of the Way and enlightenment.[39] What is most noteworthy in connection with the ritual of eating is Dōgen's "metaphysic of eating." He says the following:

It is said in a sūtra [*Vimalakīrti-nirdeśa sūtra*]: "When humans are enlightened in their eating, all things are enlightened as well; if all dharmas are nondual, we are also nondual in our eating."

Indeed, Dharma is identified with one's eating, and one's eating is identified with Dharma. For this reason, if Dharma is the Dharma-nature, a meal is also the Dharma-nature. If Dharma is thusness, food is likewise thusness. If Dharma is One Mind, a meal is also One Mind. Similarly, if Dharma is enlightenment, food is enlightenment. . . . Therefore, the act of eating constitutes the truth of all dharmas. This can be fully comprehended only by and among Buddhas. At the very moment when we eat, we are possessed of ultimate reality, essence, substance, energy, activity, causation. So Dharma is eating, and eating is Dharma. This Dharma is enjoyed by Buddhas of past and future. This eating is full of holy joy and ecstasy.[40]

Eating (*jiki*) is the celebration of Dharma (*hō*) with no hiatus between them in the samādhi of self-fulfilling activity (*jijuyū-zammai*) and in the samādhi of play (*yuge-zammai*).

Dōgen's treatment of the monastic's bowl (*hatsuu* or *hau*), originally the begging bowl, is also characteristic of his metaphysic of eating. He declares:

The Buddhist's bowl is the Buddhist's bowl—you should never regard it as [made of] stone or tile or iron or wood.

Indeed, the Buddha bowl is not an artifact: it neither arises nor perishes, neither comes nor goes, neither gains nor loses. It does not range over new or old, nor does it concern itself with past or present.[41]

The bowl is called a "miraculous utensil (*kidoku no chōdo*)—miraculous, because it is used in a "miraculous event" (*kidoku no koto*), in a "miraculous season" (*kidoku no jisetsu*), by a "miraculous person" (*kidoku no hito*). Thus: "On this account, where a miraculous event is realized, there is a miraculous bowl."[42]

Absolute simplicity, poverty, and purity are also epitomized in Dōgen's treatment of the monastic's robes. Traditionally, the Buddhist monastic is allowed to possess only three robes, called "tattered robes" (*funzōe* or *nōe*) because they are made of dirty, useless rags thrown away by the common people. The lowliest material, symbolic of worldly defilement, is transformed into the monastic's robes (*kesa*), the symbol of purity.[43] "What the world abandons, the Way uses."[44] And Dōgen writes:

Such materials, obtained from discarded clothes and/or through undefiled livelihood, are neither silk nor cotton. They are not gold or silver, not gems or brocades, or the like; they are nothing other than tattered clothes. This tattered robe is neither for shabbiness nor for finery, but only for the Buddha-dharma.[45]

Again and again Dōgen exalts the mysterious merits and efficacies of the robe.[46] He observes that the monastic's robe is called the "robe of liberation" (*gedatsu-buku*), the "robe of blessing-field" (*fukuden'e*), the "robe of no-thought" (*musōe*), the "robe of great compassion" (*daiji-daihi-e*), and so on. The robe of liberation is the body-mind of the Buddhas and ancestors. He exalts the so-called "ten victories" or merits of the monastic's robe—for example, the covering and protection of the body. Furthermore, the robe is the symbol of Buddha's purity (*hyōshiki*) in destroying, for the monastic as well as for others, passions, delusions, greed, and guilt.[47]

Dōgen gives detailed instructions as to how to make, wear, and wash robes and what materials to choose for them. When monastics wear, take off, or wash their robes, they are advised to place them on their heads and recite, with the hands in gasshō, the following gāthā:

> Great is the robe of liberation,
> The robe of blessing-field and of no-thought.
> Wearing it, we shall uphold the teachings
>   of Tathāgata,
> And liberate all sentient beings.[48]

In Dōgen's thought, even the matter of monastics' clothing had metaphysical significance, as we have seen. To Dōgen what one wears is what one is. Unless this is the case, purity is not total and complete. As we have mentioned already, a monastic's robe, which is "tattered," is a monastic's robe which assumes a revolutionary significance, precisely because it does not depend on purity and defilement, or "silk and cotton." The tattered robe is undefiled by the duality of purity and impurity and of finery and shabbiness. Dōgen writes, for instance:

For the clothing materials, you use silk or cotton according to circumstances. Cotton is not necessarily pure nor is silk impure. There is no reason why you should dislike cotton and select silk. It is a laughable thing to do. Buddhas' unchanging principle is always that the tattered clothes are best. . . . Rejecting a [dualistic] view of silk and cotton, you must penetrate into the meaning of "tattered." . . .

You should understand this: Among the tattered clothes a monastic picks up may be the cotton materials that resemble the silk ones, or the silk fabrics that look like the cotton ones. The people are all different, and what they make and wear are hard to imagine. Your naked eyes cannot figure them out well. Upon obtaining some such materials, you shall not argue over whether they are silk or cotton: they shall be called the tattered fabrics. . . . When you accept faithfully the truth that the tattered robe is neither silk nor cotton, neither gold-silver nor gems, such will be realized. Unless the dualistic understanding of silk and cotton is cast off, the tattered robe will not even be dreamed of.[49]

Elsewhere, Dōgen holds: "This [purity] not only surpasses the limits of purity and defilement, but transcends the realm of enlightenment and delusion. It does not contend with the dualism of form and mind; it has no bearing upon merits or demerits."[50] This purity is not a matter of clothes but of being; the monastic's tattered robe is the embodiment of this being. Dōgen's import is not a critique of materialism over against spiritualism; though severe indictments of the materialism of the worldly minded in Kyōto and Kamakura in those days are by no means lacking in his writings. It is abundantly clear to us by now that Dōgen almost despaired of the insatiable and inveterate search for fame, wealth, power, knowledge, and so forth. Yet he himself did not fall into this pitfall of worldliness. The nondualistic metaphysic of clothing makes possible absolute freedom from greed and delusion in material as well as spiritual life.

Zen monastics are called "clouds and water" (*unsui*), symbolizing their homelessness (*shukke*) and possession of only absolutely minimal necessities and belongings like floating clouds and flowing water.

"Monastics are like the clouds and have no fixed abode; like flowing water, they have nothing to depend on—hence they are called monastics."⁵¹ The monastic dwelling for the community of monks and nuns, therefore, must be consistent with this ideal of poverty, simplicity, and purity. As in other cases, Dōgen exalts the ancient tradition of living under a tree and in the forest, asserting its continuity in Zen monasticism.⁵² For example, Ejō put the following speech in Dōgen's mouth in *Shōbōgenzō zuimonki*:

Dōgen said: "When Zen teacher Fang-hui [992–1049] of Mt. Yang-ch'i became the head of the monastery, its buildings were so dilapidated that the monastics were quite worried about them. Then the officer in charge of the matter recommended to him: 'The buildings should be repaired.' Fang-hui said: 'Even though the buildings are crumbling, it is still better than living in the open air or under the trees. If one place is damaged and the rain leaks in, you should sit in another where the rain does not leak in and practice zazen. If monastics' enlightenment is dependent on building temples and edifices, they should be built even with gold and gems. Enlightenment does not depend on the features of your dwelling-place but solely on the quality of merits of zazen.' The next day he preached as follows: 'When Yang-ch'i first became the monastery's head, the roofs and walls were falling to pieces. The rare gems of snow were scattered all over the floors, and the monastics ducked their heads and sighed in lamentation. We thought all the more of ancient sages who lived under the trees.'

"This is true not only of the Buddha-way but also of the way of government. Emperor T'ai-tsung [of the T'ang dynasty] did not build a new palace [but lived in the old one instead].

"Lung-ya Chü-tun [835–923] once said: 'To study the Way, it is imperative that you learn poverty before everything. Only after you study poverty and become poor can you become intimate with the Way.' Ever since the time of Buddha till today we have neither seen nor heard of any true student of the Way in possession of wealth."⁵³

Elsewhere, Dōgen admonishes his disciples in connection with his exaltation of the deeds of Kuei-shan Ling-yu (771–853):

Even when you want to build temples, do not exercise human judgments, but strengthen the practice and preservation of Dharma. The ancient Buddhas' training hall was comprised of spiritual discipline, not of temples or edifices. The tradition of living in the open air and under the trees reverberates from a distance. Such places have become the boundaries [of the training hall] for ages. When there is even a single person's spiritual practice, it is imparted to the training hall of Buddhas. So, fools of these latter days, don't be obsessed uselessly with the architectural splendors of temples. The Buddhas and ancestors have never desired temples and pavilions. Aimlessly erecting temples, edifices, and monasteries without clearing your own eyes, you do not consecrate abodes to Buddhas at all, but use them as the caves of your own fame and wealth.[54]

Idealizing a shabby hut or a poor thatched cottage, which to him was most consistent with the tradition of living in the open air and under a tree, Dōgen considered that such a shelter was essentially the training hall (*dōjō*—literally, "the field of the Way"), with a boundary (*kekkai*) founded upon absolute emptiness. The sanctity of this boundary signified not so much a dualism of the sacred and profane as an expression of the nonduality of emptiness. Paradoxically, this boundary was an expression of boundary-less-ness. As Dōgen writes, "When a quarter of land forms a boundary, the entire reality is completely joined by it."[55] Moreover, the dwelling he proposed was the prototype for both monastics and laity: "The ancients lived under the trees and dwelled in the forest. Such is the abode both lay people and monastics love."[56]

The Zen monastery (*sōrin* or *zenrin*) was patterned after the ideal of a primitive Buddhist settlement (*vihāra*; *shōja*), culminating in Zen Buddhism in the form of seven halls (*shichidō-garan*). We are told: "The layout and structure of what we now call a Zen monastery are nothing other than the personal instruction of the ancestors, hence the direct transmission of the right heirs [of the Way]. Thus, the Seven Buddhas' old rule is entirely embodied in a Zen monastery."[57] And: "If you plan to build a training hall or establish a monastery, you shall follow the principles rightly transmitted by the Buddhas and ancestors."[58] From these statements we can reasonably conjecture that Dōgen was faithful to the basic building pattern of the Zen monastery, particularly that of the Ching-tê-ssŭ monastery on Mt. T'ien-t'ung, where he had studied previously.[59]

The basic layout of a seven-hall monastery consists of the entrance (*sammon*), the Buddha hall (*butsuden*), the Dharma hall (*hattō*)—in ascending order on the central axis—and, the latrine (*tōsu* or *shiijin*), the bath (*yokushitsu* or *yūshitsu*), the monastics' hall (*sōdō*), and the kitchen (*kuri* or *kuin*)—on both sides of the axis. These halls are connected with each other by corridors. The entrance to the monastery is called the "mountain gate" (*sammon*), symbolizing the entrance into the realm of purity, liberation, and emptiness through the purging of passions and delusions. It is also called the "three gates" (*sammon*) or the "gate of threefold liberation" (*san-gedatsu-mon*). The Buddha hall is designed for the worship of the image of Śākyamuni Buddha and his two attendant bodhisattvas: Mañjuśrī (Monju) to his left and Samantabhadra (Fugen) to his right. The Dharma hall, behind the Buddha hall, is the place where lectures and sermons are given by the monastic head to the monks and nuns. Between the entrance and the Buddha hall are situated the bath to the right and the latrine to the left, both of which epitomize the purification of bodily defilement; the use of these two is minutely specified as we have discussed before. The activities in the bath and the latrine are the rites of purification. Above these buildings are the monastics' hall to the left and the kitchen to the right—both symbolizing the nourishment of mind and body. This design is analogous to the human body.[60] Or, more in line with Dōgen's thought, the physical layout of the monastery is designed for the casting-off of the body-mind. Incidentally, the monastics are ordered to be silent in the monastics' hall, the bath, and the latrine; thus they are called the "three halls of silence" (*sammokudō*).

The actual buildings of the monastery are more than these seven halls, because there are other additions to them. At the top of the central axis is the monastic head's quarters (*hōjō*), for example. Also prominent in the Sōtō tradition are the washroom (*goka*), at the back of the monastics' hall, and the library (*shuryō*) where monastics study the sūtras and classics. These edifices are the functional equivalent of the shabby huts and poor thatched cottages which were the habitats of the ancient sages.

What distinguishes Dōgen's Sōtō tradition from other Zen traditions, with respect to the problem of monastic building, is twofold: the restoration of the monastics' hall, and the emphasis on the monastic library. Dōgen's conception of the monastic ideal of Po-chang Huai-hai revolved around the monastics' hall where trainees not only meditated but ate and slept—that is, carried out their daily activities. When he founded the Kōshō-hōrinji temple, with the building of the monastics' hall in 1236, this was the first instance in Japan of the Zen monastic tradition of Po-chang, which regarded the monastics' hall as the center of the monastery.[61] In the tradition of the meditation hall (*zendō*) arrangement, sleeping and eating are done in separate halls; the meditation hall is used strictly for zazen.[62] Therefore, there are considerable structural differences between the monastics' hall and the meditation hall.

In the monastics' hall, each trainee is assigned to a seat (*zashō*) which occupies an absolutely minimal space for meditation, eating, and sleeping, and which is provided with a small closet (*kanki*) where belongings are stored, and which includes a portion of the edge of the seat (*jōen*), serving as both a table for meals and as a place to lay the head for sleep. The monastics' hall enshrines Mañjuśri as the holy mentor (*shōsō*)—not as an attendant of Śākyamuni Buddha, as we see in the Buddha hall, but as a spiritual guide for monastics. Also, the monastics' hall is annexed to the washroom which was restored by Dōgen as the place for washing face and hands, particularly for cleansing the teeth with the wooden tooth cleaner. As we have noted, Dōgen was especially proud of restoring the washroom.

Another important place for the monastic life is the library (*shuryō*) where the monastics engage in silent reading of Buddhist sūtras and Zen classics. (It was also used for occasional tea drinking and other activities, but they were secondary.) It represented the academic side of the monastic life, but certainly did not encourage a purely academic or scholarly pursuit of scriptural and doctrinal studies of Buddhism, as we shall see later in a different context. Its function was to guide monastics to reflect upon their minds and hearts, through the study of sūtras, in accordance with a family precept (*kakun*) of Zen, that is, "the teaching of the ancient sages as a guide to the illumination of the mind" (*kokyō-shōshin*). This enterprise was carried out around the image of Avalokiteśvara (Kannon) as the "holy monastic of the library" (*shuryō no shōsō*) who is enshrined in it. As Miyasaka points out, the monastic library was separated from the monastics' hall probably during the Southern Sung period (1127–1279) when each major monastery in China had a large-scale library, indicating the rigor of scriptural studies in those days—an important factor that should not be forgotten. Dōgen's introduction of the monastic library in Japan, after the pattern of Chinese Zen, became the precursor of Zen educational institutions in the modern period of Japan.[63]

Nature: The Mountains and Waters

Dōgen once wrote:

From the timeless beginning have mountains been the habitat of great sagas. Wise ones and holy persons have all made mountains their secret chambers and their bodies and minds; by them mountains are fulfilled. . . . When sages and wise ones reside in mountains, mountains belong to them [i.e., there is no hiatus between them and mountains], and therefore trees and

rocks reside in their luxuriance, birds and animals are full of divine aus-
piciousness. This is so precisely because they are transfigured by the virtues
of these sages and wise ones.

You must know this: It truly is that mountains favor wise ones and are
fond of sages.[64]

Dōgen chose a monastery near the mountains and waters (*sansui*) instead of near a city, with its worldly people and their activities. However, Dōgen's relationship to "the mountains and waters" is not the
romantic exaltation of them which we see, for example, in the religion of nature mysticism, any more than it is the scientific and technological manipulation and exploitation of nature. Temperamentally
and culturally, Dōgen could not think of religion other than in the
context of the mountains and waters; yet this was not the same as the
naive veneration or exaltation of nature, which was to him a defiled
view of nature, enslaving humans in a new captivity. Hence, he was
not a sort of nature mystic, as we shall show in what follows.

In *Shōbōgenzō*, "Mujō-seppō," Dōgen presents a rather unusual
view of nature. Speaking of "discourse on Dharma" (*seppō*) and "insentient beings" (*mujō*) in an extraordinary way, similar to his approach to other words and symbols, he writes:

The way insentient beings expound Dharma should not be understood to be
necessarily like the way sentient beings expound Dharma. The voices of sentient beings should follow the principle of their discourse on Dharma.

Even so, it is contrary to the Buddha-way to usurp the voices of the living
and conjecture about those of the nonliving in terms of them. . . . Even
though our judgment now tries to recognize grasses, trees, and the like, and
liken them to nonliving things, they too cannot be measured by the ordinary mind.[65]

Insentient beings are often conceived of as comprising the physical
universe, or what we call nature, which we think of as actually dead,
and only figuratively and anthropomorphically speak of in human
terms. Human beings, unwittingly or selfishly, anthropomorphize
nature but think that nature is, after all, lifeless. To put it another way,
we draw a boundary between the sentient and the insentient, to the
degree that we perceive and judge in a particular way with a particular
nature. This might lead us to judge that the insentient is not able
to communicate. Dōgen revolts against such a conception of nature. From the standpoint of the Way, insentient beings do elucidate
Dharma, not in human languages but in their own expressions (*dō-*

toku). Hence, they are "alive" in their own way; in Dōgen's phraseology, the insentient beings are "sentient."[66] In line with his thesis that all existence is sentient beings, which we have examined earlier in this study, Dōgen's use of the term "sentient beings" (*shujō* or *ujō*) here subsumes both the sentient and the insentient, constituting all existence and, in turn, being one with Buddha-nature (*shitsuu-busshō*). This is not the same as confounding the two as having a certain psychic commonality, in the fashion of panpsychism, but, rather, entails seeing them within the context of Buddha-nature, which defies any metaphysical commitment to such a substantialistic resolution.

Dōgen tells the story of Su Tung-p'o (1036–1101), a well-known Sung poet of China, who was enlightened one night by the sounds of brooks. The occasion is explained by Dōgen himself: One day Chao-chio Ch'ang-tsung (1025–1091), the Zen mentor of the poet, preached on the discourse of insentient beings and its great importance for poetic creativity, but Su Tung-p'o could not quite understand its full significance. One day when Su Tung-p'o visited the famous resort of Lu-shan and spent a night there, he was suddenly awakened by the sounds of mountain brooks flowing in the silence of the night. This was the moment of his enlightenment; he composed the following poem:

> Sounds of brooks are nothing but a gigantic tongue
> [i.e., Buddha's discourse on Dharma],
> Figures of mountains are none other than Buddha's body of purity;
> Eighty-four thousand gāthās since last night—
> How shall I explain them to others at another time?[67]

And Dōgen comments:

The night when this lay poet was enlightened is [related to the fact] that previously he heard from Teacher Ch'ang-tsung about insentient beings' sermons on Dharma. Although he was not immediately enlightened by his teacher's discourse, the sounds of currents struck him as if raging waves were soaring into the sky. Thus the sounds of streams now awaken Su Tung-p'o. Is this the working of the brooks' sounds, or is it Chao-chio's discourse flowing into [the ears of Su Tung-p'o]? I suspect that Chao-chio's talk on the sermon of insentient beings, still reverberating, may secretly be intermingled with the nightly sounds of streams. Dare anyone say that this is a pint of water, or an ocean into which all rivers enter? Ultimately speaking, is it the poet that is enlightened, or is it mountains and waters that are enlightened? Those who have discerning eyes should apprehend the gigantic tongue and the body of purity.[68]

Here, Chao-chio's discourse and the sounds of brooks are inseparably interfused so as to make Su Tung-p'o's enlightenment possible. As Dōgen observed, it is very diifficult to say whether this is Su Tung-p'o's enlightenment or the enlightenment of the mountains and waters.[69] Humanity and nature, however, mutually partake of each other and co-work with one another as the twin activities of Buddha-nature and emptiness; they are not two separate entities, but one. Nature is alive in its own right and speaks to us through its own expressions. Thus:

When you endeavor in right practice, the voices and figures of streams and the sounds and shapes of mountains, together with you, bounteously deliver eighty-four thousand gāthās. Just as you are unsparing in surrendering fame and wealth and the body-mind, so are the brooks and mountains.[70]

In short, humans and nature co-work and co-create "eighty-four thousand gāthās" by being enlightened together and by becoming Buddha contemporaneously.

Dōgen deals with many subjects of nature in his works, such as mountains, waters, flowers, the moon, the four seasons, and so on. However, he uses these quite common words or metaphors in a unique way, in that their ordinary meanings are not extended or expanded to describe extraordinary events other than themselves; instead, their ordinary meanings are radicalized through the logic of the total exertion of a single thing (*ippō-gūjin*) within his mystical realist framework. A mountain, for example, is affirmed not in the ordinary sense of the mountain as an object of knowing by a subject; a mountain, which can be perceptually or intellectually manipulated, is not the mountain Dōgen has in mind. He says:

You must know this: Mountains are neither the human world nor the heavenly world. Do not judge mountains by human standards. If you do not apply human standards to them, who can entertain a doubt about the flowing or nonflowing of mountains?[71]

In the radical living of total exertion, the ordinary metaphor of a mountain is undefiled by subject-object dualism and realizes the totality of the universe in the single moment or event of thusness. This total exertion is the choosing of one thing at a time, to live in its total thusness—nothing else. This is why Dōgen quotes the following from Yün-mên Wên-yen (864–949): "A mountain is a mountain; water is water." This statement represents the essence of Zen itself. It is a special way of life that renders, to nonhuman and nonliving beings, their full-fledged metaphysical and religious status, and sees to it that these insentient beings are, ultimately speaking, regarded as neither sentient nor insentient, neither created nor uncreated, just like human beings. After all, all existence is empty, and unobtainable (*fukatoku*), in Dōgen's thought.[72]

The logical structure of Dōgen's view of nature, explained above, can be amply substantiated by illustrations from his works. Dōgen writes:

Consequently, water is the palace of a true dragon [the truly enlightened]. It is not that which flows down. To regard water as flowing only [which has also, in Chinese, the meaning of sinking down in fortune] is tantamount to slandering water. In other words, [that position] will force you to say not-flowing. Water is water only in its thusness and ultimate reality (*nyoze-jissō*): this is the merit of "water is water." It is not flowing. As you penetrate the flowing and not-flowing of water, the ultimate character of all things is instantly realized.[73]

Inasmuch as water, here, is not ordinary water as we speak of it in ordinary conversation, it is "absolute water," so to speak. For this reason, Dōgen holds that water may "flow up"; thus, water flows up and down, freely in all directions.[74] Water, as we perceive and name it, is dependent on the conditions and causes that constitute the situation of functional interdependence, in which we happen to live. By the same token, a fish sees water as a palace, a heavenly being as a riviere, a hungry demon as raging flames or thick blood. What we designate as water, is seen differently by a fish, a demon, and a heavenly being.[75] Hence, the water in question is not that water which we name, but that water—empty and indeterminate—out of which all these possibilities are created according to given conditions and causes. Primordial water in its emptiness is what Dōgen apprehends in and through ordinary water. Dōgen writes: "Water is neither strong nor weak, neither wet nor dry, neither dynamic nor static. Nor is it warm or cold, being or nonbeing, enlightenment or delusion."[76] It goes without saying that such an absolute water, or Water, is not the denial of ordinary water so much as the radicalization of it in its total exertion.

Having such a perspective, Dōgen was not disquieted by such statements as "an eastern mountain walks on the water."[77] The miraculous and the extraordinary were quite natural from his standpoint.

The "love" of nature, in Dōgen's thought, is not a deification of nature, but the radicalization of nature—nature in its selflessness. Only then is nature undefiled and natural. This is the reason that Dōgen was not inhibited from making such fantastic statements as "mountains ride on the clouds and walk in the heavens."[78] The mountains and waters become absolutely ordinary only in their thusness.

Such is the case of Dōgen's view of the moon. "A step of the moon is Tathágata's perfect enlightenment; Tathágata's perfect enlightenment is the moon's movement."[79] When Dōgen observers the moon, all things of the universe become the moon (*sho-getsu*).[80] Speaking of the moonlight, Dōgen asserts that when the universe is lit by moonlight, the dualism of the universe and moonlight is overcome and duality becomes undefiled. "Both light (*kō*) and environment (*kyō*) go away (*kō-kyō tomoni bōzu*)."[81] As we have touched on previously in a different context, metaphor in Dogen's sense is not that which points to something other than itself, but that in which something realizes itself. This is quite evident in his analysis of the moon reflected on the water:

Śākyamuni Buddha said: "The true Dharma-body of Buddha is like the empty sky, and it manifests itself according to sentient beings like the moon [reflected] on the water."

"Like" in "like the moon [reflected] on the water" should mean the water-moon (*sui-getsu*) [i.e., the nonduality of the moon and the water]. It should be the water-thusness (*sui-nyo*), the moon-thusness (*getsu-nyo*), thusness-on (*nyo-chū*), on-thusness (*chū-nyo*). We are not construing "like" as resemblance: "like" (*nyo*) is "thusness" (*ze*).[82]

Dōgen is well aware of the difference between likeness and thusness and warns against the confounding of the two. Yet, ultimately, likeness is thusness as the former is radically naturalized in its total exertion. Thus, Dōgen says: "Already the moon's movement is not a metaphor; therefore, it is the essence and attributes of solitary perfection."[83]

Tung-shan Liang-chieh (807–869) was asked by a monastic one day: "When cold and heat come, how shall I escape them?" "Why don't you go to a place where there are not cold or heat?" said the teacher. "Where is such a place where neither cold nor heat exists?" asked the monastic. The teacher's answer was: "When it is cold, it makes one exceedingly cold; when it is hot, exceedingly hot."[84] Dōgen used this kōan as a text for the exposition of his view on the four seasons, commenting as follows: "This cold and this heat mean the whole of cold and the whole of heat, both being cold and heat in their thusness (*kansho zukara*)."[85] "Cold and heat in thusness" is precisely the place where there exist no cold and no heat. While living in cold, the enlightened person lives cold totally in absolute freedom; while living in heat, one lives heat totally in the same way.[86] It is not an escape but a choice—the choice of duality, though not dualism, undefiled and free. Therefore this statement ensues: "Where there is the body-mind cast off, there is an escape from cold and heat. . . . You know the signs of this cold and heat, live in the seasons of cold and heat, and make use of cold and heat."[87]

On November 6, 1243, three feet of snow fell over the compound of the Kippōji temple where Dōgen happened to be staying. Recollecting Ju-ching's sermons on the old plum blossoms, Dōgen wrote: "When an old plum tree blooms unexpectedly, just then the world unfolds itself with the flowering."[88] Here again Dōgen sees the whole world in terms of the old plum blossoms blooming in their total exertion. That is, the blossom shares its merits with its five petals within itself, and with countless other blossoms without itself, yet it does not boast of its own efficacy. Both within and without constitute the unfolding of one and the same plum blossom which is in turn the locus where the absolute now is realized (*nikon no tōsho*); thus, it regenerates and restores all things of the universe. This renewal, however, is that which casts off even the "new" in contrast to the "old" in ordinary dualism.[89]

The thusness of the blossoms blooming (*kakai*) and the world unfolding (*sekaiki*) is compared to Buddha's raising an *udumbara* (*udonge*) before the multitude of congregations on Mt. Gṛdhrakūṭa. The *udumbara* is said to bloom once in three thousand years; hence, it is the symbol of extreme rarity.[90] Thus, all things are *udumbaras* at the moment of thusness. Moreover, they are the "flowers of emptiness" (*kūge*), originally interpreted as the "flowers blooming in the sky"— the illusory flowers, or perceptions, attributed to the epistemological errors of humans owing to our diseased perception.[91] Dōgen argued that what others viewed as illusions were, in reality, the flowers of emptiness, and that the ignorance of the perceivers was based on their ignorance of emptiness. For this reason, "the flowers of nothingness" may be a contradiction in terms, but "the flowers of emptiness" is not. Thus "the flowers of emptiness open and disclose both the earth and the sky."[92] Things, events, beings—sentient and insentient—

each is an *udumbara*, an incomparably rare occasion to meet, grow, and create.

You must surely know emptiness is a perfect grass. This emptiness is bound to bloom, like hundreds of grasses blossoming. As you come to grasp this truth, the Tathāgata-way is understood as emptiness, originally having no flower. Although originally having no flower, it now has flowers—peaches and damsons are all like this, and plums and willows are all like this. It is, as it were, a plum tree that some days ago did not have flowers but blooms when spring arrives. Thus, when the time comes, it immediately blooms. It is the time of flowers, and flowers have arrived. At this moment of the flowers' arrival, wanton occurrences never happen. The blossoms of plum trees and willow trees flourish always on plum trees and willow trees. Seeing the blossoms, we know the plum and the willow; when we see the plum and the willow, we judge them by their flowers. No blossoms of peaches and no blossoms of damsons ever bloom on plum trees or willow trees. The flowering of plum trees and willow trees happens to plum trees and willow trees; that of peach trees and damson trees to peach trees and damson trees. Indeed, the way the flowers of emptiness open is also like this. They bloom on no other plants, flower on no other trees.[93]

Such flowers of emptiness are beyond birth and death, beyond past, present, and future, beyond beginning, middle, and end.[94] Nonetheless, the following is also true: "Seeing a dazzling variety of the flowers of emptiness, we surmise an infinity of the fruits of emptiness (*kūka*). We observe the bloom and fall of the flowers of emptiness and learn the spring and autumn of them."[95] All in all, "Nirvāṇa and birth-and-death are none other than the flowers of emptiness."[96]

It is clear from the foregoing observations that Dōgen does not approach nature either from the standpoint of human beings, nor of the scientific method, nor of the romantic method of nature mysticism. His is neither the humanization of nature, the mechanistic, scientific manipulation of nature, nor the paradisiac absorption into nature. Whether he speaks of humans or nature, Dōgen inevitably (and quite consistently) returns to the nondualistic metaphysics of Buddha-nature, radically conceived with the logic of realization, rather than the logic of transcendence. Humans and nature, in myriad configurations and forms, share their destinies, while coming into existence and perishing, as the flowers of emptiness, characterized in Dōgen's favorite expression as "the whole body of emptiness leaping out of itself" (*konshin-chōshutsu*). They leave no traces behind, like birds flying in the sky. Such was Dōgen's view of the "radical love" of nature.[97]

The Bodhisattva Ideal

The essence of bodhisattvahood resides in the bodhisattvas' aspirations for self-perfection in enlightenment (*jōgu-bodai*), as well as in their descending to the level of sentient beings in order to liberate them, thus, remaining among sentient beings for their well-being (*geke-shujō*). The bodhisattva's four great vows (*shi-guzeigan*) resound again and again throughout the writings of Mahāyāna Buddhism, summarizing the bodhisattva ideal:

> However innumerable sentient beings are,
>   I vow to save them;
> However inexhaustible the passions are,
>   I vow to extinguish them;
> However limitless the dharmas are,
>   I vow to study them;
> However infinite the Buddha-truth is,
>   I vow to attain it.[98]

These vows are recited, reflected upon, and meditated on, by monastics, day and night, to such an extent that the lives of monastics are, in essence, the embodiments of vows. The noblest expression of the selfless bodhisattva's wisdom and compassion is found in the phrase, "nirvāṇa with no fixed abode" (*mujūsho-nehan*). Accordingly, the bodhisattva, out of wisdom, abides neither in the birth-and-death realm, nor, out of compassion, in the realm of nirvāṇa. The life of the bodhisattva is the embodiment of the nonduality of wisdom and compassion.

The bodhisattva has been variously interpreted in Buddhist tradition. For Dōgen's part there is evidence that he distinguishes, for example, between the Seven Past Buddhas, the twenty-eight Indian ancestors, and the six Chinese ancestors (from Bodhidharma to Hui-nêng), and regards the latter categories as bodhisattvas, rather than Buddhas.[99] Doctrinally speaking, bodhisattva differs from Buddha, as we see in the scheme of the fifty-two stages of bodhisattvahood (*gojūnii*), in which the stage of approaching Buddhahood (*tōgaku*) and the stage of Buddhahood itself (*myōgaku*) are clearly differentiated.[100] Dōgen seems to follow, occasionally and advisedly, some such conception of the Buddhas and bodhisattvas, in a manner similar to his approach to the doctrine of the Age of Degenerate Law. However, this is not his real view. This is made clear by the fact that, throughout his writings, Dōgen is most emphatic in denying the traditional distinction between the Buddhas and bodhisattvas. He contends:

What you call bodhisattvas are all Buddhas. Buddhas and bodhisattvas are not different types of beings. Old and young, superior and inferior do not obtain. Even though this bodhisattva and that Buddha are not two beings, nor the self, nor the other, and do not bear upon the past, present, or future, to become a Buddha (*sabutsu*) is the supreme model for the practice of the bodhisattva-way. At the time of the initial desire for enlightenment, one becomes a Buddha (*jōbutsu*), and at the stage of Buddha-hood one [still] becomes a Buddha. There are bodhisattvas who became Buddhas countless billions and billions of times. The assertion that after becoming a Buddha, one should discontinue spiritual discipline and engage in no further endeavor, is due to an ordinary worldly person's view which does not yet understand the way of Buddhas and ancestors.[101]

Dōgen further has this to say: "All bodhisattvas are the original forebears of all Buddhas; all Buddhas are the original mentors of all bodhisattvas."[102] The view of the bodhisattva as a provisional stage to Buddhahood is flatly rejected, as Dōgen contends, quite consistently, that expediency or provisionality in this traditional scheme must be seen in the light of thusness; that is, the expedient, the provisional, and the like are not the means to the end of enlightenment, but, rather, the "supreme merit of enlightenment" (*bukka no mujō-kudoku*), as the following statement indicates:

The gate of means (*hōben-mon*) is the supreme merit of enlightenment. Dharma abides in its Dharma-position; and the [momentary and shifting] aspect of life is permanent and lasting. The gate of means is not a temporary skill; it is the entire ten quarters of the world which learn—by making use of all things themselves as ultimate reality (*shohō-jissō*). Even if this gate of means appears and embraces the whole universe by being one with it (*jin-jippōkai no gaijippōkai-su*), no one except bodhisattvas can use it freely.[103]

It appears to be perfectly legitimate for Dōgen to maintain this position once we recall his fundamental view of Buddha-nature: that being Buddha and becoming Buddha are contemporaneous and nondual.

The bodhisattva can be considered in two different contexts: one is the person of the bodhisattva as the object of faith and devotion; the other, the way of the bodhisattva as the model for the Mahāyāna believer's life.[104] Dōgen gives his most explicit view on this matter in his exposition on the myth of Avalokiteśvara (Kannon), one of the most popular bodhisattvas in East Asia. He defines Kannon, the bodhisattva of great compassion (*daihi-bosatsu*), as the bodhisattva who responds to sentient beings' recitation of his name (*kanzeon-bosatsu*), as well as the bodhisattva who observes and liberates sentient beings (*kanjizai-bosatsu*).[105] In this regard, Dōgen takes up a Zen kōan, attributed to Yün-yen T'an-shêng (780–841) and Tao-wu Yüan-chih (769–835). Yün-yen one day asked Tao-wu: "What does Avalokiteśvara use his myriad arms and eyes for?" Tao-wu answered: "It is as if a person were groping at night for a pillow with his/her arms behind his/her back." "I understand! I understand!" exclaimed Yün-yen. "How did you understand it?" asked Tao-wu. "The arms and eyes are all over the body," was the answer. Tao-wu said: "Well said. You hit the mark well." Yün-yen then asked: "How do you understand it?" "The whole body is all arms and eyes," was Tao-wu's answer.[106] Dōgen analyzes this kōan and reasons as follows:

As we attempt to examine Tao-wu's remark "groping at night for a pillow with his/her arms behind his/her back," we should understand without fail that the eyes see freely at night. The arms grope for a pillow, and no bounds are yet touched. If the arms behind the back are wondrously working, there should be the wondrous working of the eyes on the back. You must clearly understand the nocturnal eyes. . . . Having said thus, we can ask: What does the bodhisattva of arms and eyes (*shugen-bosatsu*) use myriad bodhisattvas of great compassion (*daihi-bosatsu*) for? You should realize that although the arms and eyes do not impede one another, "for what use?" (*yō-somo*) means "thusness that uses" (*immo-yō*) and "to use thusness" (*yō-immo*).[107]

Avalokiteśvara's arms and eyes (traditionally a thousand arms and a thousand eyes) are not something attached to his body, in which case they would be two separate entities. Furthermore, the "body" and the "arms and eyes" are not just two different designations for something underlying them, say, great compassion, either. Dōgen further reasons:

When Yün-yen says "The arms and eyes are all over the body," he does not mean that the arms and eyes cover the whole body. "All over" (*hen*) may be understood as entirety, as in the "entire world" (*henkai*), yet, at the time when the body is comprised of nothing but the arms and eyes, "all over" is not an objectified omni-presence. . . . For this reason, Yün-yen's saying should be: "The entire body is the arms and eyes" (*henshin-ze-shugen*); it is not that the arms and eyes become the entire body. You must study this.[108]

By the same token, Tao-wu's statement is understood nondualistically as "the-whole-body-itself-is-all-arms-and-eyes" (*tsūshin-ze-shugen*).

Yün-yen's "all over the body" and Tao-wu's "the whole body" point up the same truth—the mystery of Avalokiteśvara's—all bodhisattvas' and all humans' for that matter—compassion in its dynamic operation throughout the universe, in which infinite compassion, myriad arms and eyes, and body-mind are one indivisible thusness. Avalokiteśvara in this view is not an object of faith the ordinary individual believes in, but the way of bodhisattvahood which every one can exemplify by and for oneself. In brief, Avalokiteśvara is not the object but the subject of faith. The object of faith and the model of living in question are not two discrete concerns, but one and the same in the nonduality of infinite compassion and of the thousand arms and thousand eyes of Avalokiteśvara.[109]

In view of the foregoing observations and others made before, it is clear that Buddhas, bodhisattvas, and ancestors are one and the same, and, in turn, are characterized in the context of Dōgen's "active Buddha" (*gyōbutsu*).

The "longevity" of the way of the bodhisattva is limitless and beyond time.[110] Dōgen writes:

The religious asceticism of infinite kalpas is the efforts and movements of the Buddha-womb and the Buddha-abdomen, and of Buddha's skin-flesh-bones-marrow. We have already been told: "It never, never ends." Reaching Buddha, it is ever more assiduous; even after it has been transformed into myriad worlds, it advances further.[111]

Such a spiritual evolution should not be construed in a futuristic framework, with the image of the bodhisattva steadily progressing towards the other shore (*pāramitā; higan*). Dōgen ingeniously reinterprets this metaphor of "reaching the other shore" (*tō-higan*), turning it around by saying "the other shore has arrived" (*higan-tō*).[112] He writes:

Haramitsu [*pāramitā*] means "the other shore has arrived." Although "the other shore" [nirvāṇa] is not something that is conventionally associated with forms and traces, "arrival" is realized. Arrival is a kōan. Do not ever think that your practice will let you reach the other shore. Because there is practice in the other shore [i.e., in enlightenment], the other shore "has arrived" if you practice the Way. For this practice is unfailingly possessed of the ability to realize the entire universe.[113]

In short, "the other shore" is brought forth here and now on the earth in and through the practice of bodhisattvahood; it is not a matter of the future but a matter of the present.

The essence of the bodhisattva ideal is great compassion (*mahā-karuṇā; daihi*). It is essentially the reconciliation of the dualistic opposites of self and nonself, sentient and insentient, Buddhas and sentient beings, man and woman, and so forth. As Dōgen writes, "The way of the bodhisattva is 'I am thusness; you are thusness.'"[114] The identity of "I" and "you" in thusness, rather than identity in substance, status, or the like, is the fundamental metaphysical and religious ground of great compassion.[115] This is why Dōgen says that when we study ourselves thoroughly, we understand others thoroughly as well; as a result, we cast off the self and the other.[116]

The self-other nonduality is most eloquently expressed in Dōgen's exposition on the four virtues of the bodhisattva (*bodaisatta-shishōbō*), which are (1) giving (*fuse*), (2) loving speech (*aigo*), (3) service for the welfare of all beings (*rigyō*), and (4) identity with others (*dōji*).[117] Giving, material and spiritual, is expounded by Dōgen as follows:

What we call giving means nongreed. Nongreed is not to crave. Not to crave speaks of what people ordinarily regard as the opposite of flattery. Even if you govern the four continents [the whole world], you should be in no way greedy so that you may edify the people in accordance with the right Way. For example, it is likened to people who give strangers the treasures they abandon. [They are neither attached to the treasures nor expectant of receiving any return from the strangers.] Let us offer the flowers of distant mountains to Tathāgata or share the treasures of past lives with sentient beings. In spiritual teachings as well as in material things, each and every giving is innately provided with the merit that corresponds to it. It is true that if a thing is not one's own possession, it does not hinder one's act of giving. It does not matter whether a thing is cheap or small; its merit must be authentic. When the Way is surrendered to the Way, you attain the Way. Upon being enlightened, you necessarily let the Way come through itself. When riches are what they truly are, they invariably become giving. The self gives the self for the sake of giving the self; the other gives the other for the sake of giving the other. [Giving is purposeless and noninstrumental.] The karmic force of such giving prevails as far as the heavenly world and the human world, and reaches out as far as to the wise ones and sages who attained the fruits of enlightenment. The reason is that in the act of giving, one who gives and one who receives form a connection with each other . . . you must give even a phrase or a gāthā of Buddhist teachings; it will become the seeds of goodness in this life and in the coming lives. Offer even a penny or even an unimportant bit of wealth, and it will germinate the roots of goodness in the present life, as well as in the next. Spiritual teachings are material wealth; likewise, material wealth is spiritual teachings. [Which you choose] should be considered according to one's desires and preferences. . . .

To row a boat, or to construct a bridge over a river is equally the bodhi-sattva's practice of giving. If you study giving carefully, [you realize that] living as well as dying are both giving. To be sure, to make a living and regulate a business is none other than giving. Flowers are innocently fondled by the wind, and birds trust freely to time—these too are feats of giving. . . .

Indeed, by reason of being originally gifted with the power of giving, one's present self came into being. . . .[118]

Dōgen advocates the act of giving, free and undefiled of dualism, be-tween the giver and the receiver, between Dharma and wealth, be-tween mind and matter. In this view, our birth-and-death itself is a supreme example of the nonduality of giving and the given, for the sake of the self's as well as others' liberation.

Loving speech is explained:

Loving speech means that as you meet sentient beings, you first arouse the sense of compassion in your mind and treat them with considerate, affec-tionate words. It is altogether devoid of any violent and spiteful language. . . . You should talk keeping your mind on the thought that Buddha cares for sentient beings tenderly as if he is handling babies. This is loving speech. Praise the virtuous, and have compassion for the wicked. As you take de-light in affectionate words, they will gradually flourish; then even those loving words which were hitherto unknown and unperceived will show themselves. As long as your present life lasts, you should take pleasure in speaking compassionately. Generation after generation, let us exert our-selves unremittingly. Compassionate speech is fundamental to the pacifica-tion of enemies and the reconciliation of rulers. . . .

You should ponder that thoughtful words arise from the mind of lov-ing kindness. The mind of loving kindness has compassion as its seed. Con-sider this: loving speech [of remonstrance] has the power to influence even the imperial mind. It is not just to speak highly of others' strengths and achievements.[119]

In this connection, as we have mentioned briefly, philosophic endeav-ors in words and letters are no longer to be feared, but, rather, to be cultivated as part of loving speech. What we need, Dōgen would say, is a compassionate philosophy or a philosophic compassion in which wisdom and compassion are nondually harmonized.

Dōgen also speaks of service for the welfare of all beings:

Working for the welfare of all beings means that you contrive ways to benefit all sentient beings, high and low. In other words, you carefully investigate others' distant and near futures, and think of the various means which will be the most congenial to their well-being. Commiserate with a turtle in trouble, and take care of a sparrow suffering from injury. When you see the distressed turtle or watch the sick sparrow, you do not expect any repayment for your favor, but you are moved entirely by your desire to help others.

Fools may think that if another's benefit is given priority, their own good must be lost. This is not the case. The practice of benefiting others is the total truth (*ippō*), hence, it serves both self and others far and wide. . . .

Therefore, serve enemies and friends equally, and assist self and others without discrimination. If you grasp this truth, [you will see that] this is the reason that even grass and trees, the wind and water are all naturally engaged in the activity of profiting others, and your understanding will certainly serve others' benefit. You should endeavor single-mindedly to save foolish minds.[120]

And lastly, of identity with others, Dōgen says:

Identity with others is nondifference. This applies equally to the self and to others. For example, Tathāgata was born into the human world, and lived a human life. In view of his identity with human beings, we can know that this principle of identity holds true of other nonhuman worlds. As we understand identity with others, self and others are one indivisible thusness.

[Po-Chü-i's] lute, poetry, and wine make friends of human beings, companions of heavenly beings, and comrades of gods. We turn the lute, poetry, and wine into friends. The lute, poetry, and wine make themselves acquaintances, we make ourselves friends, heavenly beings make themselves companions, gods make themselves comrades. In such a truth lies the learning of identity with others.

In other words, *ji* [in *dōji,* "identity with others"] refers to manner, dignity, and posture. There is a truth that after self assimilates others to itself, self lets itself be assimilated by others. The relationship of self and others is infinitely [varied] according to circumstances.

You must know this [as stated in *Kuan-tzŭ*]: The sea does not refuse water, because of its identity with water. You should further understand that water is originally endowed with the virtue of not rejecting the sea. On this account, water habitually gathers itself, flowing into the sea, and earth accumulates itself, forming a mountain.[121]

Underlying these cardinal virtues is the principle of the nonduality of self and others in the context of which, alone, the selfless activities of the bodhisattva become undefiled, free, and natural.[122] The hallmark of great compassion lies in this. Yet as we examine Dōgen's thought more closely, we note distinctive characteristics of his view of compassion. He observes: "To have the desire for enlightenment means that before one crosses to the other shore of nirvāṇa, one makes a vow to carry all sentient beings there, and endeavors accordingly. Even if one's personal appearance is lowly, upon being awakened to this mind, one is already a guide of all sentient beings."[123] This means, in the final analysis, that individual liberation is a contradiction in terms; liberation is fulfilled only in the context of social liberation. Dōgen's monastic ideal can be adequately interpreted only in the light of such a social interpretation of liberation. In apparent contradiction, Dōgen's view of compassion is unique because of his emphasis on Dharma for the sake of Dharma, rather than on applying Dharma to the needs of the common people; thus he underscores an exclusive elitism. Such an exclusionary attitude is usually construed as contradictory to the spirit of universal compassion expounded in the bodhisattva ideal. This conclusion, however, is premature. It is true that Dōgen chose monasticism instead of city life, a select few instead of the common folk, and this elitism is undeniably clear in the latter half of his life. It is also true that Dōgen once wrote to the effect that the Buddhas and ancestors were not without the bonds of worldly affections and obligations, yet abandoned them resolutely.[124] There was not the slightest concern with making accommodations to the mediocre or inferior capacities of the masses in the cities and villages. As we have pointed out previously, such an elitism represents not so much the absence of compassion as a mode of great compassion. Dōgen's relentless rigorism and disciplinarianism, though not without a tinge of authoritarianism, were motivated by the search for Dharma for the sake of Dharma, which in turn was the core of Dōgen's view of compassion, because it held up an example to the common people.

The Problem of Good and Evil

Monastic asceticism was based on moral precepts (*śīla; kai*) and monastic rules (*vinaya; ritsu*), carefully formulated by Dōgen in many of his writings. They were designed not for legalistic conformity or authoritarian regimentation but for the practice of the Way (*bendō*), in realization of and faith in Buddha-nature. As Dōgen put it, they represented the reenactment of the "ancient Buddhas' conducts" (*kobutsu no anri*) or the "ancient teachers' conducts" (*kosen no anri*). Thus, the Buddhist monastic order (*saṃgha; sōgya*) was the religious and educational community of seekers, in which the teacher and the disciples challenged one another in a shared search for the Way. Dōgen's warning was this: "Those who have believing minds and give up desire for worldly fame and gain shall enter. Those who lack sincerity shall not join; entering mistakenly, they shall depart after due deliberation."[125] It was an exclusive community of religious elite with unflinching determination to become members of a "family" in the family tradition of the Buddhas and ancestors (*busso no kafū*). In his passionate pursuit of the utopian vision of monastic idealism, Dōgen increasingly placed emphasis upon the minute specifications of monastic life, rather than on the general principles that had characterized his earlier writings in the Kōshōji period (1233–1243).[126]

It is imperative for us to understand the nature of moral precepts and their relation to monastic rules prior to our examination of Dōgen's view of morality. The word *kairitsu*, which is frequently used in the Chinese and Japanese Buddhist writings, is compounded by the two characters *kai* and *ritsu*. The original Sanscrit word for *kai* is usually rendered *śīla*, whereas that for *ritsu*, *vinaya*. *Kai* refers to moral precepts which should be followed by the Buddhist believers, and *ritsu* to the monastic rules that are designed to maintain the order of the community. While the latter are accompanied by some provisions of punishment for violators, the former (*kai*) are not. That is to say, moral precepts are guidelines which are dependent upon a monastic's motive, disposition, and conscience as a Buddhist believer. On the other hand, monastic rules have to do primarily with external regulations as to a monastic's behavior and conduct. Telling a lie, for example, can be considered from these two standpoints, that is, legal and moral: According to the legal standpoint, telling a lie may be an evil act regardless of the situation in which the act is committed and the motive of the person who committed it; from the moral standpoint, on the other hand, the same precept can be interpreted flexibly in the spirit of understanding and compassion. In short, the monastic rules, though indispensable in the monastic way of life, tend to induce legalism, conformism, and heteronomy, in contradistinction to the spirit of moral precepts, which take heed of individual moral autonomy and freedom.[127]

These two separate concepts are combined in the compound word *kairitsu* which, though frequently used in Chinese and Japanese sources, but not in Indian sources, is rather obscure in its origin and precise meaning. Hirakawa observes that the compound word, while retaining the meanings of its components, emphasizes that monastic rules must be subordinate and contributory to moral precepts and that a tension between the two—between freedom and order—must be creatively maintained.[128]

Dōgen's approach to this matter bears some similarities to Hirakawa's interpretation. Although relentlessly rigorous about every minute aspect of a monastic's deeds and words, which had to be consistent with the rightly transmitted Buddha–dharma as he interpreted it, Dōgen's intention was anything but the inducement of legalism, conformity, or heteronomy. What he intended to do was, as we have remarked briefly before, to implement the spirit of the precepts in the rules concerning the actuality of monastic life—to ritualize morality. Furthermore, Dōgen endeavored in this direction by subsuming both precepts and rules under the umbrella of zazen-only (*shikan-taza*), which in turn liberated the two—cult and morality.

As we have pointed out frequently, Dōgen firmly believed in the indispensability of monasticism, though this does not necessarily contradict his equal concern with the spiritual welfare of the laity. He often approvingly quotes, from Ch'ang-lu Tsung-che's *Ch'an-yüan ch'ing-kuei*, the statement that enlightenment is attained only in the monastic's life, and monastic precepts and rules should be given priority in the practice of the Way.[129] Thus, Dōgen writes:

Wherever the Dharma of the Buddhas and ancestors is transmitted, whether in India or in China, there is always the rite of receiving the precepts at the beginning of initiation into Dharma. Without receiving the precepts, you are not yet the disciples of Buddhas, nor the children of ancestors. For to avoid mistakes and keep off evils, constitutes the study and practice of the Way. Indeed, [Tsung-che's] saying that the precepts be given priority (*kai-ritsu-isen*) is already the treasury of the true Dharma eye (*shōbō-genzō*).[130]

The transmission of Dharma is inseparably connected with that of the precepts. The latter, however, are not so much commandments or codes as vows that are accepted by the monk or nun who is initiated into the Way.

Although the bodhisattva precepts (*bosatsu-kai*) were variously adopted by different Mahāyanists in the place of the Hīnayāna precepts (*biku-kai* or *gusoku-kai*),[131] Dōgen conceived them to be the sixteen precepts or vows: (I) the three precepts of faith (*san-kie-kai*): (1) faith in Buddha (*kie-butsu*), (2) faith in Dharma (*kie-hō*), and (3) faith in Saṃgha (*kie-sō*); (II) the three precepts of purity (*sanju-shōjō-kai*): (1) to eradicate all evils (*shōritsugi-kai*), (2) to exert oneself for all things that are good (*shōzembō-kai*), and (3) to liberate all sentient beings (*shōshujō-kai*); (III) the ten major precepts (*jū-jūkin-kai*): (1) not to destroy life (*fusesshō-kai*), (2) not to steal (*fuchūtō-kai*), (3) not to commit sexual acts (*fuin'yoku-kai*), (4) not to lie (*fumōgo-kai*), (5) not to deal in intoxicating liquors (*fukoshu-kai*), (6) not to report the wrongdoings of anyone among the four groups (monks, nuns, male lay-believers, and female lay-believers) (*fusetsu-zaike-shukke-bosatsu-zaika-kai*), (7) not to praise oneself or to slander others (*fu-jisan-kita-kai*), (8) not to covet (*fukendon-kai*), (9) not to be stirred to anger (*fushin'i-kai*), and (10) not to revile the three treasures (Buddha, Dharma, and Saṃgha) (*fubō-sambō-kai*).[132]

These precepts are given and received between the administrator of ordination (and initiation) and the monastic who is ordained (and initiated), in compliance with prescribed manners, before the congregation of monastics in a reverential setting. The receiving of the bodhisattva precepts signals a radical parting with the secular world—a rite of passage from the secular life to the monastic's life as a chosen path, which means "leaving home" (*shukke*) in order to live the life of the homeless. Dōgen exalts the day of receiving the precepts as the day of supreme enlightenment for all the sentient and the insentient beings, for the well-being of the self and others.[133] The initiation into monasticism, however, is not the ordinary path of withdrawal from the world—the path on which so many contemporaries of Dōgen left footsteps—but the path of the pathless, so extraordinary, indeed, that it transcends one and many, identity and difference, self and other.[134] As Dōgen writes, "The inheritance of Dharma transcends past, present, and future; the vow of enlightenment continues in unbroken succession for all ages."[135]

The precepts reflect Buddhist moral and spiritual aspirations and visions of embodying the way of the bodhisattva, intent on liberating all sentient beings through acts of wisdom and compassion. But these precepts are not always observed consistently and faithfully, due to our native frailty and wretchedness, of which Zen monastics are acutely aware. Inasmuch as the Zen monastery is called the "community of purity" (*shōjōsō*), defilement by sins and guilts must be cleansed and purified as well. It is well known that the gāthā of repentance is recited by Zen monastics at confession:

> All the evil karmas ever committed by me
> since of old,

On account of greed, anger, and folly,
   which have no beginning,
Born of my body, mouth, and thought—
I now make full open confession of it.[136]

The matter of repentance, confession, and forgiveness (*sange* or *keka*) becomes very important in Dōgen's thought.[137] Dōgen wrote:

While both your mind and your flesh may be at times in idleness or in unbelief, confess such in utter sincerity to the Buddhas who come before you. When you repent in this manner, the meritorious power of confession on the part of those Buddhas who come before you, will liberate and purify you. This merit will richly nurture undefiled faith and spiritual endeavor, which are unobstructed. As pure faith is realized, both the self and others will be changed, and sentient and insentient beings shall enjoy its efficacy far and wide.[138]

Immediately after this assertion, Dōgen continues, regarding the efficacy of confession:

The leading thought [of confession] is a sincere desire that, although owing to evil karmic effects accumulated from the past, I may have many obstacles to the Way, the Buddhas and ancestors, who were enlightened through the Buddha-way, have compassion for me, deliver me from karmic shackles, and eliminate any hindrances to my learning of the Way; and that they make the Dharma-gate of their merits completely pervade and fill the boundless reality, and apportion this compassion to me. . . .

   If you repent in this way, you will certainly have the invisible assistance of the Buddhas and ancestors. Confess your thoughts and your deeds, disclose yourself in words, relate them before Buddhas, and your sins shall be altogether rooted out.[139]

Coming from a Zen Buddhist context, these words on the efficacy of repentance, confession, and forgiveness might surprise us.[140] Yet, these are an integral part of the right practice and the right faith, not extraneous to them.

   Zen Buddhists are as acutely aware of the finitude and ambiguity of human existence as any other Buddhists or any other religious persons. Their sorrow for their sins is as profound as that of any other religionists'. Yet, the metaphysical and religious context of confession in Dōgen's case is radically different from that of others. These acts of repentance and confession are performed in the context of the nondualism of the I who confesses and the Buddhas who receive the confession. The phrase "before Buddhas" becomes "before one's self," and, hence, ultimately one confesses, repents, and is forgiven in the nondual purity of the self and Buddha. The purity of a contrite heart in its confession is identical with the confession of Buddha-nature in its purity. The act of confession is the disclosure of original purity. For this reason, the guilt intrinsic to Buddha-nature becomes "guiltless" and "pure" (*isshiki no*).[141]

Thus far, we have been slowly preparing ourselves for an examination of the problem of religion and morality in Dōgen's thought. Before we plunge into this matter, let us make the following preliminary observation: The problem of enlightenment cannot be properly understood without considering the problem of morality and ethics. Morality and enlightenment are inseparably related to one another, so much so that one without the other is not authentic so far as Dōgen is concerned. For nirvāṇa is not beyond good and evil as it is usually—indeed, too often—interpreted in the popular parlance, but is, rather, a mode of existence with a definite moral commitment which is realized in and through the realm of good and evil (and of cause and effect as well), yet undefiled by them. The secret to this undefiled freedom lies in the method of the total exertion of a single thing (*ippō-gūjin*) which appropriates the traditional Buddhist ideas of emptiness and nondualism, existentially, practically, and religiously, rather than theoretically. Unadulterated spiritual freedom, the authenticity of which is tested by the samādhi of self-fulfilling activity, demands, paradoxically enough (to those who interpret Zen as beyond good and evil), an equally unadulterated moral commitment. In brief, spiritual freedom demands moral commitment, as far as Dōgen is concerned.

One of the clues to Dōgen's view of this problem is his treatment of the traditional Buddhist idea of causation, or more exactly, moral causation (*inga* or *goppō*).[142] Dōgen gives his comments on one of his favorite kōans which runs something like this: In the monastery where Po-chang Huai-hai presided, there was an old man, who had been attending Po-chang's lecture sessions all the time with other monastics. One day after the lecture, the old man stayed in the Dharma hall instead of retiring from the hall with others as he usually did. Noticing the man, Po-chang asked: "Who is this man who is standing in front of me?" The old man said, recounting his past: "I am not a man, though I appear to be. I had been the head of this monastery on Mt. Po-chang ever since the time of Kāśyapa Buddha, one of the Seven

Buddhas of the past. However, one day when someone asked me whether or not persons of great spiritual discipline fall into causation, I answered by saying that they do not fall into causation (*furaku-inga*). As a result of the sin of saying this, I have been a fox throughout five hundred rebirths. Please deliver me from this misery with your mighty words." Po-chang answered: "Persons of great spiritual discipline do not obscure causation (*fumai-inga*)." The old man was instantly enlightened and freed from the state of a fox.[143] Dōgen analyzes and comments on the terms "not falling into causation" and "not obscuring causation." The former is a denial of moral causation, whereas the latter is an affirmation of it. Dōgen's own view on this matter is traditional, to a certain extent, but goes beyond the conventional.

One of the hallmarks of Buddhism from its inception has been its advocacy of the law of causation in the moral sphere. In its simplest formulation, the law holds that "evil deeds cause evil consequences" (*akuin-akka*), and "good deeds cause good consequences" (*zen'in-zenka*). The inexorable law of cause and effect governs the succession of rebirths through our deeds, speech, and thought. Both the fate and hope of humanity lie in the domain of our own responsibility; in this sense the law is deeply personal, despite its impersonal appearance as an iron law. Accordingly, we cannot escape the consequence of our actions, words, and thoughts—good or evil. A most devoted Buddhist, Dōgen shows his appreciation for the profundity and mystery of causation, when he writes:

Foremost in the study of the Buddha–dharma is to comprehend the law of causation. An act, such as the denial of causation, is tantamount to trying to arouse a wild, erroneous view in order to eradicate the root of goodness.

Indeed, the truth of causation is manifestly impartial: The evil person lapses, the good one evolves. There is absolutely no exception.[144]

Dōgen profoundly deplored the state of affairs in Buddhism that ignored the fundamentality of causation, resulting in moral laxity, complacency, and antinomianism.[145]

From such a perspective, Dōgen subscribed to the traditional interpretation of "not falling into causation," as the view rejecting the law of causation, and of "not obscuring causation," as the one advocating a deep faith in it. Thus, he repudiates the attempt to identify and hence confound "not falling into" and "not obscuring" with each other.[146] There is no doubt, here, about Dōgen's faith in the law of causation as inexorable, relentless, and impartial—as well as his faith in our inescapable responsibility for what we feel, think, and do. Dōgen uses the phrase "causation of common world" (*kugai no inga*) to refer to the absolute impartiality and justice that prevail in the universe.[147] Elsewhere he writes: "The law of causation is neither an original being, nor something that emerges at a particular time; it is not the case that causation is unavailing, and hence waits for us."[148] Then, if such is the case, how can we conceive of our moral and spiritual freedom in such a "deterministic" framework?

In *Shōbōgenzō*, "Daishugyō," however, Dōgen offers an interpretation of the problem which is quite different from the above description. In this chapter he attempts to expound the "great spiritual discipline" (*daishugyō*) that defines that discipline which transcends the law of causation. He writes, for example:

"Not falling into causation" is traditionally construed as entailing a rejection of causation and, consequently, as lapsing into [a heresy]. This view is groundless, and is what the ignorant person says. . . . Also, some, speaking of "not obscuring the law of causation" in its conventional sense, hold that great spiritual discipline transcends cause and effect, and, hence, liberates [the old man of Mt. Po-chang] from the body of a fox. But this misses the mark.[149]

Thus, Dōgen contends:

Great spiritual discipline, as we probe into its meaning, is none other than the great law of cause and effect. Because this causation consists unfailingly of the realized cause and the realized effect, there cannot ever be any argument about "falling into" or "not falling into," nor about the way of "obscuring" or "not obscuring."[150]

This position may appear contradictory to the previous one which was based on the conventional and common-sensical interpretation. However, Dōgen at this point interprets the law of causation from an entirely different perspective in which the realized cause and the realized effect are spoken of. That is, cause and effect are arranged not temporally or linearly in terms of before and after, but as absolute events or moments discrete from each other, each of which abides in its own Dharma-position and in its total exertion. That is to say, causation is viewed not merely as a moral category but as a metaphysical and soteriological one.[151] This is explicitly expressed in the following:

Cause is not before and effect is not after; the cause is perfect and the effect is perfect. Cause is nondual, Dharma is nondual; effect is nondual, Dharma is nondual. Though effect is occasioned by cause, they are not before or after, because the before and the after are nondual in the Way.[152]

Thus, Dōgen calls them the "wondrous cause" (*myōin*) and the "wondrous effect" (*myōka*), or the "Buddha cause" (*butsuin*) and the "Buddha effect" (*bukka*).[153]

This view can be further elucidated by considering Dōgen's analysis and interpretation of the three periods for the consequences of human deeds (*sanjigō*). Traditionally interpreted, the karmic effects of our actions, speech, and thought will be received (1) in the present life (*jungenhōjugō*), (2) in the next life (*junjishōjugō*), and (3) during rebirths after the next life (*jungo-jijugō*).[154] This doctrine is a further extension of moral causation in a larger scheme, that is, in the framework of the Buddhist doctrine of rebirth (*saṃsāra; rinne*). Deeds are bound to have their results, according to the law of causation, though with differences in the time of their maturity in the course of the spiritual journey in the three worlds and the six realms of existence. The scheme of things in which we are destined to reap what we have sown was, to Dōgen, part of his conception of reason and reasonableness (*dōri*). He says that those who commit the five cardinal sins (killing a father, killing a mother, killing an arahat, injuring the body of Śākyamuni Buddha, and destroying the Buddhist order) will be sent to the avīci hell (*muken-jigoku* or *abi-jigoku*), immediately after their death, where they will endure incessant suffering and torture.[155] On the other hand, bodhisattvas who practice the six perfections for three asaṃkhyeya-kalpas and one hundred kalpas (*sangi-hyakkō*), in order to attain the thirty-two distinguishing marks and the eighty minor characteristics of Buddha, will receive their fruits during the innumerable rebirths after the next life.[156] As is evident from these observations, Dōgen seems to have believed in the fact, or myth, of rebirth as traditionally understood in Buddhism.

Dōgen, however, is not interested in any theoretical involvement with the problem of rebirth, but simply accepts the doctrine and uses it practically as a mythopoeic framework for our moral freedom and responsibility in determining our own destiny. This is stated as follows: "It is a pity that even if you remember a thousand or ten thousand lives [of your own past], it is not necessarily the Buddha-dharma. Heretics already know [the rebirths of] eighty thousand kalpas; still it is not yet thought to be the Buddha-dharma." [157] Good deeds for the sake of acquiring good results or for the sake of avoiding bad results, in the conventional understanding of cause and effect as means and end (and, certainly, heavens and hells loom largely in ordinary minds in this connection), become utterly irrelevant in Dōgen's thought. Cause and effect are absolutely discontinuous moments which are, at once, cause and effect, in the sense that in each are realized all the causes and all the effects of the three periods of the past, present, and future. Cause is the cause of thusness, effect the effect of thusness. In a very special sense, no sooner does one choose and act according to a particular course of action than are the results thereof (heavens, hells, or otherwise) realized in it. Only when we realize this can we transcend the "falling into" and the "not falling into" regarding the law of causation, and attain perfect serenity of mind. [158]

The moment of action, as a cause or an effect, is the moment lived in thusness. This is the meaning of what we have quoted already: "Cause is not before and effect is not after." Also as Dōgen writes, "That effect which exists for its own sake (*kaka no ka*) is not the effect of causation (*inga no ka*); accordingly, the effect of causal law is the same as the effect for effect's sake." [159] We live in the midst of causation from which we cannot escape even for a moment; nevertheless, we can live from moment to moment in such a way that these moments are the fulfilled moments of moral and spiritual freedom and purity in thusness. This is exactly what Dōgen meant by using (*shitoku suru*) birth-and-death, and the law of causation for that matter, yet not being hindered or defiled by them. [160] Thus, returning to Po-chang's kōan, the "not falling into" and the "not obscuring" are transcended, and nonduality is realized. Here, causal necessity and spiritual freedom are reconciled in a uniquely paradoxical way, in Dōgen's mystical realism.

At long last we are prepared to proceed to the investigation of Dōgen's view of good and evil, which is inseparably related to the problem of moral causation. As we might well expect of him, in light of various observations we have made in the foregoing, Dōgen is vehemently opposed to a popular interpretation of Buddhist ethics as "beyond good and evil." Ejō quoted Dōgen as saying:

What is good and what is bad are difficult to determine. They say that it is good to wear silk garments and embroidered brocades, and bad to wear those clothes made of discarded and tattered rags. However, the Buddha-dharma regards the tattered ones as good and pure, and gold, silver, silk and brocade as bad and soiled. In the same manner, this holds true of all other things without exception.

Someone like me writes a few rhymed verses and composes prose one way or another; some secular people speak of this as quite proper, while others criticize me for knowing such things as these despite being a monastic who studies the Way. How can we determine which is to be accepted as good and which is to be rejected as bad?

It is said in a sūtra: "Things that are praised by people and reckoned among things pure are called good; things that are disparaged by people and included among things impure are called evil."

Also it is written: "To undergo suffering as karmic consequence is evil, whereas to invite joy is good." In this way you should judge carefully, and, thereby, practice what you deem to be truly good and discard what you find to be really bad.

Because monastics come from the midst of purity, they consider as good and pure those things which do not arouse thirst and craving on the part of humans.[161]

Matters of good and evil are indeed difficult to determine, as Dōgen acknowledges here. Moral norms and values are relative to the biological make-up of the species, personal preferences, social customs, cultural patterns, and so on. Dōgen is aware of this situation when he writes:

More about various evils: The evils of this world and those of other worlds have similarities and dissimilarities; evils are alike as well as different according to the times preceding and following; the evils of heavenly beings and those of human beings are at once similar and dissimilar—not to speak of the tremendous differences between the good, evil, and neutral of the Buddha-way and [those of] the worldly way.[162]

One undeniable facet of values is their relativity to the conditions of a given situation; quite often, "good is understood differently in different worlds."[163]

What particular course of action am I to choose here and now in this particular situation?—this is a perennial question in Dōgen's thought, and Dōgen himself was acutely aware of the enormous difficulties involved in answering the question. Ejō—referring to Myō-zen's journey to China with Dōgen and others, despite his teacher Myōyū's earnest request to nurse him on account of his critical condition[164]—asked Dōgen the following question:

"In order to truly seek Dharma, it is a matter of course to renounce the bonds and encumbrances of parents and mentors in this world. However, even if we completely cast aside obligations and affections towards our parents, when we reflect further upon the bodhisattva way of life, should we not set aside our own benefits and give priority to others' welfare? When [Myōyū] was old and sick, and there was no one to nurse him, and [Myōzen] was the only person who was in a position to help him—under such circumstances, was it not contrary to the compassionate act of a bodhisattva to think only of his own spiritual matter and not take care of Myōyū? Moreover, a bodhisattva must not discriminate in his good deeds. Should we not understand the Buddha-dharma according to particular conditions and particular circumstances? Following this reasoning, should Myōzen not have stayed and helped his teacher? What do you think about this matter?"[165]

Dōgen replied as follows:

"In both the act of benefiting others and the way of one's own discipline, to discard the inferior and adopt the superior comprises the good deeds of a bodhisattva. To offer a diet of beans and water in an effort to save the old and infirm merely caters to the misguided love and deluded passions of this brief life. If you turn your back on them and study the Way of liberation, even though you may have cause for some regret, you will have a good opportunity for an enlightened life. Consider this well, consider this well!"[166]

Here we get a glimpse of a typically Dōgen-like view of compassion which is as stern and unrelenting as it could be—almost to the point of cruelty. Yet we should not miss his rather "impersonal" search for moral excellence in Dharma for the sake of Dharma. To be sure, moral precepts, norms, and values are the concrete expressions of the way of bodhisattvahood, governed by wisdom and compassion. Fundamental as they may be, these norms are not fixed values to which we legalistically conform, but living expressions of the bodhisattva's free and pure activities in accordance with circumstances and occasions. This is why Dōgen says, consistent with the Buddhist doctrine of functional interdependence:

The human mind is originally neither good nor evil. Good and evil arise in accordance with circumstances. For instance, when you have the thought of enlightenment and enter the forest, you think that the forest life is good and the secular life is bad. On the other hand, when you depart from the forest as a result of your discouragement, you see it as bad. That is to say, the mind has no fixed form and becomes either good or evil depending on the given circumstances. Hence, the mind becomes good when it meets good conditions, bad when it approaches bad conditions. So do not think your mind is inherently bad. Only follow good circumstances.[167]

Be that as it may, Dōgen never forgot to admonish his disciples to discard the inferior and adopt the superior—relentlessly pushing them towards moral and spiritual excellence. Any conformity to worldly values such as power, wealth, fame, and knowledge was a sign of heresy; any compromise with the bonds of worldly affections and obligations was a sign of sentimentality and moral weakness. Filial piety, for example, was not confined to one's parents but extended to all sentient beings.[168] Herein lies an important characteristic of Dōgen's sense of moral reason (*dōri*) which radically rejects "human feelings" (*ninjō*), compounded with the bonds of affections and obligations.[169]

Morality does not end here, however. For moral excellence is not enough. Buddhism's unique philosophical contribution is that it goes beyond moral excellence. The problem is how to save morality from legalism, conformism, and moralism so as to attain authenticity, freedom, and purity, without retreating from moral involvement. For Dōgen's part, he considers the famous "Hymn for the Seven Buddhas' Precepts" (*shichibutsu-tsūkaige*) which reads:

> Not to commit any evil,
> To do everything good,
> And to purify one's mind,
> This is the teaching of all the Buddhas.[170]

As explained earlier in this section, good and evil are the temporary, not illusory, result of circumstances, conditions, causes, motives, and so forth, of a given situation, having no self-identical nature of their own. Like any phenomena, good and evil come and go as circumstances and conditions change in the impermanent scheme of things. Relationality seems to be an inevitable characteristic of these values; accordingly, the ultimate nature of moral values is emptiness. However, this recognition does not lend itself to moral relativism or anarchism so far as Dōgen is concerned, because his concern is with how to live relativity without falling into the trap of relativism, or how to realize absolute freedom and purity amid relationality. Dōgen says:

Each of the evils now under investigation is of one of the three moral natures—good, evil, and neutral. Their nature is unborn (*mushō*). Although the good nature, the neutral nature, and so on are also unborn, undefiled, and ultimately real, there are many particular forms [of moral values] in these three natures.[171]

The moral values of good, evil, and neutral do not exist in themselves or for themselves with any independent metaphysical status, because they are nothing more than the temporary configurations consequent upon infinitely complex interactions of conditions. In brief, good and evil have no self-same metaphysical ground or source—no self-nature (*mujishō*), unobtainable (*fukatoku*), and so forth, in the customary Buddhist phraseology.[172]

Dōgen continues:

Thus, in the learning process of supreme enlightenment, to hear the teaching, practice the Way, and attain the fruits of enlightenment, are profound, lofty, and wondrous. We hear about this supreme enlightenment through good teachers or through sūtras. Then, at first "not to commit any evil" is heard. If it is not heard, there is no right Buddha-dharma, but a demon's teaching.

You must know that what is heard as "not to commit any evil" is precisely the right Dharma of Buddhism. This "not to commit any evil" is not something which the ordinary worldly person contrives [through his/her moral deliberation]. Rather, when you hear and teach wisdom, in its concrete expression, it is naturally heard as this [i.e., as "not to commit any evil"]. This is so because it is the direct expression of supreme wisdom itself. It is intrinsically the talk of enlightenment; accordingly, it talks about enlightenment. Supreme wisdom expresses itself and is heard, whereby, one is moved to desire "not to commit any evil" and to live "not to commit any evil." Where no evil is any longer committed, the power of spiritual discipline is realized at once. This realization is attained with the entire earth, the entire world, all time, and all dharmas as its limits. Its limits are none other than [the primordial reality of] "not-committing."[173]

"Not to commit any evil" is intrinsic to enlightenment; or, enlightenment is biased toward "not to commit any evil." In other words, to commit evil is incompatible with enlightenment, contrary to what is thought by those students of Zen who might be vulnerable to the charge of "evil nondualism" (*akumuge*).[174] From the standpoint of the contemporaneity of being-Buddha (the Buddha-nature) and becoming-Buddha (moral efforts), it is contradictory to commit evil while one is enlightened; yet this does not imply the denial of the human propensity to failure and guilt. The ideal of "not to commit any evil" and the fact of human guilt are paradoxically conjoined in the structure of enlightenment. "Not to commit any evil," then, is the moral as well as transmoral sensibility that is intrinsic to enlightenment.

We are still to live with our native frailty, ambiguity, and sinfulness, that is, our karma-boundness, but no longer bound by them, in absolute freedom and purity in the samādhi of self-fulfilling activity. We must live with the law of causation as well as with human nature, as given us at this particular stage of evolution. Morality cannot escape this fact.[175] This is why, as we have noted before in this chapter, we must constantly repent and be forgiven. Though it may sound paradoxical, confession is an essential part of enlightenment, not a pre-enlightenment condition. Perhaps the problem may be clarified better from a slightly different angle. In the course of his comments on the famous kōan of the killing of a cat by Nan-ch'üan P'u-yüan (748–835),[176] Dōgen maintains that Nan-ch'üan's killing of the cat was at once a sinful act (zaisō) and a Buddha act (butsu-gyō). Dōgen goes on to qualify this by saying that the Buddha act and the sinful act co-exist in one and the same act, that is, the killing of the cat, in this case. This is why an act that is a flagrant violation of a Buddhist precept can be used transmorally as a kōan, or as a decisive word for enlightenment (ittengo)—rendering liberation to those who know how to use it.[177] Good and evil, ideality and actuality, means and end—and all the accompanying conflicts and contradictions—are very real and never illusory; yet it is the transmoral quality of life that liberates and authenticates them. When we incorporate this observation into the present context, it seems to follow that while not-to-commit-any-evil is an intrinsic, primordial part of enlightenment which disavows any possibilities of committing evil from the purview of Buddha-nature, enlightenment is such that the good and evil, of the existential states of the human being, become absolutely transparent to Buddha-nature and absolute emptiness, so that the enlightened person is able to use evil freely for the ultimate good. Dōgen says:

Even though such people of thusness, as they are authentically enlightened, appear to live, to come and go in the environment that conduces to evil, or to encounter those circumstances which engender evil, or to be associated with those who commit evil, they no longer commit evil. Because the efficacious power of "not committing" [any evil] unfolds itself, evil loses its character as evil, being deprived of its grounds.[178]

In this respect, "Good and evil are Dharma, but Dharma is not good or evil. Dharma is nondual, evil is nondual; Dharma is nondual, good is nondual." [179] In this lies the mystery of evil.

Thus, Dōgen declares:

. . . [the principle of] cause and effect in [the context of] good and evil is realized by virtue of our practice of the Way. This does not mean, however, that we can alter causes and effects or create new ones. Rather, by virtue of causation, we are able to practice the Way. The original countenance of such causation is unambiguously clear, precisely because of [the primordial] "not-committing," which is birthless and impermanent, as well as of "not obscuring" [causation] and of "not falling into" [causation]: [causation] is completely cast off.

As we investigate the matter in this way, it becomes clear to us that "all evil" has always been [embraced by] this [primordial] "not-committing." Being aided by such realization, we see clearly [the true meaning of] "not to commit any evil," thereby cutting off [all delusions] through zazen.

At such a time, the beginning, middle, and end [of our practice and enlightenment] are actualized as "not to commit any evil." Consequently, evil does not arise from direct and indirect causes, but is solely of "not-committing"; evil does not perish by direct and indirect causes, but is only of "not-committing." If all evil is nondual, all dharmas are nondual as well. Pitiful are those who know that evil is produced by various causes, but who fail to see that these causes are intrinsically of "not-committing." Since the seed of Buddhahood arises from conditions, conditions arise from the seed of Buddhahood.

Evil is not nonexistent, but simply of "not committing"; evil is not existent, but only of "not-committing." Neither is evil formless but it is of "not-committing," nor is it form but it is of "not-committing." Ultimately speaking, evil is not so much something that "thou shalt not commit" as it is something that resides in [the primordial reality of] "not-committing." . . .

Such an understanding of the problem [of evil] constitutes the kōan realized—the kōan realizing itself. The problem is examined from the standpoint of subject as well as from the standpoint of object. Such being the case, even if you feel remorse for having committed what ought not to have been committed, you are never alienated [from the primordial reality of "not-committing"], for this very feeling is unmistakably the striving power of "not-committing." [180]

The essence of the foregoing statements is that "not to commit any evil" is neither the heteronomous "Thou shalt not" nor the autonomous "I will not," but is non-contrivance. Morality, if it be authentic, must and can arise spontaneously from enlightenment. Morality and enlightenment are not to be conceived in terms of cause and effect, nor in terms of means and end. At this level of discourse, morality is not a contrivance of the ordinary worldly mind (*ushin no shukō*). Both morality and enlightenment are intrinsic to the structure of Dharma. When morality becomes effortless, purposeless, and playful, it becomes a nonmoral morality which is the culmination of Zen practice of the Way, in which morality, art, and play merge together.[181] When *ought* becomes *is* in the transparency of thusness, only then do we come to the highest morality. Moral excellence, as such, does not constitute absolute freedom and purity, from the religious and metaphysical standpoint. Only when an ought becomes an expression of thusness, does it reach the highest morality. To Dōgen, as to Shinran, the ultimate height humanity can hope for in morality is fidelity to thusness.[182]

The logic of morality outlined in the foregoing is also applied to the problem of goodness. "To do everything good" (*shuzen-bugyō*) is similarly expounded:

The "everything good" here under investigation refers to good nature as one of the three [moral] natures. Although all good exists in good nature, there is not a single instance of good actualized prior to and in anticipation of one who does [good]. At the very moment when a good deed is accomplished, all good invariably comes forth. Formless as the myriad kinds of good may be, a good act, wherever it is done, assembles them all, faster than a magnet attracts iron. Its force is stronger than a stormy wind that destroys everything in the universe. Even the great earth, mountains, and rivers, even the world, countries, and lands, as well as karma-accelerating forces, cannot hinder this confluence of all good.[183]

Furthermore, Dōgen argues:

Even though "everything good" is "to be done" [by us], [one who does good] is not one's self nor is [good] known to this self; neither is [one who does good] another self, nor is [good] known to this other. The intellectual understanding of self and other is such that [the distinction between] self and other concerns our judgments as well as our perceptions; for this reason, each and every being's living eyeball [essence] must be involved in [exerting] days and months: such is the meaning of [the primordial] "doing" [in "to do everything good"]. At the very moment of [the primordial] "doing," the kōan is realized. This does not mean, however, that the kōan is now actualized for the first time or has endured as a fixed entity. If such were the case, ["doing"] would not deserve to be called the original activity. . . . "Good" is neither being nor nonbeing, neither form nor formlessness, but is solely of "doing." Wherever and whenever realized, it is invariably of "doing." In this "doing" is "all good" unmistakably realized. Although the realization of "doing" is itself the kōan, it is neither birth nor extinction, neither direct conditions nor indirect conditions. The same holds true for the entering, dwelling, and departing of "doing." As you endeavor to do even a single good act among many forms of good, all dharmas, all bodies, the true state [of enlightenment], and all the rest will be realized in and through this "doing" (*bugyō seraruru nari*). The causes and effects of such goodness are each the kōan realized in life.[184]

Good is not an entity which the moral agent deals with as an object. The moral agent and the value of good partake of the event of valuational creation which is said to be neither coming into being nor coming out of being, nor even reducible to the outcome of functional interdependence.[185] Here again, "to do everything good" is play, in the samādhi of self-fulfilling activity, that transcends ought and is. This is a radical ritualization of morality, amounting to the liberation of morality. In this spirit we can understand the "fourfold right efforts" (*shishōgon* or *shishōdan*): (1) to prevent the evil that has not yet arisen, (2) to abandon the evil that has already arisen, (3) to produce the good that has not yet arisen, and (4) to promote the good that has already arisen.[186] Cult and morality are indistinguishably fused in Dōgen's conception of the practice of the Way.

Monastic Education

The monastic order is the community of bodhisattvas who seek and realize the Way through the communal life of discipline, reflection, and efforts—not to mention fears and hopes, joys and sorrows—and who share a common fate and destiny. Although there are divisions of labor and differentiations of function, for the sake of economy of life, these are reconciled in the shared status of the seekers and fulfillers of the Way in an egalitarian situation. Even the status of teacher and disciple become ultimately insignificant, for "Everyone must be enlightened without a teacher" (*mushi-dokugo*), despite there being so much emphasis placed on meeting a right teacher (*shōshi*) and on mutual assistance between teacher and disciple (*shishi-sōjō*) in Zen Buddhism. Each member is ultimately alone and solitary in this communal setting.

Since the monastic community is the community that seeks and realizes truth (*shinjitsusō*) (truth, or Dharma, meaning wisdom and compassion in emptiness), the monastic life constitutes the educational community in which individuals are trained in wisdom and compassion, or in the compassion of wisdom and in the wisdom of compassion. This educational process is deeply personal and social. Let us examine the personal and the social aspects of monastic education.

Dōgen writes:

As one studies the Way by following sūtras or becoming a teacher's disciple, one is enlightened without a teacher (*mushi-dokugo*). To be enlightened without a teacher is due to the work of the Dharma-nature (*hosshō*). Even though you are possessed of natural intelligence (*shōchi*), you must always seek a teacher's spiritual guidance for the Way. Even if you are in possession of the knowledge of the unborn Dharma (*mushōchi*), still you must study and practice the Way. Who is not naturally endowed [with the Dharma-nature]? Yet you must follow the sūtras and teachers as far as you realize the fruit of wisdom.[187]

Dōgen modifies the meaning of the Confucian idea of innate knowledge (*shōchi*) in such a way that humans become naturally intelligent by virtue of the Dharma-nature, rather than of intellect. He then argues that, even if we encounter the Dharma-nature and are instructed by the sūtras and teachers, we cannot understand the Dharma-nature unless we are already endowed with it; this is, indeed, a very special kind of "endowment" of emptiness, as will become clearer in the course of our investigation.[188] To follow a right master and study the sūtras—a personal encounter and an intellectual enterprise—are the two most important conditions that make the Dharma-nature flower in a person's life.

The study of sūtras must be understood in the context of what we have previously observed in connection with Dōgen's view on Buddhist teachings and sūtras, in his conception of the rightly transmitted Buddha-dharma. We noted that Dōgen rejected the distinctions between Tathāgata Zen and Ancestral Zen, between the Zen sect and other Buddhist sects, between Silent-illumination Zen and Kōan-introspection Zen, and so forth, and that he attempted to restore the classical Zen tradition which thrived during the T'ang period. Although the vicissitudes of sūtra study in the history of Zen Buddhism are indeed intriguing,[189] we simply make note of a problem, in this connection, which is rather unique, in view of the peculiarities of Zen history. In the history of Zen, a wholesome skepticism concerning intellectual learning (*gaku*) and an emphasis on spiritual practice (*gyō*) tended, more often than not, to be so dichotomized that the former was rejected entirely; this rejection was even regarded as the hallmark of Zen. Lin-chi I-hsüan (d. 850?), Tê-shan Hsüan-chien (780–865), and Yang-shan Hui-chi (807–883) towards the end of the T'ang period seem to have been largely responsible for this extreme position.[190] The literalistic, dogmatic interpretation of the two Zen principles, "a special tradition outside the sūtras" (*kyōge-betsuden*) and "no dependence upon words and letters" (*furyū-monji*), went so far as to cause the burning of sūtras and images as being utterly useless. As time went on, the so-called Kōan-introspection Zen discussed in Chapter 3 of this book—the predominant form of Zen in the Sung period—replaced scriptural study by the kōan method, with its accompanying strengths and weaknesses. The point noteworthy in this connection, however, is that although Zen Buddhists used kōans as a meditational method, in the course of time they engaged in the study of kōans (that consisted of selected stories, parables, sayings from the ancestral records and the sūtras, though predominantly from the former), which became the Zen substitute for the scriptural study of other Buddhist schools and sects. The kōan method was a form of sūtra study.[191] It seems as though even Zen could not avoid words and letters, no matter how vigorously it may have opposed them. Thus, by virtue of the peculiar turns of its history, Zen Buddhism constantly confronted the problem of how to deal with the sūtras and the kōans, and ultimately with language and symbols, as well as with intellectual endeavors in general, in a more acute way than any other schools of Buddhism. The place of language and intellect, in Zen, is the issue—an educational issue in this particular context.

In light of this background, the building of the monastic library and the codification of monastics' attitudes and behaviors in connection with it, indicate Dōgen's answer to this problem. It is true that Dōgen, in following the Zen tradition, emphasized the spirit rather than the letter of the sūtras. No one could have been more vehement in denouncing the futility of "counting words and letters" (*monji o kazouru*) and the foolishness of those "teachers of dead letters" (*monji no hosshi*) than was Dōgen.[192] On the other hand, Dōgen was also aware of the fact that the spirit in question did not function in a vacuum, but only by its interaction with words and letters. Thus, Dōgen detected in the Zen extremist's view the fundamental weakness that alienated spirit and letter—or Zen Buddhistically speaking, Buddha-mind (*busshin*) and Buddha-word (*butsugo*).[193] Spirit can be activated only by symbols; symbols can be redeemed only by spirit. Therefore, Dōgen saw the necessity of sūtra studies provided that they were understood in and through the practice of the Way.[194] This was what he called actional understanding (*gyōge*) in contrast to intellectual understanding (*gakuge*), as we observed earlier in this study. In this respect, the study of sūtras acquired a legitimate status equal to meditation in the practice of the Way, as symbolized by the monastic library and the monastics' hall in the architectural setting of the monastery. Meditation and sūtra studies, together, constitute the substance of wisdom. At any rate, this inclusion of sūtra studies in wisdom has had a far-reaching significance in the history of Zen Buddhist education.[195]

The sūtras in Dōgen's thought were not confined, as we have seen, to the corpus of sacred texts and ancestral records, accumulated in the Buddhist tradition, but also include sentient beings and insentient beings—things, phenomena, events of the universe, which have their own languages and expressions. The universe is the language and kōan that awaits deciphering by humans. From this viewpoint, Dōgen's selection of Echizen—the mountainous region remote from cities— had an educational significance. Although education in the mountains and waters (*sansui*) was not his original idea,[196] Dōgen was deeply committed to the mountains and waters which provided an ideal educational environment for monks and nuns. In a sense it meant that complete change in value orientation was required for such a radical education as the one envisioned by Dōgen; that is, it meant a radical detachment from the secular world helplessly obsessed by, and enmeshed in, power, fame, wealth, and knowledge. More than this, however, was involved. The mountains and waters constituted not only the habitat of the sages and the wise ones, but also the kōan realized in daily activities (*genjō-kōan*). In brief, the mountains and waters were at once the living sūtras waiting to be deciphered, as well as the embodiments of the sages' and the wise ones' way of life itself. Dōgen says:

The mountains and waters, here and now, are the realization of the ancient Buddhas' way. They equally abide in their own Dharma positions, and fulfill the merit of exerting themselves totally. Since this is the primordial fact prior to the kalpa of nothingness [of the four kalpas of the world], it is the living affair of the absolute now. By reason of being the self prior to the timeless incipience, it is the transcendence of realization. As the virtues of mountains are lofty and pervasive, one is thoroughly acquainted with the way and power of riding on the clouds [spiritual freedom], necessarily, through mountains, and realizes the wondrous merit of following the breeze [spiritual guidance], surely, through mountains.[197]

Thus, the monastic library for scriptural studies and the mountains and waters as the cosmic sūtra or kōan realized in life, were essential to Dōgen's envisionment of monastic education.

Dōgen's admonition for receiving the spiritual guidance of a right teacher is familiar to us by now. Again and again he tirelessly repeats the crucial importance of meeting the right teacher. For example he states:

Students of the Way should not hold obstinately to their personal views. Even though they may have a grasp of the matter, they should reason that this understanding may not necessarily be a good one, or that there might be superior views to theirs, and should visit good teachers widely, and also examine the sayings of old teachers. However, they must not cling even to the sayings of the old teachers. Thinking that they too may be wrong, and that they should be cautious while believing them, they are to follow better views as they encounter them.[198]

Right teachers are compared to artisans who mold artifacts out of the material of their disciples. The two are indispensable to each other.[199] Once you find the right teacher, you must be absolutely obedient. The disciple's absolute dedication to the teacher, however, is not a blind obedience, but is based on the view that Dharma is invariably embodied in and transmitted through a concrete person. Dharma and person are here one.[200] Dōgen considered that the teacher, as the person embodying Dharma, is entitled, to that extent, to demand an absolute obedience from the disciple which is devoid of sentimentality—the bonds of worldly affections and obligations. For both are dedicated to Dharma for the sake of Dharma.

When this responsive communion (*kannō-dōkō*) takes place between the two, Dharma blossoms in its myriad forms. Teacher and disciple engage in a deeply personal dialogue (*mondō* or *shōryō*) in the search for truth, which can be significantly compared with the Socratic dialogue (*dialektikē*) in the West.[201] The Zen dialogue employs all possible means, such as: words (including paradoxes and nonsense); bodily gestures (even apparently rough and cruel means such as slaps, kicks, shouts, etc.); and, significantly enough, silence. These educational devices (*upāya*; *hōben*) are skillfully used, by the teacher, with compassion and understanding, whenever and wherever necessary and desirable for the disciple's self-awakening. Although some of these means have fallen into disrepute in Zen training today, the point remains significant that all these means are compassionately and judiciously used in order to guide the disciple to the goal of self-enlightenment. For this purpose the relationship of the teacher and disciple becomes, of necessity, intensely personal, so the right moment and the right occasion, when the decisive event takes place, can be discovered. Zen Buddhism compares this situation to a chick and a hen tapping a shell from both inside and outside, at the opportune moment, to enable the chick to emerge from its shell (*sottaku-dōji*).[202] Disciples' presentations of their observations and opinions must be matched by their teacher's effective employment of opportune chances (*tenji-tōki*).[203] However, the teacher is the one who is always aware of the fact that the disciple's search and endeavor seems to resemble a quest, but is the Way in actuality.[204] As we see in the question "What is this that comes thus?" (which was addressed by Ta-chien Hui-nêng to Nan-yüeh Huai-jang), "What" is always asked with the formless presupposition of "thusness"; accordingly, the purpose of education is to explicate and authenticate the What, in the transparency of thusness, through the common efforts of teacher and disciple.[205]

Dōgen's view on the educational environment goes beyond the sūtras and teachers. He says: "A person's attainment of the Way depends always on many conditions (*shuen*). Although individuals may be sharp in their own way, their practice of the Way relies on the strength of many persons (*shuriki*); accordingly, monastics now should practice and seek the Way with one accord."[206] Myriads of conditions and persons are involved in the education of a person from delusion to enlightenment. Hence, Dōgen is severely critical of those who retreat into their huts and pursue their studies or their own predilections alone, free from worldly preoccupations and worries. This is nothing but a self-conceit indicating complacency and arrogance (*zō-jōman*).[207] By contrast, the monastic life is deeply communal and social in that its practioners (*hindei*) as bodhisattvas work together for the common cause—growth in wisdom and compassion. This is a social effort to reconstitute physical and human resources for a utopian vision of society; this effort does not simply cater to individual indulgence in avocations and pleasures. Education is essentially a social enterprise.

This accounts for Dōgen's admonitions about manners and attitudes, not only on the part of monastics but also on the part of monastic leaders, which are specified in detail.[208] The monastic leaders are urged to exercise fairness, harmony, compassion, joyfulness, truthfulness, whereas the inferiors, respect, obedience, propriety, and so forth.[209] Those who lead and those who are led, though functionally differentiated, are equals as members of the community and responsible to each other for maintaining the ideal environment of harmony and peace (*wagō*), by selfless participation in the communal activities. Such a communal life is likened to the blending of milk and water or to crossing the ocean aboard a single boat.[210] Initially, members may enter into the community individually, but they gradually realize that they are born out of the common root of absolute emptiness; hence they are not an assemblage of isolated individuals but the children and flowers of emptiness. Monastic education is intended to help each of them realize this common root in emptiness.

As we turn to the personal aspects of monastic education, the problem becomes much more complicated and difficult to understand. Foremost among the personal aspects is the earnest desire and aspiration for, and thought of, enlightenment (*dōshin, bodaishin, mujōshin, hosshin,* etc.). It is the mind's resolution to cast aside all worldly and selfish concerns, and to devote itself, instead, to benefiting others, following the exemplary model of the bodhisattva ideal. Such a desire is preeminently, if not solely, a practical concern, rather than an intellectual or theoretical one. One's intellectual ability is not decisive in this matter, any more than are one's wealth, status, and the like. The criterion of educability for the monastic education is this desire for and thought of enlightenment, as well as the willingness to serve others with selflessness—not the ability of intellect for abstraction and theorization. Without this decisive factor, one is ignorant and deluded in selfishness and egocentricity, however deep one may be in abstruse learning. Despite their various idiosyncrasies and diversities in personality, background, education, and so on, the monks and nuns of the monastery all share this quality of educability for bodhisattva-hood. In this sense the monastics are a matchless elite in selflessness.

How does this thought of enlightenment arise? Is the thought innately endowed to all humans, or is it socially acquired? Dōgen at one place says: "Who has the thought of enlightenment from the beginning? Only when, in this way, you arouse what is difficult to arouse, and practice what is difficult to practice, will it develop naturally.

Everyone has Buddha-nature without exception; do not vainly abase yourself."[211] Dōgen also discussed the Confucian idea of innate knowledge, to which we referred earlier, commenting on this by saying that if there was such a native endowment of intellectual superiority at all, it would mean the repudiation of the law of moral causation; needless to say, Buddhism firmly rejects such an interpretation.[212] (Dōgen seems to be saying here that any "native endowments," whether individual or collective, are entirely the result of what we have earned individually and/or collectively through the law of moral causation.) In any event the thought of enlightenment, according to Dōgen, must be learned, cultivated, and actualized in and through a multitude of conditions—among others, personal and social efforts and exertions. Religious sentiment in this respect is personally and socially acquired, rather than universally given or endowed with certain definable forms, principles, or potentialities. In short, the thought of enlightenment is something one must earn in favorable conditions; without such conditions it may never be aroused, and accordingly it may never be expressed. In this respect we can appreciate Dōgen's persistent reminder of the importance of teacher's guidance and sūtra study, despite Zen's basic tenet of self-enlightenment without a teacher.

However, inasmuch as the thought of enlightenment is related to Buddha-nature and the Dharma-nature, its mystery deepens profoundly. As we have seen before, Buddha-nature does not come into existence or go out of existence "in proportion to" or "co-extensive with" human consciousness, or even with all existence, despite the doctrine of "All existence is Buddha-nature."[213] Further, we are told that the thought of enlightenment transcends time and space, though it is not hindered by them, and, hence, is awakened freely in any particular place and time; for this reason, its arising is due neither to environment nor to our native power.[214] An important clue can be found where Dōgen relates the whole matter to the mysterious phenomenon of "cosmic resonance" (*kannō-dōkō*):

This mind [the thought of enlightenment (*bodaishin*)] does not exist independently or rise suddenly now in a vacuum. It is neither one nor many, neither spontaneous nor accomplished. [This mind] is not in my body, and my body is not in the mind. This mind is not all-pervasive throughout the entire world. Neither before nor after, neither existent nor nonexistent obtains. It does not bear upon self-nature or other-nature, upon common nature or causeless nature. Despite all this, the arising of the thought of enlightenment occurs where cosmic resonance presents itself. It is neither furnished by the Buddhas and bodhisattvas, nor by one's own effort. Because the thought of enlightenment is awakened through cosmic resonance, it is not natural.[215]

Dōgen's view on the mystery of the thought of enlightenment (comparable to the mystery of evil and ignorance in human existence) is crystallized in these remarks. We realize that the whole problem of the arising of the thought of enlightenment (and the arising of religious sentiment or religiousness, for that matter) is far more complicated than we anticipated initially. At this level of discourse, the thought of enlightenment is neither endowed nor acquired, in the simple sense of these words. What is significant here is Dōgen's attribution of the mystery to the cosmic resonance of Buddhas and sentient beings—all existence—whose primordial urge and desire for enlightenment resonate in unison throughout the universe that exerts itself totally in this shared enterprise. Education must necessarily take into account this mystery of the thought of enlightenment, or to put it otherwise, the mystery of the human being as *homo religiosus*; without doing this education would not be total.

Thus, in the monastic education personal and social conditions work together to provide wholesome conditions (*ryōen* or *zen'en*) that lead a monk or nun to awakening. Yet this is simply the affirmation of their own innermost being, that is, Buddha-nature or Dharma-nature. As Dōgen writes,

Properly speaking, the direct and indirect conditions of the arising of the thought of enlightenment do not come from without, rather one is religiously awakened by stirring the desire for enlightenment itself. . . .

In this way, conditions of eighty thousand things and phenomena are necessarily involved in one's awakening. Some were awakened in a dream and then enlightened. Others began to aspire for wisdom in the state of drunkenness and attained the Way. Still some others have the thought of enlightenment and realize the Way in the midst of flying flowers and falling leaves, or in the midst of peach blossoms and emerald bamboos. Or again, some in the heavens, others in the sea. All these take place in the mind that aspires for enlightenment, and further, the desire for wisdom is aroused.[216]

This is also the meaning of self-enlightenment without a teacher. The conditions and factors we have discussed do not constitute any elements of new knowledge, but are simply regarded as germane to the embodiment of what has already and always been. Fundamentally speaking, nothing has been added or subtracted by the monastic education. In this sense Dōgen admits the use of the "samādhi of self-enlightenment" (*jishō-zammai*).[217]

The ultimate goal of monastic education lies in this self-awakening, and its success is to help and promote, in this regard, most effectively, and to bring about, paradoxically enough, the realization that nothing has been taught or learned. Only then is education not a means to life but life itself; education is enlightenment itself and emptiness itself.

The ideal image of humanity, in Dōgen's thought, is called the "person of thusness" (*immonin*), Dōgen's favorite phrase, which is comparable to the "original countenance" (*honrai no memmoku*) or the "person of no rank" (*mui-shinjin*).[218] The alpha and omega of education is to realize this person of thusness throughout its processes. Dōgen's emphasis, however, is, as we would expect, placed on a particularity, in absolute freedom. He refers, in his critique of Lin-chi's "person of no rank," to the "person of a particular rank" (*ui-shinjin*)— a particular, concrete individual who finds fulfillment in the process of individuation.[219] Personal and social conditions and cosmic resonance all constitute concerted efforts to define this indefinable mystery of thusness, in a concrete socio-cultural and historical situation.

Reference Material

Chronology of Dōgen's Life

(Events in parentheses are those of importance in understanding the historical context of Dōgen's life and thought.)

1185   (Final defeat of the Taira family by the Minamoto.)
1191   (Eisai transmits Rinzai Zen to Japan.)
1192   (Minamoto Yoritomo founds the Kamakura shogunate.)
1198   (*Senchaku hongan nembutsu-shū* by Hōnen and *Kōzen gokoku-ron* by Eisai.)
1200   Dōgen is born on January 2 in Kyōto.
1202   Father, Koga Michichika, dies. (Eisai founds the Kenninji temple in Kyōto.)
1207   Dōgen's mother dies. (Hōnen and Shinran are banished from Kyōto; the Kamakura regime continues to suppress Pure Realm Buddhism.)
1212   Dōgen visits Ryōkan Hōgen (or Ryōken Hōgen?), his uncle on mother's side; enters the Senkōbō at Yokawa-hannyadani on Mt. Hiei. (*Hōjōki* is completed by Kamo no Chōmei; Hōnen dies.)
1213   Kōen administers the initiation ceremony for Dōgen in April.
1214   Dōgen is troubled by the question concerning original enlightenment and spiritual practice; visits Kōin of the Onjōji temple in Miidera; studies Rinzai Zen at the Kenninji temple; travels extensively to seek a right teacher.
1215   (Eisai dies.)
1217   Dōgen settles at the Kenninji temple and studies under Myōzen.
1220   (*Gukanshō* by Jien.)

1221   Formal teacher–disciple relationship with Myōzen begins. (The Jōkyū War.)

1223   Dōgen, Myōzen, and others leave Kyōto for China in February and arrive in China in April; Dōgen meets an old chief cook of the Mt. Ayüwang monastery on board the ship; enters the Ching-tê-ssŭ temple on Mt. T'ien-t'ung in July. (Nichiren is born.)

1224   Dōgen sets out on a journey to various Zen monasteries in winter. (Shinran writes *Kyōgyōshinshō* and founds the Shin sect.)

1225   Dōgen becomes a disciple of Ju-ching in May; experiences the decisive moment of enlightenment sometime during the *geango;* Myōzen dies.

1226   Dōgen continues to study under Ju-ching and composes *Hōkyōki.*

1227   Dōgen receives the ancestral seal of the Ts'ao-tung (Sōtō) sect from Ju-ching; returns home in the fall and enters the Kenninji temple; writes *Fukan-zazengi.*

1228   Ju-ching dies.

1230   Dōgen moves to the An'yōin temple in Fukakusa. (Famine and natural calamities wreak havoc upon the entire country.)

1231   *Shōbōgenzō,* "Bendōwa." (Those dead by starvation fill Kyōto.)

1233   Dōgen founds the Kōshō-hōrinji temple in Yamashiro; *Shōbōgenzō,* "Makahannya-haramitsu" and "Genjō-kōan."

1234   *Eihei shoso gakudō-yōjinshū* in March; Ejō becomes Dōgen's disciple.

1236   The monastics' hall opens, and Ejō is appointed the head monastic.

1237   *Tenzo-kyōkun.*

1238   *Shōbōgenzō,* "Ikka-myōju"; Ejō completes *Shōbōgenzō zuimonki.* (Jōkō constructs the statue of Amida Buddha at Kamakura.)

1239   *Shōbōgenzō,* "Sokushin-zebutsu," "Senjō," and "Semmen"; *Kannon-dōri Kōshō-gokokuji jūundōshiki.*

1240   *Shōbōgenzō,* "Raihai-tokuzui," "Keisei-sanshoku," "Shoaku-makusa," "Sansuikyō," "Uji," "Kesa-kudoku," and "Den'e."

1241   Ekan, Gikai, Giin, Gijun, Gien, and others become disciples; *Shōbōgenzō,* "Busso," "Shisho," "Hokke-ten-Hokke," "Shin-fukatoku," "Kokyō," "Kankin," "Busshō," "Gyōbutsu-igi," "Bukkyō" (34), and "Jinzū."

1242   *Shōbōgenzō,* "Daigo," "Zazenshin," "Bukkōjōji," "Immo," "Gyōji," "Kaiin-zammai," "Juki," "Kannon," "Arakan," "Hakujushi," "Kōmyō," "Shinjin-gakudō," "Muchū-setsumu," "Dōtoku," "Gabyō," and "Zenki."

1243   *Shōbōgenzō,* "Tsuki," "Kūge," "Kobusshin," "Bodaisatta-shishōbō," and "Kattō" at the Kōshōji temple and the Rokuharamitsuji temple between January and July; Dōgen moves to Shihinoshō in Echizen in July; *Shōbōgenzō,* "Sangai-yuishin," "Butsudō," "Mitsugo," "Shohō-jissō," "Bukkyō" (47), "Mujō-seppō," "Menju," "Semmen" (second presentation), "Hosshō," "Baika," "Jippō," "Kembutsu," "Hensan," "Zazengi," "Ganzei," "Kajō," "Ryūgin," "Sesshin-sesshō," and "Darani" at the Kippōji temple and Yamashibu in Echizen. (Enni Ben'en becomes the head of the Tōfukuji temple.)

1244   The Daibutsuji temple opens in July; *Shōbōgenzō*, "Daigo" (second presentation), "Soshi-seiraii," "Udonge," "Hotsu-mujōshin," "Hotsu-bodaishin," "Nyorai-zenshin," "Zammai-ōzammai," "Sanjūshichihon-bodaibumpō," "Tembōrin," "Jishō-zammai," "Daishugyō," and "Shunjū" at the Kippōji temple; *Taidaiko-goge-jarihō*.

1245   *Shōbōgenzō*, "Kokū," "Hatsuu," "Ango," "Tashintsū," and "Ōsaku-sendaba."

1246   The name is changed from the Daibutsuji to the Eiheiji temple in June; *Nihonkoku Echizen Eiheiji chiji-shingi*; *Shōbōgenzō*, "Shukke." (Lan-hsi Tao-lung, namely, Rankei Dōryū arrives in Japan.)

1247   Dōgen visits Hōjō Tokiyori in Kamakura in August.

1248   Dōgen returns to Echizen in March.

1249   *Kichijōzan Eiheiji shuryō-shingi* in January.

1250   *Shōbōgenzō*, "Semmen" (third presentation).

1252   Dōgen suffers from ill health.

1253   *Shōbōgenzō*, "Sanjigō" and "Hachi-dainingaku"; Dōgen moves to Kyōto for medical treatment; dies on August 28. (Nichiren founds the Nichiren sect; Rankei Dōryū founds the Kenchōji temple in Kamakura.)

Note to Appendix A

This chronology does not include the following chapters of *Shōbōgenzō* because the dates and places of their presentation or composition are not certain: "Shukke-kudoku," "Jukai," "Kuyō-shobutsu," "Kie-buppōsōbō," "Jinshin-inga," "Shime," "Shizenbiku," "Ippyakuhachi-hōmyōmon," "Yuibutsu-yobutsu," and "Shōji."

Major Works by Dōgen

1. *Hōkyōki* (*Memoirs of the Hōkyō Period*). One volume. This is the oldest of Dōgen's works, being the memoirs that consist of questions and answers on various matters exchanged between Ju-ching and Dōgen. The book bears its name because it was written in the Hōkyō (Chinese: Pao-ch'ing) period (1225–1227) of the Sung dynasty when Dōgen was studying under Ju-ching on Mt. T'ien-t'ung. *Hōkyōki* was discovered in December 1253 by Ejō, while he was arranging Dōgen's works; later it was edited and published by Menzan Zuihō (1683–1769).

2. *Fukan-zazengi* (*General Advice on the Principles of Zazen*). One volume. The work was written perhaps immediately after Dōgen returned home in 1227 from his four-year period of study in China. It attempts to propagate the method and virtues of zazen-only as the rightly transmitted Buddha-dharma. It may be regarded, with *Shōbōgenzō*, "Bendōwa," as the manifesto of Dōgen's view of Buddhism. According to his *Fukan-zazengi senjutsu yurai* (*Reasons for Writing Fukan-zazengi*), Dōgen evidently intended to modify and improve the principles of zazen expounded by Tsung-che in the eighth volume of his *Ch'an yüan-ch'ing-kuei* (1103) and thereby to restore the spirit of the monastic ideal envisioned by Po-chang Huai-hai. There exists a copy of *Fukan-zazengi* in Dōgen's own handwriting called the "fair copy edition" (jōsho-bon) dated July 15, 1233. This manuscript is considerably different in its content and style from the popular edition (rufu-bon) which we can see in *Eihei Gen-zenji goroku* (1358) and *Dōgen oshō kōroku* (or *Eihei kōroku*; 1672). It is the general consensus among scholars that Dōgen wrote the original copy immediately after his return from China and refined and pol-

ished it during the twenty years before his death. Thus the present popular edition is the more refined and mature version of *Fukan-zazengi*.[1]

3. *Shōbōgenzō* (*Treasury of the True Dharma Eye*). Ninety-two chapters. This is Dōgen's magnum opus, written between August 1231 and January 1253. The currently popular ninety-five-chapter edition was edited in 1690 by Kōzen (1648–1693) who arranged each chapter according to the chronological order of its oral presentation and/or writing. Traditionally well-known, prior to the appearance of the Kōzen-bon, were: Ejō's seventy-five-chapter edition; Giun's sixty-chapter edition (1329); and Bonsei's eighty-four-chapter edition (1419). According to Mizuno Yaoko's recent textual studies based on the oldest extant manuscripts,[2] the total picture of the formation of *Shōbōgenzō* seems significantly different. Mizuno maintains that the following four were the oldest: (1) the seventy-five-chapter edition, (2) the sixty-chapter edition, (3) the twelve-chapter edition, and (4) the twenty-eight-chapter edition. Dōgen seems to have undertaken, sometime toward the end of his life, to compose a hundred chapters, altogether, for *Shōbō-genzō* by adding some new chapters to the old manuscripts, at the same time revising the old ones. In all probability (so conjectures Mizuno) this was the seventy-five-chapter edition, which had been projected and arranged by Dōgen himself with Ejō's assistance. When he died in August 1253, Dōgen had completed only twelve new (some rewritten) chapters, constituting the twelve-chapter edition, and had again been working on the aforementioned seventy-five-chapter corpus. In short, Dōgen died prematurely without seeing the completion of his projected one-hundred-chapter version of *Shōbō-genzō*. In view of the fact that Dōgen attempted to arrange the chapters of the two editions, not chronologically, but systematically in terms of the contents of his thought, they deserve serious attention from anyone attempting to understand that thought. On the other hand, the sixty-chapter and the twenty-eight-chapter editions, according to Mizuno, belong together, complementing each other in their contents, and both might have been derived from a common hypothetical source, very possibly copied by Ejō. According to this interpretation, the eighty-four-chapter edition and the ninety-five-chapter edition, and others, are derivatives from these four oldest editions. Of the four, the seventy-five-chapter edition and the twelve-chapter edition seem to reflect Dōgen's original intention most truly.[3]

4. *Eihei shoso gakudō-yōjinshū* (*Advice on Studying the Way*). One volume. The work consists of ten sections which treat, systematically, various problems of faith, zazen, and many other subjects. It was probably written in 1234 when Dōgen stayed at the Kannon-dōriin temple in Yamashiro. It is surmised by some scholars that its present form was collected and edited by Ejō. However, this is still open to further investigation. The book was published in 1357—the earliest in the history of publication of Dōgen's

works, indicating that it was very highly regarded by sectarians in the Sōtō tradition.[4]

5. *Shōbōgenzō zuimonki* (*Gleanings from Master Dōgen's Sayings*). Six volumes. This is a collection of Dōgen's talks given to Ejō after the latter became a disciple in 1234. They were recorded and edited by Ejō himself (c. 1235–38). The work is regarded as the best introduction to the understanding of Dōgen's life and thought as a whole. It was not until 1651 that the book was published for the first time in the Keian edition (Keian-bon). Later, in 1770, the so-called popular edition (Meiwa-bon or rufu-bon), with the preface by Menzan Zuihō, was published and it was the most widely used edition thereafter. However, Okubo Dōshū, a leading authority on Dōgen's life, discovered the manuscript now called the Chōenji edition (Chōenji-bon), at the famous Chōenji temple in Aichi prefecture in 1941. This edition (1644) is allegedly based on a manuscript dated 1380. A number of issues and problems surrounding *Shōbōgenzō zuimonki* have been clarified since then.[5]

6. *Tenzo-kyōkun* (*Instructions to the Chief Cook*). One volume. This was written in 1237, admonishing monastics in general and the chief cook in particular to regard every detail of cookery as sacred. Dōgen exhorts the sanctity of the apparently ignoble duty of cooking in the monastic life.

7. *Taidaiko-goge-jarihō* or *Taidaiko no hō* (*Instructions on Revering the Monastic Superiors*). One volume. It was written in 1244 at the Kippōji temple in Echizen, and consists of sixty-two rules and instructions for the inferiors' conduct towards their superiors (*taiko*).

8. *Bendōhō* (*Rules for the Practice of the Way*). One volume. Detailed instructions on zazen, on washing the face, on wearing the robe, and so on. Written between 1244 and 1246 at the Daibutsuji temple in Echizen.

9. *Nihonkoku Echizen Eiheiji chiji-shingi* (*Instructions for Eiheiji Administrators*). One volume. Written in 1246 at the Eiheiji temple. Six administrators (*chiji*) of the monastery are instructed with respect to the treatment of monastics and inferiors. In contrast to *Taidaiko-goge-jarihō*, this work was written for the monastic leaders.[6]

10. *Fushukuhampō* (*Rules for Table Manners*). One volume. Written between 1246 and 1253. It gives minute instructions for table manners and other related conduct.

11. *Kichijōzan Eiheiji shuryō-shingi* (*Rules for the Eiheiji Library*). One volume. *Shuryō*, separate from the monastics' hall, is a special building for the reading of sūtras and Buddhist classics; accordingly, it is the center of Buddhist studies in the monastery. The book is comprised of rules for conduct in the library. Written in 1249 at the Eiheiji temple.

12. *Dōgen oshō kōroku* (*The Extensive Record of Teacher Dōgen's Sayings*). Ten volumes. This work is a collection of Dōgen's sermons, lectures, sayings, and so forth, which were edited by Ejō, Senne, and Gien perhaps im-

mediately after Dōgen's death. It also includes *Fukan-zazengi* and "Zazen-shin." There are three different editions of the text of *Dōgen oshō kōroku:* (1) the Rinnōji edition copied in 1598, (2) the popular edition printed in 1672 by Manzan Dōhaku (1636–1714), and (3) the Sozan edition (Sozan-bon), a manuscript discovered at the Eiheiji temple in 1937, which has been proven to be older than the Rinnōji edition. An increasing number of students of Dōgen in the post-war period feel that the work is comparable in its importance to *Shōbōgenzō* and, hence, must be investigated thoroughly. Research in this regard has been progressing very vigorously in recent years.[7]

13. *Eihei Gen-zenji goroku* (*The Record of Dōgen Zenji's Sayings*). One volume. The work contains Dōgen's sayings from the Kōshōji and Eiheiji period, and also *Fukan-zazengi* and "Zazenshin." Its contents were selected from the original version of *Dōgen oshō kōroku* (or *Eihei kōroku*) by Wu-wai I-yüan of China, as requested by Dōgen's disciple, Giin, in 1264. It is about one-tenth the size of *Kōroku*. It was first published in 1358, and reprinted on several occasions. Of these editions the Shōhō edition, extant at the Tōzenji temple in Aichi prefecture, is said to be oldest, having been printed not later than 1649.[8]

Notes to Appendix B

1. Ōkubo Dōshū, ed., *Dōgen zenji goroku*, pp. 207–14; idem, ed., *Dōgen zenji zenshū*, vol. 2, pp. 519–22.

2. Mizuno Yaoko, "Shōbōgenzō no shohon sono ta ni tsuite," in Nishio Minoru and others, eds., *Shōbōgenzō zuimonki*, pp. 34–56; see also Ōkubo, *Zenshū*, vol. 1, pp. 789–810.

3. *Shōbōgenzō* in Ōkubo's *Zenshū* reflects the foregoing findings of recent research in this area. See Appendix C of the present work.

4. Ōkubo, *Goroku*, pp. 215–22; idem, *Zenshū*, vol. 2, pp. 524–28.

5. Mizuno Yaoko, "Kaisetsu," in Nishio Minoru and others, eds., *Shōbōgenzō Bendōwa Shōbōgenzō zuimonki hoka*, pp. 306–22; idem, "Chōenji-bon Shōbōgenzō zuimonki no hombun ni tsuite," *Bungaku*, vol. 29, no. 6 (June 1961), pp. 100–108; Ōkubo, *Zenshū*, vol. 2, pp. 551–54.

6. In a Zen monastic community there are two groups of leaders who support and cooperate with its head (*jūji*): (1) the six administrative leaders (*chiji*)—head supervisor (*tsūsu*), supervisor (*kansu*), accountant (*fūsu*), clerk (*ino*), chief cook (*tenzo*), and maintenance manager (*shissui*); (2) the six disciplinary leaders (*chōshu*)—head monastic (*shuso*), secretary (*shoki*), head librarian (*chizō*), head of reception (*shika*), manager of the bath (*chiyoku*), and manager of the worship hall (*chiden*). The administrative leaders constitute the "Eastern Order," whereas the disciplinary leaders constitute the "Western Order." See Jimbo Nyoten and Andō Bun'ei, eds., *Zengaku jiten*.

7. Itō Shunkō, ed., *Eihei-kōroku chūkai zensho*, 3 vols. (1961–63), and many works and articles on *Kōroku*.

8. Ōkubo, *Goroku*, pp. 222–28.

Names of the
Ninety-two Chapters
of *Shōbōgenzō*[1]

I. The Seventy-five-Chapter Edition

1. Genjō-kōan (Kōan Realized in Life)
2. Maka-hannya-haramitsu or Moko-hoja-horomi (The Perfection of Great Wisdom)
3. Busshō (Buddha-nature)
4. Shinjin-gakudō (Understanding the Way Through the Body-Mind)
5. Sokushin-zebutsu (This Mind Itself Is Buddha)
6. Gyōbutsu-igi (Majestic Activities of the Active Buddha)
7. Ikka-myōju (One Luminous Pearl)
8. Shin-fukatoku (The Mind Unobtainable)[2]
9. Kobusshin (The Minds of Ancient Buddhas)
10. Daigo (Great Enlightenment)
11. Zazengi (Principles of Zazen)
12. Zazenshin (Admonitions for Zazen)
13. Kaiin-zammai (Ocean-reflections Samādhi)
14. Kūge (Flowers of Emptiness)
15. Kōmyō (Light)
16. Gyōji (I and II) (Creative Activities)
17. Immo (Thusness)
18. Kannon (Avalokiteśvara)
19. Kokyō (The Primordial Mirror)
20. Uji or Yūji (Existence-Time)
21. Juki (The Assurance of Enlightenment)
22. Zenki (Total Dynamism)

23. Tsuki or Toki (The Moon)
24. Gabyō or Gabei (Pictured Cakes)
25. Keisei-sanshoku (Sounds of Brooks and Figures of Mountains)
26. Bukkōjōji (Ongoing Enlightenment)[2]
27. Muchū-setsumu (Expounding Dreams in Dreams)
28. Raihai-tokuzui (Attainment of the Marrow Through Worship)
29. Sansuikyō (The Sūtra of the Mountains and Waters)
30. Kankin (Sūtra-Reading)
31. Shoaku-makusa (Not to Commit Any Evil)
32. Den'e (Transmission of the Robe)
33. Dōtoku (Creative Expressions)
34. Bukkyō (34) (Buddhist Teachings)[3]
35. Jinzū (Super normal Powers)
36. Arakan (Arahat)
37. Shunjū (Spring and Autumn)
38. Kattō (Vines)
39. Shisho (Genealogical Records)
40. Hakujushi (Cypress Trees)
41. Sangai-yuishin (The Triple World Is Mind-Only)
42. Sesshin-sesshō (Discourse on Mind and Its Essence)
43. Shohō-jissō (All Things Themselves Are Their Ultimate Nature)
44. Butsudō (The Buddha-Way)[2]
45. Mitsugo (Intimate Words)
46. Mujō-seppō (Sermons of Insentient Beings)
47. Bukkyō (47) (Buddhist Sūtras)[3]
48. Hosshō (The Dharma-Nature)
49. Darani (Charms and Spells)
50. Semmen (Washing the Face)[2]
51. Menju (Face-to-Face Transmission)
52. Busso (The Buddhas and Ancestors)
53. Baika (Plum Blossoms)
54. Senjō (Washing and Cleansing)
55. Jippō (Ten Quarters)
56. Kembutsu (Meeting the Buddhas)
57. Hensan (Extensive Pilgrimages)
58. Ganzei (The Eyeball)
59. Kajō (Daily Living)
60. Sanjūshichihon-bodaibumpō (Thirty-seven Virtues of Bodhisattva-hood)
61. Ryūgin (Sounds of a Flute)
62. Soshi-seiraii (The Meaning of Bodhidharma's Coming from the West)
63. Hotsu-mujōshin (The Awakening of the Supreme Mind)
64. Udonge (*Udumbara*)

65. Nyorai-zenshin (The Whole Being of Tathāgata)
66. Zammai-ōzammai (The Samādhi of Samādhis)
67. Tembōrin (Turning the Wheel of Dharma)
68. Daishugyō (Great Spiritual Discipline)
69. Jishō-zammai (The Samādhi of Self-Enlightenment)
70. Kokū (The Empty Space)
71. Hatsuu, Hau, or Hou (An Alms Bowl)
72. Ango (The Monastic Retreat)
73. Tashintsū (The Power of Knowing Other Minds)
74. Ōsaku-sendaba (The Ruler Seeking the *Sendaba*)
75. Shukke (The Monastic's Life)

II. The Twelve-Chapter Edition

1. Shukke-kudoku (Merits of the Monastic's Life)
2. Jukai (Receiving the Precepts)
3. Kesa-kudoku (Merits of the Monastic's Robe)
4. Hotsu-bodaishin (The Awakening of the Thought of Enlightenment)
5. Kuyō-shobutsu (Honoring the Buddhas)
6. Kie-buppōsōbō (Taking Refuge in the Three Treasures) [4]
7. Jinshin-inga (Deep Faith in the Law of Causation)
8. Sanjigō (The Three Periods for Karmic Consequences) [2]
9. Shime (Four Horses)
10. Shizenbiku (A Monastic in the Fourth Dhyāna)
11. Ippyakuhachi-hōmyōmon (One Hundred and Eight Teachings) [5]
12. Hachi-dainingaku (The Eight Awarenesses of Great Persons)

III. Others

1. Bendōwa (Discourse on the Practice of the Way) [2]
2. Bodaisatta-shishōbō (Four Virtues of the Bodhisattva)
3. Hokke-ten-Hokke (The *Lotus Sūtra* Turning Itself)
4. Shōji (Birth and Death)
5. Yuibutsu-yobutsu (Only Between a Buddha and a Buddha)

Notes to Appendix C

1. See Appendix B on *Shōbōgenzō*.
2. These chapters have appended chapters (*betsubon*) with the same titles. Of them, the appended chapter of Shin-fukatoku corresponds with Go-shin-fukatoku or Shin-fukatoku II of the ninety-five-chapter edition, and that of Butsudō with Dōshin.
3. Bukkyō (34) and Bukkyō (47), which signify the thirty-fourth and the forty-seventh chapters of the seventy-five-chapter edition, respectively, are adopted in the present study, because they are homophones.
4. This chapter is called Kie-sambō or Kie-sanhō in the ninety-five-chapter edition.

5. This chapter is not included in the ninety-five-chapter edition. Likewise, two chapters of the latter edition, Jūundōshiki (Rules for an Annex to the Monastics' Hall) and Jikuimmon (Manners at the Monastic Kitchen) are not included in the seventy-five-chapter edition. See Ōkubo Dōshū, ed., *Dōgen zenji zenshū*, vol. 2 for these two works which Ōkubo thinks were not originally intended to be part of *Shōbōgenzō*. Their full titles are: *Kannon-dōri-Kōshō-gokokuji jūundōshiki* and *Eiheiji jikuimmon*.

NOTES

Foreword: The Way of Dōgen Zenji

1. Simon Pétrement, *Simone Weil: A Life*, trans. by Raymond Rossenthal. (New York: Pantheon, 1976), pp. 39–40.

2. This and subsequent passages which I quote from the *Genjō Kōan* do not appear in Dr. Kim's text, and are my own translations.

3. This story was told during a talk at the Koko An Zendo by Yamada Kōun Rōshi.

4. Cf. Kōun Yamada, *Gateless Gate* (Los Angeles: Center Publications, 1979), p. 45.

5. Dōgen Kigen, *Kyōjūkaimon*. See Robert Aitken, *The Mind of Clover: Essays in Zen Buddhist Ethics* (San Francisco: North Point Press, 1984), p. 50.

Chapter One: Toward a Total Understanding of Zen

1. Masunaga Reihō, *Eihei Shōbōgenzō—Dōgen no shūkyō*, p. 3.

2. These quotations are from Tanabe Hajime, *Shobōgenzō no tetsugaku shikan* (1939), reprinted in Nishitani Keiji and others, eds., *Tanabe Hajime zenshū*, vol. 5, pp. 445–94.

3. Heinrich Dumoulin, *A History of Zen Buddhism*, p. 174.

4. This essay was carried in *Shin-shōsetsu* and *Shisō* between 1920 and 1923, and later published in his *Nihon seishinshi kenkyū*, pp. 251–404. It was reprinted recently in Nishio Minoru, ed., *Shōbōgenzō Bendōva Shōbōgenzō zuimankihoka*, pp. 325–77.

5. For my summary of the history of Dōgen studies, I am indebted to the following works: Kagamishima Genryū, "Dōgen zenji kenkyū no kaiko

to tembō," *Bungaku*, vol. 29, no. 6 (June 1961), pp. 109–17; Kagamishima Hiroyuki, "Dōgen zenji kenkyū no dōkō kaiko," *Dōgen zenji kenkyū*, vol. 1, no. 1 (January 1941), pp. 341–68; Takeuchi Michio, "Saikin no Dōgen ni kansuru kenkyū ni tsuite," *Nihon Bukkyō-shi*, no. 4 (May 1958), pp. 46–55; Fueoka Jishō, "Saikin ni okeru Dōgen zenji kenkyū sangyō no kaiko," *Dōgen zenji godenki*, vol. 1, no. 1 (June 1949), pp. 132–49; Ikebe Minoru, "Dōgen kankei kenkyū bunken mokuroku," *Bungaku*, vol. 29, no. 6 (June 1961), pp. 742–67; Ōkubo Dōshū, "Dōgen zenji sangyō no rekishi-teki kaiko," in his *Dōgen zenji-den no kenkyū* (revised edition), pp. 470–500; Okada Gihō, "Shōbōgenzō no hensan narabini chūso-shi," "Shōbōgenzō no kenkyū bunken ni tsuite," in his *Shōbōgenzō shisō taikei*, vol. 1, pp. 12–43 and vol. 8, pp. 431–40, respectively; Jimbo Nyoten and Andō Bun'ei, "Shōbōgenzō chūkai-zensho naiyō shomoku kaidai," in their *Shōbōgenzō chūkai-zensho*, vol. 11, pp. 7–78.

6. Akamatsu Toshihide and others, *Nihon Bukkyō-shi*, vol. 2, pp. 199–210; Imaeda Aishin, *Zenshū no rekishi*, pp. 151–87; Ōkubo Dōshū, op. cit., 406–68; Kurebayashi Kōdō, "Dōgen Keizan ryōso igo ni okeru Sōtō-shūgaku no shuryū," *Journal of Indian and Buddhist Studies*, vol. 6, no. 2 (March 1958), pp. 12–20. Concerning Gozan Zen, see Akamatsu and others, op. cit., pp. 173–96; Imaeda, op. cit., pp. 72–150.

7. For this period see Imaeda, op. cit., Chapter 5; Tamamuro Taijō and others, *Nihon Bukkyō-shi*, vol. 3, *Kinsei-kindai-hen*.

8. See Kishimoto Hideo, ed., *Japanese Religion in the Meiji Era*; Tamamuro Taijō and others, op. cit.

9. Kagamishima Hiroyuki, "Dōgen zenji kenkyū no dōkō kaiko," *Dōgen zenji kenkyū*, vol. 1, no. 1 (January 1941), p. 345.

10. Loc. cit., where Kagamishima observes that only two works, namely Murakami Sensei's *Bukkyō tōitsu-ron* (1901) and Ōkawa Shūmei's *Nihon bummei-shi* (1921), discussed Dōgen and then only very briefly.

11. *Keiteki* is a collection of Nishiari's lectures on twenty-nine chapters of *Shōbōgenzō* which were recorded by his disciple, Toyama Soei, and later edited by Kurebayashi Kōdō in 1930. It is one of the best commentaries on *Shōbōgenzō*.

12. This book was originally designed to be a manual for Sōtō believers' daily devotional life. However, the task of making the work required some unexpectedly painstaking efforts relative to linguistic, textual, and literary studies of *Shōbōgenzō*. These efforts gave an impetus in subsequent years to genuinely scholarly and systematic endeavors for basic research. Kagamishima Hiroyuki, "Dōgen zenji kenkyū no dōkō kaiko," pp. 364–67.

13. Akiyama later wrote another work of importance, *Dōgen zenji to gyō* in 1940.

14. Tanabe also writes: "Viewed from the philosophical standpoint, Dōgen's *Shōbōgenzō* is matchless in its command of Japanese language and

logic with the power to realize the ineffable in and through speech and discourse."

15. The subsequent volumes 2, 3, and 4 appeared in 1940, 1944, and 1950, respectively. Hashida viewed Dōgen's thought as providing science with its metaphysical foundation.

16. Kagamishima Genryū, "Dōgen zenji kenkyū no kaiko to tembō," *Bungaku*, vol. 29, no. 6 (June 1961), pp. 111–13.

17. The element of faith in Dōgen's thought is also emphasized by Kurebayashi Kōdō in his *Dōgen-zen no kenkyū* (1963), and it has been a general tendency on the part of the sectarian circle to emphasize (or over-emphasize, as some critics would say) this aspect of Dōgen's thought. The problem will be treated later in this study.

A notable activity of the sect during this period was the establishment of Dōgen zenji sangyōkai in 1936, and the publication of *Dōgen zenji kenkyū*, vol. 1, no. 1 (1941), a culmination of members' scholarly efforts in the field.

18. Some additional works of importance in the post-war period: Nakamura Hajime, *Tōyōjin no shii-hōhō*, part 2 (1949); Masunaga Reihō, op. cit. (1956); Kurebayashi Kōdō, op. cit. (1963); Miyasaka Tetsubun, *Zen ni okeru ningen keisei* (revised edition; 1970); and numerous articles and essays in the *Journal of Indian and Buddhist Studies*, *Journal of Sōtō Studies*, *Komazawa daigaku kenkyū kiyō*, etc.

19. The broadly philological studies have produced numerous works: among others, Okada Gihō, op. cit., 8 volumes (1953); Andō Bun'ei and Jimbo Nyoten, eds., *Shōbōgenzō chūkai-zensho*, 11 volumes (originally published in 1913–14, and reprinted in 1956–57); Katō Shūkō, ed., *Shōbōgenzō yōgo sakuin*, 2 volumes (1962–63). Concerning other articles and works, see the aforementioned articles by Takeuchi Michio, Kagamishima Genryū, Kagamishima Hiroyuki, Fueoka Jishō in note 5 above.

20. The following are some of the works on Dōgen and translations of his works in Western languages: Masunaga Reihō, *The Sōtō Approach to Zen*; idem, *A Primer of Sōtō Zen: A Translation of Dōgen's Shōbōgenzō zuimonki*; Katō Kazumitsu, "The Life and Teaching of Dōgen" (an unpublished Ph.D. dissertation); Philip Kapleau, *The Three Pillars of Zen*; Heinrich Dumoulin, *A History of Zen Buddhism*, pp. 151–74; idem, "Das Buch Genjōkōan Aus dem Shōbōgenzo des Zen-Meisters Dōgen," *Monumenta Nipponica*, vol. 15, nos. 3–4 (October 1959–January 1960), pp. 217–32; Oscar Benl, "Die Anfange der Sōtō-Mönchgemeinschaften," *Oriens Extremus*, vol. 7 (1960), pp. 31–50; idem, "Der Zen-Meister Dōgen in China," *Nachrichten der Deutschen Gesellschaft für Natur und Volkerkunde Ostasiens*, nos. 79–80, pp. 67–77; Jiyu Kennett, *Selling Water by the River: A Manual of Zen Training*; those translations referred to in note 22 below. Nakamura Hajime in his *Ways of Thinking of Eastern Peoples* quotes and translates extensively from Dōgen's works. The following anthologies contain some translated passages from

Dōgen: Tsunoda Ryūsaku and others, comp., *Sources of Japanese Tradition*;
William Th. de Bary, ed., *The Buddhist Tradition in India, China and Japan*;
Wing-tsit Chan and others, comp., *The Great Asian Religions: An Anthology*.

21. Masunaga Reihō, *The Sōtō Approach to Zen*, p. 193.

22. For example, *The Eastern Buddhist* has carried a series of translations by Norman Waddell and Abe Masao of some important chapters of
Shōbōgenzō and promises to carry further translations in the future issues.
Those which have appeared thus far are: "Bendōwa," vol. 4, no. 1 (May
1971), pp. 124–57; "Ikka-myōju," vol. 4, no. 2 (October 1971), pp. 108–
18; "Zenki" and "Shōji," vol. 5, no. 1 (May 1972), pp. 70–80; "Genjō-
kōan," vol. 5, no. 2 (October 1972), pp. 129–40; "Zazengi" (and *Fukan-
zazengi*), vol. 6, no. 2 (October 1973), pp. 115–28; "Zammai-ōzammai,"
vol. 7, no. 1 (May 1974), pp. 118–23.

23. Alan Watts, *Beat Zen, Square Zen, and Zen* for some aspects of Western appropriation of Zen Buddhism.

24. See, for example, Yamaguchi Susumu and others, *Bukkyō-gaku josetsu*;
Miyamoto Shōson, ed., *Bukkyō no kompon shinri*; Kenneth W. Morgan, ed.,
The Path of the Buddha; Sangharakshita, *A Survey of Buddhism*; and others,
for growing efforts on the part of Buddhists to see Buddhism in its diversity
as well as its unity. This is a significant departure from sectarian isolationism.

25. There are so many works relevant to methodological problems of
the history of religions in general. To cite only a few: Mircea Eliade and
Joseph M. Kitagawa, eds., *The History of Religions: Essays in Methodology*;
J. M. Kitagawa, ed., *The History of Religions: Essays on the Problem of Under-
standing*; Mircea Eliade, *The Quest: History and Meaning in Religion*; Robert
N. Bellah, *Beyond Belief: Essays on Religion in a Post-Traditional World*;
Wilfred C. Smith, *The Meaning and End of Religion*; J. M. Yinger, *The Scien-
tific Study of Religion*.

26. See Johan Huizinga, *Homo Ludens* for religion and play; the human
being as *animal symbolicum* is expounded in Ernst Cassirer, *Philosophy of
Symbolic Forms* and *An Essay on Man*, and Susanne Langer, *Philosophy in a
New Key*, etc.

27. I can cite just one example in this connection. Wilfred C. Smith, in
his essay, "Comparative Religion: Whither—and Why?" (Kitagawa and
Eliade, op. cit., pp. 31–58), rightly calls for the personalist approach to religious phenomena, and in a similar vein, distinguishes, in his *The Meaning
and End of Religion*, between "cumulative tradition" and "personal faith,"
maintaining that, while both are dynamic and diverse, the former is historically intelligible, the latter not amenable or reducible to such intelligibility.
This is no doubt salutary to our deeper understanding of religious faith. On
the other hand, Smith seems to suggest that cumulative tradition is extraneous to, while personal faith is involved with, transcendence (i.e, God to
Smith). Hence, personal faith should be the concern of any understanding of

religion. Here, Smith is unduly distrustful of any religious expressions that constitute cumulative tradition—and by implication, of any social scientific, historical, and cultural investigations of religion. Thus, his analysis does not provide us with an examination of the interrelation and interpenetration of history and faith. Faith, in my view, not only "varies" but also "evolves" just as cumulative tradition does, although Smith writes: "The traditions evolve. Men's faith varies. God endures" (ibid., p. 173).

Chapter Two: Dōgen's life

1. There are several biographies of Dōgen traditionally known in the Sōtō sect. However, their materials are uncritical, full of pious frauds and apologetic embellishments, and, hence, must be critically scrutinized and assessed. As to these traditional biographies, see Ōkubo Dōshū, *Dōgen zenji-den no kenkyū*, pp. 20–35. For my subsequent investigation of Dōgen's life I am greatly indebted to Ōkubo's work and Takeuchi Michio's *Dōgen*.

2. Ivan Morris, *The World of the Shining Prince*, p. 180. The following observations of Morris' are particularly significant in this connection: "The composition, exchange, and quotation of poems was central to the daily life of the Heian aristocracy, and it is doubtful whether any other society in the world has ever attached such importance to the poetic versatility of its members" (p. 177). And: "Not only did the rule of taste extend to every sphere of life and apply to the smallest details, but (with the single exception of good birth) it took primacy over all else. Artistic sensibility was more highly valued than ethical goodness. Despite the influence of Buddhism, Heian society was on the whole governed by style rather than by any moral principles, and good looks tended to take the place of virtue. The word *yoki* ('good') referred primarily to birth, but it also applied to a person's beauty or to his aesthetic sensibility; the one implication it lacked was that of ethical rectitude. For all their talk about 'heart' and 'feeling,' this stress on the cult of the beautiful, to the virtual exclusion of any concern with charity, sometimes lends a rather chilling impression to the people of Genji's world" (p. 195).

3. Cf. ibid., pp. 108ff. and pp. 195ff. The declining fate of aristocracy is lyrically depicted in a clear relief against the vigor of the rising samurai class in *Heike monogatari*. In *Hōjōki* by Kamo no Chōmei (1153–1216), it is written: "The flow of the river is ceaseless and its water is never the same. The bubbles that float in the pools, now vanishing, now forming, are not of long duration: so in the world are man and his dwellings." Donald Keene, comp. and ed., *Anthology of Japanese Literature*, p. 197. Such examples of the ethos and pathos of the age are replete in the Heian and Kamakura literature.

4. Ienaga Saburō, *Nihon dōtoku shisō-shi*, pp. 36–55.

5. Ibid., pp. 72–85.

6. Ibid., pp. 97–101. Ienaga associates such an awareness of the samurai class with Shinran's famous statement "Even the virtuous can attain rebirth in the Pure Land and how much more so the wicked" (*Tannishō*, III).

7. E. O. Reischauer, *Japan, Past and Present*, p. 53.

8. Murai Yasuhiko, "Shōen sei no hatten to kōzō," Ienaga Saburō and others, eds., *Nihon rekishi*, vol. 4, pp. 41–87; Watanabe Sumio, "Kōbu kenryoku to shōen-sei," Ienaga and others, eds., *Nihon rekishi*, vol. 5, pp. 179–226.

9. Morris, op. cit., p. 75. Also see George B. Sansom, *Japan: A Short Cultural History*, note on p. 273 concerning land holdings of the Tōdaiji temple and the Shimazu family as examples.

10. Ienaga Saburō and others, *Nihon Bukkyō-shi*, vol. 1, pp. 346–51; Charles Eliot, *Japanese Buddhism*, pp. 244–47.

11. Ienaga and others, *Nihon Bukkyō-shi*, vol. 1, pp. 241–58.

12. There are different theories of the lengths of the Three Ages of Right Law, Imitative Law, and Degenerate Law—e.g., 500, 1,000, and 10,000 years respectively, or 1,000, 1,000, and 10,000. In Japan the latter scheme was adopted and calculated from 949 B.C.E., the presumable date of Buddha's death. *Mappō* thought was popular in China from the sixth century on and in Japan from the tenth century on.

13. For example, see Shinran's "Hymn on the Three Ages" in *The Shinshū Seiten*, pp. 236–37.

14. The following observation from Reischauer is noteworthy: "It is, indeed, a curious fact that the popular Buddhism of feudal Japan had in many ways come to resemble Christianity more than historic Buddhism. Reversing the basic pessimism of the early faith, it had come to stress a real afterlife and salvation through faith. And the early feudal religious reformers, in their translations of the scriptures, their creation of lay congregations, their marriage of the clergy, their militant sectarianism, and their nascent nationalism, resembled to a surprising degree the Protestant reformers of Europe. These religious trends, coupled with the development of a feudal system which found much closer parallels in medieval Europe than in East Asia, make the early feudal period in Japan a time for startling comparisons with Europe and strong contrasts with other countries in the Far East." Op. cit., p. 60.

15. *Shōbōgenzō zuimonki*, I:2. Hereafter we shall refer to *Zuimonki* throughout the present study. Cf. ibid., V:6. Dōgen employs the doctrine often in his writings. For example, he writes: "In the ancient Ages of Right Law and of Imitative Law, Buddha's disciples all knew this truth, and they practiced and studied it. Nowadays of a thousand monastics not a single person knows these eight precepts of great persons (*hachi-dainingaku*). The pity is that nothing is comparable to the degeneration of these latter days" (*Shōbōgenzō*, "Hachi-dainingaku"). See also ibid., "Kesa-kudoku," "Den'e," "Shisho," etc.

16. *Zuimonki*, III : 20 and I : 8.

17. Dōgen said: "The worldly people would probably say: 'Although we desire earnestly to study the Way, it is the Age of Degenerate Law, we are degraded, and our capacities to understand the teachings of Buddhism are deficient. We cannot undergo spiritual discipline that accords with Dharma. We should simply be contented with our lot, follow an easy path, think of having a connection with Buddha, and hope to attain enlightenment in a subsequent existence.' What has just been said is altogether mistaken. In the Buddha-dharma, to advocate the divisions of the Three Ages of Right Law, Imitative Law, and Degenerate Law is a provisional means of instruction, but not the true teachings of the Way. If you practice according to the teachings, you will be enlightened without fail. Monastics during Buddha's lifetime were not necessarily superior; in fact some of them were unimaginably wretched and of low character. When Buddha set forth various rules and precepts, they were all for immoral sentient beings and wretched persons. Each of us is the working of the Buddha-dharma; do not ever think your calibre is unfit for it. If you follow the teachings in your practice, you will surely attain the Way. Once you have the right intention, you are capable of discriminating between good and evil. With hands and feet, you lack nothing for joining your hands in worship and for walking. In the practice of Dharma, you should not make distinction of classes or ranks. Indeed life in the human world is invariably endowed with ability, whereas it is not granted to other, non-human, life." Ibid., V : 12.

Elsewhere Dōgen states in a similar vein: "While the doctrinal schools of Buddhism are preoccupied with names and appearances, the true teachings of Mahāyāna Buddhism have not yet distinguished between Right Law, Imitative Law, and Degenerate Law. They teach that whenever one practices the Way, one surely attains it—much more so in this authentically transmitted Dharma, whether one enters into Dharma or attains liberation, one uses one's native treasure all the same. Whether you are enlightened or not can be known by yourself who practices the Way; it may be likened to those who use water, and thereby know by themselves whether water is cool or warm." *Shōbōgenzō*, "Bendōwa."

18. Hori Ichirō, *Folk Religion in Japan*; idem, *Minkan shinkō*.

19. Hori, *Folk Religion in Japan*, p. 103. Also see pp. 101–10.

20. Ibid., passim.

21. Ienaga and others, *Nihon Bukkyō-shi*, vol. 1, pp. 258–63; Watsuji Tetsurō, *Nihon rinri shisō-shi*, vol. 1, pp. 373–420.

22. For these subjects, see Hori's two cited works; Nakamura Hajime, *Ways of Thinking of Eastern Peoples*, part 4; *Proceedings of the XIth International Congress of the International Association for the History of Religions*, vol. 2: *Guilt or Pollution and Rites of Purification*; etc.

23. Concerning the family traditions of Dōgen's parents, see Ōkubo, op. cit., pp. 44–73; Takeuchi, op. cit., pp. 5–20.

24. *Zuimonki*, III : 17.

25. Ibid., III : 14.

26. Ōkubo, op. cit., pp. 75–76.

27. Loc. cit. See also *Zuimonki*, V : 8. In *Kannon-dōri Kōshō-gokokuji jūundōshiki* (hereafter *Jūundōshiki* throughout this study), Dōgen stated: "Father and mother are temporary parents while in this life."

28. For example, *Zuimonki* and *Eihei shoso gakudō-yōjinshū* (hereafter *Gakudō-yōjinshū* in this study).

29. Takeuchi, op. cit., p. 27.

30. In *Sanso gyōgōki*, one of the biographies of Dōgen, the name of Ryōken appears instead. See Takeuchi, op. cit., p. 28. As to Ryōken, see Okubo, op. cit., pp. 64, 76–77.

31. *Zuimonki*, III : 25.

32. *Shōbōgenzō*, "Gyōji."

33. *Zuimonki*, VI : 2. In *Gakudō-yōjinshū*, 4, Dōgen says: "The Buddha-dharma should never be practiced for one's own sake, much less for the sake of fame or gain. You should practice it solely for the sake of the Buddha-dharma."

34. Ōkubo doubts this because the regulation at Hiei concerning the bodhisattva ordination (*bosatsukai*) was that it was to be given when one reached the age of twenty. Op. cit., pp. 77–78.

35. *Zuimonki*, II : 18.

36. Ibid., II : 19. Cf. III : 22.

37. Ibid., II : 25. Cf. III : 20.

38. Ibid., III : 23.

39. Ibid., V : 8.

40. Ōkubo, op. cit., pp. 78–80.

41. For example, *The Awakening of Faith* (trans. Yoshito S. Hakeda), pp. 37ff.

42. Tamura Yoshirō, *Kamakura shin-Bukkyō shisō no kenkyū*, pp. 369–474.

43. See ibid., pp. 451–74 for the characteristics of the doctrine of original enlightenment.

44. Tamamuro Taijō, *Dōgen*, pp. 26–28.

45. Okubo, op. cit., p. 80.

46. As for Kōin himself, he increasingly became dissatisfied with the Tendai school and finally turned to Hōnen's Pure Realm Buddhism in his later life. In view of this, it is puzzling that Kōin recommended Zen rather than the Pure Realm tradition to Dōgen. We can only surmise that Kōin, a wise teacher, perceived, perhaps correctly, the advisability for Dōgen of studying Zen in view of his temperament and interests. It is also said that Kōin at this time recommended that Dōgen enter China for study immediately. Ibid., pp. 81–82. Dōgen refers to Kōin in *Zuimonki*, III : 8.

47. Ibid., V : 8.

48. Ōkubo, op. cit., pp. 83–109.

49. *Hōkyōki*, 1. See Ōkubo's defense for the significance of this passage of *Hōkyōki* that seems to substantiate a strong possibility of the meeting of Eisai and Dōgen. Ōkubo, op. cit., pp. 93–102. Concerning this issue, see Takeuchi, op. cit., pp. 53–55.

50. *Zuimonki*, III:2–3 and I:14, where Dōgen speaks of Eisai reverently. Concerning the relation of Dōgen's thought to Eisai's, see Etō Sokuō, *Shūso to shite no Dōgen zenji*, pp. 69–114.

51. See *Zuimonki*, V:8. Also in *Shōbōgenzō*, "Bendōwa," Dōgen says: "Ever since my initiation into Buddhism to seek Dharma, I had visited teachers extensively all over Japan."

52. Ibid., "Bendōwa."

53. *Zuimonki*, V:8.

54. *Gakudō-yōjinshū*, 5.

55. Takeuchi, op. cit., pp. 61–69. Also see his article, "Dōgen no rekishi-teki seikaku," *Bungaku*, vol. 29, no. 6 (June 1961), pp. 42–50.

56. According to *Zuimonki*, VI:15, Myōyū, Myōzen's teacher on Mt. Hiei, realizing that his time had come, sent a message to Myōzen, asking for the postponement of the latter's departure so that he could administer his teacher's death-watch. Myōzen seems to have been greatly agonized by this request: he was in a dilemma about whether he should accede to the old mentor's request, as human compassion prompted, or leave for China to seek the truth of Buddhism. Thus, Myōzen consulted with his disciples about this matter. The majority of them earnestly recommended that he defer the journey to the following year, while Dōgen was the only person who urged him to leave for China immediately as they had planned. Myōzen finally followed Dōgen's advice and went to China.

57. Ibid., VI:19. Dōgen recalled: "Years ago when I was crossing the sea to enter China, I suffered while aboard from severe diarrhea. When the whole ship was in a great turmoil owing to a terrible storm, I forgot the illness and found myself healed."

58. The question as to why Dōgen stayed on board for a full three months cannot be answered.

59. *Tenzo-kyōkun*. In this document, written fourteen years after this incident, the sanctity of cooking in the monastic kitchen was exhorted. We shall consider this problem later in Chapter 5.

60. Tsuji Zennosuke, *Nihon Bukkyō-shi*, vol. 3, p. 272.

61. *Tenzo-kyōkun*.

62. Ibid.

63. Kenneth K. S. Ch'en, *Buddhism in China*, pp. 389–400.

64. Heinrich Dumoulin, *A History of Zen Buddhism*, p. 123.

65. Ibid., pp. 123ff.

66. Ibid., p. 124.

67. Ch'en, op. cit., p. 403.
68. *Shōbōgenzō,* "Den'e."
69. Ibid., "Jishō-zammai."
70. Ibid., "Kembutsu."
71. Ibid., "Shohō-jissō." On the same subject, see also ibid., "Buk-kyō" (47).
72. Ibid., "Bendōwa."
73. Concerning Tsung-kao, see also ibid., "Jishō-zammai" and "Ōsaku-sendaba." Dōgen's attitude towards Rinzai Zen was somewhat puzzling, not always free from his sectarian consciousness and sense of rivalry with Rinzai. In this connection, see Rikukawa Taiun, "Dōgen zenji no Daie zenji hihan ni tsuite," *Zengaku kenkyū,* no. 55 (February 1966), pp. 56–70; Tama-mura Takeji, "Eihei Dōgen no Rinzai-shū ni taisuru kanjō," *Nihon rekishi,* no. 47 (April 1952), pp. 26–31; Furuta Shōkin, *Nihon Bukkyō shisō-shi no shomondai,* pp. 145–61. Although Ju-ching's relations with Rinzai Zen are difficult to determine, Tamamura conjectures that Dōgen's hostility to Rinzai Zen might have been influenced by Ju-ching, whereas Furuta thinks that Ju-ching had no anti-Rinzai sentiments and hence Dōgen's hostility had to do with his sense of rivalry with the opposing sect, particularly around 1243 and thereafter. Concerning Dōgen's mistaken observations of Tsung-kao, see Rikukawa Taiun's aforementioned article.
74. *Shōbōgenzō,* "Busshō." Dōgen describes his visit in the fall of 1223 to the Kuang-li-ssǔ temple on Mt. Ayüwang where the aforementioned chief cook had once stayed, and where Dōgen was thoroughly disappointed. It was during this period that Dōgen had the quite unusual privilege of seeing the genealogical documents (*shisho*) of various sects, and also that of his mentor, Wu-chi Liao-p'ai. The genealogical documents represented the Zen Buddhist version of "apostolic succession" and were not shown except to very special persons on exceptional occasions. See ibid., "Shisho."
75. Takeuchi, op. cit., pp. 128–48. Between the winter of 1224 and May 1, 1225, Dōgen visited, among others, Che-wêng Ju-yen at the Ching-shan Wan-shou-ssǔ temple and Yüan-tzǔ at the Wan-nien-ssǔ temple in P'ing-t'ien.
76. Ibid., p. 147.
77. *Shōbōgenzō,* "Menju."
78. Ibid., "Gyōji."
79. Ibid., "Baika." Later Dōgen wrote: "How fortunate I was, although a nameless monastic from a remote foreign country, not only to be per-mitted to become his disciple but also to be granted free access to his private quarters, witness his reverend face, and listen to his discourse on the Way! Slow-minded as I was, this was a precious opportunity that I could not pos-sibly waste."
80. *Gakudō-yōjinshū,* 5.

81. *Shōbōgenzō*, "Hotsu-bodaishin."

82. *Gakudō-yōjinshū.*

83. The verb "meet" (*au, ou, aiou,* etc.) was used by Dōgen not only with respect to person but also with respect to Dharma, the Way, sūtras, the seasons, and so on. Thus he often used such phrases as "to meet Dharma," "to meet the sūtras," "to meet the seasons," and the like.

84. *Shōbōgenzō*, "Mitsugo."

85. The other line was the line of Hung-chih Chêng-chüeh (1091–1157), which was transmitted to Japan by Tōmyō E'nichi (1272–1340) in 1309.

86. Ibid., "Gyōji."

87. *Zuimonki*, III:30.

88. Ibid., II:9. Dōgen also reminisced: "Also one day Ju-ching's attendants told him: 'Monastics in the monastics' hall are suffering from fatigue and insufficient sleep, which might damage their health as well as morale. This seems due to the long practice of zazen. We would like to ask you to shorten zazen practice.' However, Ju-ching sternly admonished them: 'You are mistaken. Those who do not have earnestness in zazen and just nominally appear in the monastics' hall will, after all, doze after even a short while. Those who have willingness to practice zazen with a believing mind, on the other hand, will be glad to discipline themselves no matter how long it may last. When I was young, I presided over various monasteries and advised in this manner, and struck those drowsing monastics so hard that I almost broke my fist. Now I am advanced in age and weakened in physical strength, so I cannot strike others as hard as before; consequently, good monastics have not been produced. Because leaders of various monastic communities likewise are too easy with their students in the practice of zazen, the Buddha-dharma is on the decline. I ought to strike more than ever.' That was all." Ibid., III:30.

89. *Shōbōgenzō*, "Gyōji."

90. Ibid., "Gyōji."

91. Ibid., "Gyōji." Dōgen observed: "An ancient sage said that we should not care a bit about gold, silver, or jewels. Even if monastics appreciate gold and silver, it befits their way of life best not to receive them. I witness this in my deceased teacher, and no others."

92. Ibid., "Butsudō."

93. Ibid., "Butsudō."

94. Ibid., "Shohō-jissō." Concerning Dōgen's own view on this matter, see particularly ibid., "Shizenbiku."

95. The relation between Ju-ching's thought and Dōgen's is still very much a moot question in Dōgen studies, primarily owing to the scarcity of historical materials on Ju-ching. Many of Dōgen's observations and claims reveal more of Dōgen himself than of Ju-ching. This is Nakamura Hajime's contention. For example, he writes in the context of his discussion of Dōgen's

Hōkyōki: "It is commonly considered that Dōgen's religion is a faithful continuation of its Chinese counterpart. But the fact that the thought of the *Shōbōgenzō* coincides with the teachings of Ju-ching, as recorded in the *Hōkyōki* . . ., does not justify this opinion. . . . It is feared that in the sayings of Ju-ching quoted there, Dōgen's wishful interpretations have probably been added." Op. cit., p. 672, note 229; also see p. 667, note 163. Furuta Shōkin is of the opinion that, judging from the records of Ju-ching's acts and sayings, he appears to have been inclined rather to kōan Zen. This is contrary to Dōgen's insistence that Ju-ching advocated zazen-only. See "The Development of Zen Thought in Japan," *Philosophical Studies of Japan*, vol. 3 (1961), pp. 41–42.

As to Ju-ching's thought, see the following: Itō Keidō, *Dōgen zenji kenkyū*, vol. 1; Ōkubo Dōshū, op. cit., pp. 502–38; Ui Hakuju, *Zenshū-shi kenkyū*, vol. 3, pp. 463–67; Nukariya Kaiten, *Zengaku shisō-shi*, vol. 2, pp. 403–20.

96. *Gakudō-yōjinshū*, 5.

97. For example: "In the past two or three hundred years of the great Sung dynasty there appeared no old Buddha like my deceased teacher" *Shōbōgenzō*, "Hensan." Elsewhere: "In the past four or five hundred years, my deceased teacher alone gouged out the eyeball [elucidated and verified the wisdom] of the Buddhas and ancestors and sat in meditation in their eyeball. Few can compare with him in China. It is rare indeed to find those who comprehend clearly that sitting in zazen is the Buddha-dharma, and the Buddha-dharma is sitting in zazen. Even if one may understand sitting in zazen as the Buddha-dharma, no one has as yet penetrated sitting as sitting [sitting for the sake of sitting], much less maintained the Buddha-dharma as the Buddha-dharma." Ibid., "Zammai-ōzammai."

98. In this connection, see Nakamura, op. cit., pp. 452–54. Nakamura contends that absolute devotion to a specific person cannot be found even in the feudalistic societies of India and China but is unique to Japan. In this respect Dōgen differed from Ju-ching.

99. *Zuimonki*, I:1.

100. *Shōbōgenzō*, "Kattō." Cf. ibid., "Menju." See Takeuchi, op. cit., pp. 161–63.

101. *Zuimonki*, II:16.

102. Jimbo Nyoten and Andō Bun'ei, eds., *Zengaku jiten*, "ango."

103. Takeuchi, op. cit., pp. 167–69; Ōkubo, op. cit., pp. 154–55.

104. Etō Sokuō, *Shūso to shite no Dōgen zenji*, pp. 162–63.

105. This is kept at present as a national treasure in the repository of the Eiheiji temple.

106. In Zen Buddhism there was a traditional custom that teachers give succeeding disciples their own portraits with eulogies as tokens of the transmission of Dharma.

107. *Shōbōgenzō*, "Bendōwa."

108. With respect to the Kenninji temple specifically, Dōgen observed: "As I compare what I saw when I entered the Kenninji temple for the first time with what I saw some seven or eight years later, some gradual changes were noticeable. Monastics made, in each of their huts, elaborate closets, had personal belongings, cared for beautiful clothes, amassed fortunes, enjoyed licentious talks, and defaulted on greetings and worship. From this I could surmise the situation of other temples." *Zuimonki*, IV:4. Also see further II:21.

109. *Shōbōgenzō*, "Bendōwa."

110. *Fukan-zazengi.*

111. Ōkubo, op. cit., pp. 185ff.; Takeuchi, op. cit., pp. 198–203.

112. *Shōbōgenzō*, "Bendōwa." In those days zazen seems to have been novel, and curious believers valued it highly. Tsuji, op. cit., pp. 275–76.

113. *Shuso* functioned as assistant abbot of the monastery.

114. Shōkū was Dōgen's elder brother and one of the ablest disciples of Hōnen. He later founded the Kōmyōji temple.

115. *Zuimonki*, III:12. "People nowadays are apt to think that the propagation of the Buddha-dharma consists of making Buddha images, building pagodas, and the like. This too is a mistake. Even though a soaring temple inlaid with gems and plated with gold boasts of its grand view, one cannot attain the Way by it. . . . Even in a hut or under a tree you contemplate upon even a phrase of Dharma and practice zazen even for a short while. That is the very thing for the true prosperity of the Buddha-dharma." Loc. cit.

116. Ibid., V:5.

117. *Kannon-dōriin sōdō konryū kanjinsho.*

118. *Shōbōgenzō*, "Bendōwa."

119. Ibid., "Shōji."

120. *Zuimonki*, II:2.

121. Ibid., III:20.

122. *Shōbōgenzō*, "Bendōwa."

123. Ibid., "Bendōwa."

124. Ibid., "Shukke-kudoku." Such a strong repudiation of laity in favor of monasticism is expressed also in ibid., "Sanjūshichihon-bodaibumpo," "Shukke," "Jukai," and "Kie-buppōsōbō."

125. Ibid., "Shukke-kudoku."

126. As to Dōgen's view on this problem, see Hosaka Gyokusen, "Shukke-Bukkyō zaike-Bukkyō to Dōgen zenji no tachiba," *Komazawa daigaku kenkyū kiyō*, no. 15 (March 1957), pp. 1–14; Tamura Yoshirō, *Kamakura shin-Bukkyō shisō no kenkyū*, pp. 315–24.

127. *Shōbōgenzō*, "Den'e."

128. Ibid., "Bendōwa."

129. Ibid., "Raihai-tokuzui."

130. Ibid., "Raihai-tokuzui."

131. Ibid., "Raihai-tokuzui." Cf. ibid., "Shukke-kudoku": "There is also the notion that woman can attain Buddhahood, but this too is not the authentic teaching."

132. *Jūundōshiki.*

133. *Shōbōgenzō*, "Bendōwa."

134. Ibid., "Bendōwa."

135. Satō Tetsugen, *Dōgen no shōgai*, pp. 142–43. *Zuimonki*, III:13 records Dōgen's conviction on this matter: "Also someone approached Dōgen and advised him to visit the province of Kantō for the propagation of the Buddha-dharma. Dōgen replied: 'No. If people have the will to study Dharma, they should come and study even though they must cross mountains and rivers and oceans. If I go out to counsel those who have no such intent, I am not so sure whether they will accept it at all. Then is it merely for the purpose of deceiving them to obtain material help for myself and to acquire riches? Since it brings me nothing but pains, I feel I need not go.'" Who "someone" in this quotation was is not certain. This may have been Hatano Yoshishige as Tsuji conjectures. See Tsuji, op. cit., p. 284.

136. Cf. Ōkubo, op. cit., pp. 184–98; Takeuchi, op. cit., pp. 254–55; Tsuji, op. cit., pp. 278–79.

137. Furuta Shōkin, *Nihon Bukkyō shisō-shi no shomondai*, pp. 145–61.

138. Kenzei, *Kenzeiki.* Quoted in Nakamura, op. cit., p. 251.

139. *Shōbōgenzō*, "Sansuikyō."

140. Mircea Eliade, *Patterns in Comparative Religion*, pp. 367–87; Hori, *Folk Religion in Japan*, pp. 141–79.

141. It is noteworthy, in this connection, that Dōgen advised his disciples to shun talks on politics, peace and the order of the nation, and other secular matters. Dōgen was completely apolitical. Moreover, he cautioned the monastics against keeping or owning bows, arrows, swords, or any other weapons. He emphatically prohibited the possession of all weapons for immoral purposes in the monastic compound.

142. Nakamura, op. cit., pp. 407–530, in which he discusses the Japanese tendency to stress a limited social nexus. As to the traditional folk belief and practice of *dōzoku*, which is the foundation of the sentiment of loyalty to a limited social nexus, see Hori, *Folk Religions in Japan*, pp. 52–63.

143. Takeuchi, op. cit., pp. 284–86.

144. Ibid., pp. 285–86.

145. Cf. Tsuji, *Nihon Bukkyō-shi no kenkyū zokuhen*, pp. 93–111; Ōkubo, op. cit., pp. 259–79; Takeuchi, op. cit., pp. 290–91.

146. Takeuchi, op. cit., pp. 306–7.

147. *Shōbōgenzō*, "Hachi-dainingaku."

Chapter Three: Activity, Expression, and Understanding

1. The *Dhammapada*, Verse 372. Adapted for gender-free diction.

2. The *Nirvāṇa sūtra*. Quoted in Philip Yampolsky, trans., *The Platform Sutra of the Sixth Patriarch*, p. 135, note 54.

3. The tension between meditation and wisdom has been perennial since the inception of Buddhism on Indian soil. As E. Conze observes, this tension can be seen already in the canonical texts such as the *Saṃyutta-Nikaya* in which the "people of trance" and the "people of wisdom" are represented by Musila and Narada, respectively. Both the people of trance and the people of wisdom have been equally vital forces in the development of Buddhist thought. See Conze, *Buddhism: Its Essence and Development*, pp. 161–62.

4. Zen Buddhism is called the school of the Buddha-mind because Dharma is transmitted from mind to mind or through personal encounter not depending on doctrines and scriptures. Other Buddhist sects belong to the school of the Buddha-word because the transmission of Dharma, according to Zen interpretation, relies heavily upon the study of scriptures and doctrines. As to Dōgen's attack on this distinction, see *Shōbōgenzō*, "Butsudō."

5. According to the classification of meditation by Kuei-fêng Tsung-mi (780–841), there are five types: (1) Non-Buddhist Zen (*gedō-zen*), (2) Ordinary Person's Zen (*bombu-zen*), (3) Small Vehicle Zen (*shōjō-zen*), (4) Great Vehicle Zen (*daijō-zen*), and (5) Highest Vehicle Zen or Tathāgata Zen (*saijōjō-zen* or *nyorai-shōjō-zen*). In this scheme, Tathāgata Zen was superior to other types of meditation. Yang-shan Hui-chi (807–883) probably first made the distinction between Tathāgata Zen and Ancestral Zen, but the distinction became widely accepted by Zen Buddhists in the Sung period. The result was an exaltation of Ancestral Zen, which was allegedly taught by Bodhidharma and transmitted by the ancestors who followed him, in opposition to Tsung-mi's Tathāgata Zen which was regarded as quietistic, doctrinal, and scriptural.

6. I. Miura and R. F. Sasaki, *Zen Dust*, pp. 13–14, 171–72.

7. *Shōbōgenzō*, "Butsudō."

8. Ibid., "Butsudō." Also see ibid., "Bukkyō" (47) and "Kembutsu." For his criticism of the doctrine of the Five Ranks, see "Shunjū." For the Five Houses of Chinese Zen, see H. Dumoulin, *A History of Zen Buddhism*, pp. 106–22.

9. *Shōbōgenzō*, "Butsudō."

10. Miyasaka Tetsubun, *Zen ni okeru ningen keisei*, pp. 102–45 for Zen thought on the scriptural studies.

11. *Shōbōgenzō*, "Bukkyō" (34).

12. Ibid., "Bukkyō" (47).

13. Ibid., "Bukkyō" (47). In the same chapter, Dōgen also writes: "In the country of great Sung today, some such people hold the title of Teacher and function in the position of Zen teacher, yet because they do not feel humbled by the past and present, they absurdly distort the Buddha-way, so much so that the Buddha-dharma hardly exists. These elders say in unison: 'The original intention of the Buddha-way resides not in sūtras but in the very ancestral tradition in which the supernal wonder and profound mystery have been imparted.' Such a statement is just a wretched stupidity in the extreme and a lunatic's allegation. In the authentically transmitted ancestral tradition, not even a single word or phrase is strange for its being in discord with the sūtras. Both the sūtras and the ancestral way have been rightly imparted and disseminated from Śākyamuni Buddha. The ancestral heritage is simply an uninterrupted succession from him. Even so, how could we not understand the sūtras? How could we not elucidate them? How could we not read and recite them?"

14. See ibid., "Bukkyō" (34), "Immo," etc.

15. Ibid., "Zazenshin."

16. Etō Sokuō, *Shūso to shite no Dōgen zenji*, pp. 269–72.

17. *Shōbōgenzō*, "Raihai-tokuzui."

18. Ibid., "Sanjūshichihon-bodaibumpō."

19. Ibid., "Arakan."

20. Ibid., "Sanjūshichihon-bodaibumpō." Cf. Etō, op. cit., pp. 275–78 concerning Dōgen's view of Theravāda Buddhism. As we have seen already, Dōgen rejected the doctrine of the unity of three religions (Confucianism, Taoism, and Buddhism). He once said: "What we call ongoing enlightenment (*bukkōjōji*) is to reach Buddha and advance further to see Buddha." *Shōbōgenzō*, "Bukkōjōji."

21. Ibid., "Bendōwa." In this sense the distinction between the two forms of samādhi is similar to the distinction between esoteric and exoteric Buddhism which was made by Kūkai (774–835). However, in the context of Dōgen's thought, the samādhi of self-fulfilling activity is realized in the concrete historical body of Buddha, which defied any interpretation in terms of traditional "trinitarian" categories of the Buddha-body. As an unconditioned freedom, the samādhi of self-fulfilling activity is also extremely akin to Shinran's "naturalness" (*jinen-hōni*), meaning the spontaneous working of Tathāgata's vow-power without human contrivance.

22. Ibid., "Bendōwa." This statement is made as a criticism of the Tendai, Kegon, and Shingon schools of Buddhism; Dōgen clearly emphasizes practice rather than doctrine. Cf. Etō, *Shōbōgenzō josetsu*, pp. 175–85.

23. *Shōbōgenzō*, "Bendōwa."

24. Yampolsky, op. cit., Sections 13 and 15.

25. *Shōbōgenzō*, "Shizen-biku." The passage in this chapter raised con-

siderable controversy among Dōgen students concerning his real intent and his relation to Hui-nêng. See works cited in note 26 below.

26. See Sakai Tokugen, "Rokuso Dankyō ni okeru jushō ni tsuite," *Shūgaku kenkyū*, no. 7 (April 1965), pp. 35–41; idem, "Rokuso Dankyō ni okeru kenshō no igi," *Shūgaku kenkyū*, no. 6 (April 1964), pp. 18–26; Harada Kōdō, "Rokuso Dankyō no jishō no shisō to Dōgen zenji no tachiba," *Shūgaku kenkyū*, no. 8 (April 1966), pp. 115–20; Kurebayashi Kōdō, "Dankyō no hannya-shisō to Dōgen zenji," *Shūgaku kenkyū*, no. 6 (April 1964), pp. 5–11; Ōkubo Dōshu, "Dōgen-shobon Rokuso Dankyō (Kaga Daijōji zōhon) no kenkyū," *Dōgen zenji-den no kenkyū*, pp. 539–63; Nakagawa Takashi, "Dōgen zenji to Rokuso Dankyō," *Journal of Indian and Buddhist Studies*, vol. 4, no. 1 (January 1956), pp. 212–15.

It was traditionally believed that the present Daijōji edition of the *Platform Sūtra* was copied by Dōgen himself from an unknown Sung edition and brought to Japan. However, this has been generally refuted. The edition or text of the sūtra Dōgen read cannot be determined at the present time, but Ōkubo maintains that Dōgen's text was different from all other editions— the Tun-huang, Daijōji, Kōshōji, and popular editions.

27. *Shōbōgenzō*, "Kobusshin."

28. Kagamishima Genryū, "Honshō-myōshu no shisō-shi-teki haikei," *Shūgaku kenkyū*, no. 7 (April 1965), pp. 24–29. Also see in this connection, Tamura Yoshirō, "Nihon Tendai hongaku-shisō no keisei-katei," *Journal of Indian and Buddhist Studies*, vol. 10, no. 2 (March 1962), pp. 661–72; and his *Kamakura shin-Bukkyō shisō no kenkyū*; Ōkubo Dōshu, "Sōtō-shū no taisei to Tendō Nyojō no shimpu," *Dōgen zenji-den no kenkyū*, pp. 502–38.

29. Conze, *Buddhist Meditation*, p. 11.

30. Masunaga, *Zenjō shisōshi*, p. 23.

31. Nakamura, "Unity and Diversity in Buddhism," Morgan, ed., *The Path of the Buddha*, p. 400.

32. The historical and cultural background of Buddhist meditation is an enormously complex and difficult subject which I do not wish to treat in this work. Nevertheless we should always keep in mind this vast background against which Dōgen's thought becomes truly significant. Buddhism is deeply indebted to the yogic tradition of pre-Buddhist India. Śākyamuni Buddha himself was acquainted with the yogic traditions, and the practice of yogic exercises by his followers appears in the earliest canonical texts of Buddhism. See Eliade, *Yoga*, pp. 162ff. and Thomas, *The History of Buddhist Thought*, p. 17 and pp. 42–57. As to Buddhist meditation, the following works in addition to those already cited above are important: Hauer, *Der Yoga: Ein indischer Weg zum Selbst*; Heiler, *Die Stufen der buddhistischen Versenkung*; Nyanaponika Thera, *The Heart of Buddhist Meditation*; Conze, *Buddhist Meditation*; Masunaga, *Zenjō shisōshi*; Reichelt, *Meditation and Piety in the Far East*; the works of D. T. Suzuki.

33. Cf. Kishizawa Ian who once said: "The ninety-five chapters of *Shōbōgenzō* are footnotes on zazen-only." Etō, ed., *Shōbōgenzō*, vol. 3, p. 328.

34. This point is made quite clearly in his *Fukan-zazengi senjutsu yurai*.

35. *Fukan-zazengi*. Instructions on zazen are also given in *Shōbōgenzō*, "Zazengi" and "Zazenshin," and in *Gakudō-yōjinshū*, *Eihei-shingi*, *Hōkyōki*, etc.

36. As regards comparative studies of Dōgen's *Fukan-zazengi* and Ch'ang-lu Tsung-che's "Tso-ch'an-i" in the *Ch'an-yüan ch'ing-kuei*, see Kinoshita Jun'ichi, "Fukan-zazengi no kenkyū," *Shūgaku kenkyū*, no. 7 (April 1965), pp. 132–37.

37. *Shōbōgenzō*, "Bendōwa": "As the authentic transmission of the Buddhist tradition says, this Buddha–dharma which has been imparted authoritatively from teacher to disciple is the very best of all. From the beginning of your training under a teacher, do not ever use incense burning, worship, nembutsu, confession, or recitation of sūtras, but sit intently in zazen and attain the casting-off of body and mind." The same view appears also in *Hōkyōki*, *Shōbōgenzō zuimonki*, *Shōbōgenzō*, "Bukkyō" (47), "Gyōji," etc.

38. *Shōbōgenzō*, "Zammai-ōzammai."

39. Ibid., "Bendōwa."

40. Ibid., "Bendōwa." See also *Fukan-zazengi*.

41. *Shōbōgenzō*, "Bendōwa," in which Dōgen says: "You now regard the samādhi of Buddhas, the supreme Dharma, as just idly sitting for nothing. This we call those who slander the Great Vehicle. Their abysmal delusion is like that of the one who finds no water in the midst of a great sea."

42. Ibid., "Bendōwa."

43. Ibid., "Bendōwa."

44. Kinoshita, "Fukan-zazengi no kenkyū." According to Kondō Ryōichi, Ch'ang-lu Tsung-che advocated a mixed Zen in which nembutsu and zazen were recommended, though the former was a preparatory step to the latter for an attainment of a higher spiritual goal. See Kondō, "Chōro Sōsaku ni tsuite," *Journal of Indian and Buddhist Studies*, vol. 14, no. 2 (March 1966), pp. 280–83.

45. Kinoshita, "Fukan-zazengi no kenkyū"; Furuta Shōkin, "Fukan-zazengi ni tsuite," *Nihon Bukkyō shisō-shi no shomondai*, pp. 137–44; Ōkubo Dōshu, *Dōgen zenji goroku*, pp. 207–14.

46. Kinoshita, "Fukan-zazengi no kenkyū"; Kiyono Munemoto, "Dōgen zenji no busso-shōden-kan no ichi-kōsatsu—Fukan-zazengi ni kanren shite—," *Shūgaku kenkyū*, no. 6 (April 1964), pp. 145–52; Yamanouchi Shun'yū, "Zazengi to Tendai shōshikan," *Shūgaku kenkyū*, no. 8 (April 1966), pp. 29–50.

47. *Fukan-zazengi*. See also *Shōbōgenzō*, "Zazengi."

48. *Shōbōgenzō*, "Zazenshin."

49. The story in the *Ching-tê-ch'uan-têng-lu*, vol. 14 runs: A monastic

asked Yüeh-shan: "What must I think in zazen?" The teacher answered: "Think of not-thinking." Then the monastic asked again: "How can I think of this not-thinking?" "Non-thinking," was the answer. Thinking, not-thinking, non-thinking are expounded in *Shōbōgenzō*, "Zazengi," "Zazen-shin," "Sanjūshichihon-bodaibumpō," *Fukan-zazengi, Dōgen oshō kōroku,* etc.

50. *Shōbōgenzō*, "Zazenshin."

51. Cf. Itō Shungen, "Hi-shiryō no kaishaku ni tsuite," *Shūgaku kenkyū*, no. 5 (April 1963), pp. 84–91; Etō Tarō, "Dōgen tetsugaku to Heidegger," *Risō*, no. 349 (June 1962), pp. 1–11 for comparison of Dōgen and Heidegger in connection with the former's idea of non thinking.

52. *Zuimonki*, III:31.

53. *Shōbōgenzō*, "Kokū."

54. Ibid., "Sanjūshichihon-bodaibumpō."

55. Cf. Itō, "Hi-shiryō no kaishaku ni tsuite"; Sakai Tokugen, "Shōbō-genzō ni okeru shimo no igi," *Komazawa daigaku kenkyū kiyō*, no. 15 (March 1957), pp. 112–26. Sakai, in this essay, holds that the logic of interrogation is to overcome the logic of negation which was characteristic of Indian Buddhism.

56. *Shōbōgenzō*, "Bendōwa." The authenticity of zazen is also character-ized in terms of "killing the Buddhas" (*setsubutsu*). This means killing the Buddhas besides, beyond, in front of, outside, or apart from, the actuality of sitting in meditation, which is itself enlightenment.

57. *Shōbōgenzō*, "Genjō-kōan" and "Zazenshin." See Furuta Shōkin, "Genjō-kōan no igi," *Journal of Indian and Buddhist Studies*, vol. 5, no. 1 (January 1957), pp. 102–7; idem, "Kōan no rekishiteki hatten keitai ni okeru shinri-sei no mondai," in Miyamoto Shōson, ed., *Bukkyō no kompon shinri*, pp. 807–40; Takahashi Masanobu, *Dōgen no jissen-tetsugaku kōzo*, pp. 98–126. I will have more to say on this subject later: see note 112 in this chapter.

58. *Shōbōgenzō*, "Bendōwa" and others.

59. Ibid., "Sesshin-sesshō."

60. Ibid., "Bendōwa." Dōgen calls his Zen "the boundless gate of com-passion" and "the easy path" which is wide open to everyone in the mun-dane life.

61. *Gakudō-yōjinshū*, 9. It continues as follows: "Its manner and principle is such that it cuts off the working of your consciousness and prevents you from heading for the path of intellectual understanding. This is precisely a method of inducement for the beginner. Thereafter, it enables you to cast off your body and mind and transcend delusion and enlightenment. This is the second aspect. Generally speaking, it is the hardest thing for us to meet those who believe that they are in the Buddha-way. If you believe in your undoubtedly being in the Way, you will naturally understand the passage and

blockage of the great Way and apprehend the reasons of delusion and enlightenment. So experiment to cut off the working of your consciousness, and eight or nine times out of ten, you will be able to find the Way in an instant.

A few illustrations in relation to Dōgen's view of faith are quoted in the following: "Indeed the life of Buddhas is incomprehensible and beyond the reach of mind and consciousness, let alone those minds with unbelief and inferior apprehension. Only the great mind of right faith can legitimately enter it. Those of no faith, even if they are instructed, have difficulty in accepting it. Even on the Vulture Peak [where Buddha is said to have expounded the *Saddharma-puṇḍarīka sūtra*] there were those who were allowed to retire from the congregation. Thus when right faith arises in your mind, you should practice and study; otherwise, you should quit for a while, and regret for yourself the want of Dharma's benefit from olden times" (*Shōbōgenzō*, "Bendōwa"). "While both your mind and your flesh may be at times in idleness or in unbelief, confess it in utter sincerity to the Buddhas who come before you. When you repent in this manner, the meritorious power of confession to the Buddhas who come before you will liberate and purify you. This merit will richly nurture undefiled faith and spiritual endeavor, which are unobstructed. As pure faith is realized, both the self and others will be changed, and the sentient and the insentient shall enjoy its efficacy far and wide" (ibid., "Keisei-sanshoku"). "What we call *kie* means this: *ki* is surrender, and *e* obedience. Thus the double form *kie*. The characteristic of surrender is, for instance, like a son returning to his father. Obedience is likened to the subject's obedience to the ruler. It is the word of salvation. We take refuge in Buddha because he is a great teacher; we take refuge in Dharma because it is a good medicine; and we take refuge in Saṃgha because it is a superior fellowship" (ibid., "Kie-buppōsōbō"). "We revere the Buddhas of the past, renounce the mundane life, and follow their way of life—such acts surely enable us to become Buddhas. One becomes a Buddha by virtue of the merit of one's veneration of the Buddhas. How can the sentient beings that have never honored a Buddha attain Buddhahood? Without cause no Buddhahood shall be attained" (ibid., "Kuyō-shobutsu"). "Even during Buddha's lifetime there were an old monk who attained the Four Fruits by [being hit by jesting young monks'] handballs, and a nun who attained the great Way as a result of wearing a surplice [in her previous life as a prostitute]. Both were wretchedly idiotic persons, being as good as insane brutes. Only through the assistance of right faith is there a way to be severed from delusion. Furthermore, a devout woman, who served a meal to a senile monk [in order to hear a sermon from him], saw his silent sitting in meditation [which he pretended, because he did not know anything to preach], yet she was enlightened. These cases did not depend on knowledge or letters; nor did they wait for words or speeches. They were aided solely by right faith" (ibid., "Bendōwa"). Cf. *Zuimonki*, II:15. In these illustrations Dōgen's view of faith in terms of trust, obedience, dependence, surrender, and commitment is clear.

62. *Shōbōgenzō*, "Sanjūshichihon-bodaibumpō."

63. As a result, Pure Realm Buddhism is often construed by some as a deviation from the fundamental Buddhist religion.

64. As Etō Sokuō observes, the element of faith is almost entirely overlooked in the study of Zen. *Shūso to shite no Dōgen zenji*, pp. 221–29. Also see Yamanouchi Shun'yū, "Dōgen zenji ni okeru shingyō no mondai," *Journal of Indian and Buddhist Studies*, vol. 13, no. 1 (January 1965), pp. 80–85; idem, "Sōtō-shū ni okeru shin-Bukkyō no tenkai ni tsuite," *Shūgaku kenkyū*, no. 7 (April 1965), pp. 63–72; Kurebayashi Kōdō, *Dōgen-zen no kenkyū*.

65. *Shōbōgenzō*, "Gabyō." See also ibid., "Shoaku-makusa."

66. The *Ching-tê-ch'uan-têng-lu*, vol. 5. Dōgen deals with this story in some detail in *Shōbōgenzō*,"Kokyō" and "Zazenshin."

67. Ibid., "Kokyō." Also see ibid., "Zazenshin," and *Zuimonki*, III:28.

68. *Shōbōgenzō*, "Bendōwa."

69. Ibid., "Busshō."

70. Ibid., "Busshō."

71. Ibid., "Genjō-kōan."

72. Ibid., "Genjō-kōan."

73. *Zuimonki*, I:6. Cf. ibid., III:28.

74. Nagao Gajin, "On the Theory of Buddha-Body (*Buddha-kāya*)," *The Eastern Buddhist*, vol. 6, no. 1 (May 1973), pp. 25–53.

75. Sangharakshita, op. cit., p. 281. Cf. E. Conze, *Buddhism: Its Essence and Development*, p. 38. Conze says: "To the Christian and agnostic historian, only the human Buddha is real, and the spiritual and the magical Buddha are to him nothing but fictions. The perspective of the believer is quite different. The Buddha-nature and the Buddha's 'glorious body' stand out most clearly, and the Buddha's human body and historical existence appear like a few rags thrown over this spiritual glory." Quoted in Sangharakshita, op. cit., p. 281.

76. *Shōbōgenzō*, "Ango"; *Fushukuhampō*.

77. Concerning the importance of the historical Buddha and related matters, see Yamada Reirin, "Dōgen zenji no butsumen sōjō-kan," Miyamoto, ed., *Bukkyō no kompon shinri*, pp. 1169–90, especially, 1173–78. Also see Abe Masao, "A Buddhism of Self-Awakening Not a Buddhism of Faith," in J. Tilakasiri, ed., *Añjali: Papers on Indology and Buddhism*, pp. 33–39.

78. *Shōbōgenzō*, "Gyōbutsu-igi."

79. This is most clearly shown in his discussion of the relation between Kāśyapa Buddha (the sixth of the Seven Past Buddhas) and Śākyamuni Bud-

dha. From the "historical" standpoint, Śākyamuni Buddha inherited Dharma from Kāśyapa Buddha, but from the transcendental standpoint the order is reversed. See ibid., "Shisho."

80. Ibid., "Shisho" and "Jinzū."

81. Ibid., "Sokushin-zebutsu," "Kembutsu," and "Hokke-ten-Hokke."

82. Ibid., "Gyōbutsu-igi."

83. Ibid., "Yuibutsu-yobutsu." See also ibid., "Shinjin-gakudō," "Sangai-yuishin," "Hensan," and other chapters.

84. Ibid., "Gyōbutsu-igi."

85. Ibid., "Yuibutsu-yobutsu."

86. Ibid., "Hotsu-mujōshin."

87. Ibid., "Gyōbutsu-igi."

88. Ibid., "Gyōbutsu-igi."

89. Ibid., "Gyōbutsu-igi."

90. Ibid., "Gyōbutsu-igi."

91. Kōchi Eigaku, "Dōgen-zen no busshin-ron," *Komazawa daigaku Bukkyō-gakubu kenkyū kiyō*, no. 19 (March 1961), pp. 34–47. Kōchi suggests similarities between Dōgen and Shingon thought on the problem of Buddha-body. The doctrine of "This mind itself is Buddha" is the Zen counterpart of "This body itself is Buddha" of Tendai and Shingon esotericism.

92. *Shōbōgenzō*, "Bendōwa."

93. Ibid., "Gyōji." "Because" in ". . . functional interdependence (*engi*) is activity, because activity is not functionally interdependent" sounds rather illogical in this context. But this translation follows the original text.

94. Cf. Nakayama Nobuji, *Bukkyō ni okeru toki no kenkyū*, pp. 177–78.

95. *Shōbōgenzō*, "Gyōji."

96. Ibid., "Gyōji."

97. Ibid., "Gyōji."

98. Ibid., "Bukkyō" (47).

99. Ibid., "Hokke-ten-Hokke." Cf. ibid., "Kankin": "Thus the mind's delusion is moved by the *Saddharma-puṇḍarīka sūtra*, whereas the mind's en-lightenment moves it. Furthermore, when mind transcends both enlighten-ment and delusion, the sūtra moves itself." Elsewhere Dōgen goes so far as to say that even the *Śūraṃgama sūtra*, which he regarded as "apocryphal," can be "extraordinary words"—the words of the Buddhas and ancestors. See ibid., "Tembōrin." In addition to the *Śūraṃgama sūtra*, Dōgen regarded the *Engaku-kyō* as apocryphal as well.

100. *Shōbōgenzō*, "Bukkyō" (47).

101. Ibid., "Jishō-zammai." Cf. ibid., "Nyorai-zenshin" and "Hotsu-mujōshin."

102. Ibid., "Bendōwa."

103. Ibid., "Hokke-ten-Hokke."

104. Ibid., "Bukkyō" (47).

105. Ibid., "Nyorai-zenshin." "Reflect quietly upon this: Life lasts not too long. To express the words of the Buddhas and ancestors, even just two or three, is tantamount to signifying the Buddhas and ancestors. The reason for this is that because their bodies and minds are one, a phrase or two constitutes perfectly their warm body-mind. That body-mind comes forth and represents my body-mind. It is exactly at the very moment of such an experience that expression comes forth and delineates my body-mind. This life shows the previous cycles of rebirth. For this reason, on becoming the Buddhas and ancestors, they surpass the Buddhas and outdo the ancestors. Two or three expressions of activity are precisely like this" (ibid., "Gyōji").

106. Ibid., "Kembutsu."

107. Ibid., "Bukkyō" (47).

108. Ibid., "Bendōwa."

109. *Jūundōshiki.*

110. For example, see Miyasaka Tetsubun, op. cit., pp. 125–30.

111. For this problem and observations on the following, I am indebted to Furuta, "Genjō-kōan no igi" and "Kōan no rekishi-teki hatten-keitai ni okeru shinrisei no mondai," both of which are cited previously.

112. Furuta observes in the above cited essays that both Ta-hui Tsung-kao and Hung-chih Chêng-chüeh used *kosoku-kōan* in the light of *genjō-kōan* and also adopted zazen as essential; in short, both used kōan and zazen freely. Furuta further observes that to distinguish between Kōan-introspection Zen and Silent-illumination Zen on the basis of the existence or nonexistence of kōan is rather erroneous and historically unfounded; the distinction arose from the existence of abuses of both kōan and zazen which became rather conspicuous later in the Sung period. It is interesting to note in this connection that Ta-hui burned the *Pi-yen-lu* when he realized the evil effects of the kōan method and Hung-chih edited the *Ts'ung-yung-lu*, another important collection of kōans, despite or because of his association with that sub-sect of Zen—Silent-illumination Zen—to which he was supposed to belong. All in all, sectarian conflicts between the two traditions have been unduly exaggerated by Zen Buddhists themselves as well as by the historians of Zen. As to Dōgen's view on this matter, see further *Zuimonki*, III:15 and VI:27.

113. This is quite evident in Dōgen's extensive use of kōans in the *Shōbōgenzō* and other works. Dōgen also compiled and edited three hundred important kōans in his *Shōbōgenzō sambyakusoku*, the authenticity of which was definitively established as a result of the discovery in 1935 of the second of the three volume work at the Kanazawa bunko.

114. Dōgen's high praise of Yüan-wu and denunciation of Ta-hui Tsung-kao (e.g., in *Shōbōgenzō*, "Jishō-zammai"), who both belonged to Kōan-introspection Zen, and his adoption of the idea of "total dynamism" (*zenki*), which was Yüan-wu's, and to which Dōgen devoted a chapter in *Shōbō-*

genzō, seem to indicate that Yüan-wu had great influence upon Dōgen's thought. See Furuta, "Genjō-kōan no igi."

115. Furuta, "Genjō-kōan no igi."

116. Cf. D. T. Suzuki, *Essays in Zen Buddhism*, Second Series, pp. 17–211 for his exposition of the kōan method from historical, psychological, and systematic standpoints. The following statement, for example, is suggestive of Suzuki's interpretation: "Zen has its definite object, which is 'to open our minds to satori' as we say, and in order to bring about this state of consciousness a kōan is held out before the mental eye, not to meditate on, nor to keep the mind in a state of receptivity, but to use the kōan as a kind of pole with which to leap over the stream of relativity to the other side of the Absolute." Ibid., p. 99, note 1.

117. *Shōbōgenzō*, "Mitsugo."

118. L. Wittgenstein, *Philosophical Investigations*, I, 23. Also see J. L. Austin, "Performative Utterances," in *Philosophical Papers*, pp. 220–39; idem, *How To Do Things with Words*, ed. by J. O. Urmson. From the standpoint of the analysis of ordinary language, Austin explores numerous possibilities for "doing things with words," in contrast to the conventional function of language, as describing and reporting some state of affairs and, hence, as being either true or false. Although vastly different from Austin in his philosophical and religious orientation and method, Dōgen too is aware of the limitations of a traditional Buddhist view of language (which is comparable to Austin's descriptive or constative fallacy), and points to the performative possibilities of words in the realm of religion.

119. *Shōbōgenzō*, "Kaiin-zammai."

120. Ibid., "Dōtoku." Cf. ibid., "Kaiin-zammai" concerning the three-year-old's expressions.

121. Ibid., "Dōtoku."

122. Ibid., "Mujō-seppō." Cf. ibid., "Ikka-myōju" and "Kobusshin."

123. This aspect of Buddha-nature will be explored further in connection with the analysis of the Buddha-nature of expression (*setsu-busshō*) in Chapter 4.

124. See ibid., "Shohō-jissō," where Dōgen refers to the idea of provisionality and instrumentality of symbols, doctrines, ideas, and so on (*upāya; hōben*) which is predominant in the *Saddharma-puṇḍarīka sūtra*, and presents his view that events and expressions themselves are ultimately reality (*jissō*). In this view means and realities are nondualistically conceived. Or to put it differently, the means and the end are mediated and purified by emptiness, and thereby realized in thusness. More will follow in the subsequent pages.

125. Ibid., "Tsuki."

126. Ibid., "Muchū-setsumu." See also ibid., "Tsuki."

127. Ibid., "Mitsugo."

128. Ibid., "Mitsugo."

129. Ibid., "Bukkōjōji."
130. Ibid., "Bukkōjōji."
131. Ibid., "Bukkōjōji."
132. Ibid., "Bukkōjōji."
133. Cf. H. Bergson who maintains in his *The Two Sources of Morality and Religion* that "complete mysticism is action" but who nevertheless regards language as antithetical to action. Both Dōgen and Bergson would concur in recognizing action or activity as fundamental in mysticism, but the former parts with the latter in viewing language and activity as not antithetical to each other. Dōgen views the use of language and symbols as linguistic and symbolic activity.
134. *Shōbōgenzō*, "Jippō."
135. Ibid., "Ōsaku-sendaba."
136. Ibid., "Muchū-setsumu."
137. Ibid., "Muchū-setsumu."
138. Ibid., "Muchū-setsumu."
139. Ibid., "Muchū-setsumu."
140. Ibid., "Kūge."
141. Ibid., "Kūge."
142. Ibid., "Kūge."
143. Ibid., "Kūge."
144. Ibid., "Gabyō."
145. Ibid., "Gabyō."
146. Ibid., "Gabyō."
147. Ibid., "Gabyō."
148. Dōgen wrote the "Jinzū" and "Darani" chapters of *Shōbōgenzō* on these subjects.
149. Ibid., "Dōtoku."
150. J. Wisdom, *Philosophy and Psycho-analysis*, p. 50. Cf. the following statements of Wittgenstein: "Whereof one cannot speak, thereof one must be silent." *Tractatus Logico-Philosophicus*, 7. "There is indeed the inexpressible. This *shows* itself; it is the mystical." Ibid., 6.5222.
151. To express at all is an impossible task, hence a most miraculous event, just as we see in the kōans of Tê-shan's "thirty blows if you cannot speak, thirty blows if you can" and Fêng-hsüeh's speech and silence.
152. Concerning loving speech, see Chapter 5.
153. *Shōbōgenzō*, "Dōtoku."
154. Ibid., "Dōtoku."
155. Ibid., "Dōtoku."
156. Watsuji's essay "Shamon Dōgen" deals with this aspect of Dōgen's thought from the standpoint of the idea of logos. However, he does not distinguish logos clearly enough from Dōgen's conception of expression which is firmly rooted in the Buddhist idea of absolute emptiness. In the

history of Western philosophy the term logos has been associated with the immutable intelligible order of everchanging nature. Such an absolute immutability of intelligible order has often tended to divorce itself from its original roots in nature and to claim its own metaphysical status independent of nature.

If Heidegger's analysis of the fate of the logos in the history of Western philosophy is correct, what he calls the "secession of the logos" (which took place in Plato and Aristotle and was completed in Hegel) has resulted in a complete separation between thought and reality and has been responsible for the hegemony of reason and thought. M. Heidegger, *An Introduction to Metaphysics*, pp. 98–164.

Expression in Dōgen is impermanent—arises and perishes in accordance with the functional interdependence of the universe; hence it is empty—has no self-nature and absolute validity. However, as will become clearer later, Dōgen radicalizes the Buddhist idea of absolute emptiness by eliminating every possible vestige of idealism, monism, and pantheism.

157. I am indebted to Watsuji's aforementioned essay for some aspects of the observations made here with respect to *dōtoku* and *kattō*.

158. *Shōbōgenzō*, "Kattō." Cf. ibid., "Genjō-kōan": "When our bodies and minds are not yet fully saturated with Dharma, we believe that they are already sufficient. If Dharma fills our bodies and minds, we think something is still missing. For example, as you take a boat to the vast expanse of a sea where no mountains are visible, and look around in all directions, only the roundness of the expanse will strike you, and no other characteristics whatever will be seen. However, this great ocean is neither round nor square; its other characteristics are inexhaustible. It is like a palace for some and like jewels for others. Only insofar as our vision can reach does it appear to be round for the time being. Analogously, this holds true of all things. Although the world, whether mundane or otherwise, is pregnant with myriad characteristics, we see and understand only to the extent of our power of penetration and vision. To understand the ways of the family of all dharmas, we must know that in addition to what appears to be round or square, other features of oceans and qualities of mountains are indeed infinite, and there are many worlds on all sides. You should note that not only the environments around us are like this, but the same holds true even of the place right beneath our feet and even of a drop of water."

159. Ibid., "Kattō."

160. Ibid., "Kattō."

161. Ibid., "Kattō."

162. Compare this with the following statements selected at random: D. T. Suzuki: "The truth can be reached when it is neither asserted nor negated. This is indeed the dilemma of life, but the Zen masters are ever insistent on escaping the dilemma." *Zen Buddhism* (ed. by W. Barrett), p. 118.

E. Conze: "Nothing is more alien to the mentality of the sage than to fight or contend for or against anything. This peacefulness of the true sage is the germ of the Mādhyamika dialectics." *Buddhism: Its Essence and Development*, p. 136. Sangharakshita: "So long as the mind oscillates between contradictory statements, trying to determine which of them is true and which false, the aspirant remains immured within the mundane; but no sooner does he embark upon a bold identification of opposites than, bypassing the intellect, he disappears from the phenomenal plane and reappears in the Transcendental, in the domain and dimension of Emptiness." Op. cit., p. 218. Despite their legitimate intention, Suzuki, Conze, and Sangharakshita do not adequately cope with the question of how dilemmas and conflicts (unmistakably real, not illusory in life) can be legitimately accepted in the enlightened life. From this standpoint, Dōgen's Zen was governed not by the logic of transcendence so much as by the logic of realization.

163. *Shōbōgenzō*, "Kattō."

164. Ibid., "Kattō."

165. Ibid., "Kattō."

166. Such a view of philosophic activity is comparable to Asaṅga's "acquired wisdom" (*tat-pṛṣṭha-labdha-jñāna*), which refers to that wisdom which is no longer just beyond the expressions of human thought but embedded within them, and regarded as superior to mere silence or ineffability. See Ueda Yoshifumi, "Thinking in Buddhist Philosophy," *Philosophical Studies of Japan*, vol. 5 (1964), pp. 69–94. It is also comparable to the dynamic relationship between the sixth Perfection (*prajñā*) and the tenth Perfection (*jñāna*) of bodhisattvahood, in which wisdom is not replaced by knowledge, or vice versa, but the two are functionally interdependent in the structure of the bodhisattva's awareness or in the activities of both the going aspect (*ōsō*) and the returning aspect (*gensō*). In this connection, see D. T. Suzuki, "Reason and Intuition in Buddhist Philosophy," in his *Studies in Zen*, pp. 85–128. In this treatment, Suzuki emphasizes the dynamic nature of prajñā and the static and passive nature of vijñāna, and does not succeed in showing a dialectical interpretation of the two in the structure of Buddhist awareness.

167. Conze, *Buddhism*, p. 97. Conze further writes: "The truth is within the body, and arises out of it." Ibid., p. 199.

168. For example, Buddhaghosa's comment on the "thirty-two parts" of the body in his *Visuddhi-magga*, which is quoted in Conze, *Buddhist Meditation*, p. 95.

169. *Shōbōgenzō*, "Sanjūshichihon-bodaibumpō."

170. Ibid., "Sanjūshichihon-bodaibumpō."

171. Ibid., "Shinjin-gakudō."

172. *Zuimonki*, III:31. Dōgen sometimes, though not often, doubles the character *shin* (body), thus using the phrase "body-body" (*shinjin*) in the

place of "body-mind" (*shinjin*). See for example, *Shōbōgenzō*, "Jishō-zammai."

173. *Shōbōgenzō*, "Juki."

174. Perhaps A. N. Whitehead is most vocal in recognizing the meta-physical importance of the body. As he rightly observes, bodily participation is always implied in any human experience. For instance, although we do not see our eyes, and we do not say we see with our eyes unless an un-usual circumstance arises, it is a truism that we see with our eyes. *Modes of Thought*, p. 156. See also pp. 155 and 158.

175. *Shōbōgenzō*, "Bendōwa." Cf. "Sokushin-zebutsu."

176. Ibid., "Hotsu-mujōshin."

177. Ibid., "Yuibutsu-yobutsu."

178. Whitehead, *Modes of Thought*, p. 221.

179. *Shōbōgenzō*, "Semmen." This is why every minute act of bodily cleansing becomes so crucially important in the monastic life. Dōgen wrote the "Semmen" and "Senjō" chapters of *Shōbōgenzō* for this purpose.

180. Dōgen writes in *Shōbōgenzō*, "Busshō": "'If you want to know the meaning of Buddha-nature' does not imply solely intellectualization. You can say also: 'if you want to act,' 'if you want to experience,' 'if you want to elucidate,' 'if you want to forget,' and so on."

181. Ibid., "Shinjin-gakudō."

182. Ibid., "Shinjin-gakudō." Concerning these three minds, also see ibid., "Hotsu-bodaishin." Apparently Dōgen adopted this classification of the mind from Tendai Buddhism. However, except for the conscious mind, they are ambiguous in their exact meanings. See Okada Gihō, *Shōbōgenzō shisō takei*, vol. 6, pp. 110–12.

183. *Shōbōgenzō*, "Hotsu-bodaishin."

184. Ibid., "Shinjin-gakudō."

185. Ibid., "Genjō-kōan."

186. Ibid., "Genjō-kōan."

187. *Gakudō-yōjinshū*, 9.

188. *Shōbōgenzō*, "Kembutsu."

189. Ibid., "Kembutsu."

Chapter Four: The Religion and Metaphysics of Buddha-Nature

1. Karaki Junzō, *Karaki Junzō zenshū*, vols. 5 and 7, to which I am greatly indebted for the following observations.

2. Karaki observes that *Hōjōki*, *Heike-monogatari*, and the first half of *Tsure-zure-gusa* represent this view of impermanence.

3. Karaki, op. cit., vol. 7, "Mujō no keijijō-gaku."

4. Karaki maintains that it is a charateristic of the Japanese that when they talk about impermanence, they become notably eloquent, and that Dōgen

was no exception in this respect. Ibid., p. 143. This is so, despite Dōgen's discouragement of rhetoric in his *Zuimonki*, which we have noted before.

5. Watsuji Tetsurō, *Nihon rinri shisō-shi*, vol. 1, pp. 319–49, where he discusses *Gukanshō* (1223) by Jien or Jichin (1155-1225), *Jōei-shikimoku* (1232), *Heike-monogatari* (1198?), and other works, and delineates the evolution of the idea of reason in medieval Japanese thought. Cf. Muraoka Tsunetsugu, *Nihon shisō-shi kenkyū*, vol. 2, pp. 111–209 for his interpretation of *Gukanshō* and *Jōei-shikimoku*.

6. Tamura Yoshirō, *Kamakura shin-Bukkyō shisō no kenkyū*, p. 237.

7. According to Katō Shūkō, *Shōbōgenzō yōgo-sakuin*, *dōri* appears 272 times and *kotowari* (which also means reason) 12 times—hence the total of 284 times in *Shōbōgenzō*. This would be an unusual frequency for the use of any single word.

8. Tamura, op. cit., pp. 234–55 concerning the general conception of the reason of naturalness in Kamakura Buddhism.

9. Cf. Miyamoto Shōson's comments on the so-called "Japanese irrationality" in Charles A. Moore, ed., *The Japanese Mind*, pp. 60–65. For better or worse, the act of philosophizing is often mistakenly attributed solely to the Western mind, or depending on one's conception of philosophy, to the Chinese and the Indian minds, but not to the Japanese mind. The latter may not have produced philosophical systems, but has never relinquished the activities of philosophizing, hence, of reasoning, in its own way. Cf. ibid., pp. 290–93.

10. See Charles A. Moore, ed., *The Indian Mind*, p. 15.

11. The *Dhammapada* (S. Radhakrishnan's translation), pp. 58–59.

12. William Th. de Bary, ed., *The Buddhist Tradition in India, China and Japan*, p. 100. Adapted for gender-free diction.

13. Nyanaponika Thera, *The Heart of Buddhist Meditation*, p. 21.

14. Jean Felliozat in his "The Psychological Discoveries of Buddhism" attributes to Buddhism "the discovery of the importance of the unconscious element of the psychism and the composite nature of the whole psychic being, manifesting both conscious mental phenomena as well as unconscious continuing potentiality." *University of Ceylon Review*, vol. 13, nos. 2 and 3 (April-July 1955), p. 78.

15. We shall not get into the discussion of these matters in this study. Detailed discussion is presented in Katsumata Shunkyō, *Bukkyō ni okeru shinshiki-setsu no kenkyū*.

16. See Ueda Yoshifumi, *Yuishiki-shisō nyūmon*, pp. 9–52 concerning the use of "idealism" in the context of Buddhist philosophy and religion.

17. D. T. Suzuki observes that the doctrine expounded in the *Laṅkāvatāra sūtra* and the *Avataṃsaka sūtra* is mind-only (*citta-mātra*; *yuishin*) in contrast to the consciousness-only (*vijñāna-mātra*; *yuishiki*) or representation-only (*vijñapti-mātra*; *yuishiki*) of the Yogācāra school of Mahāyāna Bud-

dhism. See *Studies in the Lankavatara Sutra*, p. 181 and pp. 279–82. On the other hand, mind-only (the Buddhist equivalent of idealism) can be interpreted in such a way as to subsume under it the doctrine of "the triple world is mind-only" of the *Avataṃsaka sūtra*, the doctrine of "manifestation of one's own mind" (*svacitta-dṛśya-mātra*) of the *Laṅkāvatāra sūtra*, the doctrine of the original purity of mind (*jishō-shōjōshin*) of the *tathāgata-garbha* thought, the doctrine of the store-consciousness of the Yogācāra school, etc.

18. Surendranath Dasgupta, *Indian Idealism*, p. 74.

19. As to these different theories see Katsumata, op. cit., pp. 513–59; E. Conze, *Buddhist Thought in India*, pp. 122–34.

20. Katsumata, op. cit., pp. 568–89. Cf. Conze's observations on this matter: "The climax of this combination of the uncombinable [to combine the doctrine of 'not-self' with the almost instinctive belief in a 'self'] is reached in such conceptual monstrosities as the 'store-consciousness' . . ., which performs all the functions of a 'self.' The 'store-consciousness' is a fine example of 'running with the hare, and hunting with the hounds.'" Op. cit., pp. 133–34.

21. Suzuki, *Studies in the Lankavatara Sutra*, pp. 258–60.

22. Ibid., p. 181 and pp. 279–82.

23. Katsumata, op. cit., pp. 593–637.

24. Ibid., pp. 464–73. To what extent the primitive Buddhists considered two other possibilities—the mind as originally both pure and defiled, and the mind as originally neutral, though phenomenally both pure and defiled—is not too clear, according to Katsumata.

25. Ibid., pp. 473–84.

26. Ibid., pp. 504–6.

27. Ibid., pp. 485–511.

28. Ui Hakuju, *Bukkyō shisō kenkyū*, pp. 207–8. Vasubandhu in his *Buddhatva-śāstra* gives three meanings of *tathāgata-garbha*: (1) Tathāgata covered by illusions (*ompuku-zō*), (2) Tathāgata embracing sentient beings (*shoshō-zō*), and (3) Tathāgata's merits as contained in the minds of sentient beings (*nōshō-zō*). See Masunaga Reihō, "Dōgen's Idea of Buddha-nature," *Komazawa daigaku kenkyū kiyō*, no. 18 (March 1960), p. 13; idem, *Bukkyō ni okeru jikan-ron*, p. 177.

29. Katsumata, op. cit., pp. 631–32.

30. Yoshito S. Hakeda, trans., *The Awakening of Faith*, pp. 36–37.

31. Ibid., pp. 43–45.

32. Ibid., pp. 47–48.

33. Ibid., pp. 50–51.

34. Ibid., pp. 37ff.

35. Ibid., pp. 45–46.

36. Ibid., pp. 56–64.

37. Ibid., p. 64.

38. Ibid., p. 59.

39. It is well known that Fa-tsang (643–712), the third ancestor of the Chinese Hua-yen sect and a most important systematizer of Hua-yen philosophy, was the first to note the importance of the *tathāgata-garbha* tradition, along with the Mādhyamika and the Vijñānavāda school in Indian Mahāyāna Buddhism, and regarded this tradition as central in his interpretation of Hua-yen idealism. See K. Kawada and H. Nakamura, eds., *Kegon shisō*, pp. 279–81. In this connection, see Takahashi Jikidō's article, "Kegon-kyōgaku to nyorai-shisō—Indo ni okeru shōki-shisō no tenkai—," ibid., pp. 277–332, which delineates the historical relation between the *Tathā-gatôtpattisaṃbhava-nirdeśa sūtra*, one of the oldest independent sūtras which was later incorporated into the *Avataṃsaka sūtra*, and various sūtras and treatises of the *tathāgata-garbha* tradition, in the light of the idea of "manifestation of essence" (*gotra-saṃbhava*; *shōki*).

40. Ibid., p. 280. Concerning the interpretations of this tenet by the Hua-yen thinkers, see Tamaki Kōshiro, "Yuishin no tsuikyū—shisō to taiken no kōshō—," ibid., pp. 335–416.

41. *Shōbōgenzō*, "Sesshin-sesshō."

42. Ibid., "Sokushin-zebutsu," "Shin-fukatoku," "Kokyō," "Busshō," "Tsuki," "Kobusshin," "Sangai-yuishin," "Sesshin-sesshō," "Hosshō," "Hotsu-bodaishin," "Hotsu-mujōshin," "Tashintsū," and other chapters.

43. Concerning Dōgen's view of mind, see Akiyama Hanji, op. cit., pp. 85–105.

44. *Shōbōgenzō*, "Sokushin-zebutsu," "Shinjin-gakudō," "Busshō," "Sangai-yuishin," etc. In addition he refers to mind in various ways: "walls, tiles, and stones" ("Sangai-yuishin," "Kobusshin"); "birth and death, coming and going" ("Sokushin-zebutsu," "Sangai-yuishin"); "the skin, flesh, bones, and marrow" ("Sangai-yuishin"); "the three periods" (the appended chapter of "Shin-fukatoku").

45. Ibid., "Immo."

46. Ibid., "Immo." Immediately after this, Dōgen also comments on the kōan in which, when two monastics were arguing about whether a banner moved or the wind moved, Hui-nêng observed that the mind moved. He makes essentially the same point as we have seen in the case of the bell. Warning against a subjectivistic interpretation, Dōgen interprets Hui-nêng's "the mind moves" as meaning the movement of thusness that transcends the banner, the wind, and the mind—subject and object.

47. Ibid., "Bendōwa." Dōgen applies this view to the Dharma-nature, and observes that the Dharma-nature has to do with the flow of water or with the rise and fall of trees, or the bloom of blossoms and fall of leaves.

48. Ibid., "Sokushin-zebutsu." Also see "Bendōwa."

49. Ibid., "Busshō."

50. Ibid., "Bendōwa."

51. In this connection, Akiyama observes, in his op. cit., pp. 80–81, that Dōgen's view of the nondualism of body and mind is connected with his repudiation of rebirth and of the immortality of the soul. This observation is correct, though there are, as Akiyama himself concedes, some minor evidences contrary to it. (We shall examine Dōgen's view of moral causation and rebirth on a later occasion.) Dōgen's assertion of the nondualism of body and mind, which is firmly grounded in the ideas of functional interdependence and absolute emptiness, does not necessarily exclude the possibility of some "ethereal" or "spiritual" mode of existence that might be quite different from the present make-up of the human mind-body. However, such a mode of existence must be interpreted differently from those interpretations given in the conventional doctrines of rebirth or reincarnation and of the immortality of the soul. But this problem was not a focal point in Dōgen's thought.

52. *Shōbōgenzō*, "Sesshin-sesshō."

53. Ibid., "Sesshin-sesshō."

54. Ibid., "Sesshin-sesshō."

55. Nakagawa Takashi, "Dōgen zenji to Rokuso Dankyō."

56. *Shōbōgenzō*, "Sesshin-sesshō."

57. Akiyama, op. cit., pp. 81–85. A similar dualism appears in Conze, *Buddhist Meditation*, pp. 17–18 and pp. 22–23.

58. Kurebayashi Kōdō, "Dōgen-zen ni okeru shin ni tsuite," *Komazawa daigaku Bukkyō-gakubu kenkyū kiyō*, no. 20 (March 1962), pp. 1–11. This essay tries to show that Dōgen's view of mind should not be interpreted as "the ground of being."

59. *Shōbōgenzō*, "Sokushin-zebutsu."

60. Ibid., "Hotsu-bodaishin."

61. Ibid., "Sesshin-sesshō."

62. Ibid., "Sangai-yuishin."

63. Ibid., "Sangai-yuishin."

64. Ibid., "Sangai-yuishin."

65. Ui Hakuju, *Bukkyō shisō kenkyū*, pp. 12–14. In Ui's view, to translate the idea of functional interdependence as a kind of causation is highly misleading, and he thinks that the misplaced and exclusive emphasis of early Buddhism on moral causation (karma and rebirth) which has influenced the subsequent history of Buddhist thought is also erroneous. He further thinks that the doctrine of karma and rebirth (*rinne*) is not a fact but a religious postulate, hence, it should not be overly emphasized in Buddhism. What is pivotally important, according to Ui, is the metaphysical insight of functional interdependence rather than a strictly moral causation. Ibid., pp. 87–103.

66. *Shōbōgenzō*, "Shin-fukatoku" and its appended chapter, where Dōgen criticizes the assumption of an old woman who addressed a question to Tê-shan Hsüan-chien (780/2–865) about a passage in the *Diamond Sūtra*,

"The past mind is unattainable, the present mind is unattainable, and the future mind is unattainable." That is, the old woman asked Tē-shan: "Which mind would you nourish with refreshments?"

67. *Shōbōgenzō*, "Hensan."

68. Ibid., "Genjō-kōan."

69. In Buddhism, expressions such as *ekō-henshō* and *kyakka-shōko*, meaning "self-illumination" or "illuminate thy self," are frequently used. They are the Buddhist equivalents of the dictum "Know thyself."

70. Ibid., "Busshō."

71. The Buddhists apparently adopted the idea of *gotra* (family lineage, predisposition, potentiality, etc.) from Hinduism, but it was free from any implications of the caste system. However, as time went on, they were not always consistent with the original spirit, as we see in the theory of the five groups. Har Dayal says: "The Buddhist philosophers developed the theory of *gotra* in order to explain why all persons do not try or desire to become *bodhisattvas*." *The Bodhisattva Doctrine in Buddhist Sanskrit Literature*, p. 53.

72. *Shōbōgenzō*, "Busshō."

73. Ibid., "Busshō."

74. Ibid., "Busshō."

75. Ibid., "Busshō."

76. Cf. Akiyama, op. cit., pp. 108–9.

77. *Shōbōgenzō*, "Zenki."

78. If we were forced to classify Dōgen's religious and philosophical position, panentheism might be the term we would have to choose. But even this term should be discreetly and judiciously used when we apply it to Dōgen's thought. Concerning panentheism, see C. Hartshorne and W. L. Reese, eds., *Philosophers Speak of God*, particularly pp. 1–25, pp. 499–514.

79. *Shōbōgenzō*, "Busshō."

80. Ibid., "Sangai-yuishin."

81. See Okada Gihō, op. cit., vol. 2, pp. 156–58.

82. *Shōbōgenzō*, "Sangai-yuishin."

83. Ibid., "Busshō."

84. In addition to his rejection of the theory of the five groups (*goshō*), Dōgen did not subscribe literally to the theory of the six realms, which arranges sentient beings and insentient beings biocentrically or anthropocentrically in a hierarchical model, although he often uses this traditional theory as he does other traditional concepts. As we have noted often and will more later, Dōgen's religious and philosophical thought as a whole is highly antagonistic to models of hierarchies, layers, levels, degrees, strata, etc., although this does not mean the denial of their usefulness and even validity to a certain extent. Also Dōgen's view of sentient beings differs from so-called panpsychism, which is quite clear from our expositions of mind and Buddhanature.

85. The living dynamism of the one-many relationship in connection with Buddha-nature is discussed in his exposition of the ocean-reflection samādhi (*kaiin-zammai*), in which Dōgen refers to Ts'ao-shan Pên-chi's kōan of the great sea that is said to neither "keep a corpse" nor "retain the expired." More specifically, Dōgen refers to Ts'ao-shan's statement "[The sea] includes all nature" (*hōgan-ban'u*), and comments as follows: "Teacher's [Ts'ao-shan's] '*hōgan-ban'u*' signifies the sea. Its import does not imply that a person or a thing embraces all nature, but that inclusion (*hōgan*) itself is all nature (*ban'u*). It does not mean the great sea contains all nature; the great sea only embodies inclusion-itself-is-all-nature . . . inclusion-itself-is-all-nature means that inclusion includes inclusion-itself-is-all-nature (*hōgan-u-hōgan-ban'u*)." Ibid., "Kaiin-zammai." The net result is: Inclusion includes inclusion. A theoretical question is transformed into a practical realization without losing its theoretical import.

86. Ibid., "Busshō."

87. Ibid., "Kattō."

88. Ibid., "Sesshin-sesshō."

89. Ibid., "Busshō."

90. Ibid., Sesshin-sesshō. Cf. ibid., "Busshō": "You should always devote yourself to the way of the Buddha-nature of nonexistence. Do not recoil from it." "At the initial stage of meeting Buddhas and hearing of Dharma, the most difficult thing to grasp and heed is the notion that sentient beings are the Buddha-nature of nonexistence. While following a teacher or studying the sūtras, this truth is a joyful thing to hear. Unless in your learning and apprehension you are thoroughly filled with the truth of all the sentient beings as the Buddha-nature of nonexistence, you have not as yet learned or apprehended Buddha-nature. . . . You must be aware that to understand and hear of the Buddha-nature of nonexistence is the right path to becoming a Buddha. Consequently, at the very moment when the Buddha-nature of nonexistence is realized, you attain Buddhahood. As you do not yet see, hear, or apprehend the Buddha-nature of nonexistence, you are still far from becoming a Buddha."

91. Ibid., "Busshō."

92. Ibid., "Busshō."

93. Ibid., "Busshō." In the same chapter Dōgen also writes: "Furthermore, to think that Buddha-nature exists only in life but not in death is the view of little learning and superficial comprehension. Both in life and in death are the Buddha-nature of existence and the Buddha-nature of nonexistence. If you argue the formation or nonformation of wind and fire [the four elements], the formation or nonformation of Buddha-nature should obtain. Even at the time of dissolution, it is the Buddha-nature-existence and the Buddha-nature-nonexistence. At the time of construction, too, it is the Buddha-nature-existence as well as the Buddha-nature-nonexistence. De-

spite this, it is heretical to misconstrue Buddha-nature as existing or not existing, according to whether it moves or not, or as working or not working its wonder in proportion to human consciousness or unconsciousness, or to misconstrue its nature as depending upon human knowing or not-knowing."

94. Throughout our study we have belabored this point and will do so in the subsequent pages. Specifically in reference to emptiness, Dōgen writes: "Inasmuch as the Buddhas and ancestors fulfill the Way, whereby it is, of itself, authentically transmitted, the total being of the skin-flesh-bones-marrow is suspended in emptiness. Emptiness is not of the kind which has been characterized by the twenty-modes, and the like. After all, should emptiness have only twenty modes? It can have eighty-four thousand modes, and many more." Ibid., "Kokū."

95. Ibid., "Kokū."

96. Ibid., "Kokū."

97. Ibid., "Immo."

98. Ibid., "Busshō."

99. Ibid., "Busshō."

100. Ibid., "Busshō."

101. Ibid., "Busshō."

102. Ibid., "Busshō."

103. Ibid., "Busshō."

104. Ibid., "Maka-hannya-haramitsu." Also in the same chapter Dōgen says: "As this truth [of prajñā] unfolds and realizes itself, it tells us that form is emptiness, emptiness is form; form is form, emptiness is emptiness."

105. Abe Masao compares Dōgen's view of the relationship between all existence and Buddha-nature to Heidegger's "ontological difference" (*ontologische Differenz*) between Being (*Sein*) and beings (*Seiendes*) and "ontic difference" (*ontische Differenz*) among beings, and denies ontological difference in Dōgen's case. See "Dōgen on Buddha Nature," *The Eastern Buddhist*, vol. 4, no. 1 (May 1971), pp. 50–51. An opposite interpretation is presented by Sugimori Mamoru, "Dōgen to Heidegger: Hosshō to sonzai—josetsu," *Risō*, no. 369 (February 1964), pp. 35–43.

106. In *Shōbōgenzō*, "Busshō," Dōgen discusses these seven categories of Buddha-nature. For a general discussion of them, see Akiyama, op. cit., pp. 101–43; Masunaga Reihō, "Dōgen's Idea of Buddha-nature," pp. 1–14; Abe, "Dōgen on Buddha Nature."

107. *Shōbōgenzō*, "Sesshin-sesshō."

108. Ibid., "Busshō."

109. Ibid., "Busshō."

110. Ibid., "Busshō."

111. Ibid., "Busshō."

112. Ibid.. "Busshō."

113. Ibid., "Busshō." Cf. ibid., "Hakujushi."

114. Ibid., "Busshō."

115. Ibid., "Busshō."

116. Ibid., "Busshō." Also see ibid., "Sanjūshichihon-bodaibumpō."

117. Ibid., "Sansuikyō."

118. Ibid., "Uji."

119. Dōgen's vision is extremely akin to Alfred N. Whitehead's metaphysical vision of what he phrases as the "creative advance of the universe into novelty" from moment to moment which emerges from the interaction of actualities. Unity in multiplicity in Whitehead's vision is not a static completed state of being but a dynamic process of becoming. Dōgen would concur with Whitehead in this general metaphysical vision of the universe. See Whitehead, *Process and Reality*, passim.

120. For example, Nakamura Hajime's analysis of "the phenomenal world as Absolute" in his *Ways of Thinking of Eastern Peoples* does not refer to this aspect, that is, the logic of negation, which is crucially important, especially in Dōgen's thought. Cf. Yūki Sazuku, "Nihon Bukkyō no rinrisei," in Miyamoto Shōson, ed., *Bukkyō no kompon shinri*, pp. 933–50; Ienaga Saburō, *Nihon shisō-shi ni okeru hitei no ronri no hattatsu.*

121. See Karaki Junzō, *Chūsei no bungaku*; Nishio Minoru, *Nihon bungeishi ni okeru chūseiteki na mono*. Karaki and Nishio are most vocal in stressing Dōgen's place in the history of Japanese literature. From this standpoint they appraise Dōgen's use of Japanese in his writings.

122. Karaki Junzō, *Mujō*, pp. 5–130. Karaki observes that *hakanashi* or *hakanaki*, etymologically speaking, had the meaning of the failure to "measure" the pace of environmental changes by certain standards or norms. The sense of transience, despair, and emptiness was intimately related to such an "anomic" state of mind and state of affairs.

123. Ibid., pp. 294–302.

124. A rather crude attempt at speculating on time appears in *The Questions of King Milinda*, II.2.9 and 3.1–2, in which the distinction between the three periods and that between the "time which exists" and the "time which does not" are made. The root of time is said to be ignorance, and liberation evolves from the time which exists to the time which does not.

125. Nakayama Nobuji, *Bukkyō ni okeru toki no kenkyū*, passim. I am greatly indebted to this work for my historical review of the concept of time in Buddhism, and also for my exposition of Hua-yen philosophy of time, which follows it.

126. The distinction between *kāla* and *samaya* (both of which mean time) and the Buddhist's preference for the latter indicate this typically Buddhistic sensibility very well. A well-known analogy to this substantialistic view is a fruit in a pot.

127. Andre Bareau, "The Notion of Time in Early Buddhism," *East and*

West, vol. 7, no. 4 (January 1957), pp. 353–64, discusses the various views of early Buddhist schools. See also Nakayama, op. cit., pp. 1–49.

128. Ibid., pp. 50–79.

129. Ibid., pp. 80–100. Also see F. Streng, *Emptiness: A Study in Religious Meaning*, pp. 49–50.

130. For a general discussion of Hua-yen philosophy in English, see D. T. Suzuki, *Essays in Zen Buddhism*, Third Series, pp. 21–214; Takakusu Junjirō, *The Essentials of Buddhist Philosophy*, pp. 108–25; Garma C. C. Chang, *The Buddhist Teaching of Totality: The Philosophy of Hwa Yen Buddhism*; Fung Yu-lan, *A History of Chinese Philosophy*, vol. 2, pp. 339–59.

131. Change, op. cit., pp. 141–70 as to the four dharma-realms of (1) phenomena, (2) principles, (3) the nonobstruction of principles and phenomena, and (4) the nonobstruction of all phenomena; especially pp. 153ff. Cf. Nakayama, op. cit., pp. 101ff.

132. Chang, op. cit., pp. 136–40.

133. Ibid., pp. 121–24.

134. Ibid., pp. 155–67 for the exposition of the ten mysteries.

135. These orders are taken from the new version by Fa-tsang (643–712) revised from the previous one coming down from Tu-shun (558–640) and Chih-yen (602–668).

136. Nakayama, op. cit., pp. 112–15.

137. Chang, op. cit., pp. 160–61.

138. Nakayama, op. cit., pp. 124–28.

139. Ibid., pp. 128–29.

140. Ibid., pp. 138–46.

141. Fa-tsang, *Hua-yen i-hai pai-men*. Quoted by Chang in his op. cit., p. 160.

142. This thesis is quite clearly expounded in Takahashi Masanobu, *Dōgen no jissen tetsugaku kōzō*.

143. Tamaki Kōshiro, "Bukkyō no jikanron," *Risō*, no. 460 (September 1971), pp. 64–78.

144. *Shōbōgenzō*, "Uji."

145. Ibid., "Uji."

146. Ibid., "Uji." Takahashi, op. cit., pp. 299–301 concerning interpretations of the word "interval," which is often taken to mean intervals between different times. Takahashi thinks that the word refers to the interval between the self and time.

147. *Shōbōgenzō*, "Uji."

148. Ibid., "Uji." One *jō* and six *shaku* are equivalent to about sixteen feet.

149. Ibid., "Uji."

150. Ibid., "Kūge."

151. Ibid., "Shoaku-makusa."

152. Ibid., "Uji."

153. Ibid., "Uji."

154. Here we note a striking similarity between Dōgen and Heidegger, who maintains "the temporality of spatiality" in his *Being and Time*. Heidegger writes: "Because Dasein is 'spiritual,' and *only because of this*, it can be spatial in a way which remains essentially impossible for any extended corporeal Thing." Thus, "Dasein takes space in." Ibid., p. 419.

155. Takahashi, op. cit., pp. 287–92.

156. *Shōbōgenzō*, "Uji." In this translation we follow Takahashi's interpretation of *ware* as self, instead of, as referring to time. See op. cit., pp. 278–81.

157. The personal and existential emphasis of Dōgen's treatment is hinted at in Takahashi's commentary on the "Uji" chapter (op. cit., pp. 271–92) but not stressed as much as it should be. In this respect Nakayama's treatment (op. cit., pp. 167–79) seems to be doing more justice to the intention of Dōgen's view of time.

158. *Shōbōgenzō*, "Uji."

159. Ibid., "Uji." *Waga* in this passage is interpreted as referring to existence-time by some, to the self by others. See Akiyama, op. cit., pp. 129–30; Takahashi, op. cit., pp. 335–38; Masunaga, *Bukkyō ni okeru jikanron*, pp. 214–21.

160. *Shōbōgenzō*, "Daigo."

161. Ibid., "Shukke-kudoku." Dōgen uses the conventional figures of *setsuna* and *tanji* but has no interest in speculating on the exact length of these terms, as some earlier Buddhists did. In this connection, a single thought (*ichinen*) is said to be equivalent to 1/60 or 1/400 *tanji*. As to the Buddhist tenet of "everything perishes as soon as it arises," see also ibid., "Hotsu-bodaishin" and "Kaiin-zammai."

162. Ibid., "Genjō-kōan." Cf. ibid., "Den'e," "Kūge," "Sanjūshichihon-bodaibumpō," "Juki," etc. In his discussion of the notion of arising and perishing (*kimetsu*) Dōgen writes: "For this reason, arising and perishing mean that while the self arises in and of itself (*ga-ga-ki*) and the self perishes in and of itself (*ga-ga-metsu*), it never halts. This never-halting should be understood in such a way that arising or perishing is allowed to be totally arising or perishing (*kareni ichinin shite*). . . . Speaking of not-standing-face-to-face-with (*fusōtai*) or not-waiting-for-one-another (*fusōtai*), you should realize that arising is nothing but arising throughout its beginning, middle, and end. [As Yün-chü Tao-ying said,] officially not a single needle is admitted, but privately horses and vehicles pass through. In its beginning, middle, and end, it neither waits for nor stands face to face with perishing. Even if Dharma arises abruptly after a preceding perishing, it is not the arising of [that preceding] perishing but an arising of Dharma. Because it is Dharma's arising, it neither corresponds with nor anticipates anything

(*futaidaisō nari*). Moreover, a perishing and another perishing do not expect one another nor stand opposed to each other. Perishing too is nothing but perishing throughout its beginning, middle, and end." Ibid., "Kaiin-zammai."

163. Ibid., "Shoaku-makusa." Cf. "Gabyō," "Genjō-kōan," "Zazen-shin."

164. Ibid., "Genjō-kōan." This can be compared with Hua-yen's "mystery of the co-existence of concealment and disclosure" (*ommitsu-kenryō-kujō-mon*). On this point, see Chang, op. cit., pp. 162–64.

165. *Shōbōgenzō*, "Zenki."

166. The primacy of discontinuity is well emphasized by Takahashi, op. cit., following the tradition of Nishiari Bokusan's *Keiteki*, a well-known and important commentary on Dōgen's *Shōbōgenzō*. This position is highly critical of those taken by Tanabe Hajime, Hashida Kunihiko, and other philosophers, who attempted to see Dōgen's view of time primarily in terms of time and eternity—in which case continuity becomes primary.

167. *Shōbōgenzō*, "Uji."

168. Ibid., "Uji." See Takahashi, op. cit., p. 357 and pp. 353–54 on Dōgen's special use of the word "obstruction" in this instance.

169. This is one way to convey Dōgen's intention in English. But this is only an approximation which I think is very useful. Thus any noun can be converted into a verb form, and we can say, for example: "Eating eats eating, and thereby eating realizes itself" (in which the single activity of eating exerts itself totally to such an extent that the eating subject and immediate environment—certainly the whole universe—are "darkened," yet embodied in and through it by virtue of their mutual identity and mutual penetration). Similarly, "Dōgen dōgen-s Dōgen, and thereby Dōgen realizes himself . . .," and so forth. In this way, the subject and the predicate interpenetrate one another in *activity*, and thus: "Activity acts activity, and thereby activity realizes itself." Paradoxically, obstruction in Dōgen's thought means absolute freedom in the nonobstruction of self-obstruction.

170. *Shōbōgenzō*, "Uji."

171. Ibid., "Uji."

172. Inasmuch as the *Saddharma-puṇḍarīka sūtra* and its central doctrine of "all things themselves are ultimate reality" (*shohō-jissō*) occupy a crucially important place in Dōgen's thought in general, we can claim a direct affinity of his theory of time to it, as Takahashi does. But as Takahashi himself concedes, we cannot deny an intimate relation between Dōgen's view of time and Hua-yen philosophy. See Takahashi, op. cit., pp. 5–69, especially p. 69, note 2.

173. *Shōbōgenzō*, "Tsuki."

174. Whitehead, *Process and Reality*, p. 107.

175. *Shōbōgenzō*, "Juki." Elsewhere the unity of the three periods is de-

scribed in this way: "The past, so-called, is the mind, the present is hands, the future is the brain." Ibid., "Kembutsu."

176. Ibid., "Busshō."

177. Ibid., "Busshō."

178. Ibid., "Busshō."

179. Cf. Takahashi, op. cit., pp. 109–17.

180. *Shōbōgenzō*, "Uji." Of this paragraph, which is very difficult to understand, like many other passages in the "Uji" chapter, "The times of ancient and modern do not pile up, nor do they line up" is especially difficult to interpret. Perhaps the Hua-yen doctrine of mutual identity and mutual penetration may help us understand the meaning of this passage.

181. *Shōbōgenzō*, "Uji." What are arranged (*hairetsu seru*) are not times, but things of the world in space, for the subjectively appropriated absolute nows cannot be arranged or deployed.

182. Ibid., "Uji."

183. Ibid., "Kokū," "Daigo," "Shin-fukatoku."

184. As to the relationship between the problem of time and the idea of activity, I am indebted to Nakayama, op. cit., pp. 172–79 for his insights into the matter. However, the following exposition of mine is based on a different perspective than that of Nakayama.

185. *Shōbōgenzō*, "Gyōji."

186. Ibid., "Gyōji."

187. Cf. Nakayama, op. cit., pp. 177–78.

188. *Shōbōgenzō*, "Gyōji."

189. Thus for example, the "Shōji" chapter, which has a striking affinity to Pure Realm thought, is construed by some as spurious or as Dōgen's instruction intended for Pure Realm Buddhists. See *The Eastern Buddhist*, vol. 5, no. 1 (May 1972), pp. 79–80, note 7.

190. *Shōbōgenzō*, "Shoaku-makusa."

191. Ibid., "Yuibutsu-yobutsu."

192. Ibid., "Shōji."

193. Ibid., "Bendōwa."

194. Ibid., "Bendōwa."

195. Ibid., "Shinjin-gakudō."

196. Ibid., "Yuibutsu-yobutsu."

197. Ibid., "Genjō-kōan."

198. Ibid., "Genjō-kōan."

199. This point may be clarified by considering Martin Buber's criticism of Heidegger's anthropology. See Buber, *Between Man and Man*, pp. 163–81. Buber says that Heidegger's view of human existence, despite its emphasis on the existence in the world, is based on one's relation to oneself; one's relation to other selves is regarded solely as derivative from this individualistic conception of human existence. Heidegger's human existence is essentially

"monological." In Buber's view, the essential nature of the self is derived from its embeddedness in the matrix of communal selves. We are born not only into the world but with the world. Being is essentially social and only existentially individual, not vice versa.

200. *Shōbōgenzō*, "Shōji."

201. Ienaga Saburō considers one of the lasting contributions of Pure Realm Buddhism, especially of Shinran, to be the profound sense of sinfulness, and thinks that hope for Buddhism in the future lies in the cultivation of this sense. *Chūsei Bukkyō shisō-shi kenkyū*, pp. 230–32.

202. *Shōbōgenzō*, "Busshō."

203. To translate *zenki* into English is a difficult task. Waddell and Abe translate it as "total dynamic working" and also occasionally as "total dynamism." See *The Eastern Buddhist*, vol. 5, no. 1 (May 1972), pp. 70–80. I would like to translate *zenki* variously as "total dynamism," "total function," "total working," and so forth.

204. *Shōbōgenzō*, "Zenki."

205. In this connection it is significant to observe what A. N. Whitehead said in a surprisingly similar vein: "Each task of creation is a social effort, employing the whole universe." *Process and Reality*, p. 340. Also he writes: "The whole world conspires to produce a new creation." *Religion in the Making*, p. 99.

206. *Shōbōgenzō*, "Zenki."

207. Ibid., "Zenki."

208. Ibid., "Shōji."

209. Ibid., "Genjō-kōan."

210. Ibid., "Shōji."

211. Ibid., "Shinjin-gakudō."

212. Ibid., "Yuibutsu-yobutsu."

213. Ibid., "Gyōbutsu-igi."

214. Ibid., "Gyōbutsu-igi."

Chapter Five: Monastic Asceticism: The Way of Ritual and Morality

1. Ui Hakuju, *Zenshū shisō-shi*, vol. 1, pp. 1–90.

2. See Kenneth K. S. Ch'en, *Buddhism in China*, pp. 241–57 as regards the socioeconomic background of the Buddhist monastic order in general in those days.

3. Ui, op. cit., pp. 81–90.

4. Ui, *Zenshū shisō-shi*, vol. 2, pp. 327–423; idem, *Bukkyō shisō kenkyū*, pp. 628–45.

5. Hīnayāna Buddhism had the two divisions of the vinaya: one is the division of the inhibition of evil (*shiaku-mon*), and the other the division of the promotion of good (*sazen-mon*). The former consisted of the so-called

"precepts of seven types of Buddhists" (*shichishu-kai*), that is, the precepts of monks, nuns, women who observe the six precepts, male novices, female novices, laymen, and laywomen. The division of the promotion of good consisted of such ritual observances as receiving the precepts, *uposatha* (*fusatsu*), monastic retreats, etc. Hīnayāna vinaya was far more systematic than its Mahāyāna counterpart which was comprised of the ten major precepts (*jū-jūkin-kai*) and the forty-eight minor precepts (*shijū-hachi-kyō-kai*) and included virtually nothing in the area of the promotion of good. Pochang's contribution to the Mahāyāna division of the promotion of good in the total structure of monastic discipline must be appreciated. See Ui, *Zenshū shisō-shi*, vol. 2, pp. 390–93.

6. *Zuimonki*, II:1.

7. Concerning the differences between pure Zen and mixed Zen, see Imaeda Aishin, *Zenshū no rekishi*, Chapters 2, 3, and 4.

8. *Zuimonki*, II:26.

9. Furuta Shōkin, in his *Nihon Bukkyō shisō-shi no shomondai*, analyzes these two trends in Kamakura Buddhism. Furuta observes that Hōnen's thought on this matter was only apparently opposed to the traditional observance of the precepts as the path of sages (*shōdōmon*); at a deeper level he was far from being opposed to the precepts. Hōnen's famous statement "In the Age of Degenerate Law there is neither the observance of precepts nor the violation of precepts" should be interpreted to mean that the nondualistic conception of the precepts—which transcends observance and violation—is subsumed in the sole act of the recitation of the holy name of Amida (*shōmyō-nembutsu*). See ibid., pp. 3–17.

10. Ibid., pp. 18–35 concerning Eisai's view on the precepts. Eisai once wrote: "Zen Buddhism has precepts as its beginning and meditation as its goal" (*Kōzen gokokuron*). Compare this with Dōgen's recollection of the Kenninji temple when he studied there prior to his study in China, in *Zuimonki*, V:10.

11. See Furuta, op. cit., pp. 36–56.

12. In those days Zen was largely dependent on Tendai and Shingon Buddhism and content with reinforcing the established order of the old Buddhism. See Imaeda, op. cit., p. 14.

13. *Shōbōgenzō*, "Semmen."

14. Ibid., "Semmen."

15. Ibid., "Semmen."

16. Ibid., "Semmen."

17. Ibid., "Semmen."

18. Ibid., "Senjō."

19. Ibid., "Senjō." Cf. Shinran's view of the "rightly established state" (*shōjōju*) in which all the followers of the eighteenth vow of Amida will re-

side, and by virtue of which they will be assured of the birth in the Pure Land and of the realization of enlightenment in the after-life. See *Kyōgyō-shinshō*, IV. This notion together with his denial of the esoteric Buddhist doctrine of "This body itself is Buddha" (*sokushin-jōbutsu*) in *Tannishō*, XV show that there was a significant difference between Shinran and Dōgen as to their treatment of the worldly defiled land and the Pure Land.

20. *Shōbōgenzō*, "Senjō."

21. Ibid., "Senjō."

22. Ibid., "Semmen."

23. Ibid., "Semmen."

24. Ibid., "Semmen." A similar view with respect to the washing of clothes is presented in ibid., "Sanjūshichihon-bodaibumpō."

25. As to the theme of purification, see *Proceedings of the XIth International Congress of the International Association for the History of Religions*. Particularly, Abe Masao's statement: "There is no 'being pure' apart from 'becoming pure'" (ibid., p. 150) seems to reflect Dōgen's view well.

26. *Shōbōgenzō*, "Senjō."

27. Ibid., "Senjō."

28. Dōgen expounded the chapter in 1239, 1243, and 1250. Other than this chapter, Dōgen presented "Daigo" on two occasions in 1242 and 1244. See Okada, *Shōbōgenzō shisō taikei*, vol. 6, p. 340.

29. Besides these two meals monastics take the "evening meal," usually gruel, which is called "medicinal food" (*yakujiki*) or "medicinal stone" (*yakuseki*). This seems to be a compromise with the Buddhist vow not to eat after midday. Dōgen seems to have observed the traditional two-meal practice, permitting evening meals only in the snowy winter season. See *Eiheiji-koku-shijimon*.

30. *Zuimonki*, I:3.

31. Ibid., VI:25. In *Chiji-shingi* Dōgen refers to the traditional Buddhist notions of "four impure foods" and "five improper means of livelihood." The former are: (1) food obtained from working for the rich and the powerful, (2) food obtained from charms and fortune-telling, (3) food obtained from astrological practices, and (4) food obtained from land cultivation and selling medicines. The latter (five improper means of livelihood) are: (1) to display miraculous appearances, (2) to speak of one's own merits, (3) to engage in fortune-telling and divination, (4) to threaten others by a loud voice, and (5) to spread the news of alms and offerings. All these acts are done for the purpose of profit and livelihood. Dōgen gives strict regulations for the administration of public grain (*kugaimai*) in *Eiheiji kuin seiki*.

32. Takeuchi conjectures that the monastic economy of the Eiheiji temple must have been in very straitened circumstances. See his *Dōgen*, pp. 295–97; Ōkubo Dōshū, *Dōgen-zenji-den no kenkyū*, Chapter 9.

33. In his *Tenzo-kyōkun*, see Dōgen's severe criticism of Japanese, and high praise for Chinese, practice with respect to the status of the chief cooks and their functions.

34. Cf. D. T. Suzuki, *The Training of the Zen Buddhist Monk*.

35. *Tenzo-kyōkun*.

36. Ibid.

37. Ibid.

38. *Eiheiji jikuimmon*.

39. *Fushukuhampō*.

40. Ibid.

41. *Shōbōgenzō*, "Hatsuu."

42. Ibid., "Hatsuu."

43. Sanskrit *kaśāya* for *kesa* referred originally to the spoiled, yellowish-red color of the Buddhist robe. It was chosen to signify nonattachment to clothing.

44. *Shōbōgenzō*, "Den'e."

45. Ibid., "Kesa-kudoku."

46. Ibid., "Kesa-kudoku" and "Den'e." These two chapters are almost identical in their content.

47. Ibid., "Kesa-kudoku."

48. Ibid., "Kesa-kudoku" and "Den'e." Dōgen recounts his own experience in China, being greatly moved when he witnessed a monk's reverential handling of his robe.

49. Ibid., "Kesa-kudoku."

50. Ibid., "Den'e."

51. *Zuimonki*, VI:25.

52. The twelvefold practice of asceticism (*dvādaśa dhūtaguṇāh*; *jūni-zudagyō*) is meant to purify one's body and mind by shaking off all forms of attachment to clothes, food, and dwelling. They are (1) dwelling in the forest, (2) taking any seat which may be offered, (3) living on alms, (4) observing the rule of using only one seat for meditation and eating, (5) wearing coarse garments, (6) not eating after the time when one should cease eating, (7) wearing clothes made of rags taken from a dust heap, (8) having only three robes, (9) living in or near a cemetery, (10) living under a tree, (11) living in the open air, and (12) using the sitting posture for sleeping. See Daitō shuppansha, *Japanese-English Buddhist Dictionary*, "Jūni-zuda" on p. 152; Taya Raishun and others, eds., *Bukkyō-gaku jiten*, p. 288.

53. *Zuimonki*, V:14.

54. *Shōbōgenzō*, "Gyōji."

55. Ibid., "Raihai-tokuzui."

56. Ibid., "Gyōji." Dōgen refers to the legendary emperors of China such as Huang-ti, Yao, and Shun who are said to have lived in meager thatched huts.

57. *Hōkyōki*, 29.

58. *Shōbōgenzō*, "Senjō."

59. H. Yokoyama, "Zenshū no shichidō garan," *Zen bunka*, vol. 2, no. 4 (1956), pp. 40–45; idem, "Dōgen-zen to kenchiku," Iida Toshiyuki, ed., *Dōgen-zen*, vol. 4, pp. 218–30. Yokoyama observes that the completion of the Eiheiji temple in Echizen was seen after Tettsū Gikai (1219–1309), the third ancestor of the temple, went to China from 1259–1262 and studied Zen monasteries, particularly the Ching-tê-ssŭ temple.

60. See Yokoyama's aforementioned essays.

61. Iida, op. cit., pp. 220–21. Also read *Zuimonki*, II:6 concerning Dōgen's discourse on this matter. Instructions about manners in the monastics' hall are given in *Bendōhō*.

62. Iida, op. cit., pp. 226–30.

63. Miyasaka Tetsubun, *Zen ni okeru ningen keisei*, pp. 168–75. See *Shuryō-shingi* and *Shōbōgenzō*, "Kankin."

64. *Shōbōgenzō*, "Sansuikyō."

65. Ibid., "Mujō-seppō."

66. Ibid., "Sansuikyō."

67. Ibid., "Keisei-sanshoku." Here "a gigantic tongue" (*kōchōzetsu*) refers to one of the thirty-two major characeristics of Buddha, and in turn, to the discourse of Buddha.

68. Ibid., "Keisei-sanshoku."

69. Ibid., "Keisei-sanshoku."

70. Ibid., "Keisei-sanshoku."

71. Ibid., "Sansuikyō." Dōgen writes: "While the mountain's walking is like human walking, it fails to look like human, but you should not therefore entertain a doubt about the mountain's walking" (ibid., "Sansuikyō"). This refers to the statement of Fu-yung Tao-k'ai (1043–1118): "A blue mountain is always walking; a stone image of woman gives birth to a baby at night."

72. Ibid., "Mujō-seppō."

73. Ibid., "Sansuikyō."

74. Ibid., "Sansuikyō."

75. Ibid., "Sansuikyō." This illustration is also used in ibid., "Genjō-kōan."

76. Ibid., "Sansuikyō."

77. Yün-mên Wên-yen (864–949) was once asked by a monastic the question "Where did Buddhas come from?" Yün-mên's answer was: "An eastern mountain walks on the water."

78. Ibid., "Sansuikyō."

79. Ibid., "Tsuki."

80. Ibid., "Tsuki."

81. Ibid., "Tsuki."

82. Ibid., "Tsuki."

83. Ibid., "Tsuki."
84. Ibid., "Shunjū."
85. Ibid., "Shunjū."
86. Ibid., "Shunjū."
87. Ibid., "Shunjū."
88. Ibid., "Baika."
89. Ibid., "Baika."
90. Ibid., "Udonge."
91. Ibid., "Kūge."
92. Ibid., "Kūge."
93. Ibid., "Kūge."
94. Ibid., "Kūge."
95. Ibid., "Kūge."
96. Ibid., "Kūge."

97. Hori Ichirō discusses the significance of mountains in the history of Japanese religion in his *Folk Religion in Japan*, Chapter 4. Dōgen's fascination with the mountains and waters is not just what he inherited from Ju-ching but is deeply rooted in Japanese culture, although his view is, as we have seen in this study, mediated by the logic of Buddha-nature and emptiness.

98. The vows, or "original vows" (*pūrva-praṇidhāna; hongan*), are classified traditionally in two categories: (1) The universal vows (*sōgan*) are applicable to all bodhisattvas universally and formulated in the form of the "four universal vows" (*shi-guzeigan*). The original form of the four universal vows appears in the *Saddharma-puṇḍarīka sūtra*. (2) The special vows (*betsugan*) are various formulations particular to different Buddhas and bodhisattvas—e.g., Amitābha's forty-eight vows, Bhaiśajyaguru's twelve vows, Samantabhadra's ten vows, and so on.

99. *Shōbōgenzō*, "Busso" and "Hotsu-bodaishin." The twenty-eight Indian ancestors are called "great superiors" (*dai-oshō*), whereas the six Chinese ancestors are called "ancestral teachers" (*soshi*).

100. The fifty-two stages of bodhisattvahood consist of (1) the ten stages of faith (*jusshin*), (2) the ten stages of security (*jūjū*), (3) the ten stages of practice (*jūgyō*), (4) the ten stages of devotion (*jūekō*), (5) the ten stages of development (*jūji*), (6) the stage of approaching bodhisattvahood (*tōgaku*), and (7) the stage of Buddhahood (*myōgaku*).

101. Ibid., "Shohō-jissō."

102. Ibid., "Shohō-jissō." Cf. ibid., "Kannon," in which Kannon is said to be the parent of Buddhas (*shobutsu no bumo*).

103. Ibid., "Shohō-jissō."

104. Miyamoto, op. cit., pp. 235–40. Roughly, these two can be thought of as analogous to the division of other-power (*tariki*) and self-power (*jiriki*) in Buddhism.

105. *Shōbōgenzō*, "Kannon."

106. This kōan is taken up by Dōgen in ibid., "Kannon." The kōan was originally the fifty-fourth case of the *Ts'ung-yung-lu* (1223).

107. *Shōbōgenzō*, "Kannon."

108. Ibid., "Kannon."

109. Ibid., "Kannon." Also see Dōgen's treatment of the arahat who is ranked as Buddha, which is rather unorthodox in Buddhist thought. Ibid., "Arakan." As to the problem of the arms and eyes in relation to Dōgen's notion of "arising and perishing" (*kimetsu*), see ibid., "Kaiin-zammai."

110. Ibid., "Nyorai-zenshin."

111. Ibid., "Nyorai-zenshin."

112. Ibid., "Bukkyō" (34).

113. Ibid., "Bukkyō" (34).

114. Ibid., "Kembutsu." Also cf. ibid. "Gyōbutsu-igi," where Dōgen argues that because of thusness we transcend I and you and, hence, are Buddhas.

115. Cf. Nishitani Keiji, "On the I-Thou Relation in Zen Buddhism," *The Eastern Buddhist*, vol. 2, no. 2 (1969), pp. 71–87.

116. *Shōbōgenzō*, "Jishō-zammai."

117. Ibid., "Bodaisatta-shishōbō." These four virtues were originally advocated by the Mahāyānists as part of skillfulness in the choice of means and methods, the seventh perfection of the bodhisattva's career. In other words, the Mahāyāna Buddhists taught that a bodhisattva needed three areas of skillfulness for helping and converting the people: (1) four virtues, (2) four thorough knowledges, and (3) charms and spells. The four virtues under investigation belong to (1) of this classification. See Dayal, op. cit., pp. 251–69.

118. *Shōbōgenzō*, "Bodaisatta-shishōbō." As to the fundamental nature of giving and its relation to the Buddhist ideas of compassion and the transfer of merit, see Dayal, op. cit., pp. 172–93.

119. *Shōbōgenzō*, "Bodaisatta-shishōbō."

120. Ibid., "Bodaisatta-shishōbō."

121. Ibid., "Bodaisatta-shishōbō."

122. On the theme of the bodhisattva see further ibid., "Sanjūshichihon-bodaibumpō" and "Hachi-dainingaku"; *Zuimonki*, passim; the three minds (*sanshin*) in *Tenzo-kyōkun*; etc.

123. *Shōbōgenzō*, "Hotsu-bodaishin."

124. Ibid., "Gyōji." See also *Zuimonki*, III:6.

125. *Jūundōshiki*.

126. Miyasaka, op. cit., pp. 31–32; Furuta, op. cit., pp. 36–56; Kondō Ryōichi, "Dōgen ni okeru shisō tenkai no ichi kōsatsu—hokuetsu nyūsan o keiki to shite—," *Journal of Indian and Buddhist Studies*, vol. 12, no. 1 (January 1964), pp. 243–46.

127. Hirakawa Akira, "Kairitsu yori mitaru Bukkyō shinrikan," Miyamoto, op. cit., pp. 259–84.

128. Ibid., especially pp. 268–69, 271–83. According to Hirakawa, both terms were well distinguished by the primitive Buddhists and their relation was recognized.

129. For example, see Shōbōgenzō, "Jukai," "Shukke," and "Shukke-kudoku."

130. Ibid., "Jukai"; Busso-shōden bosatsukai kyōjukaimon (hereafter Kyōju-kaimon).

131. The term Hīnayāna here and elsewhere in this work is employed advisedly. As it is widely known today, the term is used by some Mahāyāna Buddhists with pejorative connotations to designate Southern Buddhism or Theravāda Buddhism in the South-East Asian countries. On the other hand, Mahāyāna Buddhists also used the term to designate all early Buddhist schools and sects other than Mahāyāna Buddhism. It was accordingly much broader than the term Theravāda Buddhism.

132. Ibid., "Jukai;" Busso shōden bosatsukai sahō and Eihei soshi tokudo ryaku-sahō for detailed instructions for the bodhisattva ordination.

133. Shōbōgenzō, "Shukke."

134. Ibid., "Shukke."

135. Kyōjukaimon.

136. D. T. Suzuki, Manual of Zen Buddhism, p. 13.

137. The problem of confession has occupied a very important place in Buddhism from its inception. Ordinary confession (sange or keka) could be made at any time as it was required, whereas uposatha (fusatsu) was held every fifteen days and a confessional (pavāraṇa; jishi) was held at the end of the monastic retreat (ango). As regards the practice of these rites in various Japanese Buddhist sects, see M. W. de Visser, Ancient Buddhism in Japan, 2 volumes. Heinrich Dumoulin discusses this problem in connection with Zen Buddhism in his essay "Technique and Personal Devotion in the Zen Exercise," in Joseph Roggendorf, ed., Studies in Japanese Culture, pp. 17–40.

138. Shōbōgenzō, "Keisei-sanshoku."

139. Ibid., "Keisei-sanshoku."

140. Dumoulin makes the following observation of contemporary Zen: "In the commonly accepted classification of Buddhism, Zen is placed in the category of those sects that insist on salvation through 'one's own endeavor' (jiriki) while other schools, especially the Amidists, rely on 'another's strength' (tariki). Zen is thus defined because of its consistently monistic illuminationism. That is, at any rate, the impression received from much of the literature about Zen. Suzuki Daisetsu, for example, likes to recount the anecdotes of ancient Zen masters who would burn Buddha images or sūtra scrolls in order to demonstrate dramatically that the Buddha was not to be sought outside but within the heart. In reality, such episodes are

not much more but exceptional cases; they do not permit the conclusion that Zen is in effect iconoclastic or opposed to sacred cult. No Zen master has, in the final analysis, reneged on the radical monism of Zen metaphysics. Nevertheless, the actual atmosphere of many Zen monasteries is characterized by a devotional reverence comparable to that of Amida temples." Roggendorf, op. cit., p. 30. Dumoulin's interpretation of Zen as "monistic illuminationism" or "radical monism" can be challenged. Without subscribing to this we can appreciate this noteworthy antidote to the currently much misunderstood picture of Zen.

141. *Shōbōgenzō*, "Keisei-sanshoku." There are two types of confession: repentance with regard to the facts of existence (*jisan* or *ji no sange*) such as sins, ambiguities, frailties, and so forth, and repentance with regard to the nature of the facts of existence (*risan* or *ri no sange*), namely, that sins, ambiguities, and frailties are originally and ultimately empty.

142. Cf. Ui Hakuju, *Bukkyō tetsugaku no kompon mondai*, pp. 1–35. Ui points out that when the Buddhist speaks of the law of causation it is primarily the law of moral causation (and this was true of primitive Buddhism as well), though the law of physical causation—a predominant concern on the part of Western philosophers and scientists—is implied, but generally recedes in the background if it is not totally nonexistent. Dōgen is not an exception in this regard. Throughout this study "causation" refers to the law of moral causation.

143. *Shōbōgenzō*, "Daishugyō" and "Jinshin-inga"; *Dōgen oshō kōroku*, I and III.

144. *Shōbōgenzō*, "Jinshin-inga."

145. Ibid., "Jinshin-inga," "Sanjigō," "Daishugyō," "Shoaku-makusa."

146. Ibid., "Jinshin-inga" and "Sanjigō." As will become clearer in the following exposition, Dōgen presents two different interpretations of this problem in "Jinshin-inga" and "Sanjigō" on the one hand and in "Daishugyō" on the other. See G. Okada, *Shōbōgenzō shisō-taikei*, vol. 7, p. 463.

147. *Shōbōgenzō*, "Kūge."

148. Ibid., "Daishugyō."

149. Ibid., "Daishugyō."

150. Ibid., "Daishugyō."

151. Akiyama, op. cit., pp. 163–83.

152. *Shōbōgenzō*, "Shoaku-makusa."

153. Ibid., "Shoaku-makusa."

154. Ibid., "Sanjigō."

155. Ibid., "Sanjigō." The avīci hell is one of the eight hot hells (*hachi-daijigoku* or *hachi-netsujigoku*).

156. Ibid., "Sanjigō."

157. Ibid., "Jinshin-inga."

158. Ibid., "Ikka-myōju."

159. Ibid., "Shohō-jissō."
160. Ibid., "Busshō." Cf. S. Tachibana, *The Ethics of Buddhism*, pp. 66–67 concerning Buddha's position on this issue.
161. *Zuimonki*, V:11.
162. *Shōbōgenzō*, "Shoaku-makusa."
163. Ibid., "Shoaku-makusa."
164. *Zuimonki*, VI:15.
165. Ibid., VI:15.
166. Ibid., VI:15.
167. Ibid., VI:17.
168. Ibid., III:25.
169. See ibid., III:6. In a similar vein does Dōgen also interpret *on* (favors, obligations, debts, etc.) in ibid., III:25.
170. *Dhammapada*, XIV:183.
171. *Shōbōgenzō*, "Shoaku-makusa."
172. Ibid., "Sanjūshichihon-bodaibumpō."
173. Ibid., "Shoaku-makusa."
174. This is similar to "presuming upon Amida's original vow" (*honganbokori*) to which Shinran refers in his *Tannishō*, XIII.
175. *Shōbōgenzō*, "Shoaku-makusa."
176. Ibid., "Shoaku-makusa."
177. *Zuimonki*, II:4. The kōan runs as follows: Once, when the monastics of the western and eastern halls were quarrelling about a cat, Nan-ch'üan, holding up the cat, said, "You monastics! If any of you can speak a word of Zen I will spare the cat, otherwise I will kill it!" No one could answer, so Nan-ch'üan killed it. In the evening, Chao-chou came back from somewhere, and Nan-ch'üan told him what had happened. Chao-chou thereupon took off his shoe, put it on his head, and walked off. Nan-ch'üan said, "If only you had been there, I could have saved the cat!" Adapted from R. H. Blyth's translation in his *Mumonkan* (*Zen and Zen Classics*, vol. 4), pp. 120–21. Dōgen in his comments holds that it is better not to kill the cat as a way of leading monastics to enlightenment.
178. *Zuimonki*, II:4.
179. *Shōbōgenzō*, "Shoaku-makusa."
180. Ibid., "Shoaku-makusa."
181. D. T. Suzuki once said: "Zen finds its inevitable association with art but not with morality. Zen may remain unmoral but not without art." *Zen and Japanese Culture*, p. 27. Suzuki here may not be asserting a downright antinomianism, yet comes very close to it. From Dōgen's standpoint what Suzuki has to say characterizes the transmoral aspect of enlightenment but hardly, if at all, the moral expression of it. Morality is to be liberated, not belittled, much less abandoned.
182. At this point Dōgen's thought is almost indistinguishable from

Shinran's, which envisioned "naturalness" (*jinen-hōni*) as its culmination in his *Mattōshō*, *Jinen-hōni-shō*, and so forth. The Naturalness here means the spontaneous unfolding of Amida's vow-power without human calculation or contrivance. This is also called the "reason of no reason" (*mugi o motte gi to su* or *gi naki o gi to su*)—which refers to the transcendent rationality of effortlessness, meaninglessness, purposelessness—the reason of nonduality. Also cf. *Tannishō*, VIII.

183. *Shōbōgenzō*, "Shoaku-makusa."

184. Ibid., "Shoaku-makusa."

185. Ibid., "Shoaku-makusa."

186. Ibid., "Sanjūshichihon-bodaibumpō." The fourfold right effort is a part of the thirty-seven virtues of bodhisattvahood (*saptatriṃśad bodhi-pākṣikā dharmāḥ*; *sanjūshichihon-bodaibumpō*) which are very important, along with the ten perfections, in the total scheme of the bodhisattva's career. See Dayal, op. cit., pp. 80–164 concerning the thirty-seven virtues.

187. *Shōbōgenzō*, "Hosshō." The idea of "innate knowledge" is mentioned by Confucius in his *Analects*, XVII:9 which reads: "Confucius said, 'Those who are born with knowledge are the highest type of people. Those who learn through study are the next. Those who learn through hard work are still next. Those who work hard and still do not learn are really the lowest type.'"

188. *Shōbōgenzō*, "Hosshō" and "Daigo." In "Daigo" Dōgen writes: "Therefore, you should realize that there is not a single sentient being or insentient being that is not naturally intelligent. Where there is natural intelligence, there is natural enlightenment, natural experience, and natural practice."

189. See Miyasaka, op. cit., pp. 102–67 for the historical delineation of Zen thought on the problem of scriptural studies.

190. Ibid., pp. 125–30.

191. Concerning the significance of kōan as "a form of the sūtra study" and the "resuscitation of words and letters" in Zen Buddhism, see ibid., particularly, pp. 140–41.

192. See *Shōbōgenzō*, "Bendōwa," "Hokke-ten-Hokke," "Kankin," "Bukkyō" (47), and *Jūundōshiki* on words and letters.

193. Ibid., "Bukkyō" (34) and "Bukkyō" (47) on this point.

194. Ibid., "Bukkyō" (34).

195. Miyasaka, op. cit., pp. 152–61, 168–75.

196. See Karasawa Tomitarō, *Chūsei shoki Bukkyō kyōiku-shisō no kenkyū*, pp. 339–52 about Saichō and Kūkai, who initiated the education of monastics in the mountains, that is, Mt. Hiei and Mt. Kōya, respectively, in contrast to Nara Buddhism whose activities centered around the city of Nara. This meant, according to Karasawa, an emphasis on monastic discipline rather than doctrinal theorization, avoidance of politics and other-worldly

involvement, concentration on the formation of the ideal Buddhist community, and so on.

197. *Shōbōgenzō*, "Sansuikyō."

198. *Zuimonki*, V : 1.

199. *Gakudō-yōjinshū*, 5.

200. Ibid., 5.

201. The Socratic dialogue was adopted in contrast to public speech
(*rhētorikē*), the Zen counterpart of which may be sermon or lecture (*teishō*).
At any rate, the Socratic dialogue attempted to attain universalistic definitions of ideas such as "justice," "courage," "love," and so forth, through a
dialectical progression of dialogue, as we see in the Platonic dialogues. On
the other hand, the Zen dialogue is concerned with the realization of enlightenment—a much more practical concern. Yet it is highly significant that
both employed dialogue as a pedagogic and philosophic method for the discovery and realization of truth.

202. *Shōbōgenzō*, "Menju," where this analogy is applied for the direct
transmission of Dharma through the personal encounter of teacher and disciple. Such a personal encounter is said to be the sine qua non of the transmission of Dharma.

203. Ibid., "Shinjin-gakudō" and "Gabyō."

204. Ibid., "Dōtoku."

205. "A quest is an expression of the Way" (*monsho no dōtoku*) refers to
this problem. Jimbo and Andō, eds., *Zengaku jiten*, p. 1425.

206. *Zuimonki*, V : 5.

207. Ibid., V and VI, passim; *Dōgen oshō kōroku*, V.

208. See *Chiji-shingi, Tenzo-kyōkun, Taidaiko-goge-jarihō*, and so forth,
for this aspect of monastic life.

209. Cf. Karasawa, op. cit., pp. 381–96.

210. *Zuimonki*, V : 13; *Jūundōshiki*.

211. *Zuimonki*, II : 20.

212. *Shōbōgenzō*, "Shizen-biku."

213. Ibid., "Busshō."

214. Ibid., "Shinjin-gakudō."

215. Ibid., "Hotsu-bodaishin." Cf. "Shinjin-gakudō," "Kie-buppōsōbō," and so forth, for responsive communion.

216. Ibid., "Hotsu-mujōshin."

217. Ibid., "Jishō-zammai."

218. Ibid., "Immo."

219. Ibid., "Sesshin-sesshō."

BIBLIOGRAPHY

A. Works by Dōgen Kigen

Dōgen. Nihon shisō taikei, vols. 12 and 13. Ed. Terada Tōru and Mizuno Yaoko. Tokyo: Iwanami shoten, 1970 and 1972.

Dōgen zenji goroku. Ed. Ōkubo Dōshū. Tokyo: Iwanami shoten, 1940.

Dōgen zenji shingi. Ed. Ōkubo Dōshū. Tokyo: Iwanami shoten, 1941.

Dōgen zenji zenshū. 2 vols. Ed. Ōkubo Dōshū. Tokyo: Chikuma shobō, 1969–70.

Hōkyōki. Ed. Ui Hakuju. Tokyo: Iwanami shoten, 1938.

Shōbōgenzō. 3 vols. Ed. Etō Sokuō. Tokyo: Iwanami shoten, 1939–43.

Shōbōgenzō Bendōwa Shōbōgenzō zuimonki hoka. Koten Nihon bungaku zenshū, vol. 14. Ed. with translations by Nishio Minoru. Tokyo: Chikuma shobō, 1964.

Shōbōgenzō Shōbōgenzō zuimonki. Nihon koten bungaku taikei, vol. 81. Ed. Nishio Minoru and others. Tokyo: Iwanami shoten, 1965.

Shōbōgenzō zuimonki. Ed. Watsuji Tetsurō. Tokyo: Iwanami shoten, 1929.

B. Books

Akamatsu, Toshihide. *Shinran.* Tokyo: Yoshikawa kōbunkan, 1961.

Akamatsu, Toshihide, and others. *Nihon Bukkyō-shi*, vol. 2: *Chūseihen.* Kyoto: Hōzōkan, 1967.

Akiyama, Hanji. *Dōgen no kenkyū.* Tokyo: Iwanami shoten, 1936.

———. *Dōgen zenji to gyō.* Tokyo: Sankibō busshorin, 1940.

Anesaki, Masaharu. *History of Japanese Religion.* London: Kegan Paul, Trench, Trubner & Co., Ltd., 1930.

Anesaki, Masaharu. *Religious Life of the Japanese People*. Revised by Kishimoto Hideo. Tokyo: Kokusai bunka shinkōkai, 1961.

Aston, W. D. *A History of Japanese Literature*. New York: D. Appleton and Co., 1908.

Austin, J. L. *How To Do Things with Words*. Ed. J. O. Urmson. Galaxy Book edition. New York: Oxford University Press, 1965.

———. *Philosophical Papers*. London: Oxford University Press, 1961.

Bapat, P. V., ed. *2500 Years of Buddhism*. Delhi: The Publications Division, Government of India, 1956.

Bellah, N. Robert. *Beyond Belief: Essays on Religion in a Post-Traditional World*. New York: Harper & Row, 1970.

Benoit, Hubert. *The Supreme Doctrine: Psychological Studies in Zen Thought*. New York: The Viking Press, 1959.

Bergson, Henri. *The Two Sources of Morality and Religion*. New York: Henry Holt and Co., Inc., 1935.

Blyth, R. H. *Mumonkan. Zen and Zen Classics*, vol. 4. Tokyo: The Hokuseidō Press, 1966.

Brandon, S. G. F., ed. *A Dictionary of Comparative Religion*. New York: Charles Scribner's Sons, 1970.

Briggs, William, ed. *Anthology of Zen*. New York: Grove Press, 1961.

Buber, Martin. *Between Man and Man*. Trans. R. G. Smith. London: Kegan Paul, 1947.

Bunce, W. K. *Religions in Japan*. Rutland, Vt.: Charles E. Tuttle Co., 1955.

Campbell, Joseph, ed. *Man and Time*. Bollingen Series 30, vol. 3. New York: Pantheon Books, 1957.

———, ed. *The Mystical Vision*. Bollingen Series 30, vol. 6. Princeton: Princeton University Press, 1968.

———, ed. *Spiritual Disciplines*. Bollingen Series 30, vol. 4. Princeton: Princeton University Press, 1960.

Cassirer, Ernst. *An Essay on Man*. New Haven: Yale University Press, 1944.

———. *Philosophy of Symbolic Forms*. 3 vols. Trans. Ralph Mannheim. New Haven: Yale University Press, 1953–57.

Chang, Chung-yuan. *Creativity and Taoism: A Study of Chinese Philosophy, Art, and Poetry*. Harper Colophon edition. New York: Harper & Row, 1963.

Chang, Garma C. C. *The Buddhist Teaching of Totality: The Philosophy of Hwa Yen Buddhism*. University Park and London: The Pennsylvania State University Press, 1971.

———. *The Practice of Zen*. New York: Harper & Row, 1959.

Ch'en, Kenneth K. S. *Buddhism in China: A Historical Survey*. Princeton: Princeton University Press, 1964.

———. *The Chinese Transformation of Buddhism*. Princeton: Princeton University Press, 1973.

Conze, Edward. *Buddhism: Its Essence and Development*. Harper Torchbooks edition. New York: Harper & Row, 1959.

————. *Buddhist Meditation.* London: George Allen & Unwin, Ltd., 1956.

————. *Buddhist Thought in India.* Ann Arbor Paperbacks edition. Ann Arbor: The University of Michigan Press, 1967.

Dasgupta, Surendranath. *Indian Idealism.* Cambridge: The University Press, 1962.

Dayal, Har. *The Bodhisattva Doctrine in Buddhist Sanskrit Literature.* London: Kegan Paul, Trench, Trubner & Co., Ltd., 1932.

De Bary, William Th., and others, eds. *Sources of Chinese Tradition.* New York: Columbia University Press, 1960.

De Visser, M. W. *Ancient Buddhism in Japan.* 2 vols. Leiden: E. J. Brill, 1935.

Dumoulin, Heinrich. *The Development of Chinese Zen.* Trans. with additional notes and appendices by R. F. Sasaki. New York: The First Zen Institute of America, Inc., 1953.

————. *A History of Zen Buddhism.* Trans. P. Peachey. New York: Pantheon Books, 1963.

————. *Ostlich Meditation und christliche Mystik.* Freiburg/Munchen: Verlag Karl Alber, 1966.

Earhart, H. Byron. *Japanese Religion: Unity and Diversity.* Belmont, Calif.: Dickenson Publishing Co., 1969.

Eliade, Mircea. *Patterns in Comparative Religion.* Trans. Rosemary Sheed. Meridian Books edition. Cleveland and New York: The World Publishing Co., 1963.

————. *The Quest: History and Meaning in Religion.* Chicago: The University of Chicago Press, 1969.

————. *Yoga: Immortality and Freedom.* Trans. W. R. Trask. New York: Bollingen Foundation, Inc., 1958.

Eliade, Mircea, and Kitagawa, Joseph M., eds. *The History of Religions: Essays in Methodology.* Chicago: University of Chicago Press, 1959.

Eliot, Sir Charles. *Japanese Buddhism.* New York: Barnes and Noble, Inc., 1959.

Etō, Sokuō. *Shōbōgenzō josetsu: Bendōwa gikai.* Tokyo: Iwanami shoten, 1959.

————. *Shūso to shiteno Dōgen zenji.* Tokyo: Iwanami shoten, 1944.

Fairbank, John K., ed. *Chinese Thought and Institutions.* Chicago: The University of Chicago Press, 1957.

Fraser, J. T., ed. *The Voices of Time: A Cooperative Survey of Man's Views of Time as Expressed by the Sciences and by the Humanities.* New York: George Braziller, 1966.

Fromm, E., Suzuki, D. T., and De Martino, Richard. *Zen Buddhism and Psychoanalysis.* New York: Grove Press, 1963.

Fujiki, Kunihiko. *Heian-jidai no kizoku no seikatsu.* Tokyo: Shibundō, 1960.

Fung, Yu-lan. *A History of Chinese Philosophy.* 2 vols. Princeton: Princeton University Press, 1952.

Furuta, Shōkin. *Nihon Bukkyō shisōshi no shomondai*. Tokyo: Shunjūsha, 1964.

———. *Shōbōgenzō no kenkyū*. Tokyo: Sōbunsha, 1972.

———. *Zen shisōshi-ron: Nihon-zen*. Tokyo: Shunjūsha, 1966.

Gerth, H. H., and Mills, C. Wright., eds. *From Max Weber: Essays in Sociology*. Galaxy Book edition. New York: Oxford University Press, 1958.

Hakeda, Yoshito S., trans. *The Awakening of Faith*. New York: Columbia University Press, 1967.

Hanayama, Shinshō, and others. *Kōza Bukkyō*, vol. 5: *Nihon no Bukkyō*. Tokyo: Daizō shuppansha, 1967.

Hartshorne, Charles, and Reese, W. L. *Philosophers Speak of God*. Chicago: The University of Chicago Press, 1953.

Hashida, Kunihiko. *Shōbōgenzō shakui*. 4 vols. Tokyo: Sankibō busshorin, 1930–40.

Hauer, J. W. *Der Yoga: Ein indischer Weg zum Selbst*. Stuttgart: W. Kohlhammer Verlag, 1958.

Heidegger, Martin. *Being and Time*. Trans. J. Macquarrie and E. Robinson. New York: Harper & Row, 1962.

———. *Existence and Being*. With an introduction by Werner Brock. Gateway edition. Chicago: Henry Regnery Co., 1949.

———. *An Introduction to Metaphysics*. Trans. R. Manheim. New Haven: Yale University Press, 1959.

Heiler, F. *Die Stufen der buddhistischen Versenkung*. Munchen: Reinhardt, 1922.

Herrigel, Eugen. *Zen (Zen in the Art of Archery and the Method of Zen)*. McGraw-Hill paperbacks edition. New York: McGraw-Hill Book Co., 1964.

Hisamatsu, Shin'ichi. *Tōyō-teki mu*. Tokyo: Kōbundō shobō, 1939.

Hisamatsu, Shin'ichi, and Nishitani, Keiji, eds. *Zen no honshitsu to ningen no shinri*. Tokyo: Sōbunsha, 1969.

Honpa Hongwanji Mission of Hawaii, comp. *The Shinshū seiten*. Honolulu: The Honpa Hongwanji Mission of Hawaii, 1955.

Hori, Ichirō. *Folk Religion in Japan: Continuity and Change*. Chicago: The University of Chicago Press, 1968.

———. *Minkan shinkō*. Tokyo: Iwanami shoten, 1951.

Hōzōkan, ed. *Kōza: Kindai Bukkyō*. 6 vols. Kyoto: Hōzōkan, 1961–63.

Huizinga, Johan. *Homo Ludens: A Study of the Play-Element in Culture*. Beacon Paperback edition. Boston: Beacon Press, 1955.

Hunt, Ernest Shinkaku, ed. *Gleanings from Sōtō Zen*. Honolulu: Sōtō Mission, 1960.

Hutchison, John A. *Language and Faith*. Philadelphia: The Westminster Press, n.d.

Ienaga, Saburō. *Chūsei Bukkyō shisōshi kenkyū*. Kyoto: Hōzōkan, 1955.

Ienaga, Saburō, ed. *Nihon Bukkyō-shisō no tenkai—hito to sono shisō*. Kyoto: Heirakuji shoten, 1956.

————. *Nihon dōtoku shisōshi.* Tokyo: Iwanami shoten, 1954.

————. *Nihon shisōshi ni okeru hitei no ronri no hattatsu.* Tokyo: Kōbundō, 1940.

————. *Nihon shisōshi ni okeru shūkyo-teki shizenkan no tenkai.* Tokyo: Sōgensha, 1944.

————, ed. *Nihon shūkyōshi kōza,* vol. 2: *Shūkyō no kaikaku.* Tokyo and Kyoto: San'ichi shobō, 1959.

Ienaga, Saburō, and others, eds. *Iwanami kōza: Nihon rekishi.* Vols. 4 and 5. Tokyo: Iwanami shoten, 1967.

Ienaga, Saburō, and others. *Nihon Bukkyō-shi,* vol. 1: *Kodaihen.* Kyoto: Hōzōkan, 1967.

Imaeda, Aishin. *Zenshū no rekishi.* Tokyo: Shibundō, 1966.

Itō, Keidō. *Dōgen zenji kenkyū,* vol. 1. Tokyo: Daitō shuppansha, 1939.

Itō, Shunkō, ed. *Eihei-kōroku chūkai zensho.* 3 vols. Tokyo: Eihei-kōroku chūkai zensho kankōkai and Kōmeisha, 1961–63.

Iwamoto, Hidemasa, trans. *Shōbōgenzō-Zuimonki. Wortgetreue Niederschrift der lehrreichen Worte Dogen-Zenzis über den wahren Buddhismus.* Tokyo: Sankibō, 1943.

Japanese Association for Religious Studies, ed. *Religious Studies in Japan.* Tokyo: Maruzen Co., Ltd., 1959.

Japanese-English Buddhist Dictionary. Tokyo: Daitō shuppanasha, 1965.

Jayatilleke, K. N. *Early Buddhist Theory of Knowledge.* London: Allen & Unwin, 1963.

Jimbo, Nyoten, and Andō, Bun'ei. *Shōbōgenzō chūkai zensho.* 11 vols. Tokyo: Shōbōgenzō chūkai zensho kankōkai, 1913–14; reprinted 1956–57.

Jimbo, Nyoten, and Andō, Bun'ei. *Zengaku jiten.* Tokyo: Nakayama shobō, 1958.

Kagamishima, Genryū. *Dōgen zenji to sono monryū.* Tokyo: Seishin shobō, 1961.

Kagamishima, Genryū, and others, eds. *Dōgen-zen.* 4 vols. Tokyo: Seishin shobō, 1960–62.

Kanaoka, Shūyū. *Mikkyō no tetsugaku.* Kyoto: Heirakuji shoten, 1969.

Kaneko, Daiei. *Nihon Bukkyōshi-kan.* Tokyo: Zaike Bukkyō kyōkai, 1956.

Kapleau, Philip. *The Three Pillars of Zen.* New York: Harper & Row, 1966.

Karaki, Junzō. *Karaki Junzō zenshū,* vols. 5, 7, and 9. Tokyo: Chikuma shobō, 1967–68.

Karasawa, Tomitarō. *Chūsei shoki Bukkyō kyōiku-shisō no kenkyū.* Tokyo: Tōyōkan shuppansha, 1954.

Katō, Shūkō. *Shōbōgenzō yōgo sakuin.* 2 vols. Tokyo: Risōsha, 1962–63.

Katsumata, Shunkyō. *Bukkyō ni okeru shinshiki-setsu no kenkyū.* Tokyo: Sankibō busshorin, 1961.

Kawada, Kumatarō. *Bukkyō to tetsugaku.* Kyoto: Heirakuji shoten, 1957.

Kawada, Kumatarō, and Nakamura, Hajime, eds. *Kegon shisō.* Kyoto: Hōzōkan, 1960.

Kazue, Kyōichi. *Nihon no mappō-shisō*. Tokyo: Kōbundō, 1961.

Keene, Donald. *Anthology of Japanese Literature from the Earliest Era to the Mid-nineteenth Century*. Evergreen edition. New York: Grove Press, 1955.

Kennett, Jiyu. *Selling Water by the River: A Manual of Zen Training*. New York: Pantheon Books, 1972.

King, Winston L. *Buddhism and Christianity: Some Bridges of Understanding*. Philadelphia: The Westminster Press, n.d.

Kishimoto, Hideo, ed. *Japanese Religion in the Meiji Era*. Translated and adapted by John F. Howes. Tokyo: Tōyō bunko, 1956.

Kitagawa, Joseph M., ed. *The History of Religions: Essays on the Problem of Understanding*. Chicago: The University of Chicago Press, 1967.

Kitagawa, Joseph M. *Religion in Japanese History*. New York: Columbia University Press, 1966.

Kitagawa, Joseph M., and Long, Charles H., eds. *Myths and Symbols: Studies in Mircea Eliade*. Chicago: The University of Chicago Press, 1969.

Kurebayashi, Kōdō. *Dōgen-zen no kenkyū*. Tokyo: Zengaku kenkyūkai, 1963.

————, ed. *Dōgen-zen no shisō-teki kenkyū*. Tokyo: Shunjūsha, 1973.

Luk, Charles (Lu K'uan Yu). *The Secret of Chinese Meditation*. London: Rider & Co., 1964.

Masunaga, Reihō. *Bukkyō ni okeru jikanron*. Tokyo: Sankibō busshorin, 1966.

————. *Eihei Shōbōgenzō—Dōgen no shūkyō*. Tokyo: Shunjūsha, 1956.

————. *Eihei shoso gakudō no yōjin*. Tokyo: Shunjūsha, 1960.

————, trans. *A Primer of Sōtō Zen: A Translation of Dōgen's Shōbōgenzō-zuimonki*. Honolulu: East-West Center Press, 1971.

————. *The Sōtō Approach to Zen*. Tokyo: Layman Buddhist Society Press, 1958.

————. *Zenjō shisōshi*. Tokyo: Nihon hyōronsha, 1944.

Masutani, Fumio. *A Comparative Study of Buddhism and Christianity*. Tokyo: CIIB Press, 1957.

————. *Shinran Dōgen Nichiren*. Tokyo: Shibundō, 1956.

Mathews, R. H. *A Chinese-English Dictionary*. Revised American edition. Cambridge: Harvard University Press, 1963.

Matsubara, Yūzen. *Shinran to mappō shiso*. Kyoto: Hōzōkan, 1968.

Merton, Thomas. *Zen and the Birds of Appetite*. New Directions edition. New York: New Directions Publishing Corporation, 1968.

Miura, Isshū, and Sasaki, Ruth F. *Zen Dust*. New York: Harcourt, Brace & World, Inc., 1966.

Miyamoto, Shōson, ed. *Bukkyō no kompon shinri*. Tokyo: Sanseidō, 1956.

Miyasaka, Tetsubun. *Zen ni okeru ningen keisei*. Tokyo: Hyōronsha, 1970.

Mizuno, Kōgen. *Genshi Bukkyō*. Kyoto: Heirakuji shoten, 1956.

Mizuno, Kōgen, Nakamura, Hajime, and others, eds. *Shin butten kaidai jiten*. Tokyo: Shunjūsha, 1966.

Mochizuki, Shinkō. *Bukkyō daijiten.* 7 vols. Tokyo: Bukkyō jiten kankōsho, 1931–35.

Moore, Charles A., ed. *The Chinese Mind: Essentials of Chinese Philosophy and Culture.* Honolulu: East-West Center Press, 1967.

———, ed. *The Indian Mind: Essentials of Indian Philosophy and Culture.* Honolulu: East-West Center Press, 1967.

———, .ed. *The Japanese Mind: Essentials of Japanese Philosophy and Culture.* Honolulu: East-West Center Press, 1967.

———, ed. *Philosophy—East and West.* Princeton: Princeton University Press, 1944.

Morgan, Kenneth W., ed. *The Path of the Buddha: Buddhism Interpreted by Buddhists.* New York: Ronald Press, 1956.

Morris, Ivan. *The World of the Shining Prince.* New York: Alfred A. Knopf, 1964.

Murti, T. R. V. *The Central Philosophy of Buddhism.* London: George Allen & Unwin, Ltd., 1955.

Nabata, Ōjun, and others, eds. *Shinran-shū Nichiren-shū. Nihon koten bungaku takei,* vol. 82. Tokyo: Iwanami shoten, 1964.

Nakamura, Hajime. *Hikaku shisōron.* Tokyo: Iwanami shoten, 1960.

———. *A History of the Development of Japanese Thought.* 2 vols. Tokyo: Kokusai bunka shinkōkai, 1967.

———. *Jihi.* Kyoto: Heirakuji shoten, 1956.

———. *Tōyōjin no shii-hōhō.* Tokyo: Misuzu shobō, 1949.

———. *Ways of Thinking of Eastern Peoples.* Ed. P. P. Wiener. Honolulu: East-West Center Press, 1964.

Nakamura, Hajime, and others, eds. *Shin Bukkyō jiten.* Tokyo: Seishin shobō, 1962.

Nakayama, Nobuji. *Bukkyō ni okeru toki no kenkyū.* Kyoto: Hyakkaen, 1943.

Nihon Bukkyō gakkai, ed. *Bukkyō ni okeru gyō no mondai.* Kyoto: Heirakuji shoten, 1965.

———, ed. *Bukkyō ni okeru kai no mondai.* Kyoto: Heirakuji shoten, 1967.

———, ed. *Bukkyō ni okeru shin no mondai.* Kyoto: Heirakuji shoten, 1966.

———, ed. *Bukkyō ni okeru shō no mondai.* Kyoto: Heirakuji shoten, 1966.

———, ed. *Bukkyō to kyōiku no shomondai.* Kyoto: Heirakuji shoten, 1971.

Nihon bungaku kyōkai, ed. *Nihon bungaku kenkyū hikkei—kotenhen.* Tokyo: Iwanami shoten, 1959.

Nishiari, Bokusan. *Keiteki.* 3 vols. Tokyo: Daihōrinkaku, 1965.

Nishio, Minoru. *Chūsei-teki na monoto sono tenkai.* Tokyo: Iwanami shoten, 1961.

Nishitani, Keiji, ed. *Kōza: Zen.* 8 vols. Tokyo: Chikuma shobō, 1967.

———. *Shūkyō towa nanika.* Tokyo: Sōbunsha, 1961.

Nukariya, Kaiten. *Zengaku shisōshi.* 2 vols. Tokyo: Gennōsha, 1923. Reprinted; Tokyo: Mcicho kankōkai, 1969.

Nyanaponika Thera. *The Heart of Buddhist Meditation.* London: Rider & Co., 1962.

Nyanatiloka. *Buddhist Dictionary: Manual of Buddhist Terms and Doctrines.* Colombo: Frewin & Co., Ltd., 1956.

Ogisu, Jundo. *Nihon chūsei zenrinshi.* Tokyo: Mokujisha, 1965.

————, ed. *Zen to Nihon-bunka no shomondai.* Kyoto: Heirakuji shoten, 1969.

Okada, Gihō. *Shōbōgenzō shisō taikei.* 8 vols. Tokyo: Hōsei daigaku shuppan-kyoku, 1953–55.

————. *Zengaku kenkyūhō to sono shiryō.* Tokyo: Meicho kankōkai, 1969.

Ōkubo, Dōshū. *Dōgen zenji-den no kenkyū.* Tokyo: Iwanami shoten, 1953. Revised edition; Tokyo: Chikuma shobō, 1966.

Ono, Gemmyō, ed. *Bussho kaisetsu daijiten.* 12 vols. Tokyo: Daitō shuppansha, 1931–36.

Piovesana, Gino K. *Recent Japanese Philosophical Thought, 1862–1962, a Survey.* Tokyo: Enderle Bookstore, 1963.

Proceedings of the XIth International Congress of the International Association for the History of Religions, vol. 2: *Guilt or Pollution and Rites of Purification.* Leiden: E. J. Brill, 1968.

Radhakrishnan, S., trans. *The Dhammapada.* London: Oxford University Press, 1966.

Reihelt, K. L. *Meditation and Piety in the Far East.* New York: Harper & Bros., 1954.

Reischauer, E. O. *Japan Past and Present.* New York: Alfred A. Knopf, 1946.

Reischauer, E. O., and Fairbank, J. K. *East Asia: The Great Tradition.* Boston: Houghton Mifflin Co., 1958.

Rekishi gakkai, ed. *Nihonshi nempyō.* Tokyo: Iwanami shoten, 1966.

Rhys Davids, T. W., trans. *The Questions of King Milianda.* 2 vols. (F. Max Müller, ed., *The Sacred Books of the East,* vol. 35.) New York: Dover Publications, Inc., 1963.

Robinson, Richard H. *The Buddhist Religion: A Historical Introduction.* Belmont, Calif.: Dickenson Publishing Co., 1970.

————. *Early Mādhyamika in India and China.* Madison: The University of Wisconsin Press, 1967.

Roggendorf, Joseph, ed. *Studies in Japanese Culture: Tradition and Experiment.* Tokyo: Sophia University, 1963.

Sakamoto, Yukio, ed. *Hokekyō no shisō to bunka.* Kyoto: Heirakuji shoten, 1965.

Sangharakshita. *A Survey of Buddhism.* Bangalore, India: The Indian Institute of World Culture, 1957.

Sansom, George B. *Japan, a Short Cultural History.* London: Cresset, 1946.

Sasaki, Kazuo, and Iida, Toshiyuki. *Shōbōgenzō no kenkyū.* Tokyo: Kōbunkan, 1947.

Satō, Tatsugen. *Dōgen no shōgai.* Tokyo: Tōkyō shin'yūsha, 1962.

Satō, Tokuji. *Bukkyō no Nihon-teki tenkai.* Tokyo: Iwanami shoten, 1936.

Sekiguchi, Shindai. *Tendai shikan no kenkyū.* Tokyo: Iwanami shoten, 1969.

————. *Zenshū shisōshi.* Tokyo: Sankibō busshorin, 1964.

Senzaki, Nyogen, and McCandless, Ruth S., eds. and trans. *Buddhism and Zen.* New York: Philosophical Library, 1953.

Slator, Robert Lawson. *Paradox and Nirvana.* Chicago: The University of Chicago Press, 1951.

Smart, Ninian. *Doctrine and Argument in Indian Philosophy.* London: George Allen and Unwin Ltd., 1964.

————. *Reasons and Faiths: An Investigation of Religious Discourse, Christian and Non-Christian.* London: Routledge & Kegan Paul, 1958.

Smith, Wilfred C. *The Meaning and End of Religion.* Mentor Book edition. New York: The New American Library, 1964.

Soothill, W. E., and Hodous, L. *A Dictionary of Chinese Buddhist Terms.* London: Kegan Paul, Trench, Trubner & Co., Ltd., 1937.

Stace, W. T. *Mysticism and Philosophy.* Philadelphia and New York: J. B. Lippincott Co., 1960.

Stcherbatsky, F. Th. *Buddhist Logic.* 2 vols. Dover edition. New York: Dover Publications, Inc., 1962.

————. *The Central Conception of Buddhism and the Meaning of the Word "Dharma."* London: The Royal Asiatic Society, 1924.

————. *The Conception of Buddhist Nirvana.* Leningrad: Publishing Office of the Academy of Sciences of the USSR, 1927.

Stiernotte, Alfred P., ed. *Mysticism and the Modern Mind.* New York: The Liberal Arts Press, 1959.

Streng, Frederick J. *Emptiness: A Study in Religious Meaning.* Nashville and New York: Abingdon Press, 1967.

Suzuki, Daisetz Teitarō. *Essays in Zen Buddhism.* 3 vols. London: Luzac, 1927, 1933, and 1934.

————. *Manual of Zen Buddhism.* Evergreen edition. New York: Grove Press, 1960.

————. *Studies in the Lankavatara Sutra.* London: Routledge & Kegan Paul, Ltd., 1930.

————. *Studies in Zen.* London: Rider, 1955.

————. *The Training of the Zen Buddhist Monk.* Kyoto: Eastern Buddhist Society, 1934.

————. *Zen and Japanese Culture.* New York: Pantheon Books, Inc., 1959.

Suzuki, Taizan. *Zenshū no chihō hatten.* Tokyo: Unebi shobō, 1942.

Tachibana, S. *Ethics of Buddhism.* Colombo: The Buddha Sahitya Sabha, 1961.

Tada, Kōryū, and others, eds. *Tendai hongaku-ron. Nihon shisō taikei,* vol. 9. Tokyo: Iwanami shoten, 1973.

Takahashi, Masanobu. *Dōgen no jissen-tetsugaku kōzō.* Tokyo: Sankibō bus-shorin, 1967.

———. *Gendai shisō kara mita Dōgen no jissen-tetsugaku.* Tokyo: Risōsha, 1959.

Takakusu, Junjirō. *The Essentials of Buddhist Philosophy.* Ed. W. T. Chan and C. A. Moore. Honolulu: University of Hawaii Press, 1948.

Takeda, Kiyoko. *Shisōshi no hōhō to taishō.* Tokyo: Sōbunsha, 1961.

Takeuchi, Michio. *Dōgen.* Tokyo: Yoshikawa kōbunkan, 1962.

Tamaki, Kōshirō. *Shin hasoku no tenkai.* Tokyo: Sankibō busshorin, 1961.

Tamamuro, Taijō. *Dōgen.* Tokyo: Mikasa shobō, 1941.

———. *Nihon Bukkyōshi gaisetsu.* Tokyo: Risōsha, 1940.

Tamamuro, Taijō, and others. *Nihon Bukkyōshi,* vol. 3: *Kinsei-kindai-hen.* Kyoto: Hōzōkan, 1967.

Tamura, Enchō. *Hōnen.* Tokyo: Yoshikawa kōbunkan, 1959.

Tamura, Yoshirō. *Kamakura shin-Bukkyō shisō no kenkyū.* Kyoto: Heirakuji shoten, 1965.

Tanabe, Hajime. *Shōbōgenzō no tetsugaku shikan.* Tokyo: Iwanami shoten, 1939. Reprinted in: Nishitani Keiji and others, eds., *Tanabe Hajime zenshū,* vol. 5, pp. 445–94. Tokyo: Chikuma shobō, 1963.

Tanaka, Tadao. *Kobutsu Dōgen.* Tokyo: Funi shobō, 1942.

Taya, Raishun, and others, eds. *Bukkyōgaku jiten.* Kyoto: Hōzōkan, 1955.

Thomas, E. J. *The History of Buddhist Thought.* New York: Barnes & Nobles, Inc., 1951.

Tilakasiri, J., ed. *Añjali: Papers on Indology and Buddhism.* A Felicitation Volume Presented to Oliver Hector de Alwis Wijesekera on His Sixtieth Birthday. Peradeniya: The Felicitation Volume Editorial Committee, 1970.

Tsuda, Sōkichi. *Bungaku ni arawaretaru kokumin shisō no kenkyū,* vol. 2: *Bushi bungaku no jidai.* Tokyo: Iwanami shoten, 1953.

Tsuji, Zennosuke. *Nihon Bukkyō-shi.* 11 vols. Tokyo: Iwanami shoten, 1944–53.

———. *Nihon Bukkyō-shi no kenkyū zokuhen.* Tokyo: Kinkōdō, 1931.

Tsunoda, Ryūsaku, and others, eds. *Sources of Japanese Tradition.* New York: Columbia University Press, 1958.

Ueda, Yoshifumi. *Yuishiki-shisō nyūmon.* Kyoto: Asoka shorin, 1964.

Uehara, Senroku, and others, eds. *Gendai Bukkyō kōza.* 5 vols. Tokyo: Kadokawa shoten, 1953.

Ui, Hakuju. *Bukkyō hanron.* Tokyo: Iwanami shoten, 1962.

———, ed. *Bukkyō jiten.* Tokyo: Tōsei shuppansha, 1953.

———. *Bukkyō tetsugaku no kenkyū.* Tokyo: Tōsei shuppansha, 1956.

———. *Zenshūshi kenkyū.* 3 vols. Tokyo: Iwanami shoten, 1939–43.

———. *Bukkyō shisō kenkyū.* Tokyo: Iwanami shoten, 1940.

Uno, Seiichi, and others, eds. *Kōza tōyōshisō.* 10 vols. Tokyo: Tōkyō daigaku shuppansha, 1967.

Wach, Joachim. *Types of Religious Experience: Christian and Non-Christian.* Chicago: The University of Chicago Press, 1951.

————. *Understanding and Believing: Essays by Joachim Wach.* Ed. with an introduction by Joseph M. Kitagawa. New York: Harper & Row, 1968.

Washio, Junkei. *Nihon Zenshūshi no kenkyū.* Tokyo: Kyōten shuppan kabushiki kaisha, 1945.

Watanabe, Shōkō. *Japanese Buddhism: A Critical Appraisal.* Tokyo: Kokusai bunka shinkōkai, 1968.

Watsuji, Tetsurō. *Nihon rinri shisōshi.* 2 vols. Tokyo: Iwanami shoten, 1952.

————. *Nihon seishinshi kenkyū.* 2 vols. Tokyo: Iwanami shoten, 1926 and 1935.

Welbon, Guy Richard. *The Buddhist Nirvana and Its Western Interpreters.* Chicago: The University of Chicago Press, 1968.

Welch, Holmes. *The Buddhist Revival in China.* Cambridge: Harvard University Press, 1968.

————. *The Practice of Chinese Buddhism.* Cambridge: Harvard University Press, 1967.

Wheelwright, Philip. *The Burning Foundain.* Bloomington: Indiana University Press, 1959.

Whitehead, A. N. *Adventures of Ideas.* Mentor Book edition. New York: The New American Library, 1955.

————. *Modes of Thought.* Capricorn Book edition. New York: The Macmillan Co., 1958.

————. *Process and Reality.* New York: The Macmillan Co., 1929.

Wittgenstein, Ludwig. *Philosophical Investigations.* Trans. G. E. M. Anscombe. Oxford: Basil Blackwell, 1953.

————. *Tractatus Logico-Philosophicus.* London: Routledge and Kegan Paul, Ltd., 1922.

Wogihara, U. *The Sanscrit-Chinese Dictionary of Buddhist Technical Terms.* Tokyo: Sankibō, 1959.

Wright, Arthur F., ed. *Studies in Chinese Thought.* Chicago: The University of Chicago Press, 1953.

Yamada, Reirin. *Shōbōgenzō kōwa.* Tokyo: Kawade shobō shinsha, 1960.

Yamaguchi, Minoru. *The Intuition of Zen and Bergson.* Tokyo: Enderle Bookstore, 1971.

Yamaguchi, Susumu, ed. *Buddhism and Culture: Dedicated to Dr. Daisetz Teitarō Suzuki in Commemoration of His Ninetieth Birthday.* Kyoto: The Planning Committee for the Commemoration of Dr. Suzuki's Ninetieth Birthday, 1960.

————. *Kū no sekai.* Tokyo: Risōsha, 1967.

Yamaguchi, Susumu, and others. *Bukkyōgaku josetsu.* Kyoto: Heirakuji shoten, 1961.

Yamamoto, Kiyoyuki. *Dōgen-zen no shōsatsu.* Kyoto: Heirakuji shoten, 1970.

Yampolsky, Philip, trans. *The Platform Sūtra of the Sixth Patriarch*. New York: Columbia University Press, 1967.
Yasutani, Hakuun. *Shōbōgenzō sankyū—Sansuikyō Uji*. Tokyo: Shunjūsha, 1968.
Yinger, J. Milton. *The Scientific Study of Religion*. New York: The Macmillan Co., 1970.
Zürcher, E. *The Buddhist Conquest of China*. 2 vols. Leiden: E. J. Brill, 1959.

C. Articles

Abbreviations:
    EB   *The Eastern Buddhist*
    JIBS   *Journal of Indian and Buddhist Studies*
    KDBK   *Komazawa daigaku Bukkyō-gakubu kenkyū-kiyō*
    KDK   *Komazawa daigaku kenkyū-kiyō*
    MN   *Monumenta Nipponica*
    PSJ   *Philosophical Studies of Japan*
    SK   *Shūgaku kenkyū (Journal of Sōtō Studies)*

Abe, Masao. "Dōgen on Buddha Nature." *EB*, vol. 4, no. 1 (May 1971), pp. 28–71.
———. "God, Emptiness, and the True Self." *EB*, vol. 2, no. 2 (1969), pp. 15–30.
Bareau, A. "The Notion of Time in Early Buddhism." *East and West*, vol. 7, no. 4 (January 1957), pp. 353–64.
Benl, Oscar. "Die Anfänge der Sōtō-Mönchsgemeinschaften." *Oriens Extremus*, vol. 7 (1960), pp. 31–50.
———. "Der Zen-Meister Dōgen in China." *Nachrichten der Deutschen Gesellschaft für Natur und Völkerkunde Ostasiens*, nos. 79–80, pp. 67–77.
Dumoulin, Heinrich. "Allgemeine Lehren zur Förderung des Zazen von Zen Meister Dōgen." *MN*, vol. 14 (1958/59), pp. 429–36.
———. "Die religiöse Metaphysik des japanischen Zen-Meisters Dōgen." *Saeculum*, vol. 12, no. 3 (1961), pp. 205–36.
———, trans. "Das Buch Genjōkōan Aus dem Shōbōgenzō des Zen-Meisters Dōgen." *MN*, vol. 15, nos. 3–4 (October 1959–January 1960), pp. 217–32.
———, trans. "Fukan Zazengi" (German). *MN*, vol. 12, nos. 3–4 (1956), pp. 183–90.
———, trans. "Zazen Yōjinki" (German). *MN*, vol. 13, nos. 3–4 (1957), pp. 147–67.
Fueoka, Jishō. "Saikin ni okeru Dōgen zenji kenkyū sangyō no kaiko." *Dōgen zenji godenki*, vol. 1, no. 1 (June 1949), pp. 132–49.
Furuta, Shōkin. "The Development of Zen Thought in Japan." *PSJ*, vol. 3 (1961), pp. 33–55.

————. "Genjō-kōan no igi." *JIBS*, vol. 5, no. 1 (January 1957), pp. 102–7.

Harada, Kōdō. "Rokuso Dankyō no jishō no shisō to Dōgen zenji no ta-chiba." *SK*, no. 8 (April 1966), pp. 115–20.

Hisamatsu, Shin'ichi. "Oriental Nothingness." *PSJ*, vol. 2 (1960), pp. 65–97.

————. "Zen: Its Meaning for Modern Civilization." *EB*, vol. 1, no. 1 (1965), pp. 22–47.

Hosaka, Gyokusen. "Shukke-Bukkyō zaike-Bukkyō to Dōgen zenji no ta-chiba." *KDK*, no. 15 (March 1957), pp. 1–14.

Iino, Norimoto. "Dōgen's Zen View of Independence." *Philosophy East and West*, vol. 12, no. 1 (April 1962), pp. 51–57.

Ikebe, Minoru. "Dōgen kankei kenkyū bunken mokuroku." *Bungaku*, vol. 29, no. 6 (June 1961), pp. 742–67.

Ishimoto, K., and Neberfeld, P. E., trans. "*Shushōgi*. Prinzipien der Übung und Erleuchtung. Eine Zenschrift für Laien." *MN*, vol. 6, nos. 1–2, pp. 355–69.

Itō, Shungen. "Eihei Shōbōgenzō ni okeru Daie no shinshō hihan—Mu-chaku Dōchū no Shōbōgenzō-sempyō Sesshin-sesshō no shō tono kan-ren ni oite." *SK*, no. 6 (April 1964), pp. 79–85.

————. "Hi-shiryō no kaishaku ni tsuite: hi-shiryō-kō I." *SK* no. 5 (March 1963), pp. 84–91.

Kagamishima, Genryū. "Dōgen zenji kenkyū no kaiko to tembō." *Bungaku*, vol. 29, no. 6 (June 1961), pp. 109–17.

————. "Dōgen zenji to in'yō gaiten." *KDBK*, no. 21 (October 1962), pp. 100–11.

————. "Dōgen zenji to Tendai hongaku hōmon—Hokekyō in'yō ni kanren shite." *SK*, no. 2 (January 1960), pp. 50–57.

————. "Eihei-kōroku to ryakuroku." *KDK*, no. 15 (March 1957), pp. 55–64.

————. "Honshō-myōshu no shisōshi-teki haikei." *SK*, no. 7 (April 1965), pp. 24–29.

————. "Nansō zenrin no ichi-kōsatsu." *KDBK*, no. 19 (March 1961), pp. 48–62.

————. "Shingi ni okeru zazen-kan no hensen." *JIBS*, vol. 3, no. 2 (March 1955), pp. 204–7.

Kagamishima, Hiroyuki. "Dōgen zenji kenkyū no dōkō kaiko." *Dōgen zenji kenkyū*, vol. 1, no. 1 (January 1941), pp. 341–68.

King, Winston L. "A Comparison of Theravāda and Zen Buddhist Medita-tional Methods and Goals." *History of Religions*, vol. 9, no. 4 (May 1970), pp. 304–15.

Kinoshita, Jun'ichi. "Fukan-zazengi no kenkyū." *SK*, no. 7 (April 1965), pp. 132–37.

Kiyono, Munemoto. "Dōgen zenji no busso-shōden-kan no ichi-kōsatsu:

Fukan-zazengi seiritsu no mondai ni kanren shite." *SK*, no. 6 (April 1964), pp. 145–52.

Kōchi, Eigaku. "Dōgen-zen no busshin-ron." *KDBK*, no. 19 (March 1961), pp. 34–47.

———. "Shinran kyōgaku to Dōgen-zen no shō-shisō." *KDK*, no. 17 (1959), pp. 57–84.

———. "Zen-jō nikyō no gyō-shisō." *KDK*, no. 15 (March 1957), pp. 65–94.

———. "Zen-jō nikyō no shin-shisō." *KDK*, no. 16 (March 1958), pp. 25–66.

Kondō, Ryōichi. "Dōgen ni okeru shisō tenkai no ichi-kōsatsu—hokuetsu nyūsan o keiki to shite." *JIBS*, vol. 12, no. 1 (January 1964), pp. 243–46.

Kurebayashi, Kōdō. "Dankyō no hannya-shisō to Dōgen zenji." *SK*, no. 6 (April 1964), pp. 5–11.

———. "Dōgen Keizan ryōso igo ni okeru Sōtō-shūgaku no shuryū." *JIBS*, vol. 6, no. 2 (March 1958), pp. 12–20.

———. "Dōgen-zen ni okeru shin ni tsuite." *KDBK*, no. 20 (March 1962), pp. 1–11.

Masunaga, Reihō. "Dōgen's Idea of Buddha-nature." *KDK*, no. 18 (March 1960), pp. 1–14.

Masutani, Fumio. "Dōgen ni okeru zen no shisō-teki kōzō." *Shisō*, no. 521 (November 1967), pp. 100–13.

Nagao, Gadjin. "On the Theory of Buddha-Body (*Buddha-kāya*)." *EB*, vol. 6, no. 1 (May 1973), pp. 25–53.

Nakagawa, Takashi. "Dōgen zenji to rokuso Dankyō." *JIBS*, vol. 4, no. 1 (January 1956), pp. 212–15.

Nishitani, Keiji. "On the I-Thou Relation in Zen Buddhism." *EB*, vol. 2, no. 2 (1969), pp. 71–87.

———. "The Personal and the Impersonal in Religion." *EB*, vol. 3, no. 1, pp. 1–18 and vol. 3, no. 2, pp. 71–88.

———. "What Is Religion?" *PSJ*, vol. 2 (1960), pp. 21–64.

Petzold, Bruno. "On Buddhist Meditation." *Transactions of Asiatic Society of Japan*, vol. 3, no. 1 (1948), pp. 64–100.

Rikukawa, Taiun. "Dōgen zenji no Daie zenji hihan ni tsuite." *Zengaku kenkyū*, no. 55 (February 1966), pp. 56–70.

Sakai, Tokugen. "Rokuso Dankyō ni okeru jishō ni tsuite." *SK*, no. 7 (April 1965), pp. 35–41.

———. "Rokuso Dankyō ni okeru kenshō no igi." *SK*, no. 6 (April 1964), pp. 18–26.

———. "Shōbōgenzō ni okeru shimo no igi." *KDK*, no. 15 (March 1957), pp. 112–26.

Satō, Kenjun. "Ji to ji ni tsuite—Kegonkyō no jikan-kannen." *JIBS*, vol. 3, no. 2 (March 1955), pp. 107–14.

Sugio, Mamoru. "Dōgen to Heidegger." *Risō*, no. 369 (February 1964), pp. 35–43.

Takeuchi, Michio. "Eihei Dōgen to Hekiganroku—Ichiya Hekigan no Dō-gen shōrai-setsu ni tsuite." *SK*, vol. 1, no. 1 (March 1956), pp. 110–31.

———. "Saikin no Dōgen ni kansuru kenkyū ni tsuite." *Nihon Bukkyōshi*, no. 4 (March 1958), pp. 46–55.

Tamaki, Kōshirō. "Bukkyō no jikan-ron." *Risō*, no. 460 (September 1971), pp. 64–78.

Tamamura, Takeji. "Eihei Dōgen no Rinzai-shū ni taisuru kanjō." *Nihon rekishi*, no. 47 (April 1952), pp. 26–31.

Tamura, Yoshirō. "Nihon Tendai hongaku-shisō no keisei-katei." *JIBS*, vol. 10, no. 2 (March 1962), pp. 661–72.

Ueda, Yoshifumi. "Thinking in Buddhist Philosophy." *PSJ*, vol. 5 (1964), pp. 69–94.

Ui, Hakuju. "A Study of Japanese Tendai Buddhism." *PSJ*, vol. 1 (1959), pp. 33–74.

Waddell, Norman, and Abe, Masao, trans. "Dōgen's Bendōwa." *EB*, vol. 4, no. 1 (May 1971), pp. 124–57.

———, trans. "Dōgen's *Fukanzazengi* and *Shōbōgenzō zazengi*." *EB*, vol. 6, no. 2 (October 1973), pp. 115–28.

———, trans. "Dōgen's *Shōbōgenzō Zenki* 'Total Dynamic Working' and *Shōji* 'Birth and Death.'" *EB*, vol. 5, no. 1 (May 1972), pp. 70–80.

———. trans. "The King of Samadhis Samadhi, Dōgen's *Shōbōgenzō Sammai O Zammai*." *EB*, vol. 7, no. 1 (May 1974), pp. 118–23.

———, trans. "'One Bright Pearl' Dōgen's *Shōbōgenzō Ikka Myōju*." *EB*, vol. 4, no. 2 (October 1971), pp. 108–18.

———, trans. "Shōbōgenzō Genjōkōan." *EB*, vol. 5, no. 2 (October 1972), pp. 129–40.

Yamanouchi, Shun'yū. "Dōgen-zanji ni okeru shin—sono mikkyō tono renkan ni tsuite." *KDBK*, no. 22 (March 1964), pp. 58–71.

———. "Zazengi to Tendai shō-shikan." *SK*, no. 8 (April 1966), pp. 29–50.

Monographs of the Association for Asian Studies

Published by the University of Arizona Press

XXIX. *Dōgen Kigen—Mystical Realist*, by Hee-Jin Kim. 1975.

XXVIII. *Masks of Fiction in DREAM OF THE RED CHAMBER*, by Lucien Miller. 1975.

XXVII. *Politics and Nationalist Awakening in South India, 1852–1891*, by R. Suntharalingam. 1974.

XXVI. *The Peasant Rebellions of the Late Ming Dynasty*, by James Bunyan Parsons. 1970.

XXV. *Political Centers and Cultural Regions in Early Bengal*, by Barrie M. Morrison. 1970.

XXIV. *The Restoration of Thailand Under Rama I: 1782–1809*, by Klaus Wenk. 1968.

XXIII. *K'ang Yu-wei: A Biography and a Symposium*, translated and edited by Jung-pang Lo. 1967. 541 pp.

XXII. *A Documentary Chronicle of Sino-Western Relations (1644–1820)*, by Lo-shu Fu. 1966. xviii + 792 pp.

XXI. *Before Aggression: Europeans Prepare the Japanese Army*, by Ernst L. Presseisen. 1965. O.P.

XX. *Shinran's Gospel of Pure Grace*, by Alfred Bloom. 1965.

XIX. *Chiaraijima Village: Land Tenure, Taxation, and Local Trade, 1818–1884*, by William Chambliss. 1965.

XVIII. *The British in Malaya: The First Forty Years*, by K. G. Tregonning. 1965. O.P.

XVII. *Ch'oe Pu's Diary: A Record of Drifting Across the Sea*, by John Meskill. 1965.

XVI. *Korean Literature: Topics and Themes*, by Peter H. Lee. 1965. O.P.

XV. *Reform, Rebellion, and the Heavenly Way*, by Benjamin B. Weems. 1964.

XIV. *The Malayan Tin Industry to 1914*, by Wong Lin Ken. 1965.

About the Author
HEE-JIN KIM was born in Korea and received his basic education in Japan. His life-long interest in Buddhism was expanded in the United States, where he earned a B.A. and an M.A. in philosophy from the University of California and a Ph.D. in religion from Claremont Graduate School. He served on the faculties of the University of Vermont, Wright State University, and Claremont Graduate School before joining the Department of Religious Studies at the University of Oregon, where he is professor.